Blue-Blooded Cavalryman

CIVIL WAR SOLDIERS AND STRATEGIES
Brian S. Wills, Series Editor

Blue-Blooded Cavalryman

Captain William Brooke Rawle in
the Army of the Potomac,
May 1863–August 1865

Edited by J. Gregory Acken

The Kent State University Press

Kent, Ohio

© 2019 by The Kent State University Press, Kent, Ohio 44242

All rights reserved

ISBN 978-1-60635-372-1

Manufactured in the United States of America

Cataloging information for this title is available at the Library of Congress.

23 22 21 20 19   5 4 3 2 1

CONTENTS

PREFACE AND ACKNOWLEDGMENTS

In preparing William Brooke Rawle's writings for publication, I have used his letters to form the basis of the work, supplementing them with information from his transcribed diary entries when they provide additional detail not mentioned (or adequately addressed) in his correspondence and fill time gaps in his letters. In several instances, principally where its inclusion in the proper chronological place within the body of a letter would have disrupted the composition and flow of the correspondence, an entry either follows the letter or is incorporated into the endnotes. Left out are those entries that convey information already contained in Rawle's letters or address only brief, trivial matters. The reader may find that there is occasional redundancy between a diary entry and a letter; in most of these cases, removing the duplicate information from either would have compromised its structure. In order to help the reader follow the young officer's activities, at various times I have inserted dates, in brackets, into the body of his lengthier letters.

Rawle misspelled very few words, and I have not corrected his errors except in cases where he misspelled a place or proper name. On those occasions I have left the initial mention uncorrected, noted it, and corrected future mentions. In the interest of economy, Rawle liked to abbreviate words such as "would," "should," and "could"; I have spelled these out. Other words that he shortened and whose meaning remain clear (for example, "Dep'ment" and "tho'") I left alone; abbreviated words judged to be confusing if left as written are now spelled out.

Regarding the content of the letters, matters of a purely personal nature; repetitive material; inquiries after friends, relatives, and other civilians not frequently mentioned or otherwise unidentified; and complimentary closes have been expunged. With respect to the endnotes, the reader will notice that most contain a fair amount of detail. I wrote the notes as I like to read them, and my hope is that, much like in my own experience, they will provoke curiosity, provide enlightenment, and encourage further reading and research into the topics they address.

. . .

In the same way that no one can write about the Army of the Potomac without being influenced by the works of Bruce Catton and Stephen Sears, it is impossible to chronicle any events relating to the cavalry of the Army of the Potomac, even in a work as narrow in scope as this, without acknowledging the contributions of three historians: Stephen Z. Starr, Edward G. Longacre, and Eric J. Wittenberg. Starr produced a groundbreaking, three-volume study of the Union cavalry that was published between 1979 and 1985; two of these volumes cover the war in the East and treat largely the Army of the Potomac's cavalry. Longacre wrote a seminal study on the role of the cavalry of both armies during the Gettysburg Campaign—utilizing Rawle's letters and postwar correspondence in his research—and followed it up years later with a history of the Army of the Potomac's cavalry, mining many original sources that Starr had not. Wittenberg has supplemented his excellent examination of the "coming of age" of the cavalry of the Army of the Potomac—the period from just before the Battle of Fredericksburg (December 13, 1862) to Brandy Station (June 9, 1863)—with battle studies, soldiers memoirs, and biographies of prominent cavalrymen, all of which have shed much light on the army's cavalry operations. Eric also provided encouragement after reading an early draft of the manuscript, for which I am grateful. The research, opinions, and conclusions of these three historians have informed much of the material contained in my introduction and in many of my notes.

To John J. Meko Jr., executive director of the Foundations of the Union League of Philadelphia; James G. Mundy Jr., director of education and programming; and Theresa Altieri Taplin, archivist and collections manager, go my thanks for graciously granting permission to publish the Rawle letters and diary, which compose a part of the foundations' collection. John, Jim, Theresa, and the rest of the staff have made great strides over the past decade in their ongoing efforts to preserve the archival materials of the former Civil War Library and Museum of Philadelphia.

At Fredericksburg and Spotsylvania National Military Park, Chief Historian John Hennessy and Lead Historian Frank O'Reilly were very supportive, reading preliminary chapters of the work and providing constructive feedback. O'Reilly also graciously shared the interesting—and distressing—story of Rawle's original diaries and medals, which have been lost for many years now. Clark C. "Bud" Hall of Culpeper, Virginia, an authority on all things Civil War in Northern Virginia, also provided support and helped me identify and locate obscure (and misspelled) landmarks mentioned in the letters and diary.

At the US Army Heritage and Education Center in Carlisle, Pennsylvania, Rodney Foytik provided immeasurable—and unhesitatingly cheerful—assistance in locating source materials and photographs, while Lori Wheeler facilitated the process of procuring copies of the images in the center's collection. Thanks are due to Ronn Palm of Gettysburg, Pennsylvania, who provided permission to use an elusive image from his expansive photograph collection and went to great lengths to ensure that I secured it.

Marshall Krolick of Chicago, a cavalry expert in his own right, many years ago passed Rawle's letters and diary on to me while I was serving in my capacity as a member of the Board of Governors of the former Civil War Library and Museum. Marshall had intended to edit and publish the letters himself, and the museum had loaned them to him, but pressing professional obligations prevented it. For the opportunity to have undertaken it myself, I am thankful.

George Skoch, cartographer par excellence, produced the outstanding maps from my inartistic and clumsy directions. This is the third time I have had the privilege of working with George; I hope there will be future opportunities.

At the Kent State University Press, Will Underwood has been nothing but a pleasure to work with since my first inquiry and has been more than accommodating and patient throughout the process. Thanks are also due to the anonymous readers the press enlisted to provide critical assessments of the manuscript. Their suggestions helped me explore avenues I had overlooked and thus improved the work greatly, as did the copyediting suggestions made by Kevin Brock.

To my family, as always, go my greatest thanks. To say that I appreciate their patience and forbearance as I pursue my avocation is an understatement. That they allow me to do it uncomplainingly is testament either to the fact that they get along quite well without me or, as I prefer to believe, that they are selfless enough to grant me the time I need. Regina, Brian, Will, Regina, and Cameron—thank you.

Editor's proceeds from the sale of William Brooke Rawle's writings will be donated to the nonprofit Abraham Lincoln Foundation of the Union League of Philadelphia, which is the steward of a majority of the holdings of the former Civil War Library and Museum of Philadelphia, including Rawle's letters, photographs, and diary transcript.

INTRODUCTION

The lieutenant reclined in a field of clover, just inside a belt of woods on the edge of a broad farm lot. He laid low to the ground to escape the heat of the early summer day. His saddled horse, forsaking shade for sustenance, was grazing close by. Men of his command were gathered in small groups near him; some were resting, others played cards, rummaged for scraps of food, or boiled water for coffee. Like most of them, the officer was exhausted, worn down by nearly three weeks of constant exertion under a sun that shone with such intensity that it had killed scores of infantrymen on their trek from northern Virginia into southern Pennsylvania.

The march had been hard on men and beasts alike. Two days earlier, on July 1, 1863, the cavalryman had walked much of an eleven-mile stretch between northern Maryland and southern Pennsylvania, leading his horse by the bridle to save its strength. The next day he did the same while on the march from Hanover, Pennsylvania, to the outskirts of Gettysburg, where he now lay perspiring, several miles east of the town. All told, his regiment, the 3rd Pennsylvania Cavalry, had lost seventy-two horses due to fatigue during their advance into their native state.

It was quieter now than it had been just an hour earlier, when a roar louder than he had ever experienced rose up from west of the town and continued, unabated, until just a few minutes ago. Hundreds of dueling artillery pieces were responsible for the crescendo, and though he had only been in the army for a short time, the officer knew that the ferocity of such a bombardment heralded a clash of infantry. During the shelling, an artillery caisson had been hit over five miles away, the explosion sending up a plume of smoke so high it was visible from where he lay.

Less than two months earlier, this smooth-faced, nineteen-year-old soldier named William Brooke Rawle had been completing his collegiate studies; three and a half weeks prior to this day, he had participated (albeit away from the scene of the heaviest fighting) in one of the largest cavalry battles of the war at Brandy Station, Virginia. On this very day, July 3, in Philadelphia, three days' hard ride to the east of where he lay, his classmates in the University of Pennsylvania's Class of 1863 were attending their graduation ceremony, which he had foregone to enter the service. Now he found himself again in his native state, in command of what remained of his company. Some of the men he had charge of were over twice his age; most had seen hard service since Maj. Gen. George B. McClellan's Peninsula Campaign over a year before.

Earlier in the day, at almost the same time as the artillery bombardment, a regiment of Rebel horsemen had charged across the fields in front of him but were checked by a stout fence running across their line of advance and a force of Michigan cavalrymen who had rushed up to meet them. It had been a short but savage fight, during which the men of the 3rd Pennsylvania, when the flank of the Southern advance passed from right to left along their front, took the opportunity to pour carbine and pistol fire into the riders. The outnumbered Unionists at the fence were eventually forced back, Virginians in pursuit, but the accurate fire of several sections of Federal horse artillery and other Northern cavalry regiments on both Rebel flanks eventually drove the attackers back across the field to the north and west to the farm from where they had started.

There was a lull now, broken sporadically by small-arms fire and an occasional report from an artillery piece, but it was only a brief respite. From the direction the Virginians had come earlier in the day, the lieutenant and his men heard a familiar sound, the low rumble the onrushing horses of the earlier attack had produced, only now far louder. As they looked to the northwest across the field, portions of three brigades of Southern cavalry emerged from a wood where they had been concealed, rounded a distant farmhouse, dressed their lines, and prepared to attack the Northerners. Maj. Gen. James Ewell Brown "Jeb" Stuart, the leader of the cavalry of the Army of Northern Virginia, had been positioned on the far left (northern edge) of the Southern army's position to prevent Federal cavalry from sweeping around behind its flank. Now he wanted to lure the Northerners out to battle and beat them; the charge of twelve regiments from the brigades of Brig. Gen. Wade Hampton, Col. John Chambliss, and Brig. Gen. Fitzhugh Lee that Lieutenant Rawle and others saw forming was the focus of that effort.[1]

The scene was almost medieval—flags and pennants flapping in the wind; horses arrayed ranks deep, readying to charge—but these men wore no armor and carried no shields to protect them, and they were armed with pistols, carbines, and swords instead of lances. Even though they were adversaries, the sight of the mass of horsemen advancing, sunlight reflecting off of thousands of weapons, prompted admiring comments among the Pennsylvanians and others who witnessed it.

As their mounts came into line, the Rebel pace quickened, gradually moving from a walk to a slow trot to a gallop, and they were soon rumbling down the field, heading almost directly to where the lieutenant and his squadron were resting. Union artillery positioned south of the Pennsylvanians soon opened fire, tearing gaps in the onrushing mass. These spaces were closed up as quickly as they were created by the well-disciplined Southern cavalrymen.

Not long after the charge began, the lieutenant's commanding officer, a handsome, twenty-seven-year-old veteran of two years who had grown up not far from Gettysburg, called him over to his side. He had been watching the attack as it gained momentum and realized that it was advancing at them. If it followed the path of the earlier advance, which seemed likely, it would veer away from the Pennsylvanians before it reached their position, presenting, as the 1st Virginia Cavalry had earlier, its left flank to them as it passed. The captain had been directed to hold his squadron in position near the edge of the woods, but this was too tempting a target. As they peered off to their left toward the southern end of the field, where the Union artillery was positioned, the two officers could see a lone cavalry regiment advancing to meet the Rebel onslaught. Like the defenders earlier in the day, these were also Michiganders, who would be overwhelmed if left to fight alone.

Although he could not have known it, what would later be described as the "supreme moment" of 2nd Lt. William Brooke Rawle's life was near at hand.[2] In an excited way, he would later recall, he turned to his commander, William Miller, and said, "Captain, let's rally the squadron, give 'em a volley with our carbines and then pitch in with our sabres"; he later confessed that this was "a very presumptuous and impertinent remark from a small boy to his superior officer." Despite unequivocal orders to stay in his current position, Captain Miller decided to attack the exposed flank of the Southern force. "Will you stand by me

Capt. William E. Miller of Newville, Pennsylvania. He would be awarded the Medal of Honor for his initiative at Gettysburg, where Rawle served under him. (Courtesy Civil War Collection, US Army Heritage and Education Center, Military History Institute, Carlisle, PA)

if I order a charge?" he asked Rawle. "I will stick to you till hell freezes over," the young man replied.[3]

The two officers scurried back to their horses, shouting orders as they went. Their men, veterans that they were, had anticipated them and were already scrambling into their saddles, fastening the straps of their kepis, checking their pistols and carbines for ammunition, and securing or throwing aside excess equipment. A few hundred yards in front of where the Pennsylvanians were assembling, the Southerners smashed headlong into the advance of the Michigan troopers, who were led personally by their brigade commander, Brig. Gen. George Armstrong Custer. The junction of the onrushing combatants was "so sudden and violent," Captain Miller remembered, "that many of the horses were turned end over end and crushed their riders beneath them."[4]

The men of 3rd were getting impatient; some failed to wait for their comrades to form up before rushing as fast as their horses would carry them at the unsuspecting Rebels. The section of the squadron under Miller had gotten a head start on the men of Rawle's company; to maximize the force of their charge and go in together, the lieutenant encouraged his men to advance before they were fully assembled. "Front into line, draw sabers, charge!" he yelled. Once mounted, he unholstered his pistol and dug his spurs into the side of his animal; in company with his men, some of whom by now had rushed on ahead, he galloped toward the writhing mass of horses and cavalrymen engaged in desperate combat.

William Brooke Rawle, who was then known as William Rawle Brooke (he changed the order of his last and middle names in 1867), had been born into a privileged, old-line Philadelphia family in 1843. He was the second of four children of Charles Wallace Brooke and Elizabeth Tilghman Rawle. His father was descended from John Brooke, who had emigrated to America from England in 1699 to occupy land he had purchased from William Penn. William's great-grandfather, Capt. John Brooke, had served in the Continental Army during the Revolutionary War; his grandfather, Robert Brooke, was a surveyor and civil engineer.[5] William's father, Charles, was born in 1813. A skilled attorney, he was remembered as "an able and promising member of the Philadelphia Bar."[6] At twenty-eight he was appointed deputy attorney general for Philadelphia County, and in 1844 he joined a local militia organization, the City Artillery Regiment, as a private, eventually rising to captain.[7] In what was certainly a devastating blow to the family, Charles died an untimely death in 1849, rendering his thirty-one-year-old wife, Elizabeth (1818–97), a widow and leaving six-year-old William, eight-year-old Elizabeth (called Lillie, 1841–94), three-year-old Charlotte (called Lottie, 1846–85), and one-year-old Charles (1848–54) without a father.[8]

The widowed Elizabeth was descended from Quakers who had arrived in America in 1686. Her grandfather, William Rawle (1759–1836; sometimes referred to as William Rawle, the Elder), was one of the most distinguished legal minds of his time. In 1783 he established the Rawle Law Offices in Philadelphia, a firm, now known as Rawle & Henderson, that survives to this day, giving it the distinction of being the oldest in the United States. William Rawle, the Elder was one of the founders of the Philadelphia Academy of Fine Arts and served as the first president of the Historical Society of Pennsylvania. He also served in the Pennsylvania state assembly and in 1791 was appointed by George Washington as the first US district attorney for Pennsylvania.

Elizabeth's father, William Jr. (1788–1858; William Brooke Rawle's grandfather, known also as William Rawle, the Younger), was the fourth of twelve children born to the elder William Rawle and his wife, Sarah Burge. William Jr. also became a prominent Philadelphia attorney and served on the boards of many of the leading institutions of Philadelphia during his lifetime, including the Historical Society of Pennsylvania, which he helped found. Like his father, he was a trustee of the University of Pennsylvania. William Jr. further honed the legal bona fides of the family when he married Mary Anna Tilghman (1795–1878, William Brooke Rawle's grandmother).

Mary was the daughter of Edward Tilghman (1750–1815), a successful lawyer who had sided with the Patriots during the Revolution and was the great-granddaughter of Benjamin Chew, another great legal mind. Chew learned his trade under Alexander Hamilton, maintained a nearly lifelong friendship with Washington, and served as chief justice of Pennsylvania. Though sympathetic to the Loyalists during the American Revolution, Chew would provide legal advice and guidance after the War of Independence to the founders of the fledgling nation. Mary Tilghman and William Rawle Jr. had two children, Elizabeth (1818–97; Brooke Rawle's mother) and William Henry (1823–89; Brooke Rawle's uncle, who went by his middle name). Henry served brief stints in the state militia during the Civil War and, like his father, would pursue a legal career in the firm his grandfather had founded.[9]

Perhaps as a result of the early death of his father, William Brooke Rawle seems to have more closely identified himself with his mother's side of the family, which may account in some measure for his decision to change his last name after the war. Rawle mentions his uncle, Henry, periodically during his war correspondence, relying on him for advice and occasional advances of money when the paymaster failed to show. He would join Henry's legal practice after passing the bar following the war, and he changed his name from Brooke to Rawle apparently "to avoid confusion in the family."[10]

In his youth Rawle was educated at some of the best schools in the city of Philadelphia and, after completing his college preparations, entered the University of Pennsylvania in 1859 at the age of sixteen. When the war broke out near the end of his sophomore year, the university announced that it would grant leaves of absence to students who wished to volunteer. Rawle gave notice of his intent to join the army and, during the winter of 1862–63, engaged in an unsuccessful attempt to recruit a regiment of cavalry.[11] An influential family friend was able to assist his personal efforts, though, by securing him a second lieutenant's commission in the 3rd Pennsylvania Cavalry. In May 1863 Rawle finished his studies, left school two months before his commencement ceremony, and, in the company of two friends who had also been commissioned in the 3rd, journeyed from Philadelphia to war-torn Virginia. The young man was about to trade a genteel, cultured life of wealth and comfort for two years of hardship, adventure, danger, and excitement.[12]

The 3rd Pennsylvania Cavalry had been organized during the summer of 1861, when twelve independently raised cavalry companies were combined to form the regiment. Eleven of these companies had been recruited in various Pennsylvania counties (seven of these eleven in the city of Philadelphia), while one had been raised in Washington, DC. Upon completing their respective organizations, the eleven Pennsylvania-raised companies were sent to the capital, and were joined with the company raised in the district to form a regiment named the Kentucky Light Cavalry, commanded by Col. William H. Young, a Mexican War veteran who hailed from the Bluegrass State. Much to the displeasure of the men of the regiment, this designation would cost them the distinction that would have identified them as the first regiment of cavalry raised in Pennsylvania when, subsequently, it was assigned to count against the quota of regiments raised from that state. "For what possible or sane reason [the regiment] was so named cannot now be ascertained," wrote the regimental historians regarding the unit's Kentucky cavalry designation (ignoring the fact that the original regimental commander was a Kentuckian), "for eleven of the companies composing it had been raised in Pennsylvania."[13] In actuality, the 3rd Pennsylvania Cavalry was not only the first cavalry regiment raised in the state (with the exception of its DC company) but also the very first volunteer cavalry regiment raised in the North to enter into active service.[14] Even after forty years, the fact that their unit were not designated as the 1st Pennsylvania Cavalry annoyed the men of the 3rd.

William Woods Averell, the West Point–educated colonel of the 3rd Pennsylvania Cavalry and the man responsible for implementing Regular Army traditions in the regiment. Averell is shown here as a brigadier general. (Courtesy Prints and Photographs Division, Library of Congress)

Little is known of the regiment's first commander. Colonel Young served only for a short time, resigning his commission not long after the organization of the regiment was completed and around the same time that its men were assigned to count against Pennsylvania's quota and officially designated as the 3rd Pennsylvania Cavalry.[15] In Young's place, Pennsylvania governor Andrew Curtin appointed 1st Lt. William W. Averell, a thirty-year-old New York native and 1855 graduate of West Point. Prior to his appointment, Averell was serving in the 3rd US Cavalry and in 1859 had been seriously wounded while fighting Navajo Indians in present-day New Mexico. Soon after the outbreak of the Civil War, he was assigned to serve as an aide to Brig. Gen. Andrew Porter and was present during the First Battle of Bull Run (July 21, 1861). Averell was commissioned as colonel of the 3rd to date from August 23, 1861, but did not assume command of the regiment until mid-October.[16]

A pragmatic taskmaster, Averell was determined to instill Regular Army customs and practices among his volunteers and prepare them for the duties they would be required to perform.[17] "There were some to whom the rigid requirements of military life were distasteful," wrote the regimental historians of their training under Averell during the fall and winter of 1861–62. "If the man happened to be a commissioned officer, he soon made room for another." The study of army regulations, maneuvers, picket and guard duty, recitations, and other tasks filled their waking hours. "From two to four drills a day was the order, and from earliest dawn till darkness fell, the embryo trooper knew no rest," noted an officer of the 3rd. "Mutterings of dissatisfaction . . . were loud and unceasing," other members recalled, but the rigorous training implemented by their young commander served its purpose: "The officers who were opposed to these exacting and continuous duties, or who were restive under the severe, old-time Regular Army discipline insisted upon by our martinet of a Colonel, or were deemed incompetent, or otherwise unfitted for their positions, were induced or compelled to offer their resignations which were readily accepted. This process was very effective in sieving out the useless people who had floated in without proper qualification. . . . The weeding out gave opportunity for the acquisition of excellent material." Averell was nothing if not thorough. During the first six months of his command, twenty-four officers—over half of the complement called for in the regimental table of organization—resigned their commissions. The colonel turned the 3rd Pennsylvania into arguably the most well-trained volunteer cavalry regiment in the East.[18]

To fill the vacancies he created, Averell saw to it that worthy enlisted men were commissioned from the ranks, supplementing these intraregimental promotions with the appointment of men from civil life and other units. While several of those who joined the 3rd as officers in the months and years after its establishment had prior military experience, many did not. Along with Rawle, the sons of established Philadelphia families such as the Newhalls, Treichels, Stillés, and Wetherills were also commissioned as officers with the regiment.

In Rawle's case, a member of one of Philadelphia's most prominent families, Clement Biddle Barclay, helped pave the way for his commissioning. At the time, Barclay, an independently wealthy citizen, was serving as an agent for the Pennsylvania government and was responsible for seeing after the welfare of Keystone State soldiers serving in the field. He had accepted this role from Governor Curtin on two conditions—that he receive no compensation in exchange for his efforts, and that he would pay his own expenses.[19]

The fact that Barclay was able to help secure commissions for men like Rawle directly from civil life by interceding with the governor understandably did not sit well with some of the enlisted veterans, who reasonably concluded that it prevented the promotion of qualified men from the ranks. But had commissioning citizens directly into the 3rd been the only method used to fill vacant second lieutenancies, it would certainly have precluded the advancement of worthy sergeants. The records of the regiment clearly show, though, that this was not the case. During the 3rd's term of service, at least thirty noncommissioned officers were promoted from enlisted status to officers.[20] This did not stop grumbling in the ranks, however, and one outspoken corporal produced a pamphlet after the war in which he referred to Barclay (a man above reproach in the opinion of many) as a "kind of commission broker" and implied that the agent used his influence and wealth to place civilians as officers in the regiment by bribing and deceiving the governor.[21] Barclay would also assist civilians in gaining commissions in several other Philadelphia-raised units, including the 6th Pennsylvania Cavalry and the 118th Pennsylvania Infantry.

Averell was promoted to brigadier general in September 1862 and was succeeded in command of the 3rd by another Regular Army officer, John Baillie McIntosh, a naval veteran of the Mexican War who had been serving since the war's inception in the US Cavalry, first with the 2nd and later with the 5th Regiments. Although Rawle joined the 3rd Pennsylvania twenty months after it was mustered into the service (and eight months after Averell had left it), the Regular Army traditions that Averell had instilled in the regiment—unflinching obedience to orders, limited social interaction between officers and enlisted men, and swift punishment for minor infractions—were perpetuated by McIntosh and would remain ingrained in the fabric of the 3rd throughout the war.

Rawle unhesitatingly embraced the old-army principles that guided the regiment. When his orderly sergeant, a former Regular Army cavalryman, became drunk and belligerent in camp one day in the summer of 1864, Rawle had him arrested, thrown in the guardhouse, and gagged. "The more severe and unrelenting a commanding officer is," he would explain to his mother, "the more his men think of him."

With the concepts of discipline and the unquestioned authority of officers at their core, these customs, understandably, were not as highly regarded among the enlisted men. After Averell had assumed command, remembered one of them, "the men were taught, as were the officers also, that there was a wide gulf between them; that officers were superior beings, a privileged class, who could not be approached by the rank and file with undue familiarity."[22] Many of the men chafed under the strictures put upon them; a few would later cite this perceived oppression as a factor in their decision not to reenlist as veteran volunteers later in the war.[23]

Attached to McClellan's Army of the Potomac once molded by Colonel Averell, the 3rd Pennsylvania was one of only eight full regiments of cavalry that participated in the Peninsula Campaign against Richmond during the spring and early summer of 1862.[24] The Pennsylvanians suffered relatively few casualties over the five months they spent in Virginia, but the campaigning was arduous.[25] The terrain of the Peninsula was not conducive to cavalry operations, covered as it was with intertwined thickets, swampy lowlands, and roads that rainfall quickly transformed into bogs. A paucity of open terrain prevented the movements of large bodies of mounted men and rendered their operations, in Averell's words, "affairs of squadrons," meaning that the full force of a cavalry regiment could never be brought to bear.[26]

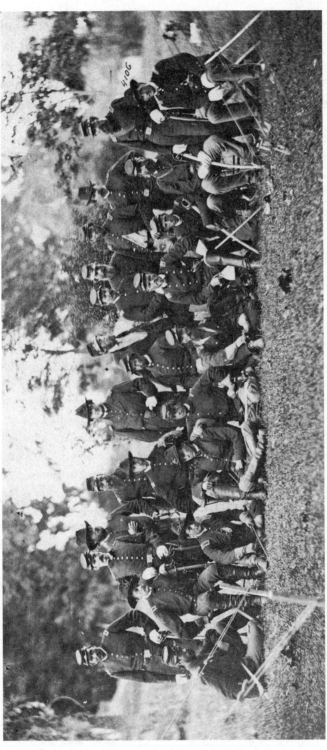

A group of officers of the 3rd Pennsylvania Cavalry, likely taken during the Peninsula Campaign of 1862. Identified individuals are, *seated on ground,* Lt. Col. Samuel Owen (*center; right arm covering right knee*), a slaveowning Virginian who left the regiment before Rawle joined it; *seated on chairs,* Charles Treichel (*second from left, hand on sword*), Col. William W. Averell (*third from right, double row of buttons*), and William E. Miller (*far right*); and *standing,* David Gilmore (*second from left*), James W. Walsh (*third from left, looking right*), Abel Wright (*fourth from left*), Oliver O. G. Robinson (*fifth from left, hand on belt*), Paul Pollard (*third from right*), and William W. Rogers (*second from right*). (Courtesy Prints and Photographs Division, Library of Congress)

As daunting as these topographical challenges proved, many of the cavalrymen were further annoyed by the duties they were assigned. Rather than fighting as a unified regiment, or for that matter in battalions or squadrons, the troopers found themselves doled out piecemeal, a handful at a time, for guard duty, special details, or service as orderlies. Worst of all, in their view, was attachment to infantry units, where they were subject to the whims of commanders who were, for the most part, unfamiliar with how to properly employ horsemen. This partitioning of cavalry was a practice that had plagued the mounted arm since the beginning of the war and one that would not be remedied until the spring of 1863, when the permanent Cavalry Corps was established. Recalling the early days with the Army of the Potomac, one cavalry officer wrote: "The smallest infantry organization had its company or more of mounted men whose duty consisted in supplying details as orderlies for mounted staff officers, following them mounted on their rapid marches for pleasure or for duty, or in camp acting as grooms or bootblacks."[27]

Much of the onus for this misuse of cavalry in the first half of the war in the East can be traced back to the Army of the Potomac's first commander. Despite having served for almost two years in the 1st US Cavalry, McClellan, who was an exceptional administrator, organizer, and leader, was confounded when it came to the utilization of his cavalry. One of his generals wrote in September 1862 that the army commander "knew precisely how to employ foot troops and cannoneers in battle" but that his "mind went blank whenever horse soldiers entered the equation."[28]

McClellan believed that it took two years to properly train a cavalryman, commenting in late 1861 that his volunteer cavalry were fit to do nothing more than "carry messages and act as vedettes."[29] Trapped in this mindset and lacking faith in their potency, McClellan distributed his cavalry regiments among the infantry divisions of his army, ensuring that opportunities for the horsemen to distinguish themselves would be limited. While carrying out courier and picket duties in camp and during times of army inaction may not have proved dispiriting to the mounted volunteers, the obligation to perform the same duties while actively campaigning certainly affected their morale.

Writing after the war, Averell amplified the responsibilities of cavalry during active service, which included monitoring the movements of opposing forces, leading the advance of the army while providing flank and rear-guard protection, and performing escort, courier, and guide duties. When supplemented with mobile horse artillery, cavalry could fight independently for periods of time against either an opposing mounted force or infantry.[30] "Cavalry should never hug the army on the march," instructed Averell, "especially in a thickly wooded country. . . . [T]he slightest obstacle in advance is liable to cause a blockade against the march of infantry." He continued: "In battle, it attacks the enemy's flanks and rear, and above all other duties in battle, it secures the fruits of victory by vigorous and unrelenting pursuit. In defeat it screens the withdrawal of the army and by its fortitude and activity baffles the enemy."[31]

While Averell's insights were written with the benefit of retrospection, the tactics he advocated stand in stark contrast to the manner in which McClellan employed his mounted arm. For much of the first half of the war in the East, the ability to baffle one's opponent that Averell emphasized seemed to be the sole purview of the cavalry of the Army of Northern Virginia and its daring leader, Jeb Stuart. During the Peninsula Campaign, Stuart had led his horseman on a four-day raid that circled around the Army of the Potomac, gathered intelligence, and destroyed supplies, all with the loss of one man. Later in 1862, a month after the Battle of Antietam (September 17), he repeated the feat, coursing through Maryland and into southern Pennsylvania, reinforcing the impression with many Northerners that their cavalry were outclassed and overmatched by their Southern counterparts. "It is a burning disgrace," opined an artillery officer of the October raid. "With the exception of the few regulars and two or three other regiments, I fear our cavalry is an awful botch." A Signal Corps officer agreed: "Our cavalry force . . . were little better than mounted monkeys." And Secretary of the Navy Gideon Welles concluded, "It is humiliating—disgraceful."[32]

Withdrawn from the Peninsula on September 3, when most of McClellan's infantry was sent to reinforce Maj. Gen. John Pope's Army of Virginia during the Second Manassas Campaign, the weary troopers of the 3rd Pennsylvania were shipped via ocean transport to Washington, arriving on the sixth. They remained in the capital until September 9, when those who still had serviceable horses joined in the westward movement to intercept Gen. Robert E. Lee on his first invasion of the North.[33] The portion of the regiment that participated in the Maryland Campaign was assigned to Maj. Gen. Joseph Hooker's I Corps and led the advance of these troops across Antietam Creek on the afternoon of September 16, when they moved into position for the attacks that would open the following day's battle.

After fording the creek, Hooker ordered elements of the 3rd to advance and develop the positions of the Rebels. Once accomplished, he then directed the Pennsylvanians to occupy a position that was so close to the enemy that they could overhear conversations. The horsemen remained there overnight, catching fits of rest while "tired, hungry and uncomfortable, in everybody's way, and of no earthly use, all because we were attached to an infantryman's command," until fighting commenced early on the seventeenth. Predictably, the companies were soon separated and assigned to different duties across the battlefield. The Pennsylvanians suffering casualties of eight wounded while carrying orders, rounding up stragglers, and supporting artillery batteries.[34]

Following Antietam, the regiment continued its service with the Army of the Potomac, establishing camp near Hagerstown, Maryland. There the men passed their time guarding the fords of the Potomac and conducting occasional scouts into western Maryland and across the river into Virginia. Those who had secured fresh horses from the dismounted camp returned, bringing the 3rd back up to fighting strength. The army, with McClellan at its head, finally moved across the Potomac into Virginia beginning on October 26. Pres. Abraham Lincoln, exasperated by seven weeks of what he believed was McClellan's torpidity, removed the general from command on November 7, replacing him with Maj. Gen. Ambrose Burnside. Colonel Averell had been officially promoted to brigadier general on September 26 (having led a brigade since July 5 on the Peninsula), and on November 15 Colonel McIntosh assumed command of the 3rd Pennsylvania.

Burnside shifted the army away from McClellan's planned route of advance along the line of the Orange & Alexandria Railroad, moving it thirty miles southeast to Fredericksburg, Virginia, where he believed that more secure waterborne supply routes were better suited to support an advance on Richmond. The leading elements of the Army of the Potomac reached Falmouth, opposite Fredericksburg, on November 17, with the 3rd Pennsylvania arriving near Potomac Creek, in Stafford County, on the twentieth. The horsemen began establishing their permanent camp there on November 24. With the exception of time away from it actively campaigning, picketing, or scouting, the regiment occupied this site for six months, the men remembering it as "the most comfortable of all our camps." Comfort aside, picket duty during the late fall and winter of 1862–63 along the Rappahannock River proved a monotonous, wearisome, and, as the cavalrymen soon learned, hazardous assignment.

The day after the Pennsylvanians began clearing the ground for their permanent camp, several companies of the 3rd were sent to picket and patrol near Hartwood Church, nine miles northwest of Fredericksburg. Three days later these outposts were surprised and routed by Confederate cavalry under General Hampton. The commander of the picket line, Capt. George Johnson of the 3rd, was making charcoal sketches on the interior walls of the church when the attack occurred; he was dismissed from the service a week later for "disgraceful and unofficerlike conduct." Five officers and seventy-seven men of the regiment were captured in the debacle, an embarrassment for the Pennsylvanians.[35] Of the Rebels who effected their capture, the regimental journal records, somewhat ruefully, "We will live in hopes of someday, sooner or later, repaying them, both principal and interest."[36]

Burnside had postponed his attack on Fredericksburg because the materials necessary to bridge the Rappahannock had been delayed; even after the equipment arrived, he vacillated. By the time the Union commander determined to cross and attempt the capture of the city on December 11, Lee was in position on the hills behind the town, from which his army had little trouble parrying the disjointed Federal assaults that took place throughout the day on December 13. The Federal cavalry was hardly engaged in this disastrous battle, suffering a total of one killed and three wounded (the 3rd Pennsylvania was held in reserve), but the infantry was battered, losing nearly 13,000 men. Six weeks later, after an attempt to outflank Lee was thwarted by a drenching winter storm, a movement known ever after as the Mud March, Burnside was relieved of command. In his place Lincoln appointed Major General Hooker.

Although Hooker is best remembered for the defeat he suffered at the Battle of Chancellorsville (May 1–4, 1863), the Army of the Potomac owed much to him, specifically for the three-month stretch between his ascension to command on January 25, 1863, and the fighting at Chancellorsville. While he may have been vainglorious, of questionable moral fiber by the standards of the times, and lacking the expansive skill set necessary to command an army, the general was, without understatement, an exceptional organizer and innovator. He recognized the problems plaguing his army and implemented the solutions that ultimately rejuvenated it.

Based on abundant personal accounts, the morale of the Army of the Potomac was at the lowest point in its existence following the tragedy of Fredericksburg and the fiasco of the Mud March. Hooker realized this and, with the assistance and direction of several key subordinates, including Chief of Staff Dan Butterfield and Medical Director Jonathan Letterman, undertook to fix it, instituting a series of reforms that, in short order, cured the Army of the Potomac of the malaise that had settled upon it. What the general and his lieutenants accomplished in just over three months was nothing short of remarkable. Dr. Letterman saw to it that supplies of fresh bread and vegetables were issued, resulting in better-fed troops. Sanitary measures were strengthened under his watch, which, when combined with the improvements in the soldier's diet, dramatically decreased sickness.[37] Hooker ordered that deserving soldiers receive leaves to visit home and took steps to suppress desertions, which had grown to troublesome proportions in the weeks after Fredericksburg.

The general also fundamentally altered his command structure in early 1863, first by dismantling the Grand Division structure Burnside had instituted (an additional level of command, with another general overseeing two corps) in favor of a corps approach, then by retiring, shelving, or reassigning a number of generals at the corps and divisional levels, many of whom had ties to McClellan.[38] When the weather improved with spring, Hooker held grand reviews that, while onerous for the men on parade, helped them see that they were part of something greater, reigniting in them an esprit de corps that had been lacking since McClellan's departure.

Hooker devoted special attention to his cavalry, where deeper operational reforms were overdue. No longer would the brigades and divisions of horsemen exist solely on an organizational chart. Two weeks after assuming command, he announced the formation of the Cavalry Corps, which would be led by Brig. Gen. George Stoneman. Going forward, the troopers of the Army of the Potomac would never again see their strength frittered away—a detail, company, or battalion at a time—to perform menial tasks that contributed little to battlefield success.

Three divisions of cavalry consisting of two brigades each were formed, supplemented by a small brigade of Regular Army horsemen under the command of Brig. Gen. John Buford. The 1st Division was put under Brig. Gen. Alfred Pleasonton, who had commanded the cavalry at Antietam and Fredericksburg. The 3rd's former colonel, William Averell, received command of the 2nd Division. Colonel McIntosh of the 3rd Pennsylvania was promoted to lead Averell's 2nd Brigade, which comprised not only the 3rd but also the 4th and 16th Pennsylvania Cavalry. The 3rd Division was commanded by a quiet, unassuming Pennsylvanian, Brig. Gen. David McMurtrie Gregg, a former Regular Army soldier and cousin of Governor Curtin. Finally, a brigade of mobile horse artillery, under the command of a seasoned regular, Capt. James M. Robertson, completed the formation of the corps. By the end of February, the Cavalry Corps counted 13,000 men and 12,000 horses in its ranks.[39]

The horses had been suffering from maladies that resulted from some of the same conditions as those that were afflicting their riders, namely poor rations and substandard care. Veterinary surgeons were assigned to the army not long after Hooker took over, treating disease and improving the overall health of the equines, while each cavalry regiment received a blacksmith to shoe its horses and a farrier to care for their hooves. The quality of the forage received by the animals improved, and more rigorous protocols were instituted to inspect mounts and replace those that could not be brought up to standards.[40]

Hooker's reforms brought with them immediate improvement, placing the cavalry of the Army of the Potomac on the path to equal footing with their Southern adversaries and providing the foundation for the successes the Cavalry Corps would experience in the coming months and years. A perceptive horse artilleryman, writing several months after Hooker had been relieved of command, echoed the thoughts of many regarding the effectiveness of these reforms: "To whom or what is this improvement due? To Gen. Joseph Hooker! From a disorderly and poorly disciplined rabble of mounted men whose only earthly benefit seemed to be as orderlies for generals or as a careless kind of picket guard he converted them into a well-disciplined and organized corps. He infused into them some of his own pluck and mettle, and they became the cavalry which since so many times have proved their prowess on rebel squadrons."[41] These plaudits, recorded in September 1863, came only after much hard campaigning, several pitched battles, and hundreds of casualties. The Cavalry Corps as formed in February 1863 had many lessons yet to learn in the crucible of conflict.

Following the defeat at Fredericksburg, the 3rd Pennsylvania resumed picketing duties and scouting the area north and west of the Rappahannock, ranging at times as far as Warrenton, thirty miles away. On February 25, in the area of Hartwood Church, Lt. Col. Edward Jones of the 3rd had command of a picket detail made up of 500 men from several regiments of McIntosh's brigade. Untested vedettes of the 16th Pennsylvania Cavalry allowed scouts of Brig. Gen. Fitzhugh Lee's 400-man force to pass through their line (the Rebels were dressed in blue). After capturing the men who let them by, the Southerners proceeded to knock out Federal picket posts one after another, penetrating to within ten miles of Army of the Potomac headquarters. Although the Northerners eventually regained their equilibrium and counterattacked, it was a repeat of the November 1862 disaster, this time with 150 soldiers from the regiments involved captured.

Division commander Averell was embarrassed, while Hooker was livid. Cavalry chief Stoneman got a shrill warning from the army commander: "You have got to stop these disgraceful cavalry 'surprises,' I'll have no more of them. . . . And by God sir if you don't do it, I give you fair notice, I'll relieve the whole of you and take command of the cavalry myself!"[42]

The first test of the newly organized Cavalry Corps came on March 17, 1863, when 2,100 troopers under Averell crossed the Rappahannock River at Kelly's Ford, seeking to avenge the surprise they had suffered at Hartwood Church. Advancing northwest from the crossing, Averell's column was attacked by Fitz Lee's brigade of cavalry, which had marched from Culpeper to meet the Federals. The fighting lasted for nine hours and ended when Averell, believing an erroneous report that Southern reinforcements were being brought up, decided to retreat.

While the action was a draw, with losses on the Federal side of approximately 80 compared with 130 for the Southerners, the fact that they had held their own in an all-cavalry engagement encouraged the Northerners. "The most substantial result of this fight was the feeling of confidence in its own ability which the volunteer cavalry gained," wrote an officer of the 3rd Pennsylvania who participated. "This feeling was not confined to the regiments engaged, but it was imparted to the whole of our cavalry. The esprit de corps and morale were greatly benefitted."[43] The soldier went on to comment that the Kelly's Ford fight was "the making of our cavalry." While his assessment may have been optimistic (less than 20 percent of the Cavalry Corps were engaged), the action undoubtedly inspired confidence in its participants.

Hooker's preliminary plans for engaging Lee's Army of Northern Virginia in the spring of 1863 called for Stoneman's cavalry to cross the Rappahannock far beyond the Rebel left, then ride cross-country to the southeast to disrupt the enemy's main supply and communication line, the Richmond, Fredericksburg, & Potomac Railroad. The Union commander believed that this raid would force Lee to shift south to address the threat, providing him an advantageous opportunity to attack the Confederate army.

The cavalry left their camps in and around Stafford County on April 13, but the next day unrelenting storms raised the Rappahannock seven feet in a few hours, rendering it impossible to cross. It took two weeks until the river was again passable, and by that time Hooker had modified his instructions to Stoneman twice. On April 22 Hooker ordered him to divide his command into detachments in an effort to confuse the enemy and "inflict a great deal of mischief."[44] Later, on the twenty-eighth, while still on the north side of the Rappahannock, Stoneman received orders to send a portion of his command to the south and west to deal with a Rebel cavalry concentration rumored to be near Culpeper, while the balance (and bulk) of his force moved as initially directed against the railroad south of Fredericksburg.

Stoneman crossed the river on April 29 and started southeast with two of his divisions, sending Averell, with the 3rd Pennsylvania, toward Culpeper and the Rebel troopers believed to be there. Stoneman's Raid, as the combined cavalry movements came to be known, delivered mixed results. Despite the presence of Union cavalry in his rear, Lee never felt threatened enough to cut loose from Fredericksburg. Ignoring the Federal horsemen, he instead delivered a shellacking to Hooker and the infantry of the Army of the Potomac at the Battle of Chancellorsville.

The divisions with Stoneman moved south and destroyed supplies and storage buildings, tore up railroad tracks and depots, and burned bridges, in the process causing the inhabitants of Richmond much uneasiness. In the raid's "strategic, and even short term tactical results," Stephen Starr has noted, "its accomplishments were insignificant." Averell's expedition to the west was separate from Stoneman's main effort, and while it achieved the object it had set out for—namely to disperse Southern cavalry near Culpeper—that was all it accomplished. Learning on May 1 that Averell was idling near Rapidan Station awaiting further instructions, Hooker ordered him back to the main body of the army, then relieved him two days later, mistakenly believing that Averell had not followed his orders.[45]

Though their efforts were bereft of outcomes that had any effect on the fighting at Chancellorsville, the Cavalry Corps had, according to an early chronicler of the effort, gained "hardihood, instruction and morale." Stephen Starr has concluded: "From the all-important standpoint of building self-confidence, self-respect and morale, the Stoneman raid, nearly barren as it was of strategic or tactical results,

... was the major step forward for the Federal cavalry." A Maine cavalryman, who voiced the opinion of many of its participants, later declared, "It was ever after a matter of pride with the boys "that they were on Stoneman's Raid."[46]

It was at this time, two weeks after the Cavalry Corps had returned to their camps in Stafford County, that 2nd Lieutenant Rawle reported for duty with the 3rd Pennsylvania. The Federal cavalry in the East, as Eric Wittenberg has fittingly described it, had nearly passed through its coming of age. Despite the uneven results of the Chancellorsville actions, the futility of the past two years would soon be gone; a time where the Union horsemen could hold their own against their Southern counterparts was within reach. Rawle's timing in joining the cavalry of the Army of the Potomac could not have been better, for the Federals would soon prove on the fields and hills of Brandy Station and Gettysburg that they could give as good as they could receive.

Following the Gettysburg Campaign, Rawle and the 3rd Pennsylvania continued to serve in the Cavalry Corps, seeing action during the Bristoe Station and Mine Run operations in the fall of 1863. When not actively campaigning, the regiment, like all of their brethren in the cavalry, was rarely immobile, with assignments to picket, outpost, and reconnaissance duty. Much of their effort was expended in chasing after Maj. John Mosby and the partisans who served under him. The incessant activity was wearisome, and during the midsummer of 1863 through the winter months of 1864, the regiment was worn down in the performance of these thankless, but necessary, tasks.

The 3rd Pennsylvania's association with the main body of the army's cavalry ended in the spring of 1864, prior to the Overland Campaign, when the regiment was assigned to duty at the headquarters of Maj. Gen. George Gordon Meade, commander of the Army of the Potomac. The Pennsylvanians replaced a regiment of Maryland cavalry and joined three infantry regiments, also attached to headquarters, to form a small brigade under the command of Provost Marshal General Marsena Patrick.[47]

The duties they assumed were very different than those they had performed over the preceding year—in fact, more reminiscent of their early war duties. Judging by their reactions, the men of the 3rd were pleased with the change. "It is considered the greatest compliment which can be paid to any regiment," Rawle told his mother of their posting to headquarters. Their new responsibilities included providing security for Meade and his headquarters staff, escorting prisoners, picketing and scouting, carrying orders, gathering up stragglers during combat, and arresting deserters and wayward Southern civilians. They were also tasked at times with guarding the large cattle herd that provided beef on the hoof for the army.

Most of the Pennsylvanians believed that their assignment to headquarters would only be temporary. "We understood that a short respite was to be allowed us to refit and recuperate," the regimental historians wrote, "in order that we might be in better condition for the arduous work of the coming campaign, which we all felt was to be a fight to the finish." Higher authorities deemed otherwise, and as the historians observed with some pride, the 3rd was a victim of its own proficiency: "So great was the esteem felt for us, and the reliance placed upon us, that no other body of cavalrymen was ever selected to replace us."[48] Over the ensuing fourteen months, reports would sporadically surface of attempts to absorb the Pennsylvanians back into the main body of the Cavalry Corps, but Lieutenant Rawle, for one, was not interested. "It would be *low*," he wrote in reaction to a rumor that the 3rd's former colonel, John McIntosh, was trying to have the regiment assigned to his brigade in the summer of 1864.

The experiences of the Pennsylvanians after their separation from the Cavalry Corps would be more closely associated with those of the infantry of the Army of the Potomac. While Gregg's 2nd Cavalry Division remained attached to the army and fought near Petersburg from August 1864 onward and the cavalry divisions under Maj. Gen. Phil Sheridan undertook independent raids and gained fame pushing Lt. Gen. Jubal Early's forces around the Shenandoah Valley, the 3rd's duties would be more commonplace and consequently less dangerous. Their relocation to headquarters, Rawle wrote, "is considered the softest of duties and is very welcome to us after being worked so hard. We can now sleep with security, without expecting to be waked up during the night by an attack on the lines." However hopeful the young officer may have been, he and his comrades would not find themselves completely immune to the hazards of combat.

As part of Meade's headquarters, the 3rd advanced into the abattoir of the Wilderness in early May 1864, providing security, rounding up stragglers, carrying orders, and shoring up lines of battle. One observer who witnessed the Pennsylvanians in action during the battle was unimpressed: "The worst feature we had to contend with was a provost guard from Meade's headquarters that kept in the rear of everything but the skirmish line. With drawn sabers they would drive the helpless sick and wounded in front of them, often striking them with their weapons."[49] The 3rd Pennsylvania continued in these duties throughout the Overland Campaign, operating along the fringes of the heaviest sustained combat of the war, witnessing the actions at Spotsylvania, along the North Anna, and around Cold Harbor before moving with the army across the James River to Petersburg. Like many of those in Meade's orbit, Rawle resented the plaudits that Lt. Gen. Ulysses S. Grant received during the battles of 1864–65. "Meade does all the fighting here and Grant gets all the credit," he complained to his mother in a letter written from Cold Harbor in June 1864.

Once near Petersburg, Rawle and the 3rd continued their provost-marshal duties, including intermittent assignments to safeguard the homes and property of Southern citizens, chiefly from marauding gangs of Federal deserters, "who hide in the woods and plunder all around the country." Their responsibilities once they occupied the lines outside of the city became routine, and, by late July, the men referred to their activities as "dull, uninteresting and unexciting."[50] There were exceptions, such as the Battle of Boydton Plank Road in late October 1864 and at Hatcher's Run in both December 1864 and February 1865, when the 3rd shed its role as provost guard and took an active part in the fighting.[51] When Lee and the Army of Northern Virginia were finally forced to vacate their fieldworks near Petersburg in April 1865, Rawle and the 3rd Pennsylvania joined in the pursuit and were near at hand when Lee surrendered his army to Grant.

William Brooke Rawle was undoubtedly a product of his environment, and his education, upbringing, wealth, and pedigree influenced the way he viewed events, narrated his experiences, and interacted with the people around him. His education alone would have set him apart from the men he served with; just over 1 percent of college-aged males in the United States in the mid-nineteenth century were enrolled in institutions of higher learning.[52] Rawle's conversion from college student to cavalry officer was remarkably smooth, and he adapted to military life with an effortlessness that would have offended the peaceful sensibilities of his Quaker ancestors. The caste system that existed within the 3rd Pennsylvania as a result of its Regular Army influences surely helped facilitate his transition; the regiment was a microcosm of the world he had grown up in, where the divide between men of wealth and standing and the rest of society was wide.

Andrew Bledsoe has explored the experiences of citizen-officers like Rawle during the Civil War and observes that many newly minted officers serving in volunteer regiments, as well as the men they commanded, were "required . . . to suppress years of instinct and custom carried forward from their civilian life" in order to adjust to life in the army. The enlisted men's "rebellious attitude toward authority, and the ideological tradition that inspired it, intensified the challenge of command." In many instances, he writes, "new officers attempting to command volunteers steeped in the citizen-soldier ethos had to alter or suspend a lifetime of accepted traditions, instincts, and peacetime prerogatives fundamental to their identities as free Americans."[53]

Second Lt. William Brooke Rawle, taken early in his war service. (From Regimental History Committee, *History of the Third Pennsylvania Cavalry* [1905])

Rawle, however, profited from the fact that the men he led had, in all probability, given up any notions of equality with their officers or democratic customs that might have influenced their conduct earlier in the war. Shaped by Regular Army officers and governed by Regular Army principles, the Pennsylvanians were acutely aware that any deviation from accepted norms of behavior and established regulations was intolerable. The unquestioning obedience to authority that guided the conduct of his men ensured that the young lieutenant's assimilation into his new role would not be disrupted by unruly, disrespectful, or rebellious members of his company.

Regrettably, Rawle left no record of the reasons behind his decision to enter the army. His letters and diary entries commence on the day he left Philadelphia to join the Army of the Potomac, nor does his earlier correspondence indicate how the military and political events that preceded his enlistment might have influenced him. Also absent is any discussion of the higher ideals or the broad themes of the war; concepts such as freedom, liberty, the Union, and states' rights go unmentioned. In this respect his writings are as noteworthy for what they omit as they are for the details of daily army life that they convey.

Rawle was similarly silent regarding the central theme of the war, slavery. The Emancipation Proclamation had gone into effect over four months before he entered the service, but any opinions he had regarding its influence he kept to himself. His personal intercourse with black Americans was limited to men he employed as servants during his military career. The infrequent mentions he does make regarding African Americans over the course of his twenty-seven months in uniform, however, reveal an attitude that can be best described as contempt. The cavalry officer was unsparing in his racially charged comments on the performance of African American troops after the Battle of the Crater (July 30, 1864); the "black rascals," he opined, performed "cowardly." At war's end, viewing the devastation wrought by the armies that passed through the countryside of Virginia west of Petersburg, he failed to note the irony when he commented on the helplessness of the Southern civilians whose slaves had deserted them. "Many of the black men," he wrote, "have got it into their heads that they are now free, and can therefore live and do nothing. A good many of them join with bands of stragglers and do a great deal of pillaging—even going so far as to rob and burn the houses of their masters." Two months later, while serving on occupation duty in the former Confederate capital, he wrote that the general commanding the department, Edward O. C. Ord, had been replaced because he "was not a strong enough abolishionist [sic] and nigger man generally, and was foolish enough to think the white man to be better than the nigger."[54] It is likely, based on the sparse evidence he supplies, that Rawle found common cause with that group of Northerners who did not expressly wage or support war to free the slaves but, as Gary Gallagher has written, "eventually accepted emancipation as a useful tool to help defeat the rebels and punish the slaveholding class most northerners blamed for secession and the outbreak of war."[55]

In his study of college-educated New Englanders who served during the Civil War, Kanisorn Wongsrichanalai has examined the gentlemanly codes of conduct and the precepts of character that were inculcated into highly educated, cultivated men like Rawle during their formative years, providing hints as to what may have prompted the young Philadelphian and men like him to serve. The "elite young men who inhabited this world," he writes, "developed their leadership class identity based on the term 'character,'" which they understood as "an idealized standard of behavior consisting most importantly of educated, independent thought and selfless action." Character, notes Wongsrichanalai, was essentially the Northern version of the "better-known code of southern honor." The level of education that Rawle had attained allowed him to "become a full man of character." While he could have sat out the war, he and other volunteers like him demonstrated that "their commitment to the Union cause as well as their dedication to behaving as honorable gentlemen compelled them to join the armed forces, even though their class positions would have shielded them from service."[56]

In a notable instance later in the war, Rawle seemed to relish the opportunity to prefer charges against a fellow officer who committed a transgression, noting that he had enough discreditable information on the offender to "knock him higher than a kite." He charged the officer in question with "disorderly conduct" and "conduct unbecoming a gentleman." While the specifics of the charges are unknown (the officer resigned before he was brought to court-martial), his behavior surely ran counter to the young Philadelphian's notions of honor, dignity, and character.

Rawle developed friendships with several officers within the regiment, a number of whom shared the education, social standing, and upbringing that he had enjoyed. One of the other lieutenants in his company was a former noncommissioned officer in the Regular Army who was commissioned in the 3rd Pennsylvania at around the same time as himself. "He is a fine fellow, a natural gentleman," Rawle wrote of the regular, though he was "probably not so polished as if he had passed his life in Phila. society." In addition, Rawle did not suffer lightly people he judged to be unqualified: he referred to a longtime commander of the regiment as "an inveterate old fogy, and very disagreeable," while another field officer he described as "a man who will let no officer of the regiment get a soft thing, but who is almost always away from his regiment himself."

Rawle would spend considerable time from August 1863 to February 1864 in northern Virginia—and later in 1864 near Petersburg—battling Confederate guerillas and guarding against their attacks. "Guerillas effectively disrupted supply lines and communications, cowed or neutralized Unionists, forced redeployment of federal forces, distracted U.S. commanders, eroded the morale of invading troops, and generally created multiple military obstacles," Daniel Sutherland has written.[57] They also picked off inattentive Northern pickets, vedettes, scouts, and outposts, variously killing or capturing individuals or small groups of soldiers.

Despite the travails and hardships he and his fellow cavalrymen experienced battling these Southern partisans and expressing disgust with their method of warfare (what he called "waylaying and murdering"), the Philadelphian voiced empathy with their conduct, which, he wrote, "tho' not justifiable, is at least excusable. I would do the same if I saw my family & property treated the way theirs is." Encountering this method of warfare was stressful for the new soldier and became more so when a fellow officer of the 3rd Pennsylvania was dismissed from the service after he was ambushed and captured in August 1863. "Orders are for every Reb found in our uniform to be hung up on the spot," Rawle wrote to his mother in February 1864, "and they in turn say they will hang one officer for every one of their men. Pleasant, isn't it? What, between a continual fear of being dismissed [from] the service for any slight delinquency, and being hung up to dry by Jonny Reb, a cavalry officer's situation is not the most agreeable in the world."

Southern partisans were not the only irregular combatants he would have to guard against. Posted to an isolated position west of Petersburg in July 1864, the nearby countryside was overrun by Northern deserters who were terrorizing Southern citizens. "To see the ravages committed by our troops often makes me disgusted with the army and with the cause," he wrote at the time. "To be sure, this is not done by the *army*. We are hanging men very often for such offenses. In any army of course there must be a proportion of rascals, and ours has its share."

Rawle's interactions with Southern civilians were mostly favorable. He spent considerable time in and around the town of Warrenton, Virginia, during the winter of 1863–64, developing friendships with several of its residents. The fact that he had relatives who lived in the South, including three who fought for the Confederacy, may have contributed to a more lenient attitude toward the Southerners he met during his army service. When the opportunity presented itself, the Pennsylvanian sought out his kinsmen, two of whom fought in the Army of Northern Virginia. One served as a sergeant in the 2nd Virginia Infantry of the famous Stonewall Brigade; the other attained the rank of major and quartermaster of the Louisiana Brigade.[58] Another "reprobate" cousin (to use Rawle's description), a native of Vicksburg, Mississippi, who also had attended the University of Pennsylvania before war broke out, was taken prisoner when Grant captured that city in July 1863. While picketing along Virginia's Rappahannock River in the fall of 1863, the cavalry officer partook in several discussions with a Rebel captain who would cross the river to converse with him.

Physically, Rawle was diminutive, and the few remaining photographs of him taken during the war show a clean-shaven, boyish-looking young man. He would cultivate a beard later in the war, although whether it was done for convenience or to combat his youthful appearance is not known. He was almost never sick, outside of an occasional cold, while serving in the field. In his adolescence he had difficulties with his hearing and wore glasses, which he stopped using after joining the army. "My eyes have improved wonderfully since I made a practice of not using spectacles," he told his mother. "When I want to see anything at a distance I use my field glasses, which I have conveniently attached at my belt." Active duty agreed with the young soldier: "I am a little taller, fuller in the face & burnt by the sun to a very dirty color," he wrote not long after joining the 3rd. "I never was in better health, and the life agrees with me immensely."

As would be expected of a man of his attainments, Rawle read widely and voraciously, favoring Scottish and English authors. "The monotony of camp life leaves a good deal of spare time on my hands," he explained to the homefolk. "When I get a good book I *devour* it, to use your expression, and I am now reading 'Oliver Twist.'" In addition to Charles Dickens, he records reading works by Sir Walter Scott, George Whyte-Melville, George Alfred Lawrence, and others and regularly received copies of popular periodicals and East Coast newspapers. He also enjoyed tobacco but drank only sparingly.

Clues to the young Philadelphian's political leanings are sprinkled throughout his correspondence and grow more frequent in the run up to the presidential election in the fall of 1864, which pitted George McClellan against Abraham Lincoln. Rawle had joined the Army of the Potomac six months after McClellan's departure, thus he was able to adopt a less biased stance regarding "Little Mac" than many who had served in the army during his tenure. "Tho' partial to McClellan personally, I think that a change would be prejudicial to the good of the cause," he wrote in September 1864, two months before the election. "Consequently if I take advantage of my right of 'exercising the election franchise,' as all the Penna troops are allowed to vote, I don't know yet whether I will or not. I don't like much the idea of soldiers meddling with politics." The presidential vote split differently between the officers of the 3rd and the enlisted men, which, Rawle noted approvingly, "shows well for the discipline of the Regiment, that is, that officers and men never have the slightest familiarity between them."

Rawle wrote 150 letters to his family during the twenty-seven months he spent in the army; collected in this work are 136 of these. The vast majority of his correspondence was written to his mother; 14 letters were written to his sister Charlotte; 10 to his sister Elizabeth; 1 to his uncle, Henry; and 1 addressed to "people at home." Portions of 12 letters and pertinent diary entries from the period between mid-May 1865 until his muster out of the service in August 1865 have been incorporated into the epilogue; 2 brief letters to his mother covering inconsequential affairs have not been included.

In order to confirm that his mail was being received at home, Rawle instructed his mother to make note in the letters she sent to him of the dates of the correspondence she had received. In this way he might know that a letter was lost or miscarried. None of the missives that he received from home have survived since he made a practice of destroying these letters after reading them, likely for fear that his private matters would be exposed should they fall into a stranger's hands.

Rawle reprimanded one of his sisters in late July 1863 for "publishing his doings," but I have been unable to ascertain that any of his letters may have been printed. "I hope hereafter," he warned, "that you will not do anything of the kind." A month later, still wary that his correspondence might be exposed to public scrutiny, he threatened to alter his content: "I write in such a way that I would prefer them to be kept private. If I find this goes on I will have to take up *formal* letter writing, which I don't think will suit you very well." Rawle was rarely pleased with the frequency of the mail he received from home and pleaded with his family to "write sooner and oftener."

Although he participated in some of the most intense combat of the war, Rawle largely omitted details of the human toll it produced in his letters home, ostensibly, it can be surmised, to both prevent his mother and sisters from despairing for his wellbeing and to avoid offending their sensibilities. It is also obvious, based on his replies to the letters received from his family, that they continually expressed fear for his safety. He, in turn, sought to reassure them: "I beg of you not to remain in anxiety about me," he wrote in October 1863. "If anything should happen to me you would hear of it soon enough, and if I were hurt, you would see me at home in a short time, you may be bound." In response to another letter that same month, he admonished, "It is actually *unkind* in you to feel so about me because it only makes me downhearted." Even the cessation of hostilities failed to assuage his family's forebodings. "You must not be anxious about not hearing from me," he wrote from Richmond in May 1865, "for the war is over and the chances are that I am all right."

While he deliberately shielded his family from details of the horrors of the combat, Rawle was, at times, taken with the pageantry that accompanied it. A mass of Confederate cavalry preparing to attack his position at Gettysburg produced a "subdued murmur of admiration" from the lieutenant and his men. A "Beautiful sight," akin to a Fourth of July fireworks display, was how he described a nighttime mortar duel near Petersburg. The teenager was enthralled when he caught a "beautiful glimpse" of a cavalry advance, flags flying, skirmishers leading the way, accompanied by artillery. What Earl Hess has described as "the terrible aesthetic appeal of combat" impressed the young man. "Awesome displays of power," for soldiers like Rawle, Hess writes, "were enormously seductive."[59]

In the postwar years, Rawle collected the letters he had written to his relatives and had them sewn into a leather-bound volume; the title on the spine reads "Letters from the Army, 1863–65." He was a diligent diarist as well, composing entries every day, and, as he wrote in the late 1800s in an introduction to a typed copy of his original diaries, used the entries in the composition of official reports. It is also apparent that he used them as the basis from which to compose his letters home. "The Original Diary," he wrote,

> was kept by me personally during the period of time which it covers, and was written in a minute hand, with lead pencil, in small printed "one-page-to-a-day" pocket journals, for the respective years. Through lapse of time, and frequent use

for reference in connection with the literature of the War, in the reading of which I have found it most valuable, the original has now become almost illegible, so much so that, in order to insure accuracy in the copying, I have found it necessary to read it myself by way of dictation to my stenographer and typewriter. . . .

The original notes were made under varied circumstances. Sometimes at night by the bivouac fire, after a hard day's march, and when utterly tired out; often by the picket fire when sleep was prohibited; at times while under artillery fire, yet compelled to remain inactive; at others during a few minutes halt on the march; and again during the quiet and occasional repose of camp life; in heat and cold; in rain and sleet and snow—at all times, and in any places, where or when the opportunity offered. The notes are necessarily brief; mere "memoires pour servir."[60] They were frequently called into requisition in the making up of official reports or other communications, and for establishing facts and dates. . . .

I now regret exceedingly that the notes are not more full. I could amplify them one hundred fold by anecdotes connected with many a stirring scene, for the details of which there was then no space or time for the writing. . . . There are abundant evidences of how ignorant one may be of military movements close at hand, how narrow were the surroundings in the midst of a large army, how false or inaccurate the information which was conveyed from mouth to mouth through the camps or the column, and in letters to those at home; what different impressions the same facts and the same scenes conveyed to different minds and memories.

The typescript copy of the diary, prepared in 1898, consists of 154 single-spaced, single-sided pages and is entitled "Diary of Service with the Army of the Potomac." Rawle retroactively employed self-censorship in the transcription of this copy, admitting that he omitted "strictly private matters, chiefly dates of correspondence with my family and friends," in the typescript version. His foresight in preparing a copy of his diary was fortunate, for while the original journals were known to have been held in private hands until sometime in the 1980s, there is no record of them since then.[61]

In addition to keeping his diary and dispatching letters home with regularity, Rawle was an enthusiastic collector of photographs, amassing a large assemblage of cartes de visite and several albumen photographs of members of the 3rd Pennsylvania Cavalry and other soldiers he served with. Once secured, he would send the photographs home for safekeeping, enclosed with his correspondence, noting in the letters the names of the individuals they depicted.

Following his discharge from the service in August 1865, Rawle returned to Philadelphia and studied law under the supervision of his uncle, Henry. In 1867, the same year that he officially declined a commission in the 7th US Cavalry, Rawle passed the bar and joined Henry's firm, the same one founded by his great-grandfather in 1783. His law practice was not devoted to litigation and trials at the bar, but instead to overseeing the economic interests of descendants of the family of William Penn, along with "the business of certain historical Philadelphia estates, some of which had passed into the hands of English owners." One relative recorded: "By reason of his methodical habits of work, and his skill in the management of trust estates, he was given charge of large holdings as a trustee, rivaling in amount some of the lesser trust companies. Coming to him as the reward for his special efficiency and high integrity, it was a particularly honorable employment."[62] After Henry's death in 1889, William would remain a member of the Rawle Law Offices until his own death.

His first foray into documenting the history of the 3rd Pennsylvania Cavalry occurred in 1869, when Rawle contributed the short historical sketch of the regiment's war service to the five-volume history of Pennsylvania volunteer regiments compiled by Samuel Bates.[63]

William Rawle wed Elizabeth Norris Pepper (1841–1926), a descendant of a line of famous Philadelphia physicians, in 1872; there is no record of any children resulting from their marriage. In the same year as his wedding, Rawle became involved in the work of the Historical Society of Pennsylvania, serving in various roles within that organization until 1900, when he was elected vice president.

Conscious of his family's deep roots in American society and mindful of his ancestors, he devoted himself throughout his postwar life to two passions. One was detailing the histories of several prominent Philadelphia families, including the Rawles, Shoemakers, Tilghmans, and Burges. The other was the study of the cavalry fighting on the Union right flank at Gettysburg on July 2–3. It was a healthy obsession for the former horse soldier, and beginning in the early 1870s, he devoted years of research and reams of correspondence to his study of the battle. "When I undertook to work up the subject," he recalled years later, "I was working in virgin fields. There was practically no literature on the subject."[64] He exchanged letters with numerous officers of the cavalry and horse artillery of both sides, wrote to the War Department to secure copies of official reports touching on the actions, and corresponded frequently with John Page Nicholson, the government-appointed historian of the Battle of Gettysburg.[65]

In 1878 Rawle produced the first history of the cavalry fighting east of Gettysburg when "The Right Flank at Gettysburg: An Account of the Operations of General David McM. Gregg's Cavalry Command and Their Important Bearing on the Results of the Battle" appeared in the Annals of the War series published in the *Philadelphia Weekly Times*. A pamphlet version of the work came out the same year, and the study was included in the book-length compilation *The Annals of the War, Written by Leading Participants North and South* in 1879. In 1883 Rawle was able to secure preliminary copies of the official Gettysburg reports that touched on the cavalry fighting on the right flank (these would not appear in print, in preliminary form, until 1889) and in February 1884 contributed another article for the *Weekly Times* Annals of the War series, entitled "With Gregg in the Gettysburg Campaign." Rawle wrote this work, he recalled, in order to correct the errors he had made in his earlier history.[66]

By this time, Rawle had established himself as the leading authority on the cavalry fighting on the right flank and in October 1884 was asked to speak at the dedication of the Cavalry Shaft monument on the East Cavalry Field at Gettysburg. The speech he gave that day was reproduced in pamphlet form the same year as *Gregg's Cavalry Fight at Gettysburg: Historical Address Delivered Oct. 15th, 1884 upon the Dedication of Monumental Shaft Erected upon the Site of the Cavalry Engagement on the Right Flank of the Army of the Potomac, July 3rd, 1863, during the Battle of Gettysburg.* Rawle also contributed two articles to the *Journal of the United States Cavalry Association* in 1891, "Gregg's Cavalry Fight at Gettysburg, July 3, 1863" and "Further Remarks on the Cavalry Fight on the Right Flank at Gettysburg."

In support of his ongoing writing and research, Rawle visited the Gettysburg battlefield throughout his life. Period photographs show him in company with a large group of veterans, including former generals Wade Hampton, David McMurtrie Gregg, and John B. McIntosh, during the 1884 monument dedication and during the 1886 reunion of veterans of the cavalry fight.

In 1893, four years after the public issuance of the Gettysburg volumes of the *Official Records,* which supported many of the conclusions he had reached in his research, Rawle would look back with satisfaction on the studies he had produced. "I have always been surprised that I made so few mistakes, groping as I had been in the dark to such an extent," he wrote to a fellow veteran.[67]

Forty years after the end of the war, in 1905, the regimental history of the 3rd Pennsylvania Cavalry was published. Despite the lapse of time between the events it covers and its publication, the book is one of the more thorough and comprehensive histories of the genre, and Rawle's influence is evident throughout its pages. Serving as the head of the Regimental History Committee, which was charged with producing the book, Rawle contributed materially to its contents, providing numerous excerpts from his diary. It is likely that he wrote much of it.

The Military Order of the Loyal Legion of the United States, a Union veteran's association to which Rawle belonged, recognized the Pennsylvanian's efforts to document the fighting on the East Cavalry Field and in 1909 raised and dedicated a fifty-five-foot flagpole there in his name. Fittingly, the flagpole stands

A group of Union and Confederate veterans of the cavalry fight on July 3, 1863, photographed in July 1886 in Lott's Woods at Gettysburg. David McM. Gregg, the Federal cavalry commander during the battle, stands in the left-center, wearing a straw hat and holding an umbrella. Standing on Gregg's left and wearing a bowler hat is John B. McIntosh, a former 3rd Pennsylvania commander, who led a Union cavalry brigade in the battle. To their left and in the center are two former Confederates. The older man in front, holding a hat and a cane, with distinctive facial hair is Wade Hampton, who commanded a cavalry brigade at Gettysburg. Behind Hampton's left shoulder and between him and the man in an overcoat is Jeb Stuart's chief of staff during the campaign, H. B. McClellan, hatless and wearing a dark suit. On the far right of the photo is Surgeon Theodore Tate of the 3rd Pennsylvania, a Gettysburg native. The tall figure (slightly blurred) over Tate's right shoulder is the government-appointed historian of the Battle of Gettysburg, John Bachelder. In front and to the left and Bachelder's right is William H. Bricker of the 3rd Pennsylvania, hatless with dark hair and a moustache. Just off the right shoulder of the one-armed veteran in front of Bricker is William Brooke Rawle, shorter than many in the group, hatless, with a full beard and glasses. The face of William Miller, the captain who ordered the charge of the 3rd at Gettysburg, is visible between Rawle and the one-armed veteran. (From Regimental History Committee, *History of the Third Pennsylvania Cavalry* [1905])

alongside modern-day Gregg Avenue, which intersects the East Cavalry Field near the point where the heaviest fighting took place on July 3. When he died six years later, a bronze plaque with the inscription "To the Memory of Bvt. Lt. Col. Wm. Brooke Rawle, 1843–1915," memorializing the flagpole to him, was affixed to it.[68] He thus enjoys the distinction of being one of the lowest-ranking officers of the Union army to have a memorial in his name on the Gettysburg battlefield.[69]

William Brooke Rawle died on December 1, 1915, survived by his wife. He had outlived his mother and both sisters. Upon his passing, his letters, his volume of transcribed diary entries, and his photographs became a part of the holdings of the War Library and Museum of the Military Order of the Loyal Legion of the United States in Philadelphia. Unfortunately, much of his extensive photographic collection vanished prior to the late 1980s, probably scattered among various un-known private collectors.[70] His extensive postwar correspondence with former Union and Confederate officers relating to the cavalry fighting at Gettysburg is now part of the collection of the Historical Society of Pennsylvania.

"Boys became men fast in those days," Rawle had written in his later years, recalling his experiences in the American Civil War. Although he may have be-lieved, as he recorded in the introduction to his diary, that his wartime writings were "crude and boyish, often of questionable grammar and unquestionable inel-egance," he was incorrect.[71] On the contrary, his letters and journal entries incor-porate the observations of an educated, astute young man and provide detailed insight into the daily life of a cavalry officer during the final, tumultuous two years of the Civil War in the East.

CHAPTER ONE

Brandy Station and the Gettysburg Campaign

May 17–July 18, 1863

Second Lt. William Brooke Rawle reported to the 3rd Pennsylvania Cavalry on May 16, 1863, ten days after the regiment had completed its participation in Stoneman's raid during the Chancellorsville Campaign. Two weeks earlier, the Army of the Potomac had been defeated at Chancellorsville by General Lee and the Army of Northern Virginia in what many regard as Lee's signature victory. Outnumbered by more than two to one and taken by surprise by Major General Hooker's opening movements, Lee reacted decisively, seized the initiative, and forced the Federals back across the fords of the Rapidan and Rappahannock Rivers after three days of heavy fighting.

In a series of sometimes contradictory orders issued in the weeks leading up to the battle, Hooker had directed Stoneman to cross the Rappahannock in mid-April and divide his 10,000-man Cavalry Corps, sending the majority of his force, under David Gregg and John Buford, to harass and disrupt Lee's supply line in the expanse between Fredericksburg and Richmond, while the balance, some 3,400 men, including the 3rd Pennsylvania, under the overall command of the 3rd's former colonel, William Averell, would advance along the Orange & Alexandria Railroad to engage Confederate cavalry located near Culpeper. After scattering that force, the division would move south and east to join with Buford and Gregg astride the Richmond, Fredericksburg, & Potomac Railroad, Lee's key supply line. Averell chased the Southern troopers through Culpeper County and across the Rapidan, but before he could advance to meet the rest of the Cavalry Corps, he was recalled to Chancellorsville by Hooker, who, frustrated that the general had not made further progress and convinced that he had disobeyed his orders, soon relieved him of command of his division.[1]

Although they had experienced relatively little combat during their twenty-four-day sojourn, the men and horses of the 3rd Pennsylvania, like most of the Cavalry Corps, were worn down by exposure to the elements and fatigue. As Rawle began to adjust to the responsibilities of life as a cavalry officer, more than half of the regiment was absent, waiting for fresh mounts. His acclimatization process, however, would be unexpectedly hastened by events he could not foresee. The cavalrymen of the Army of the Potomac were about to pass through eight of the most momentous weeks they would ever experience, fighting in the largest all-cavalry battle of the war at Brandy Station on June 9, then in the costliest battle of the conflict at Gettysburg, Pennsylvania, just over three weeks later.

On May 5, 1863, my friends Ellwood Davis and George S. Luttrel Ward and I received notice of our appointments, through the kind offices of Mr. Clement B. Barclay, and the issue of our commissions as Second Lieutenants in Companies H, M and C respectively of the Third Regiment of Pennsylvania Volunteer Cavalry.[2] We at once made our preparations to join the Regiment as soon as possible, and at midnight of Thursday, May 14th, we left our homes in Philadelphia, starting from the depot at Broad and Prime Streets by the Philadelphia, Wilmington and Baltimore Railroad. We arrived in Washington at eight o'clock on the following morning and obtained our passes to the front by way of Aquia Creek, Va., the depot of supplies for the Army of the Potomac. I was nineteen years of age at the time.[3]

———

Willard's Hotel
Washn. DC.
May 15. 63.

Dear Mother:

We arrived in the "Metropolis" at 8, this morning, after a very tedious ride of 8 hours. We were delayed about 2 hours on the road. I rode on the platform from the Susquehanna, at Perryville, to Baltimore, and saw the sun rise most beautifully. I did not get a wink of sleep on account of some babies squalling nearly all night. The delay was very acceptable, in as much as we were enabled to see the country, which I have never seen before.

We are stopping here for breakfast, (don't think us extravagant), and are now waiting for our passes through the lines. We are not able to go about without them as we have our uniforms on, & we will be arrested by the Provost Guard. Luckily, we were not stopped in coming here, although we barely "saved our bacon." Everything is "military" here.

We just missed Mr. Barclay, who passed us on the road, and so we will have to shift for ourselves. We want to get to "the Front" tonight if possible, as "Willard's" is very expensive ($3 Per diem).[4]

A good many of our friends went to the depot to see us off. I was so bothered with Grandma's mattress that I sent it back by Geo. Emlen.[5] Keep it till I want it, if I ever do. The gingerbreads were very acceptable in the cars last night. I don't know whether I will be able to look around the city. Washn. reminds me of the description of Constantinople in the "Interpreter," as it is the place where all the officers meet in going to and coming from the "Front." And Willard's reminds me of "Messirie's."[6]

I will write as soon as I reach the regiment. I send this in a carpet bag of Davis' in which he brought his uniform & is going to send back his citizen's clothes. Don't be worried about me as I will take as good care of myself as I can for your sake....

Camp near Potomac Creek, Va.

May 17. 63.

Dear Mother:

We arrived here yesterday about 1.30 PM. Our camp is situated in a pine grove, on a high hill, commanding a beautiful view, but one which I could not appreciate at first, on account of the desolation which is everywhere visible. The warm weather has dried up the roads and turned the "sacred soil" into a fine dust instead. The whole country appears to be one large road, no grass, no fences, nothing but camps everywhere. But, since you want a journal, I had better begin where I left off in my last. A short time after I sealed the letter of Friday, Ward came in with our passes "to the front" but we could not go to Aquia Creek before the next morning.

We took the opportunity of a 20 hours delay to look around Washington. We first went to the Capitol and through the magnificent grounds. The building, as you know, is unfinished as yet, but the perfect part is superb, not so much, taking it all in all, as examining every separate room and specimen of art. The views from the windows, especially from that of the room of the Reporters for the House of Representatives, are magnificent. The one particularly mentioned comprises the city of Washington with the Potomac and Gen. Lee's estate of Arlington Heights. But you, I suppose, have seen it already & I am incapable of giving an adequate description of it. We spent a couple of hours at the Capitol and then went to the White House at the other end of the town. We could not go in, but merely saw the house & grounds.

With the exception of one or two public buildings, I think Washington is one of the most wretched places I ever was in. Willard's Hotel, where we had to stay till Saturday morning, is miserably kept. To be sure, you have a bill of fare from which you can ask for almost anything, but I would enjoy my dinner at home a thousand times better. Our expenses there for 24 hours were about $5 apiece.

On Saturday morning we started by the Aquia Creek boat, down the Potomac, the scenery along the river on both sides is magnificent. I had a very fine view of Mount Vernon, Alexandria and the fortifications along the river. We arrived at Aquia Creek about noon and after a great deal of trouble with our baggage, and considerable delay, we got off. I was awfully bothered with that box of Winsor's, as it was about as much as I could do with a heavy valise alone and <u>porterage</u> was expensive. We then went to Aquia Creek Station on the Aquia Creek and Fredericksburg R.R. and then had a good deal of trouble finding the Regt.

We reported to Col. McIntosh and were introduced to the officers of the Regt., who are a fine set of gentlemen.[7] The Regt. itself is a mere skeleton, there not being more than 150 men mounted, as they have been used very hard in the late raid. The balance of the Regt. is at Dumfries, dismounted.[8] We are all waiting for a new supply of horses. We had a splendid dinner of ham & eggs, tea & shad. But that is a very unusual thing; at present we have the same for every meal, coffee is good but no milk. Some of the officers are quartered in log huts built by the men and are very comfortable. This is the old camp of the Regt., before they went out on the last raid. I am messing pro temp. with Lieut. Heyl, a nice young fellow who has the nicest hut in camp.[9] Of course this is the sunny side of camp life and it can't last forever.

Let Mrs. White and Capt. Winsor's friends know that I can't get the things to the "Lancers" yet, as they are out on picket, near Hartwood Church, where, the other day, 2 lieut's & 50 men were "gobbled up" as the camp phrase is for being captured.[10] None of our friends tho' I believe. As soon as I can I will get them to them.

We know here not even as much as you do, of things going on. We don't ever know what regiments are near us. I slept very well last night, for my first in camp. This morn. (Sunday) I was assigned to Comp. "C" and as my capt. & 1st Lieut. are detailed on the staff I am in command of the company. Rather hard on me for my 1st day.

2.30 P.M. Buford's Cav. Div. are passing with 2 or 3 squadrons of Rush's Lancers [the 6th Pennsylvania Cavalry] in the advance. They all look so dirty that I could hardly recognize them. I looked out very hard for White but I missed him although he was there. I saw Bob Morris, who was in command, Lieper, Winsor &

Edward M. Heyl rose from first sergeant to captain of Company E, 3rd Pennsylvania, during his three years of service. He had a controversial postwar career in the Regular Army. (J. Gregory Acken personal collection)

one or two of my friends.[11] I gave the letter to Winsor with White's also. He said that he would send over for the box and bundle.

I am supernumerary officer of the guard tomorrow & have more work to do than the other new officers, as they have their superior officers to do duty, but I, being in command of [the] company, have to do everything myself. I am acting captain of Comp. "C" which consists of 2 sergeants 1 corporal and 4 men. About 40 of my men are dismounted or on detached duty.

Camp near Potomac Creek, Va.

May 22. 1863

Dear Mother,

I recd. your welcome letter immediately after "Water Call" and read it during "Stables" which disagreeable duties I have to attend to, being in command of "C" Company.[12] All [are] a captain's responsibilities, I am told, which are not much diminished when I say that "C" Company consists of 2 sergeants 1 corporal & 3 men. I believe I told you that about 40 are at Dumfries dismounted awaiting horses, which we are expecting every day.

On Sunday eveng. I recd. from the Adgt. my "cocked hat" (all officer's details are folded in triangular shape, whence the name) informing me that I was detailed as "supernumerary officer of the Guard" so I was on guard from Guard Mount

(8 AM) on Monday, for 24 hours. Vernou was officer of the guard & I was on as "super[numerary]," for the purpose of becoming acquainted with the duties.[13] The guard house consists of a log & mud hut without a roof and very dirty; here we had to stay all day & night without sleeping—the Regulations require—but as we had a good sergeant—a Methodist minister bye the bye—we managed to get a wink of sleep and were waked in time to go the Grand rounds at midnight with the Officer of the day.[14] In the afternoon we recd. orders to report at Brigade Hdqrtrs to be mustered in to the U.S. service. In the eveng. we generally have officers school for the instruction (practical & theoretical) of the 2nd lieuts. We go down to bathe in the eveng. after "Tattoo," in Potomac Creek, which is very needful here, it being the dustiest & warmest place I was ever in.

May 19. Tuesday—Frank Wetherill & Lieut. Warren arrived in camp, having been lately released from Libby Prison, Richmond, Va.[15] F[rank] W[etherill] is not in command of my company ("C") but of "F" which is in the same squadron and we, being the only officers in the 6th squadron and we are as much together as if we were in the same company.[16]

———

May 19th. Tuesday. . . . In the morning Lieut. Col. Jones held a practical School of instruction for the 2nd Lieutenants.[17] We were taught to fold our overcoats, saddle and unsaddle our horses. . . . Attended theoretical officer's school in the evening.

———

May 20. Wednesday—During the afternoon Frank Wetherill & I rode over to the camp of Rush's Lancers about 3 miles from here, near Gen. Stoneman's Hdqr-trs and saw our friends.[18] Willie White looks very well indeed and so do all the others except Winsor who looks wretchedly & Geo. Pepper whose arm troubles him much. He will have to resign, or, the Drs. say, that there will be some danger of his lossing [sic] his arm. Don't mention it though.[19]

21st. Thursday—I selected a very nice bay horse for my use & had an orderly detailed from my company as my "striker," (as our enlisted servants are called).[20] In the eveng. orders were recd. to have 3 days rations & 2 of forage, to be packed on mules, 60 rounds of carbine & 20 of pistol ammunition, Reveille to sound at 2½ AM tomorrow, and to be ready to march in light marching order by 4 AM. We got everything ready, I packed my valise, took all the money I had for fear of being "gobbled up" (as being captured is called) & got everything ready. After coming from bathing we found that the order had been countermanded.

———

May 21st. Thursday. In the morning, we raw officers were drilled in the Carbine exercise. I took command of the squadron ("C" and "F") to go out to graze.

———

22d Friday. Last night it appears that some of the men stole some whisky from the Commis[sar]y and got drunk & this morng. kicked up a tremendous row. We had them put under arrest, some were compelled to carry large logs on their shoulders for hours in the hot sun & others were tied up by their thumbs. About 7.30 AM "to arms" sounded and then officer's call. I was on the point of sitting down to write this letter when I had to put on my boots, dress, put on my arms & report to the Colonel. We were ordered to have our companies out on the regimental parade [ground] and drill them at the double quick for 2 hours as a punishment. The dust & heat was tremendous and we poor officers had to suffer for the delinquencies of our men. . . .

Our officers are Col. J. B. McIntosh, a splendid, dashing West Pointer,[21] Lt. Col. Jones, an old fogy, Maj. Robinson, a jolly old fellow. My captain, Price, is Commisy. of Subsistence on the Brigade staff, a splendid fellow. He knows Henry Rawle very well and knows much about the Rawle family. 1st Lieut. Boyer a splendid fellow. Quartermaster of the regt. of course. I don't see much of them, especially my captain. The Ass[istant] Surgeon's name is Durant which is all I can say except that he is a gentleman.[22]

Don't be uneasy about me. We are living like princes here in camp. I have lately been sleeping on a bed of hay in a log hut, but now Frank W. & I have pitched a tent, which is better. I have not passed an uncomfortable night since I've been here, with the exception of the one I was on duty. I am very well, as much so at least as a continual thirst occasioned by eating ham and drinking bad water will permit. I know how to enjoy my dinner. Luckily, you will say, the commisy. whiskey is so bad that it nearly makes me sick & I would as soon drink castor oil. If you have a chance to, send me 20 or so paper collars 14½ inch turn down. Also I would like to have a toilet bag made of oiled silk (yellow round with tape) shaped about 1 ft. wide and 18 inches long to keep my brush, comb, soap, tooth brush, etc. . . .

> Camp near Deep Run, Fauquier Co. Va.
> May 30. 1863

Dear Mother:

I suppose you will be anxious about me, since I've not written for more than a week. My reason is that we have been marching & countermarching, out on picket etc. and separated from our baggage every day. I suppose the shortest way to let you know of my doings is to copy from my journal. So here is an extract.

May 23. Sat[urda]y. At dress parade at sundown, in a special order, 1st Lieut. Miles Carter was assigned to duty in Comp. "C," thereby relieving me from the command of the compy., and corresponding responsibility. He was orderly Sergt. of the compy. in the 5th Reg. Cav. in which Col. McIntosh was a lieut. and is a splendid officer. He is a Virginian, and has served on the Frontier for 5 years.[23] In the eveng. a large party of us officers rode to a beautiful waterfall in the woods and had a luxurious bathe. The fall was about 20 feet, behind which was a large cave. The natural beauties of the spot were superb. Coming home we had a regular steeple chase jumping our horses over everything in the way, such as ditches, stone walls etc.

May 24. Sunday. The only difference between Sunday & any other day is an addition to our duties in the shape of the weekly inspection by the Brigade Regimental or line officers. In the eveng. orders were issued to hold ourselves in readiness to strike camp and move tomorrow morng. early.

May 25. Monday. Reveille at 2.30 AM. Stables, breakfast etc. & about 5.30 the 2nd Brigade (Col. Gregg) of the 2nd Cavy. Divn., late Averill's now comm. by Col. Duffield, (a French army officer) formed on our Regimental Parade. Pennington's Battery of Flying Artillery accompanied.[24] The whole 2nd Divn. moved[,] I afterwards learned, not the Brigade alone. We started about 7 towards Bealeton, on the Orange & Alexandria R.R. It rained as we were starting, just sufficiently to settle the dust and the clouds kept the heat of the sun in, and made my first days march very pleasant.

At noon we halted for an hour at Hartwood Church, the place where nearly every officer in our regiment has once at least been "gobbled up." It is a place of much interest to us and every time we pass the officers point out how & where they were captured. Frank Wetherill was "paroled" here. It is a small brick building and before the war was a church, but now it is completely rooted out. The private grave yards of the F.F.V.'s [First Families of Virginia] surrounded in Virginia style by stone walls, have been torn up and terribly desecrated. Temporary fireplaces have been built by the soldiers over the graves & the trees & flowers cut down or torn up. It is a specimen of the general desolation of this beautiful country. We resumed our march and encamped for the night in a thick wood near Grove Church. Our servants have pitched us a shelter tent and we passed the night without alarm & slept well.

May 26. [Tuesday.] Another splendid day for marching. While drawn up in column of squadrons awaiting the orders to march, Adjutant Newhall handed me

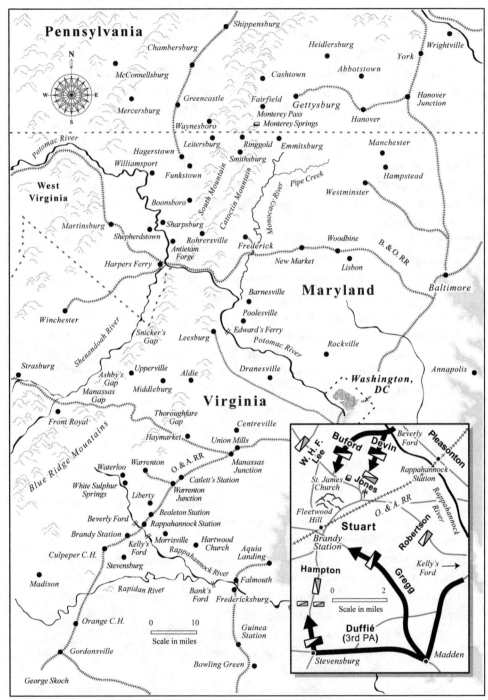

Brandy Station (inset) and the Gettysburg Campaign, May–July 1863

a letter from Mary MacCulloch which I read with much pleasure.[25] We started on the march at 8 AM & kept on steadily til we came within a short distance of Bealeton, where we encamped in a magnificent grove. Our wall tents were pitched and arrangements were made to stay some time. About 6 PM orders came to hold ourselves in readiness to move early next morng.

May 27. Wednesy. Reveille at 3 AM, and our Brigade, leaving the rest of the Division at Bealeton, started from our beautiful camp on the road we travelled yesterday. It may be "strategy" to march to a place on one day and march back the next without doing anything, but most decidedly we could not appreciate it. I was "officer of the guard," and my duty was to protect the baggage and pick up stragglers with my guard of 12 men. I had a good deal of trouble, and while I had my command in front of the trains and in rear of the Reg't. 3 or 4 men were picked up by guerillas at Morrisville.

As we marched along the other regiments were detached to picket the fords on the Rappahannock and when we had arrived near Beriah Church half the Reg't. under Major Robinson were detailed to picket Banks' Ford.[26] The rest of the Reg't. encamped near the church in a pine grove, and, as I was with the train, I accompanied it, although my company was under Major Robinson. As I was officer of the guard I had to stay awake all night at the guard house, which consisted of a large fire to keep us warm (the days here are very hot indeed and the dust terrible, while the nights are cold and blankets & fires are necessary). My instructions were, in case of an alarm—of which there was some danger—to deploy my guard across the road and to defend it until the camp was under arms. The guard was increased [and] a mounted patrol stationed outside of my guard. There was no alarm however.

May 28. Thursday. Relieved from guard at 8 AM and ordered to report immediately to Major Robinson, on picket. It is very ticklish work going through the woods alone, on account of the prowling guerilla bands, so 3 of us, with an escort, went over together. The Major, when I had reported, ordered me at present to remain with the reserve.

In the afternoon, Capt. Gilmore & I were ordered to visit the line of outside pickets.[27] We rode over to the Banks' Ford and visited the pickets. I had my first glimpse of the "Rebs," who were picketed very thickly along the Shore of the river (Rappahannock). Our pickets are not allowed to speak to the Rebs, but they call across to us. Some of them cheered for the "Red, White & Blue," and we saluted in return. The river here is about as wide as the lower part of Valley Forge Dam and the scenery resembles it much. We rode along the heights & saw the enemy's field works & heard their drums. A couple of regiment[s] of infantry arrived there for the purpose of picketing, which relieved us. During the afternoon heavy cannonading was heard up the river.

May 29. Friday. As the infantry relieved our pickets, they (our pickets) were drawn in early this morning and we rejoined the regiment near Berea Church, which we found waiting for us ready to march. We started on the march for the 2nd time in the direction of Bealeton, on the road we have travelled already twice this week. The heat and dust were terrible. (The chocolate was very acceptable when I could get no water, and the hard marching has diminished the bundle by half.) We encamped in a thick wood near Deep Run, in the extreme south of Fauquier. (You had better get one of the maps like mine, as you can follow my goings). We may stay here for 2 or 3 days.

Major Robinson informed me during the evening that Gen. Stuart, with a large force of Rebel Cavalry, was near Bealeton, 10 miles from here, and that we may soon expect warm work. Meade's 5th Corps with a lot of artillery have passed during the day.[28] Genl. M is encamped near us, I am told, but here one corps or regiment sees almost as much of any other as you or I do. The only way we get the news is from the papers up north. We are ordered to hold ourselves in readiness to move, and, until we reach a place, we never know what we are going to go. We don't know any more or even as much about movements down here as you do.

You must excuse the writing as I have not the conveniences of civilized life, and I am now writing on my valise, seated on the ground in my tent, which is dreadfully close & warm. If you don't hear from me regularly don't be uneasy, as I am often away from my baggage and sometimes have not the time to write. The postal communications with a regiment on the march are very irregular. Please don't forget to send the things I asked for, especially the photographs. Send the things when you have a chance; also a pair of buckskin cavalry gantlets about 7½ size; if you can't get that size don't get larger than 8. They can be got at Horstmann's in Cherry St. bel. 5th.[29] Riding blisters my fingers with the reins. Write soon and give my love to all.

Camp near Warrenton Junction, Va.
June 2, 1863

Dear Lottie:

I recd. letters yesterday from mother (with one enclosed from Lilly) & one from Uncle Wm. Mother says that you & she wrote to me, but I have not recd. them. The other day Gen. Stuart with a lot of "Reb" cavalry made a raid to Catlett's station, on the Orange & Alexandria RR about 4 miles from here, burnt the bridge & captured the train with our Post Master, who very prudently burned the mail to save it from falling into the hands of the Rebs.[30] Otherwise we recd. our mail very regularly except when we are on the march, when no one knows where we are. I will continue my journal for the last few days. I wrote to mother on Saturday.

May 30. Saturday. In the eveng. heavy firing was heard up the river Rappahannock at some of the fords. We heard that Gen. Stuart had burned the bridge at Catlett's Station on the O&A RR. At 10:30 PM, just as we had turned over to sleep, we recd. orders to saddle up immediately, to strike camp & march. We packed up, and got everything ready in short time. We expected an attack every minute, but were allowed a short time to lie down and take a nap, with our horses at our feet, on the damp ground, with nothing over us, as everything was packed up. We got a little sleep, notwithstanding the artillery firing and the horses & mules kicking & jumping in the midst of us.

May 31. Sunday. "To Horse" sounded at 2:30 AM, and as we were all ready, we were soon on the march. The column consisted of Col. Gregg's 2nd Brigade 2nd Cavy. Divn. We went in the direction of Bealeton, where we arrived at our beautiful campground on May 26. We had orders to pitch camp, but our servants had not quite finished when orders came to feed the horses and be ready to move in an hour. Everything had to be repacked. This packing & repacking deals hardly with my valise which is beginning to look war worn. We had a little cold ham (commissary) and bread to eat about 10, and about 11 the whole of the 2nd Divn. (the rest rejoining us in Bealeton) were on the road.

We marched along the O & A RR till we came to a small creek (which you can see on Lloyd's map) called Edwards R[iver], a branch of Elk R[un] about 2 miles from Warrenton Junction, near which we encamped in the woods.[31] The Rebel pickets were here this morning. The only way I can account for our coming here is to protect the Rail Road & cut off Stuart if possible. We don't know where he is. Always too late to do anything. I believe when he burned the bridge at Catlett's our troops took 2 pieces of artillery, but I don't know what troops were there.[32]

June 1. Monday. Recd. Mother's & Uncle's letters. Nothing happened out of the usual routine of camp life. There is some probability of our staying here from some time, but as this is a marching regiment all is uncertain. The horses are saddles and the men under arms all day. The artillery (Pennington's Battery) are in position on our right, and we are ready for an attack. I don't fear any though, as Stuart is too sensible to attack Averell's old Divn.

If you do not hear from me, don't be at all uneasy, as I can only write while I am in camp, with my baggage, which contains your writing case, which I find to be very convenient. I have not been able to get the things from Col. Smith yet as Stoneman's Hdqrs. are 40 miles off. Tell mother that if she is able, I would like her to send the mattress grandma gave me. It is not right to ask any one to take it, coming down, but if Mr. Barclay comes down soon, ask him. If it is not too much trouble, I would like him to bring it with him.

———

June 2nd. Tuesday. Fine day. In the morning I went over to Division Headquarters to see the Division Guard Mount, which was a fine sight. The band of the 1st Rhode Island Cavalry was in attendance. . . . It was a beautiful sight. 81 men and horses came from Dumfries. . . . There are some more still at Dumfries. In the afternoon there was a dress parade. In the evening Lieut. Col. Jones sent for me and I had a recitation on 3d volume and conversation.

———

General Hooker, still in command of the Army of the Potomac at this time, had been receiving intelligence since late May that some movement was afoot in the Rebel positions across the Rappahannock. During the first days of June, the Signal Corps reported that Lee was breaking camp and withdrawing his army from the vicinity of Fredericksburg.[33] Accounts soon fixed the bulk of the Confederate cavalry in Culpeper County, with much of the force gathered near the county seat, Culpeper Court House (though in reality it was grouped near the Rappahannock and east of Brandy Station, a stop on the Orange & Alexandria Railroad six miles southwest of Culpeper). On June 7 Hooker, concerned that the concentration of horsemen presaged a raid, ordered his newly appointed Cavalry Corps commander, Brig. Gen. Alfred Pleasonton, to cross the river and "disperse and destroy the rebel force."[34] In the predawn hours of June 9, the lead elements of the Federals' two-pronged advance plunged across the fords of the Rappahannock. Soon after, the largest cavalry battle of the war erupted in the fields near Brandy Station. Rawle and the 3rd Pennsylvania formed a part of Col. John Gregg's 2nd Brigade of Col. Alfred N. Duffié's 2nd Division and advanced with the left wing of the corps across Kelly's Ford.

———

June 11, 63
5:45 AM

Dear Mother:

I was in the late fight & got through all right. I have been in the saddle nearly the whole time for the last week—on a scout, a reconnaissance in force, and the fight the other day, on picket, etc. I've just been relieved from picket at Sulphur Springs.[35] I would have written earlier but I have had no chance. I will write tomorrow a full account. Send me immediately the papers containing a full account of the fight. The cavalry have suffered badly—Maj. Bob Morris reported killed & Capt. Davis of the Lancers. The Regulars lost 20 officers in killed and wounded; we are all safe. I will write tomorrow.

P.S. Maj. Bob Morris is wounded & missing, the last of him seen being he & his horse falling over struck with a piece of shell. Capt. Davis killed, Adjutant Bob Ellis wounded in leg, Lt. Tom Lennig missing, Capt. Charlie Lieper wounded, sabre cut, the others are safe, I believe.

                                            Camp near Warrenton Junc. Va.
                                                            June 12th, 1863

Dear Mother:

I wrote a few lines in haste last evening to let you know that we were in the fight of Tuesday June 9th, and that I came out all right. I have been doing a great deal since I wrote to Lottie on June 2nd. I will give you the extracts from my journal.

June 3rd Wednesday. As I was returning from watering and grazing in the afternoon, at a slow gallop, acc'g. to strict orders, an orderly galloped up with orders for me to return to camp as soon as possible. I found the Regiment had recd. orders to take one day's rations & one of forage to be ready to move in light marching order immediately. About 4.30 PM we moved out the Warrenton road on a scouting party. According to a new change, Capt. Walt. Newhall's Compy. (A) & ours (C) are in a squadron together. At present, while waiting for the rest of the men [to report back], 4 companies are put together, forming a battalion about the size of a squadron, and the regiment is divided into 3 squadrons. Ours consists of A, C, F (Capt. Wetherill) & H (Capt. Miller), under command of Capt. Newhall.[36] Although we are in the 2nd squadron, when anything is required to be done well, Newhall is detailed. He is a splendid officer and there is some talk of making him Colonel if McIntosh's resignation is accepted. (McI resigned I believe on acct. of Gen. Averell's being treated so badly).[37]

Well, I had the 3rd platoon, our squadron being in advance. We felt our way carefully, throwing out scouts in the direction of the enemy, and arrived at Warrenton at 12 o'clock midnight. The 1st platoon entered the town, while the rest of the Reg't. laid in the road outside. We heard the town clock strike all the hours. I wrapped myself up in my overcoat & laid down in the mud & marsh (there was a thunderstorm as we were starting), and slept for about 2 hours, when the cold woke me. I then got into the saddle & slept for a short time longer. About 4 AM we started back on the same road without entering the town, which I was very eager to see, it being one of the prettiest towns in Va.

June 4th Thursday. Lieut. Carter was detailed as Asst. Brigade Inspector <u>pro temp,</u> leaving me in command of the company. At the daily inspection at Retreat,

I had a bad accident in my company. I was inspecting the company, and had almost finished with the sabre of the rear rank, when I heard a report, and as I turned quickly around Private Hartenstein fell dead ay my feet. It appears that he had omitted to draw the cartridge from his carbine after returning this morning, and as he was coming from the "sling carbine" to the "order," it went off. The ball entered his mouth, and went out the top of his head. He fell dead without a sound. Dr. Tate, our new asst. surgeon, happened to be looking at me inspecting the company, but was too late, although he was on the shoe within a few seconds. I made all arrangements about trying to get leave for his brother, Sergeant H of the same compy., to take his body home.[38]

We amuse ourselves in the eveng. by singing & playing on the flute & banjo for accompaniment. There are 2 banjos & 2 flutes & several very good voices.

June 5 Friday. The compy. escorted the remains of young Hartenstein to the station. His brother has obtained leave to take them home. He was a fine fellow, one of the best we had. I attended to a good deal of business, reports of inspections, requisitions etc. having to be handed in. In the afternoon, we recd. orders to have 1 days rations & 2 of forage ready, to move at 15 min. notice. At 9 PM "Lead out" was ordered & we formed on the regiment parade as best we could in the dark. We could hardly find our companies or squadrons, it was so dark. The brigade formed on the field on the left of our camp, but it was found impracticable to move in the dark, so we returned to camp with orders to be ready to move at 3 AM. There was much joy at the prospect of a good nights sleep among the officers & men.

June 6 Saturday. The Division under Col. Duffié moved about 4 AM with Pennington's Horse Battery (M, 2nd Regt. Artillery). We passed Bealeton & struck the river road along the Rappahannock. Duffié did not want the Rebel pickets to know that a large force was in motion so he struck off towards Fayetteville. While halted previous to turning off I was ordered to move ahead of the column to take command of the pioneer corps. My instructions were (from Col. Jones) to keep on the road until I came to a creek where a bridge had been destroyed, & to rebuild the bridge as quickly as possible. He said he did not know how far off the creek was. Very indefinite, as I knew nothing of the country.

I went off in good spirits, determined to do my best. We kept on for some distance when the roads branched off. I sent a man ahead on the road past Liberty to see if there was a creek in that direction, and upon his return saying that there was none such, I took the left hand road. Roads crossed, branched, etc. in true Virginia style, and I was pretty well discomboberated [sic]. At last we arrived at Fayetteville, where I met an officer of the 16th Pa. Cav. in command of a lot of dismounted men who knew no more about the road than I did. I inquired at a house if any cavalry had passed during the day, & I was told that a squadron of the 4th N.Y. Cav. had gone out on picket. I followed their tracks as I thought they would put me to right, as they belonged to our Division. I found out afterwards that I struck the river road again near Fox's Ford.

I met the outside pickets of the 4th N.Y. near here, who directed me to the main reserve, several miles off. I followed the line of pickets along the river & came up with the reserve at Warrenton Sulphur Springs. The commanding officer said he knew nothing of the advance of the Divn. but that a squadron of the 3rd Pa. Cav. were in the immediate vicinity, having sent over for a guide to Waterloo. We went forward to meet them, & I found they were but a short distance off, and pointed out the creek I was to bridge, which was but 100 yds. off. I set the pioneers to work immediately, and had not done much when Col. Duffié & staff rode up. Another corps of Pioneers was then detailed to help us, & some dismounted men to help carry the timber from woods about 200 yds. off.

We got everything done in about an hour, & the artillery & cavalry crossed. I reported to Col. Jones, who was in a terrible stew thinking that I had been lost or captured or something. Several men were taken by guerillas on the lonesome road I came along only a day previously, & the latter are thick as hops. Col. J. questioned me about the road I had taken & requested me to draw a map of it when we returned, & also if I had seen the Rebs in any force. I told him that I had seen 4 picket posts of Rebs but that they did not appear in force, showing that they did not knew anything of our movements. The bridge (which is already called Brooke's Bridge, the Col. dubbing it) served very well. He complimented me on my success. It was all good luck, as I was utterly lost & took the road to the Springs contrary to the advice of the commander of the pioneers. The bridge consisted of heavy logs laid across the stream, and smaller logs & rails laid across, the whole covered with willows.

The column then crossed the Rappahannock at the ford at the Warrenton Sulphur Springs, about ¾ of a mile from the bridge, and we were in Rebeldom. The Springs is a beautifully situated place & was once the fashionable resort for FFV's. The buildings are partly burned, & the rest pierced with shells from a fight which occurred here some time ago. We got a splendid sip of water from the spring, the best I've tasted for some time.[39] We advanced very carefully till we came to the village of Jefferson, another dilapidated place like all others in Virginia.

Here we saw a large cloud of dust & some Rebs. We immediately drew up in line in support of our battery, under protection of a hill, expecting every minute to have a battery opened upon us, but they did not. We then advanced very carefully to about a mile beyond the town where we saw another cloud of dust in the distance. The orders [were] "4's right wheel" and we took distance to the right under protection of a beautiful grove, while the battery took up a position to our left. We were not attacked. Capt. Newhall had been sent up the river & had crossed & gone as far as Waterloo, where he had a skirmish with the Rebs, lost a horse & captured a prisoner.

The 1st Mass. Cav. also were sent out on a scout. When they had returned, and as everything has turned out successfully, (the object of the expedition being a Reconnoissance [sic] in Force to find if the Rebs were in force in that direction) about 6.30 PM we started to return, and recrossed the Rappahannock. We halted for an hour at the springs, fed our horses, explored the contents of our haversacks & then resumed the march. It was as dark as pitch, and we had much trouble in the getting along. As it was, in the thick woods, we got off the track & had to take another & cut across country. The 1st Brigade & our own advance guard also got separated from us. We arrived in camp about 1.20 AM.

June 7th Sunday. During the morning orders came from Maj. Gen. Hooker for the whole army to be in readiness to move at very short notice.

June 8th Monday. Out on picket under Capt. Hess, on the outside picket line of our Divn. camp. About 3 PM we were ordered to report to our regiments immediately, & on arriving, we found the camp struck & everything ready for an instant move. We started on the road for Morrisville, where we arrived about 9.30 and encamped for the night.

June 9th Tuesday. Reveille at 1 AM, eat a little hard tack & drank a cup of bad coffee & were on the march by 2. The Divn. marched to "Kelly's Ford," which was held & protected by Gen. Meade's Corps (5th). We crossed the Rappahannock without molestation, the Rebs having been driven back early in the morning, about 4 AM.[40] The whole force engaged was under the command of Genl. Pleasonton, the right commanded by Gen. Buford, & the left (in which we were) by Genl. Gregg (not our acting Brig., Col. [John] G[regg]).[41] We advanced very carefully for some distance in support of our (Pennington's) battery. From a hill I caught a beautiful glimpse of the advance. The skirmishers deployed in front, supported by their reserves, one column, with the artillery, advancing on our left along the road, & our regiment advancing in echelons of squadrons supporting both the battery & skirmishers. All the guidons (small American flags on lances of this shape) flying, & the effect was beautiful. . . .[42]

We drove the Reb Cavalry through the thick woods and it was a regular steeple chase, through ditches, over fences, through underbrush, getting our hands, faces, & clothes torn, till we turned their right flank. When we turned their flank they opened up on us with shell from a well posted battery about a mile off. We got our battery in a beautiful position and we were drawn up supporting it behind the crest of a hill, our skirmishers thrown out on front. For the first time I heard the shells with their nasty noise. "Bang—zzzzZZZZ—bing——boom" is the best way I can put it on paper. Sometimes they would bury themselves in the ground with a "thud" & scatter the dirt in every direction, when a general laugh would arise. None of us were hurt, tho' they came very near us. They were getting the range of us beautifully when we changed our position. I suppose all had been accomplished which was desired on the left.

We were returning to "Kelly's Ford," when orders were recd. to move to support of Buford & Gregg who had formed a junction between Beverly Ford & Brandy Station. Two regiments of Reb Cavalry had cut off our retreat to Kelly's Ford, & that had a good deal to do with moving to the right, to protect the crossing & retreat of Buford.[43] We were drawn up on a hill with our battery playing on the Rebs, when they opened on us again with shell. As we were taking position I saw Capt. Chas. Cadwalader riding by at a fast gait.[44] He had time merely to speak to Newhall. He was the only clean looking fellow I had seen all day. The rest of us were literally coated with dust, and had had no chance of making our toilets for 2 days.

After remaining for about an hour getting peppered, we withdrew to Rappahannock Station and crossed at the Ford, having moved along the road which our troops had gained. The dead and wounded Rebs were lying thick in the woods. We were the last brigade to cross with our ambulances, the rear guard of a N.J. regiment being in front of the ambulances. We had just dismounted, having been in the saddle since 1 AM (this being about 5 PM), when boom went a shell from our battery protecting the R.R. bridge & ford, & our (Newhall's) squadron were ordered to cross the river & defend the ford, the rebs having shown themselves upon the road we had just traveled, & were trying to take the ambulances with the wounded. The 1st shell just went over the last ambulance and into the foremost of the rebs, and held them in check till we could cross. We had a regular race to see who could get across the river first, & we formed as fast as we could. We deployed the 1st platoon as skirmishers & held the rebs in check until the wagons had crossed when we recrossed. Capt. Newhall was highly complimented by the Divn. & Brigade commanders for the way in which we obeyed the order. We took up our position in a wood near the Ford, to get a good night's rest, expecting a terrible battle on the morrow.

So much for our part of the fight, and what we saw of it. The hard fighting was on the right under Buford. After they had crossed they made a splendid charge in which Rush's Lancers & the Regulars lost badly. The Lancers lost Maj. Bob Morris wounded & missing (it was first reported killed), Capt. Davis killed, Adjt. Ellis wounded in the leg, Capt. Chas Lieper sabre cut, Lt. Tom Lennig missing—these are all I know. The Regulars lost 20 officers I hear.[45] Nothing more can be said against the Lancers as they at last have got into the thick of it. I know nothing about the fight except that everything that was intended turned out successfully, viz, to prevent Stuart from making the raid into Maryland & Pennsylvania for which he has been making preparations for some time. He was on the march I believe when we attacked him.

———

June 9th. Tuesday. . . . Our strikers are missing, staying most probably with the trains. I had nothing to eat all day with the exception of a few crumbs of hard tack. We had to sponge off the men for fodder. My horse ran lame in the advance through the woods. Our squadron formed along the river splendidly. . . . Tomorrow is the day which will decide many of our fates.

———

June 10th Wednesday. We woke up this morning with full expectation of having a hard battle to day, but everything turned our contrary to our expectations. Our regiment was moved down the river for the purpose of picketing near Kelly's Ford. Our reserve (the main body) was lying in a beautiful grove along the road (one of the most beautiful spots of the kind I've ever seen), the headquarters being under a chestnut tree in the circumference of whose trunk we had the curiosity to measure & found to be 22 feet. We had a good meal in prospect, (having sent some men around to buy the requisites) with strawberries for desert, when orders were recd. & we had to march back.

We marched up the river & squadrons were detailed to picket the fords along the Rappahannock, relieving the 1st Regulars. Our squadron (3 platoons at least) was detailed to picket Warrenton Sulphur Springs. We were informed that a body of Rebs were in the Springs, & we left one platoon to protect the ford while the other two made a charge through the place. We rode a mile beyond the place but saw no rebs, only their foot marks, they having left on knowing of our arrival. The reb pickets got alarmed & a large body, about 2 squadrons as far as we could distinguish, rode carefully to almost within range of the platoon protecting the ford, when they wheeled about and ran like the mischief, thinking, I suppose, that we were going to cross at the next ford above. We stationed the reserve at "Brooke's Bridge," where we lay all night.

The next morning we were relieved by the 1st Mass Cavy. We had had almost nothing to eat for about 3 days, & while on picket we sent out some men who brought us some milk & Virginia hoecakes, which we pitched into as if we were hungry. We were passed being hungry, (there is such a point), and I believe [I] could have gone without food for as long again. The men fared better than the officers, as our <u>strikers</u> had our rations, and we were separated from them.

June 11th Thursday. Relieved from picket about noon, & we set out to return to camp with our spoils, consisting of one (suspected) guerilla & 4 captured horses. We were ordered to report at Liberty, but when we arrived there we found that the Regiment had returned to our old camp near Warrenton Junction, where we proceeded immediately, got something to eat & went to bed, or rather to sleep.

Now you have my journal, which has kept me nearly all my spare time to day. I am laughed at here for my long letters, but know you want the particulars so I give them. Being in command, I don't have much time to spare, & have to write fast so you must excuse [the sloppy handwriting]. I am very well, with the exception of being a little out of order from having to drink bad water & getting starved & being in the saddle all day & every day. I've not been able to get the box from Col. Smith, as we are about 40 miles off. I am very sorry that he has to be bothered with it. I will get it as soon as I can. I recd. your letter this morning with the photographs. I don't suppose you can read this all through but you say you want particulars, so you have them. Write as often and as soon as you can. I would be much obliged if you would send me down regularly Forney's *Weekly War Press*, as I rarely see a newspaper. My last address will last as long as the regiment does, or at least until further notice. Don't be alarmed if you don't hear from me regularly, as we are a marching body.

———

Until Brandy Station, wrote a Confederate officer after the war, "the Confederate cavalry did have its own way. . . . But after that time we held our ground only by hard fighting." The contest on June 9, the same officer related in an oft-repeated statement, "<u>made</u> the Federal cavalry." Union division commander David Gregg agreed, recalling that the outcome of the fight "created the greatest enthusiasm in our regiments."[46] Brandy Station, historian Eric Wittenberg has noted, represented a turning point for the Army of the Potomac's cavalry: "Its maturation process was now complete. The Northern horsemen were finally the equals of their Southern counterparts, and they would never look back."[47]

The day after the fighting at Brandy Station, Lee began to move advance elements of his army north via the Shenandoah Valley, hoping to transfer the fighting from Virginia to the Northern states. Although Hooker was initially slow to react (he proposed moving against Richmond rather than pursuing the Army of Northern Virginia[48]), by June 15, columns of Union soldiers and horsemen were filling the roads and byways of northern Virginia, soon to pass through Maryland for the historic clash in southern Pennsylvania. While Hooker tried to make sense of conflicting reports about Lee's location and plans, his cavalry remained active. From June 15 through the Battle of Gettysburg—with the exception of a four day hiatus in late June—the bulk of the Cavalry Corps was in almost constant motion, scouting, reconnoitering, and fighting several pitched battles against Stuart's troopers in Fauquier and Loudoun Counties of Virginia as the Northerners tried to gain intelligence and pinpoint the location of the Army of Northern Virginia.

Clashes took place at Aldie on June 17, Middleburg on June 19, and several miles east of Upperville on June 21 as Pleasonton's horsemen tried to force their way past Confederate cavalry screens through gaps in the Blue Ridge Mountains and into the Shenandoah Valley to determine Lee's intentions. Acting as rear guard for Gregg's division, the 3rd Pennsylvania saw little action outside of a few scattered picket shots during these movements. Stuart was successful in blunting the Federal thrusts, and Lee continued his move north unimpeded, crossing the Potomac into Maryland and toward Pennsylvania.

According to a notation on his next letter, which Rawle sent home on June 24, a letter detailing his experiences between June 12 and 24 was captured by the Rebels. His diary entries fill the void.

———

June 12th. Friday. Everything as usual. In the afternoon we had a Brigade Dress Parade.

June 13th. Saturday. During the morning Capt. Fred Newhall, of Gen. Stoneman's staff, came over and brought me the box which Mother had sent by Col. Chas. Ross Smith of the staff. It contained, among other things, sugarplums, into which the officers pitched without mercy, and before long they were reported missing. [Newhall] was in the terrible Cavalry conflict of Tuesday on our right [Brandy Station]. He reports 140 of Rush's Lancers killed, wounded, and missing, Major Bob Morris taken prisoner while dismounted though unhurt, Capt. Davis killed, Charley Leiper sabre cut in head, and Bill White had 3 horses killed, lost 2 sabres and took 3 prisoners. Tom Lennig is missing and nothing more is known of him.

About 2.30 PM orders were issued for 3 days rations and forage and the "General" sounded and camp was struck. The Division I believe has been broken up and we are to be brigaded with Col. Sir Percy Windham.[49] *We marched along the O&A RR to Warrenton Junction and then along the W[arrenton] J[unction] RR to Warrenton and encamped with the rest of the Brigade outside the town.*

June 14th. Sunday. I presume the Brigade is stationed here for the purpose of picketing and protecting the move of the main army. Hooker has re-crossed to the N. side of the Rappahannock (Lee being reinforced, having now 90,000 men) and is moving up towards Manassas. About 4 PM our squadron went out to relieve the 1st (Walsh's) pickets, about a half a mile from the brigade. Headquarters are under a fine tree, around which are quantities of Rebel graves. In the afternoon about 5 Capt. Newhall ordered me to take 4 men of C Company and go out on a scout towards Catlett's Station to find out what a cloud of dust and smoke was. I went as far as the pickets of the 8th N.Y. a little beyond Auburn and Cedar Run. It proved to be a corps of infantry moving up towards Manassas. I had a very pleasant little ride of about 10 or 12 miles.

June 15th. Monday. For breakfast I had some rolls and milk, which my striker got for 75 cents. I could get nothing else. The reports are that Lee is crossing the Rappahannock at most of the fords and our army is falling back towards Manassas Junction. During the afternoon we received orders to rejoin the brigade, and we started in the terrible dust and heat, passing through the beautiful village of Warrenton, and took the road towards Manassas Junction, where we arrived at 9 PM, watered our horses in Broad Run, and rolled ourselves in our overcoats and slept as best we could, with our horses at our feet, upon the classic ground of the Plains of Manassas. We could see around us the camp fires of a large part of the Army of the Potomac.

June 16th. Tuesday. I got a cup of coffee and a hard tack (having eaten nothing for 24 hours) and resumed the march by 6 AM. We only went a couple of miles and encamped for the day and night on the hills below Union Mills. By the papers we see that the Rebs are advancing in three columns into Penna. and that they are in possession of Chambersburg. So much for the Generalship! While we are almost doing nothing our homes, from which we came this far to defend, are in danger.[50]

June 17th. Wednesday. Terribly dusty and warm. Early in the morning the Cavalry Corps began to move and the 3rd were detailed as rear guard and to guard the immense wagon train. Every few minutes there would be some delay—a wagon breaking down and we having to wait until it was repaired. It was the most tedious thing I ever endured. The dust was so thick that at times we could not see beyond our horses heads. It took us till late in the afternoon to go but a few miles, but we arrived at dusk near Aldie on the road to Leesburg and we encamped along side the road. We (Newhall's squadron) were detailed for picket and stationed our reserve at Little River Church, about half a mile from the rear of the column. I was detailed to form a junction with Capt. Wetherill's pickets on the left flank of the column. It was very dark and I had a very hard time to perform my task in the thick woods.

The advance of the column during the march fell in with the Rebs and captured 4 pieces of artillery and 200 prisoners.[51] *We passed along the battlefield of 2nd Bull Run and saw shells, balls, and skulls and bones in profusion.*[52]

June 18th. Thursday. Warmest day of the season. About 9 ordered to rejoin the Regiment and we advanced beyond Aldie, when we received orders to move back to where we were to protect the train and for the purpose of picketing. Our squadron formed the reserve and were stationed near the camp ground of last evening. Lt. Charles Coxe of the Lancers was stationed in the same woods and we dined together on coffee and bread.[53]

During the afternoon and night we had a hard rain storm. About 6 PM we changed the reserve camp about a mile nearer the mountains to an orchard, where we had our shelter tents pitched, and passed the night comfortably. We are in a very ticklish position here, the Rebs being in force in the mountains near us and they may attack us at any time. The fight the other day was a very hard one. Col. Duffié of the 1st R.I. Cav. with his regiment was surrounded near the gap here and cut his way through with a few officers and men, the rest being lost.[54]

June 19th. Friday. Hard rain storm. Our regiment still picketing in same place. Our squadron was divided in half and sent in two directions. We got forage and rations and then went to our posts. In [the] evening we received orders to join the column, and in the midst of one of the hardest rain storms and darkest nights I ever experienced the Brigade (Col. Wyndham's), consisting of the 1st N.J., 1st Penna., 1st Maryland and 3rd Penna., started off for Haymarket on the Manassas Junction RR near Thoroughfare Gap. It was so dark that we got off the road and had a hard time getting back. Nearly the whole column got separated, many miles and horses lost, and some wandered off in the woods thinking they were following the column. We could not see a bit before us and it rained tremendously, and we were coated with mud. We arrived at Haymarket about daybreak and built fires and laid down for a nap.

Made all arrangements for "housekeeping" as I find it best to mess by myself. Got my striker, Montgomery, to cook and a nigger to assist. I have also a horse for each and a mule.[55]

June 20th. Saturday. About 10 a place to camp pro tem. was selected and we moved and had our "flys" pitched. The intention is, I suppose, to have the brigade here for the purpose of picketing Thoroughfare Gap. During the evening Hancock's 2nd Corps passed towards the Gap, and I suppose that they will relieve us here.

June 21st. Sunday. "General" sounded at 5.30 AM and in an hour we were in the saddle. We marched along the road we travelled in the rain and dark on Friday night, arriving at Aldie at 9.30 where we found General Meade's Corps. We only halted a few moments, but crossed the mountains and took the road to Ashby's Gap. At Middleburg we stopped for a couple of hours to get rations and forage and then resumed the march. The Corps under Pleasonton, of which we form the rear guard, has been fighting for the last two or three days, driving Stuart all the way. There has been hard Cavalry fighting. When we arrived at Upperville the enemy had been driven into the Gap [from] which it is almost impossible to dislodge them. As we arrived our troops were returning from the day's fight, and I saw Col. Chas. Ross Smith of P[leasonton]'s staff, to thank him for bringing my box. Our squadron was detailed for picket and our reserve was stationed in a garden. Although we were very near the enemy there was no alarm.

June 22nd. Monday. Magnificent day. The Cavalry Corps, having accomplished all that was desired, are returning this morning. Our brigade (1st of 2nd Division, Col. Wyndham, now commanded by Col. Taylor) formed the rear guard and covered the retreat. Our position was to cover the skirmishers. We thought we would not be troubled, but we had just crossed Goose Creek when the enemy's skirmishers came up with ours, and from this spot we had artillery and skirmishing all the way back to Aldie. There was some pretty artillery firing. Both [sides] managed the guns beautifully. The sharpest fighting was just before we arrived at Aldie; also at Middleburg. We lost but one horse in our brigade. We had hard work all day with nothing to eat, and we were glad when we arrived at Aldie and bivouacked for the night and got a good night's rest.

Col. McIntosh has returned with a large squad of men. He has taken command of the Brigade.

June 23rd. Tuesday. We remained near Aldie all day. In the morning I was detailed to take all the horses that wanted shoeing to the regimental forge in the town, which kept me [occupied] a greater part of the day. Got this morning's Washington Chronicle, containing a full account of the great cavalry fight the other day (Sunday) which was gladly received in camp. Got another striker (Ward) who was recommended to me by Capt. Wright.[56]

June 24th. Wednesday. We remained in camp all day to-day also, but with orders to be in readiness to move at a moments notice. Lieut. Carter was sent on detached service to Alexandria, which leaves me in command of C Company.

June 25th. Thursday. Rainy. Another day in bivouac near Aldie, with nothing to do beyond the regular tour of duty. Rain all night and evening. El Davis is very sick with Bilious fever. I spent the afternoon with him.

———

After ascertaining that the Rebels were ranging far to his north and west and posed no threat to Washington, Hooker resumed his pursuit on June 26, ordering his infantry to cross the Potomac and concentrate near Frederick, Maryland. Having enjoyed a respite for several days near Aldie, the Cavalry Corps would also move into Maryland. Buford's 1st Division would lead and guard the left of the Union army as it advanced, while Gregg's 2nd Division, including the 3rd Pennsylvania, would guard its right. The newly formed 3rd Division, under Brig. Gen. Judson Kilpatrick, would occupy the center.

After successfully blocking Federal efforts to force the passes of the Blue Ridge Mountains, Jeb Stuart had taken the bulk of his cavalry and headed east from Salem, Virginia, on June 25, intending, as he had done twice before, to circumvent the

Yankees. During the movement, he hoped to gather supplies, confuse Hooker (who would be supplanted as commander of the Army of the Potomac by Pennsylvanian George Meade on June 28), and eventually join Lt. Gen. Richard S. Ewell's corps near York, Pennsylvania. Continually detoured farther to the east than planned and delayed by periodic resistance and the accretion of plunder his horsemen had confiscated, Stuart lost contact with Lee for eight days, depriving the Confederate commander of vital intelligence about the movements of the Federals.

Gregg's division would brush up against straggling elements of Stuart's rear guard near Westminster, Maryland, on June 30. Three days later, after both armies had concentrated at Gettysburg and experienced some of the most desperate fighting of the war, they would meet again, this time on a broad expanse of farmland three miles east of the Pennsylvania town.

—

On picket, Ringold, Pa. & Md
July 9, 1863

Dear Mother:

I have not been able to write home since June 24, from Aldie, after our grand cavalry fight. Since then we have been having very hard work. On the 26th we left Aldie & marched to Leesburg, where we bivouacked for the night, and the next day [June 27] crossed the Potomac on pontoons at Edward's Ferry. During the day in crossing the river I recd. your letter of the 17th. We crossed at 3 P.M. and were in "My Maryland."

—

June 27th. Saturday. We got some forage and about dusk we started on the march, passed Poolesville and Barnesville and marched steadily all night. It was one of the hardest day's work I ever had, as I had hardly anything to eat, our mules not being with us. It was all I could do to keep awake by lashing my face with my halter strap, etc.

—

We marched very hard all night, and arrived early in the morning [June 28] at Monocacy on the Baltimore & Ohio RR, a short distance from the beautiful town of Frederick. On the march I recd. Lily's letter of the 14th. In the afternoon we marched along the Baltimore pike to near New [Market].

The next day [June 29] we went out on a reconnaissance in force, as far as Lisbon & Woodbine, where the rebs had passed and torn up the RR the night before.

In the afternoon we got some rations and a little forage at Mt. Airy & camped about 5 m. from Westminster.

———

June 29th Monday. . . . [W]e got a short sleep. Nothing to eat except what we could get along the road. The Artillery and the horses in the rear went to sleep and we had to wait for them, which caused a halt. No wonder everyone was sleepy.[57]

June 30th. Tuesday. About daybreak we were again in the saddle, without food for man or beast, and resumed the march in the direction of Westminster, where we arrived about 7 A.M.

———

[We] made a charge through the town amid the cheers & waving of flags and handkerchiefs. 5,000 Reb cavalry had left the place during the night. We came up with their rear guard & captured about 20. During the afternoon the brigade struck the Balt. & Hanover pike at Hampstead and marched to the town of Manchester, Pennsylvania—once more in our native state.[58] I can appreciate the healthy looks of the country, which were noticeable immediately on crossing the Potomac. In Va. we saw no crops & few inhabitants, & everything looked devastated. In Maryland, & especially in Penna., we are well recd. & live almost altogether on the farmers. We fare very well indeed now—that is when we get anything at all. I have been 7 days with 3 meals, & nothing for the horses but pasture.

Next morning July 1st we left Manchester, marched along the Balt. & York RR to Hanover Junction, thence to Hanover. You can have some idea of the hard marching we have had when I say that horses fell dead along the road & many were so played out that they had to be deserted.[59] All along our march we can see how the Rebs have treated the inhabitants. Not a good horse is to be seen anywhere, and everything of use to them (& many not even that) stolen or destroyed.

———

July 1st. Wednesday. We had our breakfast (the first meal for some time) and were in the saddle by 5.30 A.M. We marched from Manchester to the B[altimore] & York R.R. to Hanover Junction, thence to Hanover. I was detailed to take charge of the dismounted men, and with those and the played out horses of the Brigade I had a terrible time. The horses and men have been worked awfully for some time, marching day and night, with food for neither horse nor man. Three of the played out horses fell dead, and as many more I had to abandon, equipments and all.[60] *We were in the saddle all day and until 1.40 A.M. when we laid down in a field outside*

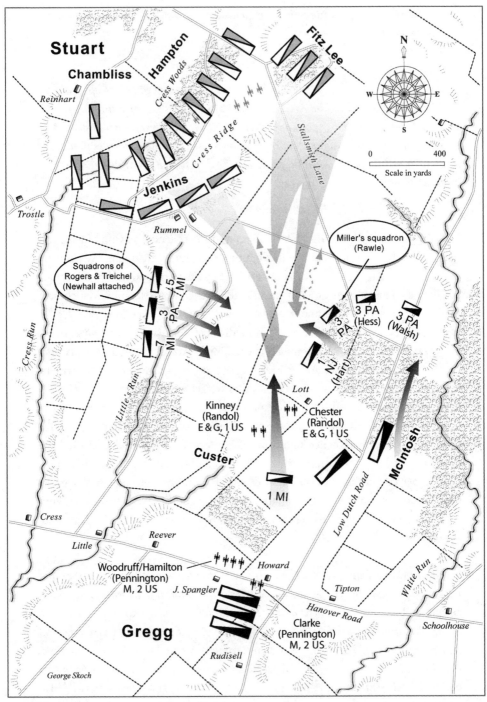

The Fight on the East Cavalry Field, July 3, 1863

of Hanover, with nothing to eat. The Rebs passed over the same road we did within
the last 24 hours, destroying the Railroad and rolling stock, taking all horses and pil-
laging everywhere. In Hanover Genl. Kilpatrick's Cavalry Brigade had a sharp fight,
and drove the Rebs like the d—l.[61]

———

July 2nd. By daybreak again in the saddle & the 1st & 3rd Brigades of the 2nd
Cavy. Divn. left Hanover & marched to near Gettysburg, where the Rebs were
in force. During the afternoon we were lying in fancied security behind a hill,
some of us unsaddled, when the report came that the Reb cavalry were coming
down on us like mischief. (This was the 1st day of our fighting at Gettysburg; the
infantry battle we could see from the hill). Well, our regiment was immediately
dismounted & deployed as skirmishers, and made a rush for the stone fence 500
yds. in front. The rebs (infantry of Ewell's Corps) saw that if they got possession
of that, we had no defense, & they also made a rush & our squadron got there
while "Johnny Reb" was but 20 feet off. It was done beautifully. We had a pretty
sharp skirmish for over an hour, with no loss however.[62] We bivouacked for the
night on the Baltimore Pike, east of Rock Creek.

Battle of Gettysburg, Pa. July 3rd. During the morning we moved to the right,
where the rest of Gen. Gregg's & Gen. Kilpatrick's (Late Stahel's) Cavy. divisions
were.[63] We were posted to prevent the Reb's turning the right flank of the army or
of escaping that way. About 3 miles off from our position we could see the most
terrible battle of the war. The artillery firing was the heaviest of any battle yet, being one continuous roar without a seconds' intermission.[64] About 2 PM the Reb
Cavy. skirmishers came up with ours & pressed them so hard that our regiment
& another were thrown out to reinforce them.[65] Our squadron was formed along
the edge of a wood on the right, my company (C) on its left.[66] Our firing was to
the right oblique, & for some time we had very hot work. Of my platoon I lost
1 man & 3 horses. For a considerable time the bullets flew around my head like
hail, & shells burst all around us.

After about an hour's hot work, during which we kept them back, a large force
of about a brigade (as best I could judge) made a charge, which Custer's Michn.
Brigade met in splendid style. We rallied our skirmishers as best we could and
gave them a good volley, & then charged down along their left flank.[67] A large
fence separated my command from the rest of the squadron, and I had to go round
in order to get to the rebs & a ploughed field went hard with my used up horses,
but we got up in time for the finish.[68] Five officers pitched in [from the other side
of the field where we were] with a few men & suffered severely.[69] Capt. Treichel

One of Rawle's fellow Philadelphia bluebloods was Charles Treichel, who would rise to major in the 3rd Pennsylvania. He was wounded at Kelly's Ford and again during the cavalry fight at Gettysburg. (Courtesy Civil War Collection, US Army Heritage and Education Center, Military History Institute, Carlisle, PA)

wounded in the arm, taken prisoner & Paroled. Capt. Rogers wounded (mortally it is feared) in chest & shoulder. He was shot while down. Capt. Walt Newhall in face. Lieut. Edmonds in head and shoulder. The regiment lost, I guess, about 25 killed wounded & missing. My company lost 1 wounded mortally, 1 corporal missing and 6 horses. We drove the rebels back & held the field of the charge.[70]

The whole loss of the army is estimated at 12,000 & that of the Rebs at 30,000 at least. They lost a great many prisoners, 10,000 at one time. The prisoners confess to a terrible thrashing. It was a peculiar thing that it was generally understood throughout the army that McClellan was in command and the enthusiasm was immense. But Meade has done splendidly.[71]

July 4th. The "Glorious Fourth." I was sent out with 30 men to report to Regl. Quarter Master Boyer to get forage for the horses & we were fired into exactly in a place where, 2 hours before, I had got some for my horse.[72] We withdrew with our wagons. In the evening we were out on picket in the woods where the rebs were supposed to be & close to their pickets. Our lines were established during the night, in the rain & dark as pitch. It was very ticklish work.[73]

———

McIntosh's brigade, including the 3rd Pennsylvania, was ordered to advance to Emmittsburg, Maryland, on July 5 to prevent any attempt by the retreating

Confederates to circle back behind the Army of the Potomac, still at Gettysburg. Soon after, they linked up with the VI Corps near Fairfield, Pennsylvania, and moved west toward Monterey Pass to join in the pursuit of the Army of Northern Virginia.[74]

———

On July 5 Sunday, about noon we recd. orders to join the regiment & we marched to the vicinity of Emmitsburg on the boundary line between Penna & Maryland, where we camped for the night. E[mmittsburg] is at the foot of the South Mountain & is beautifully situated. It is a very Catholic place, & has a beautiful convent.

Next morning (6th) I was sent out for the first time in command of a picket & had just returned from a scout & posting my pickets when I recd. orders to join the regiment. We moved out on the Hagerstown road about 2 miles, when we came up with the infantry skirmishers of the Rebs. I suppose it was the wagon guard, which consisted of a Division. After a sharp skirmish we withdrew, & moved out on a road to the right & met the 6th Corps which was after the Rebs trains. We took the road to Fairfield, where we remained during the night. I took advantage of being detailed to take some horses into town to be shod to get a good supper at the hotel.

July 7. Tuesday, in the saddle shortly after daybreak. Our brigade (Col. McIntosh) is attached to Gen. Sedgwick's 6th Corps. Gen. Neill's Brigade, with a section of artillery, & our brigade of cavalry in the advance left Fairfield, crossed the mountains, & about noon arrived at Monterey Springs, a beautiful summer resort at the summit of South Mountain. It has been shamefully treated by the rebs—almost everything stolen or destroyed. Lt. Horace Binney is on Gen. Neill's Staff, & he came over to see me.[75]

From the Springs our squadron was sent off on a scout to the right of the main road, (Pittsburg pike) to pick up stragglers from the Reb army. We captured 10 men. We rejoined the column at Waynesboro during the afternoon, beyond which place we went into camp. We were very close on the rear of the retreating Rebel army, & the citizens of W. say that they (the Rebs) were terribly scared at our force, which was following them up. Some of our troops captured 4 miles of their train & burnt the wagons. In the evening I was sent out for forage & took advantage of it to get supper at a farm house on Antietam Creek.

July 8th. Wed. We have had very hard rain since the 4th of July, & the roads are very muddy. In the morning I was attending to some business about collecting forage. In the afternoon we changed our camp to a better situation. We had just arrived when who should ride in but Uncle Wm. I was very glad indeed to see him. I went with him over to the camp of his battery (Comp. A Phila. Home Guard, Capt.

Landis), about 200 yards off, and saw a great many of my friends. Geo. Emlen, Wm. Winsor, John Thayer, John Biddle & a great many others. They had a pretty hard fight at Carlisle &, I am sorry to say, one of their number, C. Stuart Patterson, an old friend of mine, lost his hand. Uncle is Quarter Master Sergeant of the battery.[76] About midnight we were sent off on picket to this place, on the Pa & Md line.

Altogether we have been having a very hard time chasing the Rebs, with scarcely anything to eat & almost nothing for our horses. I would have written sooner, but we have as yet had no mail communications with home & have to suffer accordingly. I had just run out of money yesterday when Uncle gave me a XX [$20]. You see how irregular the mail is, so don't be uneasy when you don't hear from me. I've not recd. a letter since Lilly's of June 14th, nearly a month ago. A mail is expected to start from Waynesboro tomorrow—the first for 3 weeks— although it is a country town. This is a beautiful country here in the Cumberland valley. I suppose you are now enjoying yourselves in the country. . . . Give my love to all my friends.

Bolivar Heights near Harpers Ferry, Va
July 17, 1863

Dear Mother:

This morning I recd. your letter (with Lilly's enclosed) dated July 9th—the first I have had from home since that dated June 17th. I wrote last from Waynes- boro, Pa., which I gave to Uncle Wm., as I did not know whether you had gone out of town or not. Letter writing from the army is not prohibited, that I know of, but we have [had] no communications, postal or otherwise, for a long time. You say you can not find out anything of our movements from the papers, but if you had looked carefully over the list of killed wounded & missing you would have inferred that the "old 3rd" was in the midst of it at Gettysburg. But I gave you the account of our share in that splendid victory in my last.

We are now in the 1st Brigade of <u>Gen. Gregg's</u> Division. I believe I told you that Elwood Davis was sick with Bilious Fever in the Hospital at Frederick, Md. You ask if I have lost my valise. I've not seen it since we left Aldie, but I am told that it is with the Regimental Wagons. I've lost my <u>contraband</u> & mule, though, with my blankets & tent & cooking utensils, and forage & rations. I may consider myself lucky, though, in comparison with the loss most of the other officers have suffered, during a fight we had last evening, of which I will tell you in my journal.

I wrote to you, while on picket at a small place called [Ringold], July 9. On that day we went out on a scout, with only a few men, & captured a couple of the rebs' wagons (which had gone out stealing forage), & a few prisoners.

On July 10, the brigade went out on a reconnoissance in force, and had a sharp skirmish with the rebs near Antietam Forge. In the evening I went over to Landis' Battery—encamped 200 yds. from us. The poor fellows were nearly starved to death & I took Geo. Emlen & Wm. Windsor over to supper with me. In Penna & Maryland we lived splendidly in comparison with Virginia, having butter, 25 cts per lb., eggs, 25 cts a dozen, chickens, 18 cts a piece and bread & rolls, etc.

———

July 10th. Friday. . . . We went out on a reconnaissance in force to Smithsburg and Leitersburg, and found the enemy strongly entrenched near Old Antietam Forge. We had a fight of skirmishers and artillery for an hour or so. The Brigade lost about a dozen.

———

June [July] 11 Saty. I was over at Landis' Battery camp nearly all day & had John Thayer, David Pepper & Jim Large over to dinner. All the militia left during the evening & we recd. orders to move early in the morng.

July 12 Sunday. In the saddle soon after daybreak. Our brigade marched through Leitersburg [and] Funkstown Md. & after steady marching all day arrived at Boonsboro, near which place we encamped for the night.[77]

———

July 12th. Sunday. . . . We expect another hard fight in a day or two. We bivouacked for the night in a beautiful wood. It rained in torrents during the afternoon. I lost my darkey, Marshall, and pack mule, with all my blankets, fly and tent, mess kit and eatables, etc.[78]

———

July 13 Monday. It rained hard all yesterday & today. . . .

———

July 13th. Monday. About 10 AM we moved our camp beyond the town of Boonsboro, where we remained during the day.

———

July 14 Tuesday. I recd. a copy of Forney's *War Press,* which you kindly had sent for me. In the saddle at 7 AM, and together with the rest of Gregg's Divn.— which joined us at Boonsboro—we moved through Rohrersville, crossed the mountains near the battlefield of Antietam & crossed the Potomac on pontoons at Harper's Ferry.[79] Such scenery as at this place you never beheld. The town is a forlorn place, but the situation & surrounding scenery make it beautiful. The Shenandoah emptying into the Potomac, with Maryland Heights (the banks of which go up perpendicularly for hundreds of feet) on the one bank & Loudoun & Bolivar Heights on the other, renders the place the grandest I ever beheld. But I cannot give it a just description. We encamped for the night on Bolivar Heights—about a mile from Harper's Ferry.

July 15 Wednesday. Again in the saddle early. We left Bolivar Heights & marched to Shepherdstown, near which place we arrived in the afternoon and remained during the night. We had two brigades along, Col. Gregg's and Col. McIntosh's. The 2nd (Gregg's) was in the advance & captured some wagons & prisoners.

July 16 Thursday. We remained during the morning at the same place. About 2 PM the rebels (Fitz Hugh Lee's Cav with 2 batteries & strong infantry supports—as best we could tell), attacked Col. Gregg, & our regiment was deployed as skirmishers on his left, to guard against a flank movement, which was much to be feared. We had for a while some lively skirmishing and [at] about 5 they let fly their 2 batteries with percussion shells as fast as they could load & fire, they behaved very much as if they wanted to hurt someone. We lost about 50 or 60. The hard fighting was on our right. One of their guns was not 400 yds from where I was posted with some videttes on the extreme left. On our part the whole thing was badly managed. Col. G's brigade skirmished in fine style & drove the rebs some distance, when, in turn, they had to fall back, being left unsupported. The fighting ceased at dark, but we were kept deployed until 2 AM. We were in the saddle the whole time & the constrained position of remaining mounted without moving was decidedly uncomfortable, & the necessity of keeping awake, though awfully sleepy, made the night pass very disagreeably.

[July 17 Friday] We were ordered to join the brigade at 2.30 AM this morning, which we f[oun]d on the march. We marched by the river road along the banks of the Potomac & arrived at Bolivar Heights about 7 AM. The whole expedition seemed badly managed. Our mules with our rations & forage started out with us, but were ordered back, & neither ourselves nor our horses had anything to eat. The wagons & mules were ordered up afterwards & got up in time to be almost captured, and, in getting off in a hurry, we lost a great many things, some of the officers everything they had. The Brigade Headquarter wagon was captured with the baggage of the brigade commander & staff. What in the world we were sent out for is more than I can tell. We were completely surrounded on all sides & we were lucky in getting off as well as we did. So much for my doings.[80]

I wish you would send me an account of the commencement of our class & tell me if you have got & paid for my "sheepskin," or what you intend doing in the matter.[81] I wrote a long time ago, acknowledging the receipt of the green box, which was very welcome indeed. Tell the girls to write soon & write yourself as often as you can & I will do the same. . . .

———

July 17th. Friday. . . . Letters received from home state that they have not heard from me since June 12th and are very anxious.

———

P.S. I am terribly in want of money, the XX Uncle gave me lasted some time, but I had to pay up some back dues. In Pa. & Md. we had to pay cash for everything, & though it cost us about the same to live well there as to live badly in Va., we had to pay cash instead of getting things on credit. I am allowed $36 per mo. for rations but I can live far within that & Uncle Wm. has not returned yet. I don't know what I am to do. We won't be paid for some time yet I guess. I wish you would get him to send me about $25 as soon as possible, or I will starve.

———

July 18th. Saturday. We lay at Bolivar Heights all day.

CHAPTER TWO

Fighting Mosby and the Partisans

July 19–October 3, 1863

Following his retreat from Gettysburg into Virginia, Lee positioned his army behind the Rappahannock River, protecting his main supply line, the Orange & Alexandria Railroad. The Rebel chief had lost more than a third of his men during his invasion of Pennsylvania, and the Army of Northern Virginia needed time to resupply and to recoup some of the manpower it had lost. The Federals had also suffered—the Army of the Potomac had lost approximately a quarter of its strength—so Meade settled in around Fauquier County, near Warrenton, to refit.

While much of the Federal infantry rested, General Gregg's 2nd Division, with the 3rd Pennsylvania, was sent to picket and protect the right flank of the army and, as the eyes and ears of Union forces, was rarely sedentary. "A vast extent of the country had to be covered, comprising the greater part of what was facetiously known as 'Mosby's Confederacy,' some of the picketing being near the Blue Ridge Mountains," recalled the regiment's historians. "The entire region was infested with irregular bands of guerillas, as well as organized bodies of cavalry. As the country was perfectly familiar to them, every woodcutter's road, by-path, as well as the highways, known, the inhabitants, chiefly women, of every house friendly to them and hostile to us, we labored under great difficulties in performing our duty. Individuals, or small parties of our men, were the chief objects of their 'bushwhacking.' Vedettes were frequently captured and run off or shot, and small scouting parties ambushed."[1]

The nights spent on picket duty were especially nerve racking to Rawle, commanding a detachment in an unfamiliar countryside and liable to capture at any time. "I never slept a wink," he wrote his sister Charlotte after one of these experiences, "jumping into the saddle at every noise or alarm."

Camp near Snicker's Gap, Va
July 25th, 1863

Dear Mother:

I've recd. no letter from you since that dated July 9th, which I answered the same day, from Bolivar Heights. I suppose there are a good many for me, but as they must be sent first to the Division, & we being detached, the delay is occasioned in this manner. I promised to write once a week if I had the chance, but so far have not been able to.

We (the Brigade) left Bolivar Heights on Sunday July 19th in the tremendous heat. (By the bye, the same day I got at my valise for the first time since we left Warrenton Juncn. June 13th. It was almost battered to pieces & everything in it damp & mouldy. But I can't complain—most of the officers having lost everything). We crossed the Shenandoah at Harpers Ferry, went along the Potomac to the East side of the Blue Ridge, & then south. Our duty is to protect the immense trains of Genl. Meade's army, now moving south, along the east side of the mountains. The Rebs are on the other side in the Shenandoah Valley. As the trains move very slowly we only marched a few miles & bivouacked for the night between the Blue Ridge & Short Hills.

July 20th Monday. After some delay occasioned by the trains, we started about noon. We went through Hillsboro & encamped for the night in a wood about 5 miles beyond, on the Purcellsville Road.

July 21st Tuesday. During the morning we moved back & the brigade encamped near Hillsboro. Rations & forage were issued, & our regiment was detailed for picket, in Vestal's Gap & at Key's Ford on the Shenandoah.[2] Near the top of the mountains we found the rebs, & as it was getting dark, we threw out pickets & remained there. The woods were full of by-paths, and we picketed as carefully as possible. It was a ticklish place, they were as apprehensive of an attack as we were, & we passed the night quietly, with the exception of a few shots.

July 22nd Wednes. On picket all day. We advanced as far as the Shenandoah at Key's Ford, & threw out pickets over the mountain. I had command of my first picket of any consequence. I had 7 posts & 21 men. About midnight we were relieved by the 1st Maryland. We got a couple of hours sleep at the foot of the mountain.

July 23rd Thursday. Early in the morning we returned to camp, near Hillsboro, & soon after the Brigade took up the line of march, in a southerly direction, along the foot of the mts., to Snickersville near Snicker's Gap, where we pitched our camp. Our squadron marched on the flanks of the train, as protection against guerilla bands, which are numerous & troublesome in these mountains. Our Brigade is comd. by Col. McIntosh, who is talked of for Brig. Gen. It consists of 1st Mass., 1st New Jersey, 1st Maryland, 1st Penna & 3rd Penna.

July 24th Friday. We remained here all day & took the opportunity to make out muster rolls for pay for 2 months ending June 30th. I was hard at work all day writing. Ditto today. Our two days rest is very acceptable, not so much for ourselves as for our horses, which need rest badly. They can't leave us alone long tho', and we may move at any moment. It is tremendously warm here.

Camp near Catlett's Station, Va.
on the O&A RR
July 28th, 1863

Dear Lottie:

I postponed finishing Mother's letter, and before I had time to resume it, we were again on the march. The [next] evening [July 25] we had a tremendous rain storm. We were camped at the base of the mountains, and in a short time we were flooded. You have heard of mountain rain storms, but have never experienced one. My tent blew down & it rained too hard to have my servants put it back up again, so I put into the next one. Before long this had half a foot of water in it; I looked around the camp & found the whole place covered with rushing waters, with mess utensils & other things floating around regardless. Everything we had [was] soaking wet, [so] you may imagine what a night we had, to rest ourselves for tomorrow's march.

The next day [July 26] we left Snickersville, marched along the Mts. to Upperville, then along the pike to Middleburg (the road on which we had that running fight with Stuart & drove him into the mountains), and encamped near here. Our regiment, being in advance, was detailed for picket. Being in command of one reserve & outposts, of course I had no sleep.

Next morning (Mon. July 27th), we joined the column, marched to White Plains, New Baltimore & through the beautiful town of Warrenton, where the 2nd Corps laid. We have formed the rear guard of the whole army, & at last have got within our own lines. We camped for the night between Warrenton & Warrenton Junction.

This morning [July 28] early we resumed the march, went to the Junction, which is the base of supplies for Meade's Army. Several corps lay here. We rejoined Genl. Gregg's Divn. near Catlett's Station on the Orange & Alexandria RR, & went into camp in one of the most forlorn places for anything of the kind I've ever seen—low, hot, no shelter, great scarcity of water, and that of the worst & most untransparens kind. But we always console ourselves for the many disagreeabilities with "For what we are sojers." A mail awaited our arrival, containing your letter of the 17th. . . .

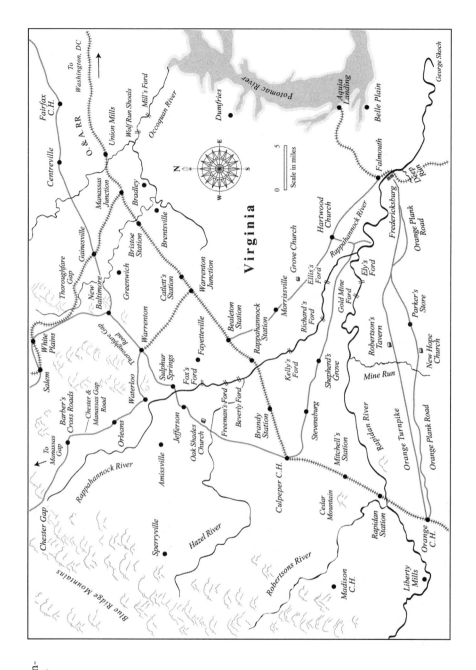

Vicinity of Warrenton, Virginia, July 1863–April 1864

George Skoch

Virginia

To Washington, DC

Fairfax C.H.

Centreville

O. & A. RR

Union Mills

Wolf Run Shoals

Mill's Ford

Occoquan River

Dumfries

Potomac River

Aquia Landing

Belle Plain

Manassas Junction

Bradley

Gainesville

Thoroughfare Gap

New Baltimore

Greenwich

Bristoe Station

Brentsville

Catlett's Station

Warrenton Junction

Bealeton Station

Rappahannock Station

Morrisville

Grove Church

Ellis's Ford

Harwood Church

Rappahannock River

Ely's Ford

Falmouth

Deep Run

Fredericksburg

Orange Plank Road

Chester & Manassas Gap Road

Thoroughfare Gap Road

Warrenton

Fayetteville

Sulphur Springs

Fox's Ford

Waterloo

Richard's Ford

Gold Mine Ford

Robertson's Tavern

Parker's Store

New Hope Church

White Plains

Salem

Barber's Cross Roads

Orleans

Jefferson

Oak Shades Church

Freeman's Ford

Beverly Ford

Brandy Station

Kelly's Ford

Shepherd's Grove

Mine Run

Stevensburg

To Manassas Gap

Chester Gap

Sperryville

Amissville

Rappahannock River

Hazel River

Culpeper C.H.

Cedar Mountain

Mitchell's Station

Rapidan River

Orange Turnpike

Orange Plank Road

Blue Ridge Mountains

Robertsons River

Madison C.H.

Rapidan Station

Liberty Mills

Orange C.H.

N
E
S
W

0 5
Scale in miles

I am sorry to see that you publish my doings. My letters are not intended to go out of the family, & I have a serious idea not to continue my journal. I have done so for your sake only. I refer to your spreading a ridiculous report, or rather exaggeration, of my building a rough crossing over a stream, one of the details I am any day liable to be sent on. I hope that hereafter you will not do anything of the kind. . . . Our mail carrier has just called at my tent for letters & I must stop. . . . Write as often as you can.

———

In an effort to pinpoint Confederate positions and strength, Meade ordered his cavalry, supported by elements of the I and VI Corps, to make a reconnaissance across the Rappahannock on August 1. Fighting continued sporadically over the succeeding week, eventually compelling Lee to reposition the Rebel army. He moved his infantry south of the Rapidan River but left his cavalry to patrol the ground between the Rapidan and Rappahannock. The retrograde movement shortened his lengthy supply line, while Meade, unwilling to extend his own supply line and render it vulnerable to guerilla attacks, chose not to follow, keeping the bulk of his army north of the Rappahannock for the ensuing six weeks.[3]

———

Camp in the Field, near
Warrenton Sulphur Springs
Aug, 8th, '63

Dear Lillie:

The last letter I wrote home was from camp near Catlett's Station, to Lottie, on July 28th. Since then I have recd. yours of July 25th & Aug 3rd, also one from Mary McCulloch of Aug 1st. The day after I wrote, we left Catlett's, and marched to near Warrenton. On the following day (30th), Gregg's Divn. passed through the town, [and] marched to Waterloo, where we forded the Rappahannock. It was very deep, up to our saddles, and of course everything got wet. We then went to Amissville, where our Divn. relieved Gen. Custer's (late Kilpatrick's) during a tremendous thunderstorm. This is the extreme right of Meade's line (the old one of the Rappahannock, I believe) & we are here for picket, etc. We went into camp near the small village of Amissville, and on Aug. 1st our regiment went out on picket for 2 days. During the night we were much bothered by rebel scouts.

———

August 1st. Saturday. About noon I was detailed with Capt. Baughman and Lieut. Heyl and 52 men for picket.[4] We had our reserve on the Winchester Pike, about two miles from Waterloo. We were much troubled during the night by Rebel cavalry scouts, and about midnight we received orders to withdraw our reserve a mile back, about a mile from Amissville.

August 2nd. Sunday. Very warm. On picket all day. My platoon went on and I was in command from 1 PM all night. 7 posts, 10 at night; visited them at 7, 11 and 3 AM. All quiet.

———

On Monday, the 3rd, we were relieved by some of the 1st Mass & returned to camp. Capt. Miller & Lieuts. Bradbury & Beaton were sent up North to have the regiment filled up with conscripts.[5] All the old regiments are to be filled in like manner.

———

August 4th. Tuesday. Infernally hot. Officer of the day. Laid in camp all day.

———

Aug 5th Wednesday. By General Orders 61 I was temporarily assigned to "L" Compy. & took command. Capt. Rogers & Lt. Edmonds were both wounded at Gettysburg, leaving no officers in the company. Rogers is reported to have died. There are in the regiment now more companies than officers—so many sick, wounded & on special service. The squadron I am in, now consists of Capt. Gilmore, "D" Compy, Lt. Bricker, "B" Compy, & myself, "L" Compy.[6]

August 6th—being a day of Thanksgiving—in the evening Sgt. Rammel of "B" Compy had camp service. He is a Baptist or Methodist preacher & a good noncommissioned officer & soldier. I never told you of "Holy Joe," our Chaplain. Dr. Hunter is a finely educated man graduating at Yale, and was in that institution at the same time as Uncle Herbert Norris. He is lazy & slovenly, drinks & smokes like a trooper. He draws the pay of a Chaplain, which is very good, & does nothing. He has held service twice since he has been in the Regt., but before my time.[7]

August 7th Friday. We struck camp near Amissville at 8.30 AM, took the road through Jefferson & went into camp near Warrenton Sulphur Springs, in a nice wood, where we are now.

Now for your letter. You are mistaken in my not having written to you. I have done so several times. We expect to be paid in a week or two, and I think we can hold out until then, so you may say to Uncle Wm. that he need not send any money yet. We may be mistaken about the supposition. Hardly anyone in the Regt. has any "spons" & we need the paymaster badly. . . . Send me 2 or 3 of my vignettes if you have any, as my "phiz" is in demand among my friends.[8] . . . Send some postage stamps. They are not to be had here.

Aug 9, '63

Dear Mother:

My letter to Lilly, enclosed with this, was too late for yesterday's mail. Shortly after finishing it I recd. yours dated Aug. 5. I have been without any money for a week or two, living without luxuries, but many (of the very few remaining) others are in the same box. It is rumored about that we will be paid within a couple of weeks and on the strength of this I have decided not to make a draft, according to Mr. B[arclay]'s very kind plan.

When Col. McIntosh took command of the Regt. he immediately ordered the Brigade Commissary to issue supplies to the officers, on credit, so I manage to get along very well. Luckily the people around here are very much in need of coffee & sugar, and that is our substitute for money. For instance I sent my cook out foraging for me yesterday & he brought me 2 pr. of spring chickens, having given 1½ lbs. of coffee in exchange. In the same manner we sometimes get vegitables, and yesterday <u>fresh bread</u> was issued. I owe my servant back pay, & I have to get my clothes washed (10 cts. a piece is the universal price!) & for these I want money principally. I will try exchanging coffee & sugar for the last. After I once get paid I think I can get along without "supplies." If I should want any however, money can be insured I believe by having it registered at the Phila P.O. (fee 15 cts.). Thank Mr. B for his very kind offer.

Today my valise came up (it is almost battered to pieces) & therefor the pen & ink. If you want me to continue the correspondence don't forget the postage stamps—half a dozen at a time will do, as none are to be had here, & lucky is the one who owns any.

You are right in denying the report of my "glorious skedaddle" at Gettysburg. You have my experiences at that glorious victory. It is only to my discredit to have stories of any kind circulated about me, so don't allow it. . . .

P.S. I wish you & the girls would write as often as possible, each once a week, if you can spare that much time to me.

Camp in the Field near
Warrenton, Va.
Aug. 16, '63 Sunday

Dear Lottie:

Just as I was starting with the rest of the regiment for picket, in a hard rain, on Thursday, your letter arrived, together with a copy of the *War Press,* (one of <u>three</u> I've recd. since mother subscribed to it for me) from Grandma. It came rather late, as I had recd. a copy four or five days before.

The last letter I wrote home was to Lilly on Sat. Aug. 8th, while laying in camp near Warrenton White Sulphur Springs.

———

August 12th. Wednesday. About noon Lieut. Hazlet and I were detailed with 70 men to report at Brigade Headquarters to Q.M. Boyer.[9] We went to Rappahannock Station about 12 miles distant and got about 54 horses. They used to belong to the Regulars, who have turned in everything and are being entirely equipped anew. It is supposed that they are going to Texas. It was very hot indeed. We marched through almost the whole of Meade's Army, which lies along from Warrenton Sulphur Springs to the S.E. along the river. We started back in the evening, and it came on to rain. The road was woody and narrow and in the dark we had a very hard time to find the roads, getting off several times. It reminded me of the march to Haymarket on June 19th. We got back to camp about 11:30, tired, soaking wet, and without anything to eat all day. Got "L" Co. striker, Hummel, for cook and Durne for horses.[10]

———

We remained there [at Warrenton Sulphur Springs] until Thursday Aug. 13, when the regiment went out on picket to relieve the 1st Maryland, the 4 squadrons posted at different points along the Hazel River picketing for 8 miles from the Gourd Vine R[iver]. The main reserve lay at Oak Shades Church, about 5 miles from Jefferson. This church is 150 years old and belongs to the parish of Dundee. It is the most substantial church for its age I've ever seen, the bricks having been imported from England. It has been terribly desecrated by both armies—nothing but the sounding board over the pulpit, and the place where the altar was, still remaining.[11] The reb pickets were on the other bank of the narrow stream, & as they were very friendly, conversations were frequent. They thought generally that the rebellion was about "played out," and were tired of the war.[12]

———

August 14th. Friday. I was on duty in command of the picket at noon for 24 hours, and made an independent scout around the country. Everything quiet during the day and night.

———

Yesterday [August 15], orders were recd. to draw in the pickets, as Gen. Gregg's Divn. had struck camp & moved in that direction. All the regiment that could possibly be spared (125 men) was sent on under my command, and the balance arrived here in camp this morning.

———

August 15th. Saturday. About 8.30 AM I was ordered to report with 125 men to Capt. Wright—Col. McIntosh's A.A.A.G.—at Brigade Headquarters. The camps of the whole of Gen. Gregg's Division were struck and an orderly was left to tell me to follow up and join the brigade. I marched as hard as I could and caught up to it at Warrenton, where it went into camp.

———

You need not talk of the heat up North. Think what it must be down here in the Sunny South. You can get some idea of it in the papers. It is a wonder that there is no[t] more sickness in the regiment. Only about one fourth of the officers are with the regiment, the rest being home, sick & wounded. I suppose my turn will come soon, tho' I never felt better in my life than at present. . . . If I ever get a chance to I will send or get you a pony. One of my horses is a little beauty only 4 years old, but he is Uncle Sam's. It would suit you beautifully & if I get through "This Cruel War" & he is still with me I will give him to you.

I heard that Willie White was taken prisoner when Buford rammed the Lancer's & 6th U.S. into the Reb waggon guard. The 6th Regulars came out with 72 men & I suppose the Lancers suffered proportionally. We ran into the same division on July 6th in the Mountains near Emmittsburg, Pa. [Maryland], but luckily we got out of it with only a small skirmish & little loss. . . . Write as often and as soon as you can. Also send some postage stamps.

———

August 17th. Monday. In camp all day. Major Sabine, Paymaster U.S.A., came around. We fixed up the pay rolls and he began to pay the regiment.[13]

August 18th. Tuesday. The whole day was taken up in paying the regiment. I got pay for half May, and June, one month and sixteen days, $170.10, the first money I ever made, and hard work earned it.[14] Settled commissary bills $40.65.

———

Camp in the Field near
Warrenton, Fauquier Co, Va.
Aug 29, 1863

Dear Lottie:

Your letter, which I recd. this morning, is my only birthday present. I accept the 20 pinches & kisses. I am very sorry to hear that mother is so unwell, but hope that it is nothing serious, and that she will soon be well. Tell her that I always thought her "moon gazing" would affect her <u>materially</u> some day, and not <u>sentimentally</u> alone.

I last wrote home on Aug. 19 enclosing a draft for $50, which I am glad you recd. safely. The same day I recd. a letter from Uncle Stephen, and the next, one from Carrie, with a superb vignette of herself, taken at Hurn's.

On the 21st (Friday) our regiment was ordered out on picket, relieving the 1st Maryland Cavy. We had the "tallest" picket duty I ever saw or want to see again. [We] formed the extreme right of Meade's line, about 9 miles from here. The main reserve was posted near Carter's Creek with two squadrons, and the other two (Capt. Gilmore's to which I belong and Lt. Carter's) were sent out to occupy the picket line, 5 miles out on an almost impassible road. Much good it would do us so far off!

Well, our reserve was posted at Orleans, and such a line was occupied! A picket line is posted for protecting the flank, front or rear of an army, to prevent or give timely notice of an offensive movement on the part of the enemy. The country around Orleans is beautiful, open and gently undulating to the foot of the Blue Mountains, about 10 or 12 miles distant. Such sunsets! They would have set mother wild with delight. Early in the morning the lower part of the mountains would be encircled by clouds, while the summit[s] were perfectly visable.

I should have said, in describing the picket line, that the commander's first duty is to establish one which will cover & protect the <u>main</u> force, <u>not</u> alone his own command. The small force sent out required us to follow out the <u>first</u> duty by regular patrols, while the videttes were required for our <u>own</u> protection. The country was infested with guerilla bands, who troubled us greatly.

About 1 AM on Saty. [August 22] Lieut. Bricker of our squadron was sent out with 20 men of my compy. ("L") (the orders were issued from Hdqrtrs by persons who knew nothing about the country) on a scout on the Chester & Manassas Gap roads. The rebs are in force in the Shenandoah Valley, on the other side of the Mts., and can throw out scouting parties in all directions. Nothing short of a regiment should have been sent out on such an expedition.

He had carried out his very indefinite orders perfectly, when, on his return, a short distance this side of Barber's X Roads,[15] (you can trace out all these places on Lloyd's Map) to which place we patrolled morning and evening, he was fired at & charged upon from 50 yds. by a superior force of Reb Cavy. Lieut. Bricker, my Orderly Sgt. Jones & 2 other men of "L" Co. were captured & the rest made their way back as best they could by another road.[16]

Lt. B is to be dismissed [from] the service for a misfortune in which he is blameless, and which is likely to happen to anyone. It is a contemptible outrage, and is done merely to prevent a too close investigation in higher circles. The penalty would fall more properly on the persons who established the line, or who sent out a squad of men into such a country.

Second Lt. William H. Bricker of Philadelphia was captured while picketing near Warrenton, Virginia, in August 1863. (From Regimental History Committee, *History of the Third Pennsylvania Cavalry* [1905])

We had three reserves, one at Orleans, one to the right, about a mile, and one to the left about a half a mile, which latter I commanded. Three such nights I never passed before. I had the pleasant knowledge that I was in a very ticklish position, in the exact spot where a reserve was "gobbled up" a few days before belonging to the 1st Mass. Cavy. I never slept a wink—jumping into the saddle at every noise or alarm, my vidette posts doubled, and the men doing double duty, send[ing] out patrols every two hours & scouting parties just before day break (the most dangerous time on picket).

Our patrols and men returning from post were fired upon from thick bushes by guerillas. These guerillas are peaceful citizens in day time, but after darkness rendezvous at certain places and try to capture or murder our men when alone or in small parties. Shortly after daybreak on Monday [August 24] a party came close up to one of my men, within 75 yards of my reserve. The man gave the alarm, and the reserve was out in an instant. It happened that at that moment I had but a very few men, about ⅔rds having been sent out scouting. We came down with a big noise, which scared the Rebs, and they put into the close underbrush in quick time. I hunted around for them some time, but to no avail. I had made up my mind to hang a "bushwacker" up to a tree if I caught one, but it appears they could not see it.

Except at night, we have nice times on picket, generally being in a place not visited by the main army, and consequently little devastated. We had chickens, fresh bread, butter, milk, young potatoes, corn, cucumbers, beans, tomatoes and such unheard of delicacies. The Virginians are, notwithstanding, in a very destitute condition, and it requires considerable maneuvering on the part of ourselves or our servants to get the above delicacies. Coffee, sugar and greenbacks are very acceptable and generally gain the day.

Speaking of the subject I may say that the coming of the army here is a perfect Godsend to the people of Warrenton. It is a beautiful town with many pretty girls, but it is rank <u>secesh.</u> The sutlers bring up goods which are eagerly bought by the inhabitants, and now the fair rebs sport new dresses, gloves and such toggery. I never go into town, however, except when the regt. passes through it, but intend to apply for a pass to go to church tomorrow. I have not asked permission to leave camp since we lay at Waynesboro when I went over to Landis' Battery, laying 200 yds. from us.

I spend my time when off duty and not attending to any business in writing, reading and <u>sleeping.</u> I find it a good plan, and so do the others, to sleep as much as possible for it is very probable that we may be ordered off and have to march all night, which is not the most agreeable thing in the world when one is tired and sleepy. But all this is apart from my journal, which you always want to see.

On the third day Monday Aug. 24th, we were relieved by the 6th Ohio Cav. and marched back to Warrenton. We found that the Brigade had just moved and we followed it to Warrenton White Sulphur Springs, crossed the Rappahannock, and encamped on the same ground we occupied before. On Wednesday however, we moved back to this place where we are now laying in a beautiful grove about half a mile from town.

We have had some "screaming" weather down her in the "Sunny South" lately, so warm, indeed, that the army has been laying inactive and the cavalry doing nothing "except picket," as the papers say. The weather now is very pleasant and the nights cold. So much for myself. The reason that I answer your letters so soon, when I have the chance, is that it is risky carrying them about, and equally so in a valise, so I answer them as soon as I can & destroy them.

The monotony of camp life leaves a good deal of spare time on my hands. When I get a good book I <u>devour</u> it, to use your expression, and I am now reading "Oliver Twist." If you want to make me a very acceptable birthday present, send me by mail the small blue & gold edition of "Scott's Poems," which is a very convenient size. . . . Don't fear about me just yet. I never was in better health, and the life agrees with me immensely. I am a little taller, fuller in the face & burnt by the sun to a very dirty color. Oh, I forgot my head, which is shaved in the style you used to admire, and which adds greatly to the "tout ensemble."

I have strung this letter out to a great length. But it appears that it is for the public benefit, so all I have to say is that they may get tired of it and ask for no more. I write in such a way that I would prefer them to be kept private. If I find this goes on I will have to take up <u>formal</u> letter writing, which I don't think will suit you very well. . . . Write as often as you can as it is a great disappointment to go to the Adjutant's office, when the mail comes in, and get nothing. I have only recd. 4 copies of the *War Press*. Grandma sends me a newspaper sometimes but always of a week back. We get the Phila. Inquirer here, only one day late, & the Balt. & Washn. papers the same afternoon.

———

August 26th. Wednesday. Cool and airy. Officer of the Day. About 8 AM "General" sounded. Camp was struck, and the Brigade moved back to the beautiful ground we occupied before, near Warrenton.

August 27th. Thursday. Pleasant weather. Relieved at "Guard Mount" by Lieut. Warren. Went up to 2nd R.I. sutler and bought a cap, pair spurs, paper, etc. $6.75. . . .

August 29th. Saturday. My twentieth birthday. . . .

August 31st. Monday. The different companies were inspected and mustered in the morning, and muster rolls sent in. Bought one pair woolen blankets $7.20 and one india rubber poncho $2.25, from "C" Company, in the name of Corporal Richardson. The beautiful pair I brought from home I lost on my mule and darkey in Maryland July 12th.

———

Warrenton, Va.

Sept. 4, 1863

In a letter I recd. a day or two ago, I see that a reprobate cousin of ours, Will Ingersoll, was captured at Vicksburg. He was a sergeant in a Miss. Regiment. I hear he intends taking the oath and coming North.[17] We have not been doing much out of the routine of camp life, since I last wrote. I told you that we were relieved by the 6th Ohio when we were on picket near Orleans. I tried to give you some faint idea of the place. The 6th Ohio lost 30 men killed, wounded & missing & a Major wounded there.[18] Col. Sergeant of the 1st Mass. was sent out with 3 regiments to picket the place where we had but 150 men, and said that it was not enough men, & that it would take the whole Cavalry Corps to do it properly.[19]

On Sept.1st when we were just thinking of going to sleep, "Boots & Saddles" sounded and the Regt. was sent out to support Col. Sargent, whose pickets had been driven in, & was expecting an attack every minute. We marched out to Orleans as fast as we could.

———

September 1st. Tuesday. In the morning there was a mounted Regimental drill. In the afternoon a photographer came over and took a group of nearly all the officers in the Regiment now present, with Col. McIntosh and 3rd Pa. Cavalry members of the Brigade staff.

———

We were on picket the next day [Sept. 2], and about 4 PM the 1st Rhode Island & 2 squadrons of the 3rd Pa. were sent out on a scout through Chester Gap in the Blue Mts. We marched fast and steadily till 2 AM, when we got back to Orleans, having marched 35 miles over terrible, rocky mountain roads. Both horses & men were completely worn out. We were ordered back to camp yesterday.

Everybody is filled with indignation in regard to Lt. Bricker's affair. In my last letter I gave an account of it. He is to be dismissed the service. It is a wonder that more of us have not gone up the spout already. The way the thing is managed is this. The commander, whether Gen. Gregg (or Col. McIntosh, who is, however, far too good an officer for anything of the kind) knows nothing about the country, most probably never having seen it. He sends out a few men to take up a line which has already been established. Wishing to know where the enemy are, in place of a large scouting party, or a reconnoisance in force, he sends out a small party, taking good care not to give them any definite instructions, thereby throwing the whole blame & responsibility upon the commander of the scouting party.

I have the whole explanation from the Adj. Gen. of the Brigade. He is not told what to do in any contingency. Thus Lt. B. was ordered out with 20 men to go out the Manassas & Chester Gap roads & give a correct report on his return. He was not told how far out these roads he was to go, whether he was to find the enemy's pickets, drive them in, charge the reserve, or find out where the enemy is posted. . . . If the scout turned out successful, all well & good. If it failed, or he was attacked by superior numbers, far from any support, he must be censured accordingly. He was attacked, & he himself & several of his men were taken prisoners.

As soon as the people at Headquarters find it out knowing that the blame rests there & before he has time to demand an investigation of the matter, or a court martial, he is dismissed [from] the service to prevent unpleasant disclosures among higher circles. Several parties have been sent out in this way, and some came near getting into trouble, but Lt. B is the only one of our regt. who has been captured as yet. If this continues some more of us will go up the spout I fear. But "for what, we are sojers!" It is a bad thing to cry before you are hurt, so I will try my best & hope for the best.

How is it, mother, that I have not recd. a regular letter from you for nearly 2 months? Don't forget me quite yet. I put my last postage stamp on this letter & must cease my correspondence until I get some more. . . . Write soon and oftener.

———

September 3rd. Tuesday. . . . During the morning the Regiment left Orleans and marched back to camp near Warrenton, where we arrived at 1 PM, pretty well tired out.

———

Camp 3rd Penna. Cav.
Near Warrenton, Va.
Sept. 10, 1863

Dear Mother:

Another mail and no letters from home. I have not heard from you since August 31, nearly two weeks. I am anxious to hear from you, knowing you are not well. The whole brigade moved this morning, shortly after daybreak, in fighting trim, but as I was Officer of the Day I was left in charge of the camp, which was not struck. They have gone on some expedition of importance.[20] All morning there has been fighting going on in the direction of Sulphur Springs, where the 2nd Brigade of our division is laying. We have heard no particulars but I should judge that it was some reconnoissance in force of the enemy. The artillery fire sounded as if we had driven them very hard, and is no longer to be heard.

I last wrote on Friday the 4th inst. On the day following a detail of 100 men under Capt. Gilmore, Lieuts. Potter, Heslet and myself, were sent out to picket the Salem road, about 1½ miles from Warrenton, where guerillas were giving trouble.

During the afternoon of the next day, Sunday [September 6], our outposts reported that a party of 6 guerillas had crossed the Salem road to the right. I was sent out the Salem road with 7 men, so as not to let them get back that way; Lieut. Potter out the Thoroughfare Gap road, with 9 men, to head them off in that direction, while Capt. Gilmore started after them with about the same number. My orders were to go about 2 miles, more or less as I thought best, and scout the country.

I had gone to a very favorable place, about 1½ miles outside the outposts, and had just turned to come back when about two dozen Rebel cavalry charged down on me in front. My rear guard was 100 yds. in rear and one of the main body got "demoralized" and ran back. I had therefor only 4 men, and seeing that the only thing to be done was to charge them, I did so. They tried to surround the small party outnumbering us 3 to 1, but I succeeded in cutting my way through. My horse was shot in the head, in the middle of the row, and sprang several feet straight up in the air, maddened with pain, and tried to unseat me, so I had to devote a great part of my energies to control him.[21]

I turned around as soon as we got through, and found that three men (i.e. the rear guard and the skulker) were captured, and I had almost made up my mind to try and rescue them, when I saw another party of about a dozen moving round with the intention of flanking me on the left & cutting me off, so I retreated in good order until reinforcements came up, at the sight of which the reb cowards ran. It was a very pressing invitation to spend part of the winter in that fine old Virginia mansion vulgarly called Libby Prison, but I declined.[22]

I state the above incident to show what I have declared before; the way they have of sending small parties beyond the lines in a mountainous country, far from any supports, almost to certain capture. I told you of Lieut. Bricker's case, which resembled the above almost exactly, with the exception that I, with God's mercy, got out of it. I have been expecting an attack of [that] kind for some time back, and took precautions which Bricker did not, that of having an advance guard out. He, having been captured, is to be ignominiously dismissed [from] the service, whilst I have been complimented by Brigade & Reg[imental] commanders & officers. So you see the great inconsistency which exists, the Scylla & Charybdis between which we are placed. . . .

[P.S.] I found out afterwards that it was a company of Mosby's Cav. numbering 48 men under D. Mountjoy.[23]

———

September 7th. Monday. All quiet during the day. About 5 PM a detachment of our regiment under Capt. Englebert relieved us and we were glad of it.[24] Upward of 50 or 75 people passed through the lines with marketing, etc. with passes from Gen. Sedgwick, and we anticipated trouble from it. I was complimented by Col. McIntosh and all the officers of the Regiment for my affair of yesterday.

September 8th. Tuesday. Orders issued to have everything in marching order.

September 9th. Wednesday. Officer of the Day. Wrote letters.

September 10th. Thursday. The brigade marched in fighting trim this morning at 6 A.M. Everything looks like work. As I was Officer of the Day I was left in charge of the camp.

September 11th. Friday. Dull work in camp, very few persons being left. In the afternoon Verny and I took a ride into town and then paid a visit to the 119th P.V. Grey Reserves. During the evening the regiment returned.

———

[P.S.]   Sept. 12
                                                                Saturday 1 P.M.

The regiment returned last evening. The expedition proved to be a reconnoissance in force in the direction of Salem, Middleburg & that country. Orders have
just been recd. to break camp at 3 P.M. There are various suppositions in regard to
the matter. The whole army is to move, it is reported. Some say that the rebs have
fallen back and torn up the RR from Brandy Station to Culpeper, and that we are
going to follow them up. I hardly believe this, as it would take us too far away from
our base of supplies, and, with such a length of R.R. to protect, our communications
are liable to be cut off at any moment. Others state that we are going to fall back. It
is generally thought that we are to be moved in the direction of Richmond. Which-
ever way we go the cavalry will have the post of honor, & therefore of danger.

——

Several weeks after Lee had moved his infantry south of the Rapidan, Confederate president Jefferson Davis directed that reinforcements from the Army
of Northern Virginia be dispatched to Georgia to aid Gen. Braxton Bragg, who
was being threatened by Federals under Maj. Gen. William Rosecrans. Much of
Lt. Gen. James Longstreet's corps was sent off beginning on September 9, and
several days later, having learned of the movement, Meade ordered his cavalry,
supported by infantry from the II Corps, to move across the Rappahannock.
Pushing the outnumbered Southern cavalry back over the course of the next
week—"break neck charging and regular bull dog fighting" was how Captain Newhall of the 3rd characterized it—the Army of the Potomac eventually occupied
a line fronting the Rapidan River but went no farther. "A passage can be forced,"
Meade wrote to Halleck after receiving reports on the Southern positions below
the river, "but it would, undoubtedly, result in a considerable sacrifice."[25] Following these movements, Gregg's division, including the 3rd Pennsylvania, was
assigned to duty guarding the Orange & Alexandria Railroad.

——

                                        Camp near Culpeper Court House
                                           Sept. 20th, 1863, Sunday
Dear Mother:

I recd. your letter of the 8th, and Lilly's of the 12th on Wednesday last (16th)
while skirmishing along the Rapidan River, near Rapidan Station. I last wrote
to you on Sep. 10th, and in a postscript [September 12] stated that we had orders to move—all preparations being made for hot work. Accordingly, "General"
sounded at 3 P.M. on Saturday Sep. 12th, and, in a hard thunderstorm, Col. Mc-

Intosh's brigade marched to join the rest of Gen. Gregg's Divn. near Warrenton White Sulphur Springs.

Before daybreak on Sunday [September 13], the whole Divn. moved, crossed the Hazel River at Oak Shades Church, where the advance (Col. Gregg's Brigade), drove in the enemy's pickets, and pushed the main body, with considerable fighting to Culpeper C.H., where McIntosh's brigade took the advance, about 4 P.M.

About a mile beyond the town we had a very hard fight of artillery and cavalry, and lost rather heavily. They let us have it most fearfully with shell, round shot (one of which went between my horse's legs without touching him), spherical case, etc., slap[ping] into our two squadrons which were supporting a battery. It is, proverbially, the hardest thing for cavalry to do, to <u>stand</u> quietly under fire. We made several charges on a reb battery, which would soon get out of the road, & we would take up a new position. Several days after we passed over the ground & saw how the woods suffered from the severity of the shelling; trees were cut clear off, limbs off & altogether badly mutilated. We fought all the way till we drove the rebs to Cedar Mountain (or "Slaughter Mountain," as it is more appropriately called), the scene of [Maj. Gen. John] Pope's terrible defeat [on August 9, 1862]. We bivouacked for the night near here—it raining hard all night, nothing to eat, no tents, overcoats or blankets, as of course our mules were sent to the rear.

Gen. Pleasonton's whole Cavalry Corps advanced simultaneously, Gen. Buford on the right, Gen. Kilpatrick in the centre, and several corps of infantry supporting, several miles in the rear. It appears that the enemy had moved their army beyond the Rapidan, and the movement above mentioned was a reconnoissance in force.

Sept. 14th, Monday. At daybreak the Divn. moved carefully, with some opposition, over the Cedar Mountain battlefield, to within a couple of miles of the Rapidan, when 3 regiments were sent down to the river to feel the enemy's position. The enemy were found to hold an impregnable position, the hills on the other side being covered with earthworks and batteries and (it was reported) A. P. Hill's Corps of Reb infantry besides a force of cavalry and artillery being on this side of the river, which is open and affords no protection for artillery or cavalry. Our line was dismounted as skirmishers, and they had a hard fight, the sharpshooters picking off our officers and men.

September 15th Tuesday. Before daybreak, our regiment and several others were ordered out to relieve those on the skirmish line. Skirmishing and picket firing all day & night, but not quite so heavy as yesterday. During the day & evening we could hear trains bringing up reinforcements to "the rebellious," their drums beating, bands playing and the rebs yelling & cheering.

September 16th Wednesday. Skirmishing and picket firing all day. The rebs are throwing up works in front of us, on this side of the river.[26] The whole command is doing terribly hard duty. We were not relieved as expected, and were without rations or forage. The regiment, on the contrary, was ordered out to the left of the line, our squadron forming the extreme left flank of the line. Passed a very anxious night on the skirmish line, it being pitch dark, and the rebs within a few yards of us.

September 17th Thursday. Much quieter along the line today. About 4 P.M. the 2nd Corps came up, and the infantry established a new line, relieving the cavalry which had been doing terribly hard duty, almost starved, and between the rebs & the government, very nearly completely killed dead.

September 18th Friday. Shortly after noon the Divn. moved back to Culpeper C.H. where we lay for the night. On the following day, the brigade moved camp about 2 miles to the right. We are now in a large elevated field, good water, and everything that could be wanted, with the exception of shade. So you see that they have been knocking us about rather hard, and now we hope to have a little rest, with only a little dose of picketing occasionally. . . .

Your inference is right in regards to the "Lloyd's Map." I have a piece, about 6 in. sq. left, of the spot where the present camp is. You cannot imagine how much service it has been to me, & I would not be without one for a good deal. Please send me one with a muslin back & made to fold up in pocket form. There are several other things that I would like to get, which I will put on a piece of paper.[27] You can put them all into a box & send them by Capt. Wetherill. I hardly like to ask him to bring them, as nothing is so troublesome to an officer joining his reg't, as bringing things. . . . It is reported that a month will be given to each Cavalry Brigade to go to Washn. to rest & recruit. So make it be, & may our turn come during the winter. I have no conveniences for writing, so excuse the calligraphy. Write as often & as soon as possible.

———

September 19th. Saturday. . . . During the afternoon the Brigade moved camp about a couple of miles to the right, and camped in a large open elevated field, a beautiful position but no shade.

September 20th. Sunday. Company inspection in the morning. Dress parade in the evening, at which an order from Brigade Headquarters was read, compliment-ing the 1st Brigade for its conduct on Sunday at Rapidan Station. Drew a beautiful black horse in a lot that came up.[28] Got seven besides for "L" Company.

———

Camp near
Bristow Station, Va.[29]
Sept. 26th, 1863

Dear Lilly:

You need not get so "rankankerous" about my not writing to you personally. What I write I intend for all of you who want to read, and I direct to any of you, just as I get the last letter. Your letter of the 22nd has just been handed to me. I received Lottie's of the 18th and Mothers of the 20th. I am glad to see that you now are doing what I requested, <u>each</u> to write once a week. I last wrote home (to Mother) on Sunday the 20th, as soon after the fighting as I could get a chance. I also wrote on the 11th, but as we moved about so much before it could be sent from the Regtl. P.O., I suppose it did not arrive before a week after.

On Tuesday (22nd), "Reveille" sounded at 2 am, and by day break the Brigade was on the march. We moved in an eastwardly direction, through Stevensburg, and went into a temporary camp about 1½ miles from that place, near where I first smelt powder at Brandy Station. We were sent here (the left flank of the army) to picket in place of Kilpatrick, who, with Buford, has gone on a Reconnoissance in Force, I believe towards Gordonsville.[30]

About 6 P.M. the next day [September 23] the Brigade was relieved, Kilpatrick & Buford having returned, and we moved back to our camp near Culpeper C.H., where we arrived at 10 pm. I lost my overcoat, and various utensils, from my pack mule in the rapid march. We have to sacrifice a good deal for our love of country, sometimes.

Thursday Sep. 24th. The whole morning was spent in making ourselves as comfortable as possible, expecting to stay here a while. Our wall tents [were] burnt at Aldie during the fight there last summer, and we have nothing but "flies" (awnings stretched on poles without back or front, meant for warm weather), and now the nights are getting very cold, and they are not going to let us have any more wall tents. We had barely got through fixing up our "houses" when the "General" sounded, camp was struck, and by 4 P.M. we were on the march. We went thro' Culpeper C.H., along the O&A RR, passed Brandy Station (where we met that veteran hero & patriot of the Union cause in Virginia—John Minor Botts,[31] riding along on horseback), crossed the Rappahannock at Rappahannock Station and bivouacked there for the night.

Sept. 25th Friday. In the saddle again by 5 am. We marched along the R.R. The brigade halted at Catlett's Station, but our regiment was sent 7 miles beyond to Bristoe Station to picket. I was immediately detailed, with Capt. Walsh & Lieut. Potter, for picket, and we went out on a scout to Greenwich, where we communicated with the pickets of the 1st Mass. We then established posts midway between G. and Bristoe. About 1 pm today [September 26] we [were] relieved by another squadron.

Gen. Gregg's Divn. has been sent back from the front to guard the O&A RR— the infantry having fallen back[;] some movement of importance is going on. Gen. Meade, I am very glad to see, has found out that it is very dangerous to carry on operations with such a long line of supplies, which is liable to be cut off at any moment, and his army is now falling back. There are a great many suppositions in regard to it, but whether the Army of the Potomac is to fall back to Alexandria to ship for the Peninsula, or to reinforce any of the Union armies, or to re-occupy the old line of the Rappahannock, or to camp along the Potomac to recuperate, I am unable to say.[32] We are now but 31 miles from Alexandria.

In my last letter I sent a list of articles that I needed, but I suppose it came too late. Some of the things can be sent by mail, as the map. I need a sack coat badly, and would like to have it if you can possibly get it down to me. As the cold weather is coming on (or rather, has come on, for the nights are very cold & 3 blankets are insufficient), I would like to have the cork mattress Grandma gave me when I left to join my regiment.[33] See if Mr. Barclay is coming soon, or El Davis or somebody. If I don't get it soon I will have to let the sutlers swindle me for one. . . . I don't need stockings as yet, but would like to have a couple of cravats, black & narrow. . . .

It is said that a brigade of cavalry will be sent, each for a month, to Washn. to recuperate, as the 6th Pa. Cav. have been doing. It is nearly time that they should be sent to the front, and not lay in idleness, while we are doing all the work. They have never seen any really hard service.[34]

Camp in the Field, near
Bristoe Station, O&A RR. Va.
Sept. 28th, 1863

Dear Mother:

Yesterday was a very lucky day for us. In the first place Maj. Staples, our Paymaster, paid us a visit, and I recd. from him $224.80 for the months of July & Aug.[35] I send enclosed a check for $50 and also one to Uncle Wm. for the same amt., thinking it best to send them separately. You can take out what I owe you or give it to Uncle, and wait, as you think best.

In the evening, who should come but Capt. Frank Wetherill, Capt. Rogers (who was almost mortally wounded at Gettysburg) & Elwood Davis. You cannot imagine how glad I was to get your box, and, as in the army everything is public property, Sallie's sugar plumbs did not last long. I hardly thought you could send all the things I wanted so soon. I was sadly in want of a coat, my old "civilian" one being in rags. It fits well but is rather large. The next stockings you get for me get them about an inch shorter in the foot. I am glad you did not send shoulder straps as I only wear them on dress occasions, on my shell jacket, they being too conspicuous in a fight. Everything was as nice as could be. I will be returned to "C" Compy. in a few days, as soon as I settle up my papers, as Capt. Rogers has returned. The birthday presents (Marmion & Lady of the Lake) are very nice indeed.[36]

We are still doing picket duty in the rear. The army is making some important move, but whether forward or backward we cannot tell.

You may think it foolish in my asking you to send such little things, but they are not to be got here, except in a few cases, at the sutlers, who ask from 50 to 400 per cent profit for their goods. Don't be so scared about me. We all say that the 1st principle of war is "Look out for No. 1 (yourself)" or self preservation, and for your sakes I <u>will</u> look out. If you get a chance to send the mattress down, it will be very acceptable during cold nights.

> Camp in the Field near
> Bristoe Station, O&A RR., Va.
> Sept. 28th, 1863

Dear Uncle:

Our new Paymaster, Maj. Staples, paid us a visit yesterday, and I am enabled to send home $100, $50 to you, in a check (No. 1376) & the same amount to Mother. Next pay day, if all goes all right, I hope to send home more, and close my a/c with you. I am very much obliged to you for helping mother to get some things for me, especially the coat, of which I was sadly in need. My old one I wore for nearly a year at home, & our hard work has made a sad havoc of it.

After our tough but beautiful fight near Culpeper CH & the Rapidan, Gen. Gregg's Divn. was sent more to the rear to guard the line of the Orange & Alexandria RR, which is the line of supplies for the Army of the Potomac, so we are doing picket duty here. Some important movement is going on, but whether Gen. Meade is advancing or withdrawing, it is hard to tell. The RR is very busy. The present line of supplies is much too long, and too subject to being cut off by a dash of the enemy.

The reports from prisoners & deserters are that the enemy have evacuated Richmond, & fallen back on their works at Lynchburg, with the intention of remaining on the defensive while a large force has been sent to reinforce the army opposed to Rosecrans. That is the most important point in the theatre of war at the present moment, and I hope that strong reinforcements from this army will be sent there. I don't suppose the above is <u>contraband</u> news, as it is merely a supposition—you, up North, knowing as much about the army as we do. One thing is certain, that

Genl. Meade does not let his plans leak out, and the army has confidence in him. Notwithstanding this, it would be the gladdest day the Army of the Potomac ever saw if McClellan was restored. He is perfectly adored by the officers & men of the army, who, of course, are the best judges in the case.

Much interest is taken in the results of the coming election, and the universal feeling is in favor of Curtin. So many patriots being away in the army strengthens the cause of the traitors in the North, but we trust to the Union party of the North to carry their candidate through successfully.[37]

On the march, near Brandy Station, I had the pleasure of seeing that fine old patriot, and upholder of the Union cause in Virginia, John Minor Botts. I felt like going up to shake hands with him. He has lost immensely for his country. . . .

Camp in the Field
Near Bristoe Stn., O&A RR, Va.
Oct. 3rd, 1863[38]

Dear Mother:

I was very glad to get your letter today, of last Sunday. Altho' we are now nearer Washn. than we have been before (but 31 miles) it appears that our mail is the more irregular, and altho' I suppose several letters have been written, this is the first one I've recd. since the one in the box wh[ich] I got last Sunday. I also recd. the *War Press* today.

As you can see, we are still laying here doing picket duty, protecting the O&A R.R. The picketing is rather easy, there being as yet no rebs around, and plenty to eat, yet they have us three days on and three off.[39]

For the first time since I've been in the army I have been excused from duty on account of sickness. I've caught my semi-annual cold, which was the only thing that ever troubled me at home. It was the worst I ever had, but wishing to get over it as quickly as possible, I took two rousing doses of salts, which broke it, and I will soon be all right. It seems strange that it should have come on with no provocation, since I have often slept in a pouring rain, in a pool of water, without any covering, and nothing to eat or drink, only "a pipe" and often not even that, and not felt the worse for wear. . . .

Our sick & wounded companions are coming back. Capt. Treichel arrived this evening, but has not yet fully recovered the use of his arm. He was wounded at Gettysburg. Frank Wetherill & I have a tent together, which is very nice. We are in the same squadron, I having got back to my old company (C) having been relieved from the command of "L" . . . by Capt. Rogers. You inquire particularly about my appearance. I've outgrown, almost, my clothes, and have grown much stouter. You would almost say I was bloated, but as I don't drink, it is perfectly natural. I like the life immensely, and have never enjoyed better health.

In the Inquirer of Oct. 1 I see that Lt. Bricker of "ours" has been dismissed [from] the service—a most contemptible outrage.[40]

The gloves are 9½, not 7, but they will do very well until the very cold weather comes on, when, if I can't get the proper kind at some sutler's, I will get you to send on a pair. I suppose you would like to know how we enjoy ourselves in camp, of an evening. Most of the officers play, but we few who do not often join the circle of darkies who have singing, banjo playing & dancing around a large wood fire. There are lots of runaway slaves in the regt., as officer's servants, who of course all dance, sing or play the banjo, and their performances are highly amusing. The scene is very picturesque.

The army seems to be laying quiet—2 or 3 corps having gone to reinforce Rosecrans. I suppose we are waiting the development of affairs in that part of the country. . . .

P.S. I would like to have a couple of each kind of photographs, as they seem to be in demand—many officers getting collections of the others. Send my cork mattress down the first opportunity.

CHAPTER THREE

Bristoe Station and Mine Run

October 4–December 5, 1863

Meade had received orders in late September to send his XI and XII Corps to reinforce the Army of the Cumberland after its defeat at the Battle of Chickamauga (September 19–20, 1863). Lee became aware of this transfer shortly afterward and began to formulate plans to strike the Federals, even though they still outnumbered him by over 20,000 men. Mimicking the opening movements of his successful Second Manassas Campaign thirteen months earlier, he planned to sweep around the Army of the Potomac's right flank, move north, and look for "an opportunity to strike a blow at the enemy." The Rebels began quietly moving to the west out of their camps on October 8. Meade, however, was not caught completely unaware. After a tentative thrust across the Rapidan River—he initially believed Lee might be retreating farther south—he had his own army on the move on October 10, backtracking along the line of the Orange & Alexandria Railroad. Lee had a head start, but Meade was marching on an interior line, moving to concentrate his forces on the heights near Centreville before the Southern commander could initiate a battle.

The 3rd Pennsylvania was picketing the area around Bristoe Station on the Orange & Alexandria Railroad and, when the retrograde movement began, was temporarily posted to Buford's division of the Cavalry Corps. Buford had been assigned to safeguard the quartermaster and ordnance wagons of the army, and, as the 3rd's historians explained, "as the guests of his division, he gave us the usual place of honor in military parades, the rear of its column." Consequently, the Pennsylvanians were nearly cut off from the rest of the army as they fought off determined Rebel attacks against the rearmost elements of the supply train.[1]

Camp on Kettle Run
Near Bristoe Stn., Va.
Oct. 8th, 1863

Dear Mother:

I have just come in from [a] three days tour of picket duty, muddy and dirty, and on my arrival at Camp your letter of Sunday was handed to me. On Tuesday I recd. your letter of the 2nd, with the receipt for the cork mattress; also one from Lottie and one from Uncle Wm. H. R[awle], both of Oct. 1st. Many thanks for sending the mattress, and I will get it as soon as possible.

I last wrote to you on Saty. (3rd). Since then we have been on picket most of the time. For a change, picket is rather pleasant, for the last 3 days we have been living on poultry, eggs, butter, milk, corn, fruit, etc. A little outside of the lines are several families of F.F.V.'s, but in a rather poor, forlorn and dilapidated condition, and several very pretty girls. Capt. Wetherill has found a relation of his, by the name of McComb, near Greenwich, but, since a party of rebs or guerillas tackled a patrol of ours on Tuesday night [October 6], wounding one & capturing two, I don't go beyond the line without an escort. We are temporarily attached to Eustice's Brigade, Terry's Divn., 6th Corps, and there is a probability of our remaining here some time.[2] They work us very hard, however.

The map is considered a very good one, but I prefer Lloyd's. You can get one to fold up at Callendar's, 3rd & Walnut. By the advertisement in the corner, they send them by mail. I would like to have one; if not one of the above kind, one like yours. I have been greatly benefitted by it, especially on scouting parties & picket, more roads being given and places marked. Martien's is more correct in regard to distances, & in many cases superior to Lloyd's.

The chocolate is very fine, and I almost made myself sick with it. I have not yet been reduced to the extremity of cooking for myself, but, in place of it, have almost starved, as our contrabands, who cook for us, lead the mules which carry our "grubb," so we have them both together, or we have neither. I intend drawing a regulation overcoat & having it fixed as it is hardly worth the while to get a fine one. You needn't send me one. . . .

P.S. I enclose also [a] small fragment of our regimental standard, which has been in many a battle, and is torn into shreds by shell & ball. The piece I found (it having fallen off) . . . contains part of a "6"—this being the 60th Regt. of Penna. Volunteers, & the 3rd Cavalry. It is as precious as gold, so don't lose it.[3]

Camp on Kettle Run
Near Bristoe Stn., Va., O&A RR
Oct. 9th, 1863

Dear Mother:

You requested me in your last letter to get my photograph taken, so I got the nearest thing I could to it—an ambrotype, the commonest kind of a picture, which, at home, costs 25 cents but here is 4 or 5 times that sum. I suddenly took it into my head to have my picture taken, so I jumped on my horse and rode over to the Station in the clothes I wear about camp. The coat is the one you sent me and the corduroy pants I bought at the Sutlers. (Almost all officers of Cavy. wear them, as they are comfortable, and may be said to last forever). Now you can see how much stouter I am. The group consists of 1st Lieut. Heyl (sitting down) and 1st Lieut. Carter of my company. Tho' both pictures are bad (they make every one look like a "Baltimore Plug"), both officers are good looking. Lieut. Carter is an old soldier, having served 5 yrs. in the 5th Regular Cavalry and is a fine officer. He is a Virginian and has a fine place on the James River near Richmond, which, but for his mother living there, would long ago have been confiscated. Heyl used to live in our block, at the cor. of 18th Sts. He is also a good officer, dashing & brave as a lion, but far too reckless. We are laying here, as you see, and, may be will stick here some time—no news. Write soon & often. . . .

———

October 10th. Saturday. "General" sounded about 10, camp was struck, and we marched a few hundred yards on the Catlett's Station Road, when another dispatch arrived and we returned to camp.

———

On the march
Gainesville, Va.
Oct. 21st, 63

Dear Mother:

I have not been able to write home lately, as we have been marching & fighting hard. Poor Elwood Davis was instantly killed in a very severe engagement on Oct. 15th. We were rear guard of Meade's Army trains, & Buford, to whom we were attached <u>pro temp</u> gave us (our Regt.) the credit of saving the army's trains. We alone held the enemy in check for an hour and a half, until supports came up. I am very well. We are marching in the direction of Warrenton, but I can't understand the <u>strategy.</u> The whole army is marching. . . . I will write a full account when we get settled.

Camp near
Warrenton, Va.
Oct. 22, 1863

Dear Mother:

I wrote a few lines home yesterday, while we were halted near Gainesville drawing rations & forage, to let you know that I was all right. Since I last wrote on Friday Oct. 9th, from camp on Kettle Run, near Bristoe Station, we have been very active and I have had no chance of writing.

On Sunday Oct. 11th, Camp was struck & we moved to Catlett's Station where Gen. Terry's Headquarters (3rd Divn. 6th Corps) were, and went into camp, but with orders to move at a moment's notice.

At Midnight of Monday, 12th, just as we had got into a comfortable sleep, camp was ordered to be struck, and we went to Warrenton Junction. We lay in a field all day of Tuesday (13th) (2 squadrons being out scouting). All the Army trains and rolling stock were being moved to the rear as quickly as possible, and a great part of the army passed also. In the evening we were relieved from Duty with Genl. Terry's Divn. and reported to Col. Devin's Brigade of Gen. Buford's (1st) Cavalry Divn., and went into bivouac for the night near the Junction.

Oct. 14 Wednesday. About 8.30 we started on the march, and came up with the army trains, parked near Brentsville opposite Bristoe Station where (the Station) a heavy fight was going on, from 2 to 5 miles off from us.[4] The rebs were trying hard to get at our trains. The particulars of the fight you already have.[5] We were mounted or standing to horse all night nearly, expecting an attack—no sleep & little or nothing to eat.

Oct. 15th Thursday. Early in the morning we started on the march, our regiment in the extreme rear. At a small place, Bradley, where we halted for some time on acct. of some delay among the wagons, the enemy fired on our rear guard. They did not trouble us until we came up with the cursed wagons, parked, 2 or 3 miles beyond, about a mile & a half East of the Manassas fortifications. Here we had a terrible fight, from about 3.30 P.M. till after dark.

Seeing a line of skirmishers approaching, Capt. Walsh, commanding the Regiment, immediately threw out the greater part of the regiment as skirmishers to hold the enemy in check. It was an hour and a half before we were reinforced, and longer before our artillery came into position. In the mean time, the enemy massed squadrons upon squadrons upon our line, but we stood to our work.[6] Almost within the first few minutes, my old friend Ellwood Davis was killed instantly by a ball from a carbine striking him in the right eye and knocking nearly the whole side of his head in. His body was brought in under a galling fire. We

Lt. Ellwood "Ned" Davis (*left*), an unidentified officer (*standing*), and Capt. William W. Rogers (*right*). Davis, Rawle's close friend and classmate at the University of Pennsylvania, was killed on October 15, 1863. Rogers, who commanded Company L, was severely wounded during the cavalry fight at Gettysburg. (Courtesy Civil War Collection, US Army Heritage and Education Center, Military History Institute, Carlisle, PA)

were, as I was saying, in a very critical position, until reinforcements & artillery came up, but we held the large force of Rebels in check.

The artillery practice on the part of the enemy was the finest I have ever seen. They got the range of us beautifully, & their 3rd shell burst in the centre of the 1st platoon of our (Wetherill's) squadron killing a couple of horses & wounding one man badly, besides several small scratches. Our skirmishers on the right were being pressed hard & our squadron was sent across as fast as we could go to reinforce & support them. There was an exposed place between two hills which we had to cross, and we had almost passed it when the reb battery took us on the wing, and sent a shell into the 3rd platoon, which went through Orderly Sgt. Dodwell ("F" Compy., Wetherill's) tearing him to pieces, within 6 feet of me. Though pressed upon by far superior numbers, we held our ground until after dark.[7]

The conduct of the 3rd Pennsylvania was the talk of everybody. Gen. Buford complimented Capt. Walsh and gave us credit for saving Gen. Meade's trains. Capt. Walsh, who is an "old regular" handled the men admirably. Our loss, besides poor Ned Davis & Sgt. Dodwell was private Bern of B compy. killed, nine wounded and five missing.[8] Davis was the first officer ever killed in the regiment, and was in it the least time. Poor fellow, he has had a very unlucky time of it.[9]

We remained on the battle field till 10 P.M., when we moved back, crossed the Bull Run, and bivouacked for the night on its banks.

Oct. 16th Friday. Col. J. W. McIntosh's brigade (now commanded by Col. Taylor, Col. McI. being on sick leave) and the 3rd Div. 3rd Corps came up to our support last evening, but we saved the trains without their aid. We rejoined our own brigade and moved over to the right, and went into temporary camp near Wolf Run Shoals on the Occoquan River to picket. I was detailed for picket in the evening. No sleep for the 6th night, of any account.

———

October 17th. Saturday. Lieut. Vandegrift relieved me at 5 PM when I returned to camp.[10] *Splendid apples and chestnuts. Lieut. Col. Jones and Major Robinson rejoined the regiment from absence on leave.*

———

The Regiment went out on Sunday 18th to picket along the river some distance down the stream. Our squadron pickets Mayhugh's & Mill's Fords. About dusk we were ordered to draw in our pickets & rejoin the brigade, but owing to some mistake, the regiment did not move on till next morning, when we rejoined the Brigade beyond Fairfax Station. After we had something to eat and our horses fed, we started on the march again. We halted for a couple of hours at Union Mills, passed over the Bull Run battlefield, fortifications, etc., and lay for the night beyond Centreville on the Warrenton Pike.

Oct. 20th Tuesday. We marched very little during the day, and camped for the night on the same road, about 2 miles beyond.

Oct. 21st Wednesday. At daybreak we were on the march again. At Gainesville we halted to draw rations & forage, then through Thoroughfare Gap, where I took advantage of a short halt to ride over to see Lt. George Heberton, who is on Gen. Rowley's staff, 1st Brig., 3rd Divn., 1st Corps, which lays here.[11] We then marched to Warrenton, & occupied for the night our old camp. The rebs have been here very lately, and cleaned it out. This morning [October 22nd] we moved camp to a beautiful wood on the road to the Sulphur Springs, about 2 or 3 miles from town.

Now I have made up for not writing for some time. I recd. your letter of Oct. 11th and Lilly's of 13th. Also, this morning, I recd. yours & Lottie's, both of Oct. 18th, with the welcome cravats. And now for your answers. With care, got over my cold in 3 days, so don't worry yourself about nothing. I have sent for the mattress. I recd. all of the letters you speak of. No chance of going up to Washington. . . . [I]t was not my little black pony "Little Mac" which was shot, but one of my company horses I happened to be riding. . . . And last of all I beg of you not to remain in anxiety about me. If anything should happen to me you would hear of it soon enough, and if I were hurt, you would see me at home in a short time, you may be bound.

You would enjoy this country much, if there was no war, now. The beautiful scenery is most magnificent now, with the multitude of different colored foliage, especially among the mountains and along the Occoquan. Chestnuts are plenty and all we have to do is to get a tree cut down. We have been spending the day in making camp comfortable, but the worst of it is that we have to clear out at any moment.

The movements of both armies are a puzzle to anyone. The rebs fall back, and we put after them—the cavalry of course in the advance, fighting hard all the way. Before long, we retreat helter skelter (the late one was very badly managed) and the rebs put after us—cavalry fighting all the time. Then they slip off under our nozes & we occupy our old line. The only way I can account for it is that both leaders want to occupy the attention of the other, to prevent Bragg or Rosecrans from being reinforced. But such is "strategy." The slip from the paper, about the cavalry, which Lottie sent, is the only thing giving the proper credit to the cavalry (which is the hardest worked branch of the service) that I have seen. In return I send a short story cut from Harper's of our campaign in Maryland & Penna. The writer appears to belong to the 1st New Jersey, which is in our brigade. It gives a description of the part our brigade took at Gettysburg, and mentions the 3rd quite condescendingly. . . .[12]

P.S. Nearly all the officers have requested me to get some of poor Ell Davis' photographs. We had them both taken at the same time at "Manger's," 12th & Chestnut, the day before we left home. If you can get a dozen & a half & send them you will do a great favor. I will pay for them.

———

Finding the Army of the Potomac secure on the high ground around Centreville, Lee turned his army south and once again moved back behind the Rappahannock, destroying the Orange & Alexandria Railroad between Manassas and the river as he retreated. The Southerners had suffered a setback when part of Hill's Corps was repulsed at Bristoe Station on October 14. Otherwise, the brief campaign was notable as the last time that Lee initiated an independent offensive action against the Federals.

Meade followed Lee into Fauquier County, repairing the vital railroad line as his army advanced, and was soon settled in the vicinity of Warrenton, Virginia. The commander would have been content to end active campaigning for the winter, but Lincoln and General in Chief Halleck, dissatisfied with Meade's actions over the previous two weeks, spurred him to action. "The President desires that you will prepare to attack Lee's army," Halleck wired him on October 24. With the railway to Warrenton restored on November 1, five days later Meade ordered an advance against two key points along the Rappahannock: the crossing near Rappahannock Station, where Lee maintained a force on the north bank protected by forts and rifle pits, and Kelly's Ford, located four miles downstream.

———

October 23rd. Friday. In the morning there was a Regimental Dress Parade, for the purpose of reading orders relative to reenlistment. The offer is $402 bounty, to be sent home now for six weeks on recruiting service, and thirty days leave during August. The men however could not see it and only a few sent in their names.

October 24th. Saturday. Rain. Camp was struck about 8 AM and the regiment went out to relieve the 1st R.I. on picket on the Rappahannock at Waterloo and below. Treichel's and Carter's squadrons picketed at Waterloo. . . .

October 25th. Sunday. Magnificent weather. All quiet during the day and night.

October 26th. Monday. Received letters from home dated Oct. 21st. They were all terribly anxious about me, having not as yet received my letters. All quiet during the day and night. The 1st and 3rd Maryland (Rebel) mounted infantry picketing opposite us. In the afternoon we changed the reserve back about three-quarters of a mile, and at midnight I went out and relieved Lieut. Potter, remaining the rest of the night. I received an officer's folding Lloyd's pocket map from home by post.

———

Camp near Warrenton, Va.

Oct. 27th, 63.

Dear Mother:

I have just returned from a three days tour of picket duty along the Rappahannock, from Sulphur Springs to Waterloo. I last wrote you on Thursday 22nd, since which time I have recd. your letter of Oct. 21st, in which you are in an awful scare, and one of the 23rd in which you are relieved. Working the way we do is not very apt to elevate a fellow's spirits, and receiving such letters as yours of the 21st don't put him in any better humor. It is actually <u>unkind</u> in you to feel so about me, because it only makes me downhearted. If anything should happen, believe me, you will hear soon enough, and if I get hurt, I will get home at the double quick. A "plug"—if not too bad, is considered rather a lucky thing, and is compensated for by a 30, 60 or 90 days leave, which is decidedly a good thing. Don't for my sake get so anxious about me.

Last night I recd. the map, which was very welcome. I had not had it but a few minutes when an orderly rode up, "Col. Jones sends his compliments and would like to see your large map." It is in great demand. A detachment was sent to Washington the other day for horses, and I expect the mattress by one of the non-commissioned officers. By the bye I hear that the mail of the Army was captured yesterday near Thoroughfare Gap, but I hope I lost nothing. Today I recd. a letter from Carrie.

Don't believe the rumors in the papers. It is the general opinion that the active campaign is closed for the Fall & winter, and we hope soon to go into winter quarters. . . . There goes "Stables," so good bye. Write soon and as often as possible.

———

October 28th. Wednesday. Regimental (dismounted) Inspection and Inspection of horses in the morning. Got Boyle of "C" Company for "Dog Robber."[13]

———

Camp near Warrenton, Va.
Oct. 31st, 1863.

Dear Lilly:

I recd. your letter of Oct. 26th last evening, and was very glad to get it. We are still laying here, but our turn for a 3 day's tour of picket comes round again on Monday. Tomorrow, if possible, I am going to the Episcopal Church in Warrenton. I have tried several times before to attend, but have been prevented every time. Nothing much is going on, except settling up our papers. This morning we had an inspection & muster, preparatory to being paid. The skirmish the other Day was with Col. Gregg's Brigade of our Division, and we have had no fight since Oct. 17th. We are not attached to any but our own (2nd) Division of the Cavalry Corps. I never was in greater want of something to write of, and can't even fill this paper.

This evening I recd. today's *War Press,* which comes very regularly now, but no letters except of a business character. It has been raining, but it has cleared off now & the wind is blowing around promiscuously. I only hope my tent won't come down tonight, which would be decidedly disagreeable. Think of having your house coming down around your ears. Since Wetherill has gone home I am all alone, keeping Bachelor's Hall. I have a board bed, with 6 blankets. A hard-tack box constitutes my table and my valise does for a wardrobe, closet, chair, etc. and some boards for my carpet. My table has a newspaper for a cover, and does for desk & library, which last consists of tactics & military works, "Marmion" & "The Antiquary,"[14] which last I was very glad to get from one of the officers, who had stolen it somewhere. There goes "Tattoo" so good night. . . .

Camp near Warrenton, Va.
Nov. 5th, 1863

Dear Mother:

We have just returned from another 3 day's tour of picket, on the Rappahannock between the Sulphur Springs & Waterloo. . . .

Last Sunday [November 1], for the first time since I've been in the Army, I succeeded in getting to Church. About 6 of us got passes from Reg'tal, Brigade & Divn. Hdqrtrs (all of which are necessary) & attended service at the Episcopal Church in Warrenton. It is quite a nice little building, not delapidated like the rest of the town. It is built something in the style of Ch. Woodbury & St. Mark's [Church, Philadelphia]. We had a very fine sermon on the communion between the Unseen & Seen worlds. Warrenton, as I have told you before, is <u>secesh</u> of the hottest kind, and the prayers used would have shocked Lilly. In place of "the President of the U.S." the pastor put "Chief Magistrates," and he also prayed for their unhappy land. Of about 30 ladies present, but 2 or 3 were in colors, the rest being in mourning for relations in the Reb army who have been killed. It looked very sad. A great many officers were there among others, Maj. Jim Biddle & Capt. Ch[arles] Cadwalader of Gen. Meade's staff, Lt. Horace Binney, Jr. of Gen. Neill's staff and an old teacher of mine at Faires, Lt. Hayden of Gen. Wright's staff.[15]

The next day, Monday [November 2], we went out on picket, relieving the Rhode Islanders. Our squadron picketed Porter's Ford. During the afternoon the Rebs in some force drove in our pickets on the right, at Waterloo, made a dash along the line & gobbled several videttes.[16] The Rebs were thick as hops on the other bank, & very friendly. Tho' strictly contrary to orders, conversations are frequent, & several men of either army crossed the river & had a chat, exchanged newspapers, etc. "Johnny Reb" wanted to swap everything almost. Two or three times, when we rode down to the river, the Reb captain came down & crossed to our side, & we sat down on the earthworks & had a talk. He belonged to the 13th Va. & was named Horner (some relation to Dr. H of Phila.). They were dressed in coarse grey stuff, but good & new. Their officers cannot be distinguished from the privates, as they dress in the same way & carry carbines as the men do. The Capt. says they are required to do so.[17]

[November 5.] We were relieved this morning by the 1st Pa. Cav, & returned to camp.

Evening. No mail has arrived, so I am greatly disappointed—its arrival being about the only pleasure to look forward to during the day—but I will content myself with the "Antiquary." I wish you would each write once a week at least.

———

November 6th. Friday. By Special Order No. 99 Maj. O. O. G. Robinson, Capt. Baughman and I, as recorder, were appointed a Military Commission to investigate charges against Sgt. Weir.[18] We got through by night. I was hard at work writing all day. As it is my turn, I became caterer of the Tycoon mess,[19] and began work by losing, through one of the "contrabands," $20.

———

Camp in the field, somewhere
Between Fayetteville & Warrenton
Fauquier Co., Va. Nov. 11th, 1863

Dear Mother:

I was very glad to get a letter from you dated Nov. 1st, and one from Lottie of Nov. 5th. They both arrived on the same day. I recd. them last Sunday while laying at Rappahannock Station. I last wrote to you on Nov. 5th, and since then we have been knocked around pretty freely.

We left Warrenton on Sat. Nov. 7th, and marched to Bealeton, where we lay for the night. When we arrived, a heavy fight was going on nearby at Rappahannock Station, in which part of the 6th Corps drove the rebs from their strong entrenchments on this side of the river, capturing 1827 prisoners & a battery.[20] The Army is making some great move, but what it is we can't yet make out. It is probably "changing its base" toward the old line of Acquia Creek & Fredericksburg. At any rate, something was going on, and there where a great many wagon trains here, which we were guarding I suppose.

The next day we moved in rear of the trains about dusk, to Rappahannock Statn., and bivouacked on the battle field of Saturday. We lay here all day, with the exception of escorting forage trains to Kelly's Ford & back, until Tuesday 10th, when the Brigade moved to Fayetteville & went into camp. This morning we moved a couple of miles nearer Warrenton.

We are posted here to guard the right flank of the army during its "big move," and have plenty of work. Gregg's Divn. has a line of 75 miles to picket!!! As I can best make out, Meade's intention is to keep Lee's attention engaged, by strategic movements, to prevent his sending troops to reinforce the Reb army at Chickamauga. If so, we do not yet expect to go into Winter Quarters. It is getting very cold down here now, the small streams freezing over at night. Yesterday morning the mountain tops were covered with snow, which looked very beautiful. . . . Orders have just come in to prepare to go on picket early tomorrow morning, so "bon soir."

[P.S.] Send Davis' Photographs as soon as you can. My vignettes were wretched. Almost every one of the officers is getting a collection of the officers of the Reg't., and I have promised a good many photogs. Send a dozen or so in uniform. Excuse my asking so many little favors, and keep an a/c of what you pay out for me.

———

Meade moved cautiously across the Rappahannock on the heels of the November 7 successes at Rappahannock Station and Kelly's Ford, providing the Army of Northern Virginia time to fall back unchallenged. Lee initially occupied a position north of Culpeper, but with both flanks vulnerable to the advancing Federals, he moved to the south side of the Rapidan and occupied the high ground overlooking the lower north side of the river. Despite the fact that the Southerners had slipped away, Lincoln was pleased with Meade: "I have seen your dispatches about operations on the Rappahannock . . . and I wish to say, 'Well done.'"[21]

———

Camp in the Field near
Fayetteville, Va.
Nov. 15th, 1863

Dear Mother:

. . . I last wrote on Thursday [sic, Wednesday, November 11] from this place. Early next morning we went out to relieve the 6th Ohio, picketing along the Rappahannock from Sulphur Springs almost to Beverly Ford. There were none of the enemy on the opposite bank, so we had an easy & uneventful tour of duty.

———

WBR was officer of the day on November 12, having charge of the pickets in the immediate vicinity of the camp, which were necessary, he noted in his diary entry of the eleventh, because "the country around here is so infested with guerillas . . . we have to establish a line of vedettes a short distance from camp, besides the dismounted camp guards." He was relieved as officer of the day on the thirteenth, and on the following afternoon rode with Lieutenant Colonel Jones, commander of the 3rd, along the picket line of the regiment, which was stationed guarding crossings of the Rappahannock at Freeman's, Fonce's, and Fox's Fords.[22] His letter below details his further actions on November 14.

———

I crossed over [the river] several times, once to arrest a marauding party of stragglers from our army, whom I caught after a considerable run. Tho' contrary to the strictest orders, these parties of stragglers of <u>our</u> army I am ashamed to say, go to houses of citizens, and unprotected females, kill the live stock & poultry, which is all the poor people have to look forward to, to keep them alive during the coming winter, tear up and destroy or steal every thing in the house and even maltreat the owners. No wonder that the men swear eternal hatred [for] every Northerner, & turn guerillas. The country around here is infested with them, and no one is safe in going alone outside of camp. This morning the officers had to send all their "Dog robbers" (enlisted men allowed to officers as servants) in a body to get commissary stores a couple of miles off.

Tho' this species of warfare (waylaying & murdering every one they can) is held in contempt by soldiers, yet when I come to think over it, tho' not justifiable, [it] is at least excusable. I would do the same if I saw my family & property treated the way theirs is. The inhabitants declare that wherever we go we make enemies, & not friends as we should do if we desired to bring them back to the Union. It is almost heartrending to view the destitution which exists in every part of Virginia I have visited. The people have not the slightest idea how they are going to live through the coming winter. They are actually starving. I have seen the genuine F.F.V.'s doing the most menial work, having no servants to do it for them. All their houses & estates have gone to ruin, no fences no crops. I cannot attempt to picture the universal wretchedness.

This morning [November 15] we were relieved by the 6th Ohio, & returned to camp. We are doing very hard duty, 3 days on & 3 days off.

This afternoon we had variety in the routine of camp life. There was a Mounted Brigade Dress Parade to carry out the sentence of a Gen. Court Martial, in the cases of two of my company who deserted shortly after entering the service. They had half their heads shaved, branded on the hip with the letter "D" & were drummed out of the service. I was in hopes they would have been shot, as a few examples would have been of service, but as it is the disgrace is greater. They formed a comical spectacle.[23]

In the letter giving an account of poor Ell Davis' death, I forgot to state that the men who went out between the enemy's & our own lines under a most terrible fire where Orderly Sergeants Whalen of Compy. "H" (Davis own compy.) and Lyons of "A" Compy.[24] I state this so that if you have a chance you may let his family know who volunteered to recover his body from the enemy's hands, though exposing themselves to almost certain death. I have not yet recd. Davis' photographs.

I am unable to say what the army is doing or intends to do. Gen. Meade wisely keeps his plans a secret, which none of his predecessors were able to do. I presume his design is to keep Lee busy so as to prevent his reinforcing Bragg.

They are cutting down our conveniences greatly. They are going to take away the officer's mules, and what we will do I cannot say. As it is, our transportation is insufficient. One of the principal duties of an officer of the U.S. Army is to support the dignity of his position, and how can he do so when he is not allowed the means?

You ask what I do for stationary. We get it from the Sutlers when there are any about. This paper I got from being recorder of a Reg'tal Military Commission, and is all I have. You must excuse my writing, as my position (sprawling on the ground) is not well adapted for that purpose. Give my love to all at home & write soon.

P.S. If a letter should come addressed to Miles G. Carter in my care send it on to me. It will be from Richmond, his home, pr. flag of truce, and as he did not want to give his address in the U.S. Army, I told him to direct to my care.

Camp in the Field near
Fayetteville, Va.
Nov. 17th, 1863

Dear Mother:

Last eveng. I recd. the 1½ doz of Ell Davis' photographs, which I gave around to the officers of the Regt, as they had requested me, and, I'm glad to say they gave universal satisfaction. A good many officers are exchanging photogs. for the purpose of making collections. I think it best not to send for an album, as my valise may be lost on any march, so I've decided to send all I get home for you to keep for me.

Enclosed are photogs of Ell Davis & Major Robinson & a very good ambrotype of my compy. commander, Carter, of whom I have often written to you. Carter expects a leave soon & if he gets it, most probably he will visit Phila. and I've asked him to make you a call. He is a fine fellow, a natural gentleman, tho' probably not so polished as if he had passed his life in Phila. society. He has served in the Regular Army since he was 18, in Texas & Virginia. He is a Virginian, his mother owning a fine estate on the James River near Richmond & he belongs to the genuine F.F.V.'s. Should he pay you a call, receive him well for my sake, if that is any inducement. He has no home now, the Rebs having confiscated his own property, negroes & all. Major Robinson lives in Pittsburg & is acquainted with the Moorhead's.

I wrote to you on Sunday Evening. Last night about 2 AM our pickets were attacked by Mosby's guerillas, and our regiment, expecting an attack every minute,

Miles G. Carter, a former Regular Army cavalryman and Virginia native, was commissioned first lieutenant in the 3rd Pennsylvania in May 1863. Rawle and Carter would serve together in Company B for sixteen months. (Courtesy Civil War Collection, US Army Heritage and Education Center, Military History Institute, Carlisle, PA)

was out in line under arms in five minutes. We remained in line until nearly 5 o'c, when we again "turned in."

As soon as you can, send me the dozen photogs in uniform I asked for, as I want to get those of the other officers by exchanging. Keep a strict a/c of what money you spend for me, & I will square it up. We expect soon to be paid off for Sep. & Oct, & I think I will be able, I hope, to pay Uncle Wm. my last installment & also what I owe you.

The authorities are treating us more like dogs now, than officers of the U.S. Army. Yesterday we had to turn in our pack mules, and at present we have no transportation, except for our valises. Even these we can't have with us, as our camp may be attacked at any moment by guerillas, & wagons are in the way. We used pack mules to carry our "grub," cooking utensils, forage for horses, blankets & tents—one animal being allowed each officer. The order is to let us have one wagon more instead, but how we are to get along till then, & even then I don't know. I believe they are even going to take our tents & flies (which last are intended only for the hottest weather) and let us have "shelter tents," which are used by the men. These are two pieces of canvas stretched . . . over a hole about 4 feet high, and covering an area about 5 feet by four.

They are in addition, I heard, to reduce our pay $23 pr mo. for the services of "Dog Robbers," which every officer is allowed one by Army Regulations. I have explained to you the meaning of the name "Dog robbers" or "Striker" before. It is one of the company who is relieved from all company duty (except inspections & dress parades) to perform the <u>chambermaid</u> work of an officer, i.e. groom & attend to his horses, clean & take care of his arms & equipments, pitch & take care of his tent, etc. So you see why they are getting pretty rough on us.

Frank Wetherill is on duty at "Dismounted Camp" near Washington D.C., the cavalry depot for supplying remounts, & a nice place, little work & no fighting or picket. I am reading over again "Devereux,"[25] which one of the officers got out of a deserted F.F.V. <u>mansion.</u> . . .

———

Rebuffed weeks earlier upon suggesting that his army should go into winter camps, Meade planned to initiate an offensive despite the imminent arrival of the cold weather that would render active campaigning difficult. Starting from its camps on November 24, the Army of the Potomac was to undertake a three-pronged assault across the lightly guarded fords of the Rapidan in an attempt to turn Lee's right. Bad weather delayed the movement for two days (and made the river crossings hazardous), while tardiness coupled with confusion by the leadership of the III Corps ruined any chance Meade had of surprising the Rebels. Lee learned of the threat beyond his flank and, after fighting throughout the day of November 27, pivoted his line back to a strong defensive position fronting a small stream known as Mine Run to await the Federals.

Rawle and the 3rd Pennsylvania experienced an eventful ten days, enduring hard fighting on November 27, when they led the advance of the army, and on the twenty-ninth, when, but for the foresight of Rawle, the entire regiment might have been captured.

———

On Picket, Fox's Ford
Rappahannock River, Va.
Nov. 22, 1863
Sunday Eveng.

Dear Mother:

Last Wednesday I recd. your Sunday letter & one from Lottie of Monday. On

Capt. Walter S. Newhall, a Philadelphian from a prominent family and renowned prewar cricketeer, was severely wounded at Gettysburg. He served both within the 3rd Pennsylvania and in brigade-level staff assignments before his death in December 1863, when his horse reared and fell on him, smothering Newhall. In this view he is hiding the right side of face, which was disfigured by his Gettysburg wound. His brother, Harrison, was the adjutant of the 3rd. (Courtesy Ronn Palm, Gettysburg, PA)

Monday I recd. Ell Davis' photograph[s], and distributed them among the officers, & thereby gave universal satisfaction. They were all very eager to get them.

I wrote to you on Tuesday, I believe, enclosing some photographs of Maj. Robinson & Ell Davis & an ambrotype of Lt. Carter, which I want you to keep for me. Today I enclose one of Capt. Walter S. Newhall, Compy. A, now Act. Asst. Adjt. Genl. of the Brigade. You have often heard me mention him. At the Episcopal Academy we were schoolmates. He is a splendid officer, and has one of the best <u>heads</u> for military matters of anyone I ever knew. It is a fine likeness. He was wounded in the face at Gettysburg, and to hide the big scar he has been taken in <u>profile.</u>

We lay in camp near Fayetteville until Friday [November 20], when we went out to relieve the 1st R.I., picketing down from the Sulphur Springs. It has rained hard until today, making it rather unpleasant. We expect to be relieved tomorrow.

I hear that 20 days rations were ordered & that the Army of the Potomac was to advance today, but I've heard or seen nothing more about it. Guerillas have again been troubling us. For several nights they gave our line a good deal of trouble, and a considerable force was put in ambush, and a section (2 guns) of our battery put in position commanding the town of Warrenton, with the intention of giving the inhabitants a taste of percussion shells should our line be attacked, but luckily for them they "kept scarce." Yesterday they attacked our wagon train in force, captured 3 mule teams & (it is reported) 30 men of our regiment. I suppose it is an exaggerated account, however. This is just the time for the annual detail for "Libby" to report, a number of officers and men being generally taken prisoners during the last part of November. We were in hopes that the cavalry would have a respite soon, but there appears to be little chance of it. Gen. Hooker used to say that cavalry was good for nothing, whereas Gen. Meade thinks too much of it, and works it a great deal too hard. He expects from it much more than it is capable of performing. It sadly needs recruiting & refitting.

Buford & Kilpatrick are down towards the Rapidan, and Gregg is doing very hard picket [duty] to prevent a flank movement, & protect the O&A RR. It is impossible to say what we are going to do. The most general belief is that the Army will change its base, and move to the Peninsula via Fredericksburg. It is reported also that the 3d Pa Cav will be sent to near Washington D.C. to refit. Col. McIntosh, who is in command at Dismounted Camp, is trying hard for it. . . . I am writing this on my lap, by the light of a fire, so excuse the writing, etc.

On the March near Bealeton, Monday [November 23] 11 AM.
Our pickets were drawn in before daylight this morning and we joined the Brigade, and marched here. We are now drawing rations & forage, expecting every minute to continue the march, wither I know not—a change of base probably.
This letter was in a mail captured by the enemy & found on the road.[26]

Bivouac near Parker's Store
Gordonsville & Fredericksburg Plank Road
Nov. 28/63. Saty.

Dear Mother:
I wrote a letter to you last Sunday (22nd), but as there has been no chance of sending a mail off lately, you will not receive it until some time after its date. The mail carrier gave it back to me, but I only wrote a few words to you on the envelope, telling you that we had had (or rather, were having) a terrible fight, a stray shell now & then busting about us at the time, but I will give you an account from my journal.

Nov. 23rd Monday. At daylight our pickets were drawn in & we rejoined the Brigade at our old camp, near Fayetteville. We marched to Bealeton, where we drew rations, forage, etc., then resumed the march, arriving at Morrisville about

8 PM (owing to a delay among the wagons) where we bivouacked for the night. The whole Army of the Potomac is in motion, & we expect important events & hard work before long. Gregg's Cavy. Divn. is moving on the left flank.

Nov. 24th Tuesday. At daybreak we left Morrisville & forded the Rappahannock at Ellis' Ford. The river was much swollen by the rain & some amusing scenes occurred. Just before crossing I recd. Lilly's letter of Nov. 10th, also the Press and *Living Age,* which I was glad to receive. We bivouacked for the night about a mile from the river.

Nov. 25th Wednesday. At 10 AM "Boots & Saddles" sounded, but about noon "Recall," and we remained there during the night.

Nov. 26th Thursday. Thanksgiving Day, to all but the Army. "Reveille" at 4 AM, but "To Horse" not till 9.15. We moved down to the Rapidan, & forded it at Ely's Ford about noon. The Division marched about 10 miles through "The Wilderness," (a large, almost uninhabited tract of underbrush) and bivouacked for the night on a farm on the road to Orange C.H. The country beyond the Wilderness is flourishing, and has not suffered from the presence of an army. It did not take long for the men to do away with a flock of sheep, pigs, chickens, vegitable gardens & forage, and we had a good supper & nights rest.

Nov. 27th Friday. Battle of New Hope Church. In the saddle at 5.30 AM and the 3d Pa took the advance of the Division. We made a junction with the 5th Corps at Parker's Store, on the Fredericksburg and Gordonsville Plank Road. We again took the advance, moved up the Road in column of platoons, & met the enemy's cavalry about 2 or 3 miles beyond. The country is very bad for cavalry fighting—thick woods, underbrush & no good positions for artillery. For an hour & a half we fought the Rebs, and drove them over a mile, when their infantry came up & relieved them.

The remainder of our regiment was thrown out as skirmishers to reinforce the rest of the 3d Pa & 1st Mass, and in the thick woods we had a terrible fight. The enemy's line was so near us that we could hear their commands and talking. Dismounted cavalry can do nothing against infantry with their long range Enfield's & bayonets, but we held our ground. Once, the rebs charged bayonets on us, and we retreated about 20 yards, when we succeeded in rallying the line, charged in turn to beyond our old position, drove the infantry, & captured 30 or 40 prisoners. Such a thing as dismounted cavalry driving infantry, I believe, has not been heard of during the war.[27]

About this time the 1st New Jersey came up to relieve us, but owing to some misunderstanding, we remained on the line for 1½ hours longer. John Kester, who used to live in the square above us, is Lieut. Col. of the 1st New Jersey Cavalry, & Peter Penn Gaskill is a captain.[28] Col. Kester and I laid flat on the ground for an

Joseph D. Galloway of Philadelphia, who served as second lieutenant of Company I and first lieutenant of Company M. (J. Gregory Acken personal collection)

hour, talking of old times & the minnies & shells flying around us like hail. After being out on the skirmish line for 5 hours, under a terrific fire, we [were] relieved, and returned to our led horses, and left the work in the hands of the 5th Corps.

We lost very severely, upwards of 25 killed & wounded in the 3d alone. Our squadron lost 2 killed & 8 wounded, some of them mortally. Capt. Englebert was shot through the hand.[29] The 1st Mass lost 2 officers on the line. The 1st, 2nd & part of the 3rd Army Corps came up during the afternoon & evening. We retired about dusk to this place (near Parker's Store) sent a squadron out to picket in the rear and went into bivouac.

The prisoners said that A. P. Hill's & Ewell's Corps were in our front, & that, on hearing of our advance, were marched for 20 miles as hard as they could. I give it for what it is worth. So much for the journal. It is raining now and we are waiting [for] orders to move, where we don't know. In front of us the "doeboys" are at work, about 3 or 4 miles off. Cavalry can do nothing in this country.

I send enclosed two more cartes de visite for my collection—1st Lieut. J. D. Galloway & 2nd Lieut. Jas. Heslett. Galloway is one of the most amusing men I ever knew. In a fight, he will make the queerest observations and keep you laughing enough to kill yourself.

The *Living Age* gave me such pleasure that I read it through twice. I would like you to subscribe to it for me & charge the amount to my a/c. . . .

On the march near Shepherd's Grove, Va.
Dec. 4th, 1863. Friday

Dear Mother:

I suppose you are very anxious about me, not having heard from me for so long. If you get this, my correspondence will arrive in a bunch. I have written twice, but as we have had no communications, my letters have not been sent off. We have been having a very hard time, you may judge from my journal.

I last wrote on Nov. 28th, giving an account of our doings up to that time, and our fights at Parker's Store & New Hope Church on the Fredericksburg & Gordonsville Plank Road. During the eveng. I was ordered out to picket along the Plank Road with a platoon, to join the pickets of the 2nd Penna, from the 2nd Brig. of our Divn. laying at New Hope Church. The infantry have gone on ahead & desultory fighting can be heard all & every day. This place, where we are posted, is very important for the safety of the army, being the left flank.

Nov. 29. Sunday. There being an unpicketed road coming in to the Plank Road in my rear, I spoke to Col. Jones, our regimental commander about it, but he told me that there was no danger, & said that it was useless to picket it. I told him that, as I was responsible for the safety of my picket reserve, I would draw back my reserve to within 500 yds. of the Store, where the 3rd Penna & 1st Mass, all under command of Col. Jones, were laying, and I threw a vidette out the branch road.

Within an hour afterwards, the whole of Fitzhugh Lee's & Hampton's Divisions of Rebel cavalry came charging in upon the bivouac by 3 roads, having dodged all the pickets except the one I had just posted on one of them & on which one of the columns advanced, cutting me off from the Regiment. I had barely time to get into the saddle, when they were in the middle of my reserve. The Rebs being in far superior numbers, & I not knowing of the other large columns which charged in upon the Regiment (as they did immediately after), I fell back towards the 2nd Brigade at the church, after exchanging several shots. My intention in doing so was to give the regiment time to be fully prepared, and also to draw the enemy on, even at the sacrifice of part of my command, and get them between the party at the Store and the 2nd Brigade, I not knowing of the attacks by the other roads. They followed me up at a dead run, & about half the party were captured and I myself nearly so. Near the church the 2nd Penna formed across the road & held them in check. I reported to Gen. Gregg, for whom I played aide de camp until my horse was used up. I was completely plastered with mud & was in a comical situation.

In the meantime an unmounted force attacked the 3rd Penna & 1st Mass which, had it not been for the alarm I had given, would have been <u>completely</u> surprized and consequently annihilated. They got out of it wonderfully well, with the loss of 31 killed, wounded & missing. Many horses & much property was lost, especially by the officers, who lost everything.[30] I lost my beautiful black horse, all my blankets, tent, rations, mess kit, etc., which were captured. As I was cut off from my regiment, I accepted the hospitality of Lt. R. Butler Price, Jr., & other officers of the 2nd Pa Cav.[31] Some prisoners (I took two in the chase after me) said that the attack was a complete failure, and that they expected to capture every man of us.

Nov. 30th Monday. At 3 AM Gen. Gregg sent me with dispatches to Col. Taylor commanding our Brigade, with some of our men whom I had picked up, by the back road via Pleasonton's Hdqts. at Robertson's Tavern. The Brigade lay at a small village called "Wilderness." Last evening our regiment had fallen back there and I returned to it. About 9 AM the Brigade moved back to Parker's Store and stationed its Hdqts. there.[32] Our squadron went out to picket the Plank Road. In the confusion incident to the surprize yesterday, the mail, both to & from here, was captured and scattered about. My letter to you dated Nov. 22d. with photographs etc. was found by one of the men & also your letter of the same date to me. As we had no blankets, etc. and the nights are bitter cold, we could get no sleep, but sat up by the fire.[33]

Dec. 1st Tuesday. The 1st Brig. 2nd Div. 3d Corps came up to support us, & help hold this very important point. During the evening & night, the army moved past, falling back. We started about midnight, in rear of the infantry.

Dec. 2d Wednesday. Slow tedious marching all night. About noon we crossed the Rapidan at Gold Mine or Culpeper Ford. The infantry moved on, but Gregg's Divn. remained to picket, etc., our Brig. Hdqts. being between Ellis' Ford on the Rappahannock & Gold Mine Ford. During the evening Capt. Walsh's Battalion (I, A, C & K) was ordered out on a scout. We went down to Ellis' Ford, but found Jonny Reb on the other side & we waited daylight.

Dec. 3d Thursday. The enemy having withdrawn from the other bank, at daylight we crossed the Rappahannock at Ellis' Ford (5.45 AM) went to Morrisville, Grove Church, Deep Run & drove in the enemy's pickets near Hartwood Church until we found them. Capt. W[etherill], from their maneuvering & having got the information that Hampton's Divn. was there, withdrew and recrossed at Ellis' Ford at 1 PM, after having marched hard all the time. It was well we got off as well as we did, as we afterwards found out that a party tried to cut us off. At midnight we were again in the saddle, and marched to Shepherd's Grove. We have no rations, living only on coffee & crackers (glad enough to get even that) & no feed for our horses & no sleep.

Dec. 4th Friday. We lay at Shepherd's Grove all day. Almost starved to death. I got the first sleep since Nov. 26th. I recd. your letter of Nov. 29th. News came of the promotion of Capt. Walsh to a Majority, and we had a joyful time over it.

Dec. 5th Saturday. Still in the same place. Rations & forage issued for the first time. Everyone sick or starved. I recd. your letter of Nov. 29th yesterday, also two copies of the *War Press*. In the one of today's date, I see some mention of our fight for a wonder. It states that we were driven back & fell back on the 5th Corps. Once the Rebs made a charge, but we rallied when we had fallen back about 20 yds., and in turn drove them much farther and held them in check until the 5th Corps came up.

———

December 5th. Saturday. Last night was the first regular sleep I have had since Nov. 26th. During the morning I made a report of my share in the attack of our regiment at Parker's Store on Nov. 29th. It seems that Col. Jones is in hot water about it and tries to shift the blame as much as possible. I wrote the report for him but put in more than he bargained for. In case of a court of inquiry I have enough evidence to cashier him, an ultimatum much desired by all parties. He is an old superannuated granny, no more fit to command a regiment than a baby. . . . By accident Carter's and my shelter tent caught fire and burnt up, ruining my coat, cap, etc.

———

What the results of the late movement forward of the Army of the Potomac are, I do not as yet know. Four miles this side of Orange Court House the enemy was posted behind lines upon lines of earthworks, which it was almost impossible to take.[34] One thing is certain, that Richmond can never be taken from this way alone. The only way the Army of the Potomac can take it is by way of the Peninsula. It is reported that Gen. Meade will be relieved. He has proved himself the most successful of our generals. There goes "Retreat" so good bye. . . .

CHAPTER FOUR

Winter at Warrenton

December 6, 1863–April 30, 1864

For the soldiers of the Army of the Potomac, the winter of 1863–64 was devoid of the uncertainty and angst that had characterized the winter of 1862–63, following as it had the defeat at Fredericksburg and the lack of confidence in the army's leadership. Though Meade was unsuccessful in bringing on a decisive engagement at Mine Run, his soldiers lauded his caution in agreeing to call off the assault on November 30, which, many acknowledged, had saved thousands of lives: "that one wise decision of the general commanding," remembered a V Corps soldier, "gave him a tremendous lift into the respect, veneration and love of the army he commanded, completely redeeming himself from the opprobrium that the army hung to his name when he allowed Lee to escape to Maryland."[1]

The Northerners established their winter camps in the war-worn area between the Rappahannock and Rapidan Rivers, where they would remain, mostly static, until the commencement of the Overland Campaign five months later. But the cavalrymen of the army, as always, were rarely sedentary, picketing, scouting, chasing guerillas, and safeguarding supply lines. "It is shameful the way the cavalry have to work," Rawle complained, "while the infantry do nothing at all in their camps." The chaplain of the 1st New Jersey Cavalry wrote, "Incessant vigilance had to be exercised against guerillas, and squadrons kept always under saddle, ready to dash out on the slightest alarm."[2] Although the duty was fatiguing, the men of the 3rd Pennsylvania were fortunate to be stationed near Warrenton, the principal settlement in Fauquier County. Rawle took advantage of his proximity to the town to attend church and develop friendships with some of its inhabitants, despite the fact that Warrenton, he wrote, "was very hot secesh."

In addition to serving a stint as adjutant of the regiment, being tentatively offered a staff position as an aide-de-camp, and enjoying two furloughs back to Philadelphia, the young lieutenant was also appointed regimental recruiting officer. In
this role he was charged with overseeing the reenlistment of veteran soldiers from
the 3rd whose terms of enlistment were expiring in August 1864.

———

Camp, Warrenton, Va.
Dec. 13th, 1863

Dear Mother:

. . . I last wrote home from Shepherd's Grove, where we lay for a day or two,
on Dec. 5th. Next morning the Brigade moved to Brandy Station, and camped in
a low, muddy, swampy wood, which soon made everyone more or less sick. We
lay here, getting a little very much needed rest, for several days.

On Dec. 11th our Paymaster, Maj. Staples, paid us a visit. Of late the Government has taken it into its head to cut down our pay. They now subtract $25.50
pr. mo. for our "Dog Robbers" (soldier servants, whom we are allowed by Army
Regulations). So, instead of $224.80, my former two month's pay, I only got
$172.05, and that in a check which here is about as good as a blank piece of paper,
no one being able to cash it. I am as poor as Job's turkey, with $172 in my pocket.
It seems hard that Uncle Sam should "go back" on Cavalry officers, the hardest
worked class of any in the Army, especially when everything is so expensive. It
costs us to live modestly, with no extravagance, $100 pr. month, viz. Rations $25,
servant $25 (clothes & food). Now, for soldier's servant $25 &, for the absolute
necessities of a soldier, tobacco and incidental expenses of the sutler, etc., etc.,
which are very numerous, say $25, gives $100, as the smallest calculation. Paying
us $86 pr. mo., how are we to get along and live contentedly, when contentment is
all a soldier has to look to? I can manage to get along, but I don't drink or gamble,
which are additional expenses. So much for my grumble.[3]

The same day that we were paid, Dec. 11th, the Brigade moved along the R.R.
to Bealeton, & bivouacked for the night. Next day, we marched to Warrenton and
occupied our old camp ground on the Waterloo Pike. This morning [December
13] we changed to a nice place, on a hill a quarter of a mile from & overlooking
the town of Warrenton, and are building Winter Quarters. It is a splendid place
to winter in, but I'm afraid we will have a very hard time doing picket duty. At
present we are the only troops here, but we expect the rest of Gregg's Divn. &
some infantry up shortly.

Last night it blew a great deal. Wetherill (who came down on Dec. 9th, having
been in hospital), Carter & I tent together. We had fixed ourselves up comfort-

Samuel Boyer, the regimental quartermaster of the 3rd Pennsylvania. (Courtesy Civil War Collection, US Army Heritage and Education Center, Military History Institute, Carlisle, PA)

ably for the night, but did not dig a ditch around the tent. In the middle of the night it blew down & the cold December rain came piling in. We succeeded in fixing it up, but it came down again in a few minutes & we passed the night as best we could, in its ruins. That was not so bad, but the water came flowing in on all sides, and as we slept on the ground of course we were nearly drowned. For the consideration of such advantages, they are gradually taking away all our pay. Luckily for us, our long looked for blankets arrived. Up to this time we have been sleeping all huddled up together to keep warm in our overcoats & horse or saddle blankets, and lived like dogs.

The man I sent for the cork mattress at Adams Express office, Washington, arrived today. He called there, but they had sent it on to the Regt. I am glad I did not get it before, as it [will] come [in] more opportunely now, & I would have lost it by capture, as almost everything I had, except my valise, which Providentially I still have, has gone. It will turn up some day. Don't send your "Christmas Box" till I write for it, and say that I am "open for such offers."

I most probably will have to buy another horse, as I lost one the other day. If so, I will not be able to send home any "spons." The paymaster expects to be around again in the beginning of January. . . . I enclose [a photograph] of our Reg'tal Quarter Master, D. R. Boyer, for my collection.

P.S. Always let me know the dates of letters you receive from me, so that I may know which ones miscarry.

Camp, Warrenton, Va.
Dec. 17th, 1863

Dear Mother:

I have recd. Lilly's letter of Dec. 11th, and your Sunday letter arrived last evening, on my return from picket. I last wrote to you on Sunday Evening, and whenever I have the chance I will always write then, so while you are writing you may imagine me being similarly occupied.

That day, as I told you, we had picked out a camping ground, and we were just setting about, getting ready, commencing to begin work at building Winter Quarters. Carter, Wetherill & I mess together, & we gave the contract to a carpenter in C Company (letting him have whatever men he required detailed from the Compy.) to build us a nice comfortable log & mud hut, giving him $20 for the job. It was very well started when orders came for picket, & we had to suspend operations.[4]

———

December 14th. Monday. A court of inquiry in the case of Col. Jones, in which I am a witness, met at 1 PM at the Warren Green Hotel, but it was postponed on account of the absence of one of the court.[5]

———

At present there are no troops around here but our Brigade, which is encamped all around the town. The picket line consists of a cordon of videttes, about ¾ of a mile from the town. A great many little bands of cavalry & guerillas continually show themselves & bother us. Should no more troops come up we would be in a rather precarious position, and a large force of cavalry could "[illegible]" us out of this in a little time, & get another supply of tents, blankets, horses, etc. An officer of the Brigade Staff told me that some infantry would be up as soon as the Junction R. Road was in running order. Trains began to run up day before yesterday.

We returned from picket last evening, and of course a cold, disagreeable, sleety rain began last night, which in our small light shelter tent, was not the most pleasant thing in the world. We might have had our house done by this time, and been comfortable today. I am writing now in the only finished house in camp with a home-made stove in it, & it is very comfortable, considering the circumstances.

I hope that we will remain near Warrenton all winter, provided some more troops come up. Our camp is beautifully situated on a gentle undulation, south of & overlooking the town, about 300 yards off, between the Junction Rail Road & the Warrenton Sulphur Springs Road. Warrenton itself was once a most beautiful town, the county seat of Fauquier County. It is very prettily situated, surrounded by hills, from which the scenery is superb, with the Blue Ridge of mountains in the distance. In the Court House steeple there is a clock, the striking of which is very pleasant, & reminds me of Woodbury. There are three churches (& one unfinished one), an Episcopalian, a Methodist and a Roman Catholic. The Episcopal Church is very pretty, & the rector, Bartiene, a fine preacher.[6] If I have the chance I will attend regularly.

The society of the place is extremely aristocratic, and there are some very pretty young ladies there. All the young men are away in the Confederate army. A very beautiful young lady, one of the extreme F.F.V.'s whose acquaintance I formed while on picket, (from the fact of her wishing to go outside the line), told me that it was the patriotism of the ladies of Warrenton alone that kept the young gentlemen in the service. She was a fiery hot secessionist (wearing grey & blue, & a Brig. Gen.'s star in her hat), and was confident in the success of her cause. She was acquainted with many persons I knew, in Phila. & in the army. Among the names she mentioned were Julia Welsh & Julia Turner, the Stockton's & many others.[7] If our picketing (cavalry is worked even in the dead of winter) is not too hard, we may pass the winter here very pleasantly. Indeed, I would rather have our winter camp where it now is than any other part of Virginia I have been in.[8]

You ask if I know anything of Frank Wetherill. He came down to the Regt. on Dec. 7th. He is still unwell. . . . Don't send the box quite yet, till we get settled down. You can send the photogs. Have you recd. those of the officers of the Regt. I have sent? The home-made stove is smoking to such a degree that I must clear out.

[P.S.] If you can send me by return of mail an india rubber Havelock from Goodyear's, Chestnut above 3rd ($1). It would be very kind.

Camp, Warrenton, Va.

Dec. 22d, 63

Dear Mother:

I have recd. Lottie's letter of Dec. 17th, and Lilly's of the 18th. So at last Lottie Lazyboots has stirred up energy to write. I was too busy to write on Sunday eveng., and this is my first opportunity.

I last wrote on Thursday Dec. 17th. We were busy at work building Winter Quarters, and indeed have hardly finished yet. The suffering from the intense cold is very great in the Regt., many of the men having no shoes & overcoats, (everything having been lost at Parker's Store Nov. 29th) and the work of the reg't is terribly hard. Very often I have tried hard to keep up the spirits of the men, even when I had "the blues" myself to an intolerable degree, but "talk" won't keep men warm. A large part of the Reg't, officers & men, are sick. We can't stand it any longer, and tomorrow the Comd'g officer will report 150 out of 300 men unfit for duty.

On Dec. 18th our Reg't, Brigade & the service generally met with a sad loss. My old school mate Capt. Walt. S. Newhall of Compy A 3d Pa Cav, late Actg. Asst. Adj. Genl. of the Brigade, was drowned in crossing a stream on his way to Corps Hdqts to join his brother Fred, Capt. & Asst. Ins. Genl. of the Corps staff. They were going home together on furlough to spend the Holiday. He attempted to swim his horse across the stream, which was much swollen by the rain, but, as I understand, sank in the mud & his horse kept him down till he was drowned. Without doubt, the finest soldier in the Brigade, his loss is universally deplored. His indomitable will, which no one could overthrow, brought him through everything, but was the cause of his premature death. I have often spoken of him as having the finest military head, (altho' so young, 22) of any one I ever knew. He gave me his photograph some time ago, & I mailed it home, but it was lost at Parker's Store.[9]

———

December 18th. Friday. . . . General Buford is dead also. A magnificent cavalry officer.[10]

———

On Sunday Dec. 20th I attended service in the Episcopal Church in Warrenton. The same day, I recd. my appointment, from Brig. Hdqts, of Regimental Recruiting officer, in the field, for the enlistment of Veteran Volunteers, and since then I have been very busy. Strong inducements are offered for the re-enlistment of veterans, but only 31 men will agree to do it under our present Reg'tal Com'der Lt. Col. Jones, who is very unpopular, and entirely unfit for the position, being far too old & incompetent.

Today, Frank Wetherill & I moved into our log huts. It is the largest in camp— about 10 by 12 ft. with a large grate stove in it, floored, & with comfortable beds. The reports are however, that we will leave in the course of a few days, and that the army will fall farther back. If there were more troops here, & less duty (which we can't stand much longer), I would rather spend the winter here than at any other

Lt. Col. Edward S. Jones of the 3rd Pennsylvania, who Rawle considered "an inveterate old fogy." (From Regimental History Committee, *History of the Third Pennsylvania Cavalry* [1905])

place. I would be very sorry to leave our comfortable log huts. Frank Wetherill is not very well.

I recd. the helmet & pulse warmers for Carter, but as he is absent on leave, I have not yet been able to give them to him. They are very nice. . . .[11]

Camp 3d Pa Cavy
Warrenton, Va.
Xmas Eve/ 63

Dear Mother:

The first Christmas Eve I've ever spent away from home, I devote to writing to you. And a beautiful Evening it is, with its blue cloudless sky & full moon, very fitting for the happiest night of the year. To us, however, it is the same as any other Evening. I am sitting in our comfortable log hut, Wetherill along side of me, carving on his "meerschaum"—his "battle pipe," (I was the first to introduce the article in the Reg't.), the names of his many hard-fought battles. He is sitting by my side, on the ground, by the cosy grate stove, which is burning cheerfully with Virginia wood. We are quite comfortably fixed up at last; you would say it was rather rude comfort, but we think it grand.

Our mansion consists of a log hut, about 10 ft. square, the cracks plastered up with the "sacred soil." The roof consists of canvass, double. In the corner is a double bunk, and opposite the grate stove, which I <u>rented</u> in Warrenton for the length of time we stay here, for $5 worth of groceries at the Commissary. A board floor, a table made of a cracker box, covered with a <u>poncho</u> for a cloth, and a door 2½ by 2 ft. finishes our <u>ranch.</u> It is the established custom of the "Upper Ten" of Warrenton to spend Xmas Eve in drinking Egg nog, and preparations have been going on for some time by the fair damsels, I suppose because they expected the rebs in town tonight. The Black Horse Cavy., whom we drove out when we last came here, have promised to spend the evening with them. They have been lurking around outside of our pickets ever since. This company, belonging to the 4th Va. Cav., was raised here & is composed of gentlemen of the first standing.[12]

I've recd. invitations to several egg-nog parties, and also to Xmas dinners tomorrow, having received accompanying hints that some whiskey from the [Commissary] (the sale of Commy. goods is strictly prohibited to citizens) would be very acceptable for the purpose of making mince pies, etc. But Frank & I will eat our humble Xmas dinner together, and we have engaged a pair of chickens & some mince pies (if we can get "the needful" whiskey, the sale of which is pro. temp. forbidden to officers or men). We tried hard to get a turkey, but "no go," altho' we have had several lately. At the post Commissary, in town, we can very often get butter, eggs, poultry, etc., as citizens bring them there to exchange for groceries, they not being able to buy them themselves.

Last evening I recd. your Sunday Eveng. letter, and also the india-rubber Havelock, for which I am very much obliged to you. I last wrote to you on Tuesday. Nothing has happened since then. I believe I told you that I was appointed Reg'tal Recruiting Officer in the field, superintending the re-enlistment of Veteran Volunteers. This has kept me very busy, I having no clerk, & doing all the work myself. The thing has hardly got started yet, only 78 names having come in. If we get 275 the regt. will be sent home on 35 days furlough, and if that number is not obtained, individual furloughs for the same time will be granted. I have given in my name to serve for 3 yrs. from the present date, it not making much difference, as when I joined the regt. last May 16th, I was mustered in for 3 years. Being on special duty, it relieves me from picket, and such nasty little things.

There is not much chance of my getting a furlough, at least before the end of the winter, as I have a good deal of work to attend to.

Francis D. Wetherill of Philadelphia, a good friend of Rawle's. Wetherill was captured at Hartwood Church in February 1863 and led Company F of the 3rd from May 1863 until his muster out in August 1864. (From Regimental History Committee, *History of the Third Pennsylvania Cavalry* [1905])

Orders have just come to saddle up with 3 days rations, & 2 of forage, to move at a moments' notice. Hdqts. seem to be scared at the preparations for dinner tomorrow, thinking the rebs may try to get in.

Did you see the Inquirer of Dec. 21st? It contained several complimentary notices of Capt. Walt. Newhall. He cannot be spoken of with too much praise. The officers of the 3d made some very good resolutions, and resolved to wear the usual badge of mourning, but as crape is scarce I wish you would send me some pieces about 1½ ft. long & 2 inches wide.

The Col. has sent an orderly to tell me he wishes to see me, so good night. A Merry Christmas to all at home.

Camp, Warrenton, Va.
Dec. 29th, 1863

Dear Lilly:

. . . Harry Wetherill came down to pay us a visit on Dec. 26th, and stayed until this morning. I'm afraid he had a rather bad time, however, as it rained all the time, almost, that he was here. As I told you before, egg nog parties are "the thing" about here about Xmas time. I was invited to several of them, & also to "several" Xmas dinners but Frank Wetherill & I spent it together, chickens for turkey, & apple for mince, pie.

On Xmas Eve information was recd. at Corps Hdqts. that Mosby was to have an egg nog party near Salem, & a large party was sent after him. He had left a couple of hours before it arrived. It captured 2 of his officers, very important men, however. Last night again a large party went after him, but with his usual luck he got off.

———

December 25th. Friday. . . . The Court of Inquiry in the Parker's Store affair came off today at the Warren Green Hotel. I was a witness in the case but let Col. Jones off as lightly as possible, so nothing came of it.

December 26th. Saturday. This reenlistment business can not be carried on without the blank forms, in the forwarding of which there is some great delay which is very detrimental to the Reg. Rec[ruiting] service. . . .

December 28th. Monday. Rainy. Busy a greater part of the day attending to Recruiting business. Lt. Carter came back from furlough. The Regiment went out on a scout towards Rectersburg [Rectortown] to catch Mosby but "no go."

———

I am very busy, with a great deal of writing to do, so excuse the brevity of this. Write soon &

Dec. 31 '63

I was suddenly stopped in my letter by firing all along the picket line. I hurried out to see some guerillas & cavalry prowling & bothering the picket line. It is raining in torrents & I am hard at work with my paper, etc. and must stop.

Camp Warrenton, Va.
Jan. 3d, 1864
Sunday Eveng.

Dear Mother:

. . . I was very glad to get that piece of poetry on Walt Newhall, the only fault was the quantity spoilt it. If it had ended at "Here ends his story," it would have been much better.[13]

Since I last wrote, nothing much has happened out of the routine of Camp life. I am very busy indeed, being Regimental Recruiting Officer, as I told you before. The only good of it is it relieves me from all duty, and therefor have no picket, scouting, etc. of which the regiment has a good deal. A day or two ago, the 2nd Divn., with the exception of our Reg't which was on picket, went on a raid, reconnaissance or something of the kind, into the Shenandoah Valley.[14] The next day one of Gen. Merritt's (late Buford's) regiments came here to occupy this place, and relieved our pickets. For the first time since we have been here our reg't is off duty.

We have been having some infernally cold weather lately, the coldest, the oldest inhabitants say, for 20 years. Our log hut is very comfortable indeed, the best one in the whole brigade, with a small camp stove, which keeps it as warm as a toast. . . .

I can't, to save my life, write an interesting letter, so there is nothing to tell. I wish you would call at O. Knipe's, No. 906 Arch Street, and get me a photog of Walt Newhall. They were taken last fall, and are a side view so that you can tell them. . . . I will try and get a furlough as soon as possible, but it can't be for a couple of months.

Camp Warrenton, Va.

Jany. 11th, 1864

Dear Mother:

I have not written home since Sunday Jany. 3d, as my time has been entirely occupied with recruiting, and the multitude of papers connected with it. And indeed I cannot find enough of interest to fill a letter with now, the dull routine of camp life not giving me the chance.

We are very comfortably fixed up now in our Winter Quarters, but officers and men are worked very hard, with little or no rest. I, for my part, can't complain on that score, as my being on Special Duty relieves me from everything of the kind, which is about the only advantage derived from the "soft" position. Of the great quantity of writing I aught not to complain, as our Reg'tal Commander offered me as many clerks as I wanted, but I prefer doing the writing myself, as then I can be sure it is done properly.

Genl. Gregg's Head Quarters are now in the town, and the 2nd Brig. which, with ours, constitutes the 2nd Divn., Cavalry Corps, lies between here and Warrenton Junction. Early Thursday morning (7th) a party of rebel cavalry, owing to the negligence of the 1st Penna. pickets, got in rear of the picket reserve of our regiment on the Sulphur Springs road, and charged in upon it, taking it, of course, unawares. Capt. Gilmore, who was in command, was wounded in the leg, [as were] 7 others, and about 20 men captured. Ward got off very nicely, playing possum, making believe he was dead, and escaped with only a little hurt in the hand from the horse of the reb officer in command. This same "chivalry" stripped Gilmore of his money, etc. The reb officers and men always do that now to their prisoners, which shows the spirit of our enemies.[15]

Yesterday, Dr. Potter, Frank Wetherill & I went to the Episcopal Church in Warrenton. . . . I am sorry you gave Capt. Coxe a bundle for me, as nothing is more troublesome to an officer going down to the army. . . . I send enclosed a good photograph of Carter, for my collection. He was glad indeed to get the helmet, and has found [it] is of great advantage. . . .

> Camp 3d Pa Cavy.
> Warrenton, Va.
> Jany. 17th, 1864
> Sunday Eveng.

Dear Mother:

. . . I can't spare time to write more than once a week, or, I should say, I <u>have</u> not had the time. Most of the work on the multitude of papers incident to my office is over now though, as the 65 Veterans have been mustered out & in, and paid off. All that remains now for them is to get their 35 days furlough, which, owing to bad management somewhere, I am afraid, will end in their not getting as much as promised. That was nearly all the inducement which got them to re-enlist, they preferring that even to the $402 bounty.[16] I have nothing to do with the furloughs now, as the applications have gone on to Corps Hdqts.

There is nothing to write about, the proverbial dull monotony of camp life affording nothing of interest. It is shameful the way the cavalry have to work while the infantry do nothing at all in their camps. Officers & men get, at the very most, 2 out of 4 or 5 nights in camp; always on duty of some kind or another. It don't trouble me much at present, as I am on Special Duty.

No sign yet of Capt. Coxe & the bundle. They will come along in time though, I suppose. I attend the Episcopal Church in Warrenton almost every Sunday. I enclose two more photographs for my collection, Capt. Gilmore (who was wounded the other day) and Capt. Frank Wetherill's, both of which are good. . . .

———

January 17th. Sunday. The Veteran Volunteers were all paid off by Maj. Staples at the Warren Green [Hotel], $100 old bounty; old account settled; discharge given, and $75 new bounty. After all was gotten through I went to Church, after which [I] took a short walk with Carter. In the evening we had a jolly time at Galloway's, music on flute and violin, singing, dancing etc. "No Sunday in War times."

Camp 3d Pa. Cavy.
Warrenton, Va.
Jan 21st, 1863

Dear Mother:

Ward arrived this evening with your letter & box, for which I am very much obliged. I gave most of the chocolate to Capt. Gilmore who is wounded. He is very fond of it, as an eatible, and his <u>contraband,</u> who used to be in a New Orleans Hotel, cooks it up superbly. I am also very much obliged for the postage stamps, of which I now have plenty.

As soon as you receive this, if possible I want you to jump into the Cars & go <u>immediately</u> to the U.S. Schuylkill Arsenal on Grey's Ferry road, about half a mile from home, and buy me a "capot," <u>alias</u> a bluish grey hooded cloak-cape, costing $4.50. They are in great demand with Cavalry Officers, and if you don't go immediately they will be gone. They were captured in a French vessel which was trying to run the blockade for the Reb. Government. They are very cheap, and the most comfortable things in the world for cavalry—much of the pattern used by the French Huzzars.[17] Don't, on any account, fail to get one. They look very much like ladies waterproofs. . . .

———

January 22nd. Friday. Dress Parade in the morning, to read orders congratulating the soldiers of the 1st Brigade, and also one to the effect that all officers whose pickets are surprised are to be dismissed, and that any of the enemy caught wearing our uniform are to be hung on the spot.

———

Camp, 3d Pa Cavy, Warrenton, Va.
Jan. 24, '64. Sunday Eveng.

Dear Mother:

. . . I wrote on Thursday principally for the purpose of asking you to get me a Huzzar Cloak at the U.S. Arsenal, as it will save me from getting a fine overcoat. Have you got it yet? If not I'm afraid you will be too late. Keep it if you get it "until further orders."

At last your bundle, per Capt. Coxe, has arrived (day before yesterday), and I was very glad to get it. The map of the Battle of Gettysburg and the description are good, but of course poor Gregg's name is not mentioned. Do you remember in that English officer's account in the *Living Age,* his stating that the rebs always made it a point of capturing (or trying to capture) as much ammunition as they expended, in a battle, and that they tried unsuccessfully at Gettysburg? During the afternoon of the 3rd days fight, when whipped at every point of the line, and with their ammunition almost expended (the cannonading there was fiercer than any battle in the world, more shells having been used than during Napoleon's wars), they tried to turn our flank, between the York & Bonaughtown Roads, and get at our ammunition trains, but with one of the hardest fights of the whole 3 days, they were repulsed and we lost severely. By studying out the map, we have come to the conclusion that what is marked as Buford's was Gregg's position.

I was at Church both this morning and afternoon. I will make it a point of calling to see the pastor for Cousin Beccy Lewis. The Church is superbly fixed up for the Xmas Holiday, more tastefully than most of those at home. A great many officers are sending up for their wives, and Warrenton is quite gay, but I never go anywhere, as at home, being not much of a lady's man. I've nothing of interest to write about, as everything is very slow.

A street scene in Warrenton, Virginia, taken in 1862. Rawle spent much of the second half of 1863 and early 1864 in and around the town. (Courtesy Prints and Photographs Division, Library of Congress)

Camp 3d Penna. Cavy.
Warrenton, Va.
Jany. 31, '64 Sunday Eveng.

Dear Mother:

I recd. your last Sunday Evening letter in due time, on Wednesday.

I am very sorry you made such a fuss, and took so much trouble about the "capot." If I had known what would follow, I would not have asked you to do it. As it is I am much obliged for the trouble you took. I was told there were only a few of them left, and that they were going very fast; but since as you say, there are several thousand still at the Arsenal, I will lay the matter on the table for the present.

I told you that I recd. Capt. Coxe's box all right. The cork mattress I have never received, and still have the receipt for it. I am afraid it is in constant use by some rascally Provost Marshall, who inspect everything that goes down to the army, to prevent any contraband whiskey from getting down, and who frequently take out what they want.

The other evening I called to see Rev. Dr. Barten, & had a very pleasant visit. He did not know that Mordy was in the Reb Army. He said that he would write a note to Cousin Beccy Lewis, for me to enclose. We have been having, until yesterday, some most delicious spring weather.

The guerillas still trouble our lines. The other day they brutally murdered & robbed a man of the 6th Ohio Cavy., after he had surrendered, and showed themselves in force out the Salem & New Baltimore roads. Our Reg't. was ordered out after them, & thinking we would probably have some fun, I went along, I being just going out to take a ride. We had a lively chase for a couple of miles, but, as usual, they were too quick for us.

As Lieut. Potter has gone home on furlough, I am Acting Adjutant in his place. I send you enclosed photographs of Lieut. Col. Jones, Commanding the Regiment, & 2nd Lieut. Bradbury, for my collection. Please take good care of all I send home. . . .

P.S. 9 P.M. I have just received the enclosed letter for Cousin Beccy Lewis from Dr. Barten, which please forward.

———

January 31st. Sunday. Damp and drizzly. In the afternoon some of us attended the Episcopal Church. I like the Adjutant's work very well, except keeping the Officer's Roster, which, as many of the officers grumble at every detail, is very disagreeable. "Old Granny" Jones, as he is called, is such an inveterate old fogy and very disagreeable. An Adjutant, some how or other, is always unpopular among the officers, for some reason or other.

February 1st. Monday. Rainy, disagreeable and muddy. In camp all day. Hereafter we are to send out outlying pickets beyond the line to catch prowling guerillas, so the work will be very hard on the men. As a general thing the men get half the night in bed, but very often much less.

———

Head Qrs. 3d Penna. Cavy.
Warrenton, Va., Feby. 7th, 1864
Sunday Eveng.

Dear People at Home:

. . . I have nothing to tell about. Everything goes on as usual. An occasional scout and capture of guerillas. Orders are for every Reb found in our uniform to be hung up on the spot, and they in turn say they will hang one officer for every one of their men. Pleasant, isn't it? What, between a continual fear of being dismissed [from] the service for any slight delinquency, and being hung up to dry by Jonny Reb, a cavalry officer's situation is not the most agreeable in the world.

I am now <u>pro temp</u> "running the masheen" for the Reg't (i.e. acting as Adjutant) and "big Injun" generally for the Colonel. An adjutant is the Chief of Staff for the Regimental Commander, and his Confidential officer. He transacts all the military business of the Regiment. Under a <u>soldier</u> I would like the position very well, but under an old <u>granny</u> it is very disagreeable.

Heavy cannonading has been heard yesterday & today in the direction of the Rapidan, and many conjectures are afloat. The prevailing opinion is, that hearing of a mutiny in the Reb camps, a force of our men pitched into them & took 8,000 prisoners. We will have to wait for the papers to get the truth of the matter.[18]

I send herewith photographs for my collection, of Lieuts. Heyl & Ward, & Asst. Surgeon Durant, all very good. I receive the *"Living Age"* & *"War Press"* very regularly, on Saturday afternoon, and they are read by all with pleasure.

———

February 9th. Tuesday. Major Walsh, Lieut. Warren and Lieut. Potter, Acting Adjutant, returned from furlough and therefore I was relieved from Acting Adjutant. Capt. Rogers gave me his photograph. My application for leave of absence came back approved.

———

Rawle went home on leave on the morning of February 10, reaching Philadelphia at 3 A.M. of the eleventh. "They did not expect me," he recorded in his diary, "so I took them all by surprise and of course they all went crazy." He stayed until

February 20, when he set out again for Virginia. "The worst of coming home on so short a furlough," he lamented, "is the bidding good bye."

Shortly after his return, the 3rd received an order that changed the course of their participation in the war. Plucked from Gregg's division, the Pennsylvanians found themselves assigned to duty at the headquarters of the Army of the Potomac and placed under the command of Brig. Gen. Marsena Patrick, provost marshal general of the army.

———

Camp 3d Pa. Cavy.
Feby. 21st/64
Eveng.

Dear Mother:

When I left you yesterday morning for the "Front," after my ten days furlough, I came through and arrived in Camp about 3 P.M. I had a good deal of trouble with the boxes, etc. coming on, as I had to change cars 4 times, to the benefit of the porters along the road. I arrived in Washington about 5 P.M. yesterday, spent the evening at Grover's Theatre (where I saw Edwin Booth in Richard III) and the night at the "Kirkwood."[19] I left W[ashington] by the U.S.M.R.R. this morning at 10 AM, & arrived in camp with baggage and boxes all right. This evening didn't mess and friends pitch into your box for supper? You should feel highly complimented at the way the things disappeared. The mess now has some chance of keeping alive for a few days on the boxes. A poorer set of dogs than the officers of the regiment, with 4 mos. pay due them, I never saw. Everything is going on as usual in camp, tomorrow there is to be a grand review of Gregg's Division.

I enclose a photograph of 1st Lieut. Howard Edmonds, "L" Co., for my album. All photogs I send, please put in as they come, with the name & Company at the beginning, like the others. Also send a couple of each of my photogs, as soon as they come. . . .

Camp 3d Pa Cavy.
Head Qrs., Army of the Potomac
Feb. 28th, 1864
Sunday Eveng.

Dear Mother:

As you see we have changed our place of residence once more. On Friday, 26th, Reveille sounded at 4 AM, and much to our astonishment & disgust, "General" at 5. We left our beautiful & comfortable Winter Qrs. at Warrenton at 8 AM, &

marched (our regiment only) via Fayetteville, Bealeton & Rappahannock to Army Head Quarters, near Brandy Station, & reported to Gen. Patrick, Pro. Marsh. Gen. of this Army for escort & Hd. Qrs. Duty, relieving the 1st Maryland Cavy.

Our Regiment was picked out of the whole Cavalry Corps by the War Department for this duty, & it is considered the greatest compliment which can be paid to any Regiment. It was picked out as one of the oldest (it is the oldest), most war worn, soldierly, hardest worked and most thinned by the casualties of war, of any Volunteer Cavalry.[20] It is considered the softest of duties and is very welcome to us after being worked so hard. We can now sleep with security, without expecting to be waked up during the night by an attack on the lines, as at Warrenton. On a march we have to escort the Genl. & guard cattle, and now have 2 companies (I & G) doing the latter. We supply orderlies for Hd. Qrs. etc., etc. As yet we are laying in bivouac, as the 1st Maryland have not "vamoosed" as yet, but expect tomorrow, so, altho' in the midst of civilization, I cannot write with ink.

We are directly in front of Capt. J. Redwood Coxe's Quarters. I called on him as soon as we arrived. I know a good many of Gen. Meade's staff—Capt's. Coxe, Cadwalader, Arthur McClellan, Geo. Meade, Jr., Maj. Jim Biddle etc. Collis' Zouaves are on the same duty here, and I know a good many officers, so it is very pleasant. The officers of Patrick's Brigade are often sent up north on duty & so I may get a little of it some day.[21]

I attended chapel today in the Hd. Qr. Church Tent. Gen. Meade & staff, & a good many big bugs were present. Services by Dr. Dorr of Ch[rist] Ch[urch] Phila.[22] When I am short of news I will furnish a description of Hd. Qrs. for your benefit. I am again Acting Adjutant pro temp. Yesterday the 6th Corps & a large command of Cavalry started out on a Grand Reconnoissance in force.[23]

I wrote last Sunday Evening. On Tuesday we had a Grand Review of Gregg's Divn. of Cavalry, and on Wednesday Eveng. had a very pleasant visit at Rev. Mr. Barten's.

Hd. Qrs. Army of the Potomac
Camp 3d Penna Cav.
March 6, 1864
Sunday Eveng.

Dear Mother:

According to custom I write home this Sunday Eveng., and I find it difficult now to fill even a weekly letter. . . . I suppose by this time you have received my first letter from Army Hdqrs., stating the why's & wherefores of our move from Warrenton.

Everything is quiet about here since the late cavalry raid, which is generally (as far as concerns old Blowhard "KilCavalry") considered a fizzle.[24] Don't be anxious about me here; we are safe as ever we were in our lives, and [have] very light duty.

On Tues. M[ar]ch. 1st, a terribly rainy & muddy day, after laying 3 or 4 days in bivouac in the dirtiest place around, the 1st Md. Cavy. moved out, and we moved in to the dirtiest camp I ever saw. Since then we have been hard at work, policing and cleaning up. Carter & I are comfortably fixed up in a wall tent, as nicely as could be desired.

You cannot imagine with what relish we pitched into your box, the ham the best I ever eat, and everything likewise. By the bye, the other day we shipped off our tremendous swindle of a sutler & got a new one, who runs an officer's mess for the regiment for $5.00 a week; very nice & convenient.

I see Capt. Coxe almost every day. His qrs. are only about 100 yds. from camp. There go "Stables," and as I am doing Carter's duty (he is acting R. Qr. Master), I must go see my people groom their "crowbales." So goodbye. . . .

———

March 7th. Monday. In the morning I took a ride over to see the Bull Guards. Carter is A.R.Q.M., so I have taken command of "C" Company, though on special duty. Our new sutler, Mathews, has begun to run a Regimental Mess. . . .

March 9th. Wednesday. Magnificent spring day. In the afternoon I took a ride over to Brandy Station and got some small articles, spurs, whip etc.

March 10th. Thursday. Raining hard all day. The application for 35 days leave of absence, on signifying my intention to serve three years longer (Veteran Volunteer!) came back approved for 25 days, as I have had ten this winter. . . . Lt. Gen. U. S. Grant arrived here today on a visit to Genl. Meade.[25]

———

Rawle went home again on a twenty-five-day leave of absence, lasting March 11 through April 7. "One of the principal objects in [my] applying for leave," he wrote, "was to secure the bounties which had been promised to the reenlisted men or 'Veteran Volunteers.' My intention in trying again and again to get North was to go to Harrisburg to try to get the Vets their District Bounties." After a short stop at home, the lieutenant traveled to the state capital on March 14 to get the muster rolls of the regiment certified, then returned to Philadelphia on the sixteenth and handed in his papers to the Bounty Fund Committee, which was responsible for disbursing the money due to the soldiers. Most of the men, he noted, "have issued or sold powers of attorney for the $250." He spent the balance of his leave in Philadelphia, beginning his journey back to the 3rd Pennsylvania on April 4, though not, he unhappily remarked, before catching "another bad cold from <u>exposure</u> of sleeping in a house and bed."

—

Camp 3d Pa. Cav.
Hd. Qrs. Army of the Potomac
Apr. 8th, 1864

Dear Mother:

Here I am back again at my old Quarters, after my extended <u>rustication</u> up North. I left Phila. on the eveng. of the 4th, & arrived in Washington early on the 5th, during the whole of which day it poured in torrents. I went to the Capitol, & saw Clinton Lloyd, (Chief Clerk of the House of Rep.) but could not get time to call at Lottie's.[26] In the evening I went to hear "Martha" pretty well performed by the German Opera Troope.

Next morning (6th) I left Washington for the "Front" via O&A RR at 9.45 AM, with a horse in tow for Lt. Warren of "ours."

—

April 6th. Wednesday. . . . Brought on a beautiful sorrel horse for Lieut. Warren of "Ours." A most shameful practice they have now of examining an officer's baggage before starting, but nevertheless I got through two bottles of old Scotch whiskey.

—

Found Virginia swallowed up in a tremendous mud hole. Arrived in camp about 4 PM. I found that Brig. Gen. Rufus Ingalls, Chief Quarter Master of the Army of the Potomac, on Gen. Meade's Staff, on the recommendation of Col. Chas. R. Smith and some friends on Meade's Staff, had applied for me to be detailed as Aide de Camp. I went over, and found him a very clever gentleman. He seemed earnest for me to accept his offer so I did. I was introduced to Gen. Seth Williams, Adjutant Gen. of the Army, who said that I would be detailed in a day or two.[27] It is a splendid position, and very desirable, as I will be able to see more of the world in a military point of view in the coming campaign, which will open shortly. Everything is to be moved to the rear by the 16th inst.

This morning [April 8] I relieved Capt. Wetherill as "Officer of the Day." This evening we had a fine Dress Parade.

The general opinion in the army about Grant is, that if he don't look out he will get tripped up by the heels. He never fought Lee before, and now has to fight the best army the Rebs have. . . .[28]

—

April 9th. Saturday. Pouring rain all day and night. In Camp all day, practicing on piccolo and reading "Holmby House." Relieved as O[fficer of the] D[ay] by Lieut. Bradbury.[29]

———

Hd. Qrs. Army of Potomac
Camp 3d Pa Cavy.
April 11th, 1864

Dear Mother:

. . . I am expecting every day my detail for the Head Qrs. Staff, which has not yet arrived. I am however very well satisfied as I am, but would like to be settled before we move.

We have been having some terribly rainy weather lately. Our Camp was completely flooded, and is now in a delightful state of knee-deep mud. The bridges over Bull Run and Cedar Run have been washed away, and the Rappahannock instead of 100 yds. is 3 miles wide. So our communications are pro temp cut off. Although camp is in such a state that you are lucky if you walk a dozen yards without losing your boots, and when you get into bunk you find your blankets soaking, and manage, with the aid of various pipes, to hang on to existence. Yesterday (Sunday) we had services in the Hd. Qr. U.S. Christian Commission Chapel Tent, by Rev. Dr. Kirk of Boston, and a fine sermon.[30] Gen. Meade and many of his staff, and a good many "stars" were present. When the weather permits we have drills, etc. . . .

P.S. Put these photographs of Maj. Robinson & Carter in my album.

Camp 3rd Penna. Cavy.
Head Qrs., Army of Potomac
Brandy Stn., Va., April 17th, 1864
Sunday Eveng.

Dear Lilly:

. . . Since I last wrote, on Monday, nothing much has happened outside of camp duties, and playing football with our next door neighbors the Zouaves (114th PV), and drilling a good deal.

On Wednesday [April 13], Will White of the 6th Pa. Cav. and Capt. Chas. Cadwalader of Gen. Meade's Staff came over to see us. White had that day received his Commission of Captain in his regiment, jumping several officers. He looked as well as usual. In the evening, I rode part of the way home with him & Capt. Joe. Ash of the 5th Reg. Cavy.[31]

Capt. Wright & I amuse ourselves by playing duetts, he on the flute & I on the piccolo.[32]

On Friday [April 15], Maj. Robinson, Capt. Baughman & a detail of men went off on Recruiting Service. Before starting, we had a photograph taken of most of the officers present, and shortly afterwards our Orderly Sergt. came up to Carter & me, & wished us to have the whole Company (C) photographed. I will send you copies of both, if they are good.

According to a late order, all sutlers had to leave the army before the 16th (yesterday), when everything was to have been ready for the opening of an active Spring Campaign. Our sutler of course left, but we are going to keep up the Regimental mess. It has been raining, and the roads are in a bad state again, and as this is a rainy month, the whole army may remain quiet for a week or two longer. There is some talk of Army Hd. Qrs. being moved to Culpeper C.H. Gen. Patrick, I heard say today, that most probably we would move during this week. If Grant attacks Mr. Lee in his present well-chosen position on the Rapidan, somebody will get hurt, & we will get abominably whipped. I know the place from personal observation and it is one of the strongest in this part of Virginia. We _felt_ the position to our heart's content, after our Culpeper Fight, last Fall.

I don't know what we are to do for tobacco, now that the sutlers have been cleared out. It [is] as indispensable an article as pork & hard tack. Many a time have I been for days & nights with little or nothing to eat, but my pipe has kept me up.

It has cleared up again this evening, & tomorrow I intend going to Warrenton to see Mr. Horner.[33] I have not been able to go yet. Enclosed is a photograph for my collection of 1st Lieut. E. Will Warren, "E" Compy., and a group of Vernou, Wright & Carter. . . .

Camp 3d Penna. Cavalry
Hd. Qrs., Army of the Potomac
April 20th, 1864

Dear Mother:

I recd. your Sunday letter this afternoon. Owing to red tape, I am beginning to think that I won't get over to Hd. Qrs. on the Staff, but any how I don't care much about the matter.

I wrote to you on Sunday Evening. On Monday [April 18], I went to Warrenton to deliver Mr. Horner's letters and bundle to his brother. I saw him and the young ladies, & had a pleasant visit, altho' they are terribly _secesh._ Let Mr. Horner know that I delivered them, but could not possibly get there sooner. I spent the evening very pleasantly at Rev. Barten's, and Mrs. B, a delightful and pretty young lady, sang for me. At the earnest solicitations of a Mr. Sedgewick, for whom I had done several favors while we were at Warrenton, I stayed at his house while I was in town.

An old classmate of mine, Capt. J. Nelson Potter (son of Bishop P.) has relieved Lt. Wagner of "ours" as C[ommissary] of S[ubsistence], 1st Brig., 2nd Cavy. Divn. He is a very fine fellow.[34]

I left Warrenton the next day, Tuesday [April 19], and returned to the regiment. We expect to move every day now. All superfluous baggage and even our company desks are being sent to Alexandria. The pontoons and engineers, and more artillery, are coming up to the front. There are all sorts of rumors afloat, but nothing is known. We are fortifying around Culpeper Court House, and everything looks like a speedy opening of the Spring Campaign.

Today we had a mounted Regimental Inspection, and then a 3 hours drill, in complicated evolutions of the regiment, which we performed very satisfactorily. . . .

———

April 20th. Wednesday. Fine day. Went on our new "dirty duty" as "Body Snatchers," alias patrolling the roads about Head Quarters to prevent unnecessarily fast riding. . . .

April 23rd. Saturday. Splendid day. Dismounted Company Drill in the morning. In afternoon a party of us rode over to 6th Corps Hd. Qrs. to a horse race. Our old sutler, C. E. Kloeber came here to collect his bills. Mine was $10.50, and as I had no money I gave him a draft for the amount on my uncle, W.H.R.

———

Camp 3d Penna Cavy.
Hd. Qrs., Army of the Potomac
Brandy Stn., Va., Apr. 24th, 1864
Sunday Eveng.

Dear Mother:

As you see, we have not moved yet, though everything indicates a speedy opening of a very determined Spring Campaign. All the Cavalry have been relieved from their very hard work, and are to have a few days of the (comparative) rest they have needed all winter. We are fortifying Culpeper, which is intended, it is supposed, to be the depot for supplies. Rumor also says that the "Condemned Yankees" (Invalid Corps) are to relieve the 5th Corps along the Rail Road, to protect the line of communications, they being relieved in turn by the Militia, a very wise movement.[35] Also that 60 days supplies are to be laid up at Culpeper, for fear the communications should be cut off.

Gen. Gregg's Divn. of Cavalry left Warrenton early on the morning of Thursday, and moved nearer to the Junction, so I got there just in time. Gen. Davies, late of Kilpatrick's Divn., has taken command of our old brigade (1st of 2nd Divn.). Gregg

& Davies both are trying very hard to get us back, but I heard on very good authority at Army Hdqrs. (Gen. Williams, A.A.G. & Gen. Ingalls, Chief Qr. Mr.) that we are all right here.

Yesterday Col. Chas. H. T. Collis of the 114th PV took command of the Brigade of the Provost Marshal Dep't.

When the weather permits, we have company, platoon, squadron & regimental drills. Today we did a full dress Regimental Inspection, and Gen. Patrick and Col. Collis, both being present, paid us great compliments, especially our company, ("C"). We have been having splendid weather, and the roads are in excellent condition, but it has begun to rain again this evening. The weather is so treacherous this month that if we attempt a move I'm afraid we'll stick in the mud.

I've heard nothing more about the appointment, and as I don't care much about it either way, I don't press the matter, but will let it take its own course.[36]

Horace Binney, Jr., Aide de Camp to Gen. Neill (Beau Neill of Phila.) of the 6th Corps paid me a visit a few days ago. . . . I must be chary of my paper as it is very scarce.

Camp, 3d Penna. Cavy.
Hd. Qrs., Army of the Potomac near Brandy Stn., Va.
April 27th, 1864

Dear Mother:

. . . This morning Frank Wetherill and I rode up to pay the "Lancer's" a visit. They are now encamped about 1½ miles beyond Culpeper C.H. I found White (now a Captain), Capts. Leiper, Windsor, Charlie Coxe and all my friends well. Windsor is on Gen. Torbert's staff. Gen. T. is in command of Buford's old Division. We returned this afternoon.

Every day, before sunset, we have a dress parade of the Provisional Brigade, Col. Collis Comd'g. As the 114th Zouaves have a fine band, it is a very pretty sight. We form, 3d Pa. Cavy. dismounted on the right, Zouaves in the centre and 68th P.V. (Scott Legion) on the left, and, on fine days, we have nearly all Head Qrs. to see it. We have been complimented very highly on our appearance. We also now mount guard by Brigade Guard Mount.

. . . We have not moved as yet, but expect it every day. Rumor says we move tomorrow. Our troops, I saw today, are fortifying all around Culpeper. I saw my old friend Lieut. Harvey Fisher of the Bucktails. Carter went up to Washington today in charge of Rebel prisoners. Nothing is going on, but it is blowing like blazes. . . . I enclose photograph for my collection of Lieut. S. C. Wagner, Regimental Comm'y. of Subsist.

CHAPTER FIVE

The Overland Campaign and the Early Actions near Petersburg

May 1–July 26, 1864

After his appointment as general in chief of all Union armies on March 9, Lieutenant General Grant developed and implemented a grand strategy for the spring campaign designed to apply military pressure to the Confederacy on multiple fronts. The two main offensives were to be conducted by Maj. Gen. William T. Sherman's force of over 100,000 men, which would move from its position at Chattanooga against Gen. Joe Johnston in northern Georgia, and Meade's Army of the Potomac, which would cross the Rapidan River and engage Lee's Army of Northern Virginia. In support of their moves, and to prevent the South from being able to transfer reinforcements to these threatened points, Maj. Gen. Franz Sigel would march up the Shenandoah Valley and Major General Butler was to advance on Richmond along the James River from the east.[1]

After meeting with Meade in March shortly after his promotion, Grant had decided that he would retain the Pennsylvanian as commander of the army but, in order to shield Meade from the political pressures that had so burdened prior commanders of the Army of the Potomac, that he would make his headquarters with that army.[2] While this unusual arrangement began harmoniously, it would eventually lead to confusion regarding the chain of command and discomfiture for Meade, who came to be perceived, not without some justification, as simply an intermediary between his army and the lieutenant general.

Prior to Grant's ascension, Meade had been planning a reorganization of his army, and on March 23, with Grant's approval, the changes were announced. Maj. Gen. Gouverneur Warren replaced Maj. Gen. George Sykes in command of the V Corps, which also absorbed the I Corps, reduced since its mauling at Gettysburg. The III Corps—also severely handled at Gettysburg—was abolished too, with its 1st and 2nd Divisions consolidated into Maj. Gen. Winfield Scott Hancock's II Corps, while its 3rd Division became a part of Maj. Gen. John Sedgwick's VI Corps. Two days later Grant placed Maj. Gen. Philip Sheridan at the head of the Cavalry Corps, replacing Pleasonton, and later in April Major General Burnside's IX Corps was attached to the army as an independent command. In all (including the IX Corps), the Army of the Potomac counted 115,000 men in its ranks, nearly twice as many as were serving with the Army of Northern Virginia. "Lee's army will be your objective point," Grant instructed Meade. "Wherever Lee goes, there you will go also."[3]

On May 4 the Army of the Potomac crossed the Rapidan and entered the tangle of the Wilderness, precipitating some of the most intense, prolonged fighting of the war. Grant had hoped to pass through the foreboding, second-growth forest before a fight was initiated, but Lee moved quickly eastward and engaged the Army of the Potomac on the fifth. "Of all the places on earth for a battle," wrote a Massachusetts soldier, "it would be hard to select one more gloomy or desolate."[4] During the next six weeks, over 90,000 casualties were incurred by the two armies (more than 60,000 of these were suffered by the Federals) as Lee repeatedly rebuffed the thrusts of Grant and Meade ever southward. Severe fighting took place in the Wilderness, at Spotsylvania, along the North Anna River, and at Cold Harbor as Grant moved by his left to the south and east, constantly looking for an opportunity to lure the Rebels from behind their field works and defeat them. Because their provost and guard duties kept them occupied primarily behind the main lines of battle, Rawle and the men of the 3rd Pennsylvania were, in a sense, witnesses to the carnage that this combat produced, rather than active participants in the fighting.

———

Camp 3d Penna. Cavy., Hd. Qrs. Army of the Potomac
near Brandy Stn., Va., May 1st, 1864

Dear Lottie:

. . . As you see, we have not moved yet. A large part of the Army is moving up to the front today, and Capt. Coxe tells me Hd. Qrs. will likely move on Tuesday. Frank Wetherill, in a letter received today, also says that all letter correspondence with the army is prohibited for 60 days. We know nothing of it here.

Col. Collis, who commands our Brigade, is very fond of the "pomp, pride & circumstance of war," and has us out every evening to a Brigade Dress Parade. As we have a very fine band, it is a beautiful sight, but too much of it is a humbug. On Friday, Gen. Patrick reviewed the Brigade, and we looked finely.[5] On Thursday, I went out to see Gen. Meade review the Reserve Artillery of the Army. We drill almost every day. Tomorrow, Collis is going to have a Brigade Drill. How in the name of common sense he is going to drill a brigade of cavalry & infantry together none of us can make out. . . .

I am officer of the day, so my letter must be short, as I have to attend to my duty. . . .

———

May 3rd. Tuesday. Fine day. In [the] morning I was detailed to report for Special Duty to Gen. Patrick. Instructions he gave were to go to Hon. John Minor Botts, beyond Brandy Station, who would give me information about several families on his property. I arrested ten persons, two old negroes, and a family (Covington) consisting of one old man, wife, three daughters and three sons, all of bad character, . . . turned them out of their houses and transferred them to Col. Gates, 20th N.Y.S.M., Pro. Mar.[6] *I had much trouble, especially with the old woman and her pretty daughters, bad characters. I got through all right. Orders for Head Quarters to move tomorrow.*

———

Hd. Qrs., Army of the Potomac
In the field, trying another
"on to Richmond," between
Chancellorsville & Spotsylvania C.H.
May 9th, 1864

Dear Mother:

As you most probably know we are moving again, with fair prospects of at last getting to Richmond. We have abandoned our communications and send or receive no mail. Our next base we expect to be Fredericksburg, which is now in rear of us. We have had terrible fighting (loss terrible), mostly by infantry, as artillery can't be used in this "Wilderness." We being at Hd. Qrs. in rear of the centre of the line of battle see & hear almost everything. Our troops fought splendidly—we being on Hd. Qr. duty, accompanying Gens. Grant & Meade, and encamp in rear of their tents. The Cavalry also had very hard fighting. Capt. Joe Ash of the 5th Regulars killed, Lt. Bob Wilson of same Regiment wounded, Major Jim Starr & Lt. Charlie Coxe of the 6th Penna., wounded, & the adjutant also, mortally.[7]

Night before last, in the face almost of the enemy, Gens. Grant & Meade made a flank movement on the left, one of the boldest & most strategical movements of the war. Gen. Longstreet of Reb army reported wounded in the left lung & Gen. Pickett killed. Gen. Sedgwick of our 6th Corps, one of our finest corps commanders, was killed this morning. Both armies are resting, it seems, after our very hard work, only skirmishing in front, and Gen. S. was killed in riding along

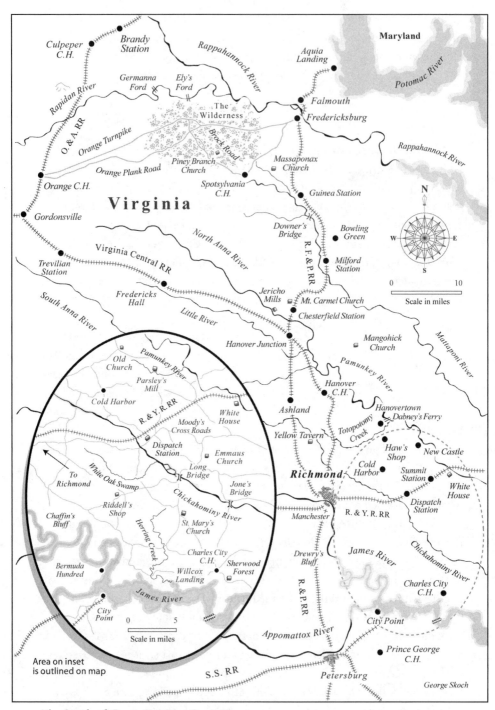

The Overland Campaign, May–June 1864

the lines. Our army has lost terribly, and a great many officers. Many wounded were burned to death in the Wilderness, where the battle took place, it catching fire from shells, etc. Hd. Qrs. during the battle were at Wilderness Tavern. So far all goes well, and all are in brilliant spirits.[8]

I only have time to write a few lines, intending to send this by a detail from our Regiment who are to escort Gen. Sedgwick's body North. I will write more fully when things get settled, and we again get into camp. I am very well, very hungry, & very rough looking. . . .

Hd. Qrs. Army of the Potomac, In bivouac
1½ miles from Spottsylvania C.H.
May 16, 1864

Dear Mother:

We now occasionally get a chance to write home, & I now take the opportunity of writing. I wrote on the 9th per the escort of Gen. Sedgwick's body, but I don't know whether you ever rec'd. it. We have been having the most terrible fighting, the hardest battle not only of the history of the war, but of the <u>world.</u> It is estimated that 40,000 will barely cover our loss, including a dozen Generals. The hard fighting lasted for 10 days and nights, and skirmishing ever since. Our army is completely used up by the hard work, and yesterday and today we have been resting, with but little fighting. The enemy's line runs within sight of (¾ of a mile) our own, but both lines are pretty quiet. We got rather the best of the bargain, but can't claim a victory. Being at Hd. Qrs. we have a good chance of seeing & hearing everything, and we can go out to the line of battle whenever we want to, to see how things are going on.

At daybreak of May 12th we charged & captured nearly the whole of the 'Stonewall" (Stonewall Jackson's) division—2 generals and 4000 prisoners, 22 pieces of artillery. Nearly the whole of Mord. Lewis' Regiment (2d Virginia) were captured, but he got off safely, as the men of his company told me. He is orderly sergeant & very well.[9]

Today we recd. our first mail—dates of May 2d & 3d. I recd. a letter from Carrie H., "*Living Age*" & "*War Press.*" It came via Fredericksburg & Belle Plain. The papers (we have them as late as the 10th) call the fight "Grant's victory." It was no victory, and Meade did all the fighting, which was splendid.

Day before yesterday as Gen. Meade & a small escort were riding along, a Major of the 13th Virginia Cavy. & 6 men tried to capture him, but were themselves taken prisoners.

My old schoolmate, Capt. Will Dorr of the 121st P.V. was killed in the battle.[10] . . . We have lost nearly ¼ of our army. I suppose there are a good many letters to me from home on the way. Don't be uneasy about me, I am very well. . . . If we ever get into camp I will write a full account of this campaign from my journal. . . .

> Hd. Qrs. Army of the Potomac
> In the field, in front of Spottsylvania C.H.
> May 19th, 1864

Dear Mother:

I have recd. two letters from home, Lilly's of the 13th and yours of the 15th. We now are getting about 2 or 3 mails a week via Belle Plain & Fredericksburg. I wrote a second pencil note on Monday last.

The army is still in line of battle, Spottsylvania C.H. being in the hands of the enemy, and not in ours, as the papers would have you believe. The 2 or 3 houses constituting the Court House, are in front of our right centre, the enemy hold a very strong line and are patiently awaiting the attack. I suppose you would like a few extracts from my diary.

May 4th Wedy. Hd. Qrs. broke camp early in the morning, the whole army on the move. Our regiment accompanied Gens. Meade and Patrick. Crossed the Rapidan at 9.30 AM, at Germanna Ford, and remained on the heights while the main army crossed. 2nd Corps crossed below at Ely's Ford. In the evening, two other officers & myself, with 100 men, ordered out to picket a very important road on the extreme right, a very pressing emergency. Very ticklish work, no fires, nothing to eat etc. The army moved up into position today.

May 5th Thurs. Reb Cavy. showed themselves outside of our line, and reporting the fact, Rickett's Divn. of 6th Corps came up to support us. I rode outside the lines to take a look with Gen. Morris. About 1.30 PM, Gen. Burnside's Corps having crossed, we were relieved by his cavalry (2nd Ohio), who were almost scared out of their boots at the sight of <u>wild</u> reb[s].[11] We then marched to Army Hd. Qrs. at the "Wilderness Tavern," almost starved, and dead beat. Heavy fighting going on on our right centre, 6th Corps.[12]

May 6th Friday. Terrific fighting. Hd. Qrs. at Wilderness Tavern. At daylight we were routed up by a terrific attack on the right of our line (6th Corps, Gen. Sedgwick). Fighting general along the line. About 1 PM our left centre on the F'dksburg & Orange Plank Road, consisting of the left of the 2nd Corps (Hancock), & right of the 9th (Burnside) was severely pressed and partially broken. The Rebs flanked and drove Stevenson's Divn. of 6th Corps, but the line was re-formed in time to prevent anything serious.[13] The Provost Martial Brigade went out and rallied the broken up regiments, and they then moved up to the front again. We immediately attacked in turn, and regained the mile & a half lost by the retreat, losing about 5000 men in the affair. We were out all day driving stragglers up to the very line of battle. Our troops fought splendidly, but suffered terribly. The battle raged in the Wilderness, a long & wide tract of country covered with almost impenetrable low underbrush. It was very dry, and catching fire from the shells, many wounded were burned to death. The fighting was almost entirely done by the infantry—no good positions for artillery. Our loss is terrible, large proportion of officers; several Generals killed & wounded.[14]

May 7th Saty. Weather very hot. Both lines remained in nearly the same position during the day, heavy fighting principally on the right. Hd. Qrs. were shelled during the afternoon, but nobody hurt. I rode out to the line of battle to see the fun. After dark the whole army moved over to the left flank. Gens. Grant & Meade, accompanied by their staffs, escorts & our regiment, started first, and went along the Plank Road within 500 yds. of the enemy's line, very ticklish in the dark & woods. We ran off the track, and nearly into the enemy's lines.[15] Marching for the most part at a gallop, we reached Todd's Tavern at 1 AM. The Cavalry Corps had a very hard fight today. After the regulars were badly whipped, our old brigade of Gregg's Divn. waded in, and gave the rebs a sound drubbing. The Cavy. were lying here when we arrived. Hd. Qrs. were here for the rest of the night.[16]

May 8th Sunday. Very hot weather. After our hard march last night, we got about 6 hours sleep, along side of our horses. We moved with Hd. Qrs. about a couple miles beyond, and lay there for 4 hours, when Hd. Qrs. moved out about 3 miles farther to the front, in the direction of Spottsylvania C.H. in rear of the 6th Corps, which occupied the left, the 5th (Warren) and 2nd (Hancock) Corps, the centre and front. Burnside with the 9th Corps in rear within supporting distance. The Cavalry moving from the right front, started on a raid, it is not known wither.[17] At dusk we went into camp in the woods, about 4 miles from Spottsylvania C. House. Fighting going on all day & during the night.

———

May 8th. Sunday. . . . Hooker is reported to be coming up with his Corps, this side of the O&A R.R.; a large force coming up the Peninsula and all closing in together on Richmond. (look out Mr. Lee!). Warren marched by the Brock Road, coming up with the enemy at Alsop's farm, where he had a very severe fight and drove the enemy.

———

May 9th Monday. We remained during the day in the same place. Fighting is going on along the line, but no severe attacks. Maj. Gen. Sedgwick of the 6th

Corps was killed this morning by a sharpshooter, while riding along the line. He was joking the men for dodging the shells when he was hit under the left eye. I saw his body. Poor "Uncle John" was one of the most popular and best of our Corps Commanders. He was sent North with a small escort from our regiment, & I took advantage of the chance by writing a few lines home. Grant, it is said, is waiting for Lee to fall back and to gain a little time. A prisoner who has just come in (6 PM) reports them moving to the rear. I saw the Richmond Enquirer of the 7th. It is very desponding, says that we are moving "slow but sure." Our loss, so far, is reported at 12,000 to 13,000.[18] The enemy have lost equally. Prisoners say that Lee has issued an order that no more supplies will be issued to them—the next to come from the Yankees. During the evening our left advanced. Hd. Qrs. remained in the same place during the night.

May 10th Tuesday. 12.30 PM, Gen. Meade has just issued an order "that Gen. Butler has whipped Beauregard at Petersburg and is advancing on Richmond." Also that Gen. Sherman has whipped the Rebel Johnson [sic], who was completely routed & left everything in his hands. Rumors are that Sheridan, with the Cavalry Corps, is at Hanover Junction. During the evening Hd. Qrs. moved to between Piney Grove Church & Spottsylvania C.H. In the evening the 6th Corps made a successful charge, captured 1000 prisoners & 2 pieces of artillery. Fighting all day.[19]

———

May 10th. Tuesday. . . . Our line formed a crescent north of the Ny [River]. The Rebels lay north of Spotsylvania C.H., left on Glady Creek and right on the Ny. We attacked the enemy's centre, driving him to his pits, but could not take them; suffered severely. In the evening a second attack was made, in which we took the works, 1000 prisoners and two guns.

———

May 11th Wednesday. Raining all day & night. Hd. Qrs. in same place all day. Fighting all along the line—nothing very severe tho'. Busy building earthworks. Our horses are getting low for want of feed. Nothing heard from the North. We are rather hard up—our baggage wagon being far in the rear. We are sadly in want of tobacco & have to smoke wretched stuff.

———

May 11th. Wednesday. . . . Escorting prisoners and collecting them from the line of battle and driving stragglers works us very hard.

———

May 12th Thursday. Rainy. At daybreak Hd. Qrs. were moved about 2 miles, in the direction of Fredericksburg. At daybreak the 2nd Corps made a glorious charge upon the enemy's works, and captured nearly the whole of "Stonewall" Jackson's old celebrated division, now in Ewell's Corps, & commanded by Gen. Johnson. Gens. Johnson & Stuart, about 6,000 prisoners, & 22 pieces of artillery, and about a dozen stand of colours were captured, and we had to escort the prisoners to the rear—about 5 miles back, in the direction of Fredericksburg.[20] Recd. a Richmond Examiner of the 8th—rather desponding yet full of brags. Nearly the whole of the 2nd Va. infantry were captured in the above fight, but from members of Mord. Lewis' company (he is an orderly sergeant) I found out that he had escaped—& no more; he was safe & well. Fighting all day. This is the 8th day of continuous fighting; the toughest battle of the war, and no decisive result, except that we have repulsed every attack (and there have been some terrific ones) and maintained our line with success. Our loss so far is estimated at 40,000. This has been the most terrific battle in the history of the world.

May 13th 1864. Friday. Raining nearly all day. Roads in [a] terrible state. Hd. Qrs. remain in the same place all day & night. Skirmishing and artillery fighting during the day. The enemy have moved more over to our left.

———

May 13th. Friday. . . . We advanced and occupied the crests of the hills south of the Ny. . . . We are now using Fredericksburg and Aquia Creek as our base.

———

May 14th Saty. At daybreak, Hd. Qrs. was moved out to within 1½ miles, & within sight of Spotsylvania C.H., on the Spotsylvania & Fredericksburg Pike. The Rebel line of battle runs just this side of the Court House. During the morning, Gen. Patrick sent me along the line of battle to take a sketch of the new positions, and the different corps. Hdqrs., the 2nd Corps on the right, the 9th on their left, 5th next, in front of the C.H., and the 6th (now commanded by Gen. Wright) on the left. I could distinctly see the rebel line. In some of the rebel breastworks which our men captured, dead rebs were piled up 4 deep. The 5th and 6th Corps moved from the right to the left of the line. Hd. Qrs. camped on the Pike, about 2½ miles from the Court House. Some heavy fighting in the direction of the 5th Corps in afternoon and Evening.

———

May 14th. Saturday. . . . From 5th Corps Hd. Qrs. on the Pike I could distinctly see the Court House and the Rebel line. . . . Hd. Qrs. camped for the night on the Spotsylvania and Fredericksburg Pike, about two miles from the Court House.

———

May 15th Sunday. I rode out to the outside line of battle, found everything the same as yesterday. Some fighting during the day. Our troops are entirely used up, and we are not in a fit condition to attack. In this terrific fight we have lost nearly ¼ of our large army. Remained for the night in the same place. Yesterday Gen. Meade and a small party were riding along, when a Major of the 13th Va. Cavy. tried to capture him, but he himself was taken prisoner.[21]

———

May 15th. Sunday. Clear in the morning, rain in the afternoon. Early in the morning I was sent out to hunt and drive up stragglers. Some fighting along the line. . . . [M]et my old classmate Lieut. Harry Lambdin, of the 5th Corps staff, out on the line.[22] We remained for the night in the same place as last.

———

May 16th Monday. Received our first mail of the campaign, letters dated of May 2nd & 3rd. Hd. Qrs. remained in the same place.

May 17th Tuesday. During the morning Hd. Qrs. moved over more to the left, in rear of centre of the line, and remained there for the night. Rather quieter along the line, getting some rest. New troops coming up from Washington.

———

May 17th. Tuesday. . . . We are getting fresh, but new, troops up from Washington and the rear. "Chin" is that Gen. Sheridan is on his way back with the Cavalry Corps, having done a great deal of damage, and that the Rebel Gen. J. E. B. Stuart, commanding the Rebel Cavalry, was killed.

———

May 18th Wednesy. Some tough fighting on the right centre during the morning, by the 6th Corps.[23] On Gen. Wright's staff are Capt. Arthur McClellan & Lt. Haydn, an old teacher. I rode out there to see the fun. Just before I got there Capt. McClellan lost a magnificent horse. He had just dismounted, when a shell exploded inside of his horse. I got into a good dose of grape and canister while out there. Hd. Qrs. in the same place.

———

May 18th. Wednesday. . . . A good many stragglers from this army were picked up in Washington, etc. and we had to send them to their corps today under guard. Hd. Qrs. moved in the morning in the direction of Spotsylvania Court House, but moved back to the same place as last night.

———

Today [May 19] we are still in the same place. This afternoon, part of Ewell's Corps came around our right flank, and got in our rear between here and trains at Fredericksburg. We got them out of that pretty quickly though.[24]

———

May 19th. Thursday. . . . Lt. Col. Jones returned to the Regiment from Recruiting service. Good bye 3rd Pa. Cav.

———

Now you have a pretty good idea of what is going on. At Hd. Qrs. we have a good chance of seeing and hearing everything, and when a tough fight is going on, we go out to the line of battle to see the fun. Our regiment is worked hard during a battle. Going out to the line of battle to get the prisoners, escorting them to the rear, driving stragglers up to their regiments, etc. The papers make out that we have obtained a glorious victory, and that Lee is in full retreat. If you were to ride out to the front rifle pits you would not think so. To be sure, we have been successful so far, in that we have repulsed the terrific attacks of the enemy, and held and gained ground. The rebs fought very obstinately, and we also, but they are still before us, patiently awaiting our attack on their very strong position.

We get several mails a week now, so that report about mail communications not being allowed is not true. I have recd. all letters from home so far, but they reach us very late. I am still with the regiment, and not on Gen. Hunt's staff, as my friends would make out.[25] As for being Gen. Ingall's aid, I don't care a bit about it. Since last Oct. 15th, when Ell. Davis was killed, I hate the sight of the army trains, and in the Qr. Master Dept., I would have too much to do with them. I am very well satisfied as I am, in the "glorious front." . . . [W]e are now to the East of "the Wilderness," and the woods are of a very different kind, but very dense nevertheless. I get the "*Living Age*" & "*Press*" regularly, and they are exceedingly welcome.

I suppose I have exhausted your patience with this long letter. It is the only chance of writing I have had, so I have taken advantage of it. Sitting on the ground writing on a box of hard tack, with a bad pen, is not very pleasant though. . . .

> Headquarters Army of the Potomac
> In the Field near Dabner's Ford, South
> of the Pamunkey River, 18 miles from
> Richmond,[26] May 29th, 1864

Dear Mother:

I have not had an opportunity of writing home since the 19th, being on the

A group of officers of the 3rd Pennsylvania, photographed on April 15, 1864, near Brandy Station, Virginia, several weeks before the Overland Campaign. *Front row, seated, left to right:* Capt. Abel Wright, Capt. William Baughman, Maj. Oliver Robinson, Lt. George S. L. Ward, and Lt. Miles Carter. *Back row, standing, left to right:* Chaplain Joel Rammel, Lt. Albert Bradbury, Lt. Samuel Green, Lt. Louis Stillé, Maj. James Walsh, Asst. Surg. Henry Durant, Lt. Eugene Cauffman, Lt. Joseph Galloway, Lt. William Potter, Lt. William Brooke Rawle, and Capt. Francis Wetherill. Rawle wears a sash denoting that he is officer of the day. (From Regimental History Committee, *History of the Third Pennsylvania Cavalry* [1905])

march, and the army having no communications. We were then in front of Spottsylvania Court House, fighting the enemy every day, and we remained there until the morning of the 21st.

May 21st Saty. The army is making another flank movement to the left. Hancock's 2nd Corps marched last night for Guinney's [Guinea] Station, and meeting with no opposition, moved on to Bowling Green & Milford. Hd. Qrs. started around 12 m. via Massaponax Church to Guinea Station, on the Fredericksburg & Richmond RR. When we arrived there a brigade of Rebel Cavalry was there. The Provost Marshall's Brigade attacked them, 114th & 68th P.V. as skirmishers, and the 3d Pa. Cavy. supporting. We drove them across the Pony [Mattaponi] River, and about 2 miles, when Warren's (5th) Corps came up. Hd. Qrs. for the night near the Station.

May 22d Sunday. About noon Hd. Qrs. moved and camped for the night near Downer's Bridge, on the Tapony [Mattaponi] River, a beautiful place belonging to a rank secesher, Mr. Tyler, about 2½ miles from Bowling Green.[27] This is a beautiful country we are now passing through, the army never having visited it, and it is in good condition. The army is moving on fast, Hancock with the advance near Hanover Junction, Warren & Burnside following by parallel roads, Wright in the rear. Everything going on finely.

———

The "heavy fighting" and skirmishing that WBR alludes to in his letters and diary entries between May 23 and May 26 became known as the Battle of the North Anna. These took place when Grant, hoping to lure Lee from behind his works at Spotsylvania, sent the II Corps to threaten a key Confederate rail hub, Hanover Junction, located below the North Anna River. Hancock advanced on May 21, but instead of attacking as Grant had hoped, Lee fell back to positions south of the North Anna. Fighting began on May 23 and eventually involved all four Union infantry corps, some of which were able to gain footholds south of the river. Lee fell back into strong defensive positions on the twenty-fourth. With his army spread out and separated along both banks of the North Anna, Grant chose not to fight, instead opting on May 26 to move east toward Cold Harbor.

———

May 23d Monday. Very warm. On the march again. Hd. Qrs. for the night about 4 miles north of the North Anna River. Heavy fighting on the left flank during the afternoon.

———

May 23rd. Monday. . . . We went with Gen. Patrick and the Hd. Qr. Train and poked along the road. Very tiresome work. . . . Warren succeeding in getting across the North Anna at Jericho Bridge by turning the enemy's left flank.

———

May 24th Tuesday. Exceedingly warm. Hd. Qrs. moved about 2 miles, to "Carmel Church" and remained there till the afternoon, when we again moved across the North Anna River, near Jericho Bridge, and camped for the night. Hard fighting all day. Our line of battle in front of Hanover Junction, where the enemy have very strong works.[28]

———

May 24th. Tuesday. . . . I was doing a little case of "picket" during the day. . . . I borrowed $20 from R.Q.M. Boyer. We are as poor as Job's turkey, "divil-a-cent in the mess." This is called Jericho Bridge I suppose because there is no bridge here, and no ford either. Our base of supplies has been shifted to Port Royal on the Rappahannock.

———

May 25th Wednesday. Considerable fighting during the day. I rode out to the line of battle on the left, resting on the River, and got some splendid natural leaf tobacco, and I spent the rest of the day manufacturing it for smoking. This is a splendid tobacco country, and plenty of it.[29] In the afternoon Hd. Qrs. moved back across the river, and more to the left, and we went into camp on a high hill on the bank. A thunderstorm came up and down went our "shebeens."

May 26th Thursday. Hd. Qrs. remained in the same place all day. Considerable infantry and artillery fighting during the day. Another case of "flank by the left" for tomorrow.

———

May 26th. Thursday. . . . At dark the 2nd, 5th and 6th Corps re-crossed the river and marched, heading S.E., the 6th in advance with Sheridan's Cavalry.

———

May 27th Friday. We followed Grant & Meade, who marched ahead of the main army, the Cavy. and 1st Divn. 6th Corps being in front. Crossed the Fredericksburg & Richmond RR at Chesterfield Station and marched about 10 miles on the road to the White House, leaving the Hanover C.H. road to the right. Hd. Qrs. camped for the night at Mangohick Church.[30]

May 28th Saturday. Very warm & roads terribly dusty. Hd. Qrs. moved at 8 AM, crossed the Pamunkey River at Dabner's Bridge [Dabney's Ferry], and camped about a mile from there. The 1st & 2d Cav Divn. had a hard fight in front today—dismounted, with Reb cavalry & infantry. Gregg's Divn. lost 400 men and many officers, especially Gen. Davies brigade (our old one).[31]

Today [May 29] we are in the same place, the army in line of battle in front, 5th Corps on the right, 9th & 2nd in centre & 6th on the left, resting on the River. We are taking advantage of the <u>Sunday</u> I suppose, for rest. I presume we will march for Richmond tomorrow. Our new base, I suppose, will be White House on the York River.[32]

———

May 29th. Sunday. . . . The enemy are in our front again, by marching fast and on interior lines. It is said that Col. McIntosh of the 3rd Pa. Cav., now commanding a Brigade of raw troops in the 3rd Division Cavalry Corps (Gen. Wilson) is trying to get us with him. If he succeeds it will be low.[33]

———

So now you are "au fait" of our long, and, so far, successful march. We have done what no army has yet done—by a continuation of bold strategical movements, abandoning and marching without our communications, uncovering Washington, engaging first the enemy in front, and then dodging around his right flank, compelling him to fall back, coming upon him again, he having the shorter road to march (militaricé—holding interior lines) and trying the same over again, we have reached this point, communicated with Butler and are but 18 miles from Richmond.

I suppose of course you have been worrying about me. In Lilly's letter of [the] 19th, which I recd. on the 25th, she wants to know whether our regiment was actually engaged during the late battles. Our duty at Hd. Qrs. does not put us as a regiment into the fight, but is more of a staff duty character. Although not really fighting as a general thing, we are always in it individually as much as any of the staff of the Hd. Qrs. are.

We expect to have some more terrible fighting in front of Richmond in a few days. Everything is going on finely, and the army is in the best of spirits, having entire confidence in Meade, who does all of the fighting while Grant gets the credit for it.[34] Meade is continually in the saddle, looking to everything himself, riding around with only one aid[e] and a couple of orderlies. . . .

———

Sheridan's cavalry seized the crossroads of Cold Harbor, ten miles east of Richmond, on May 31. Over the next two days, the infantry of the Army of the Potomac, supported by a corps from the Army of the James, filed into hastily built fortifications and prepared to assault the Army of Northern Virginia. The attack, it was hoped, would turn Lee's right, severing the supply and communication lines that tethered his army to Richmond. Grant had planned to assault on June 2, before the balance of Lee's forces could be brought up, but Hancock's battle-thinned II Corps was not ready. The consequent postponement of the advance until June 3 provided Lee with the time both to bring his army to full strength and to prepare entrenchments to repel the Federals. The ensuing attacks were nothing short of a disaster for the Northerners. "Its management," wrote a VI Corps officer of the battle, "would have shamed a cadet in his first year at West Point." Grant admitted in his memoirs, "I have always regretted that the last assault at Cold Harbor was ever made."[35]

Following the setback, the armies remained entrenched at Cold Harbor for the better part of nine days. Grant initiated siege operations against the Southern positions on June 4, but after several days of labor abandoned the idea, favoring instead a move south to the James River. Scores of dead and wounded soldiers lay between the opposing lines, and any efforts to provide succor to the suffering of either side were met by snipers' bullets. Finally, on June 7 a truce was implemented, and the few wounded who had survived dozens of hours of exposure were recovered.

———

Camp, Hd. Qrs. Army of the Potomac
near "Cold Harbor" in front of Richmond
June 5th, 1864 Sunday

Dear Mother:

I wrote to you last Sunday [May 29] from Dabney's Ferry (or Hanover Town) on the Pamunkey River, and since then we have been very busy persuading the "Rebellious" to let us pay Richmond a visit. Contrary to the saying "No Sunday's in War times," the last was given to resting the army, and giving time for our heavy trains to move up nearer, and today, at least so far (10 AM), with the exception of a morning salute of a few guns to the gentlemen on the other side at daybreak, everything is quiet.

The day after I wrote (Monday [May 30]), early in the morning, Gens. Grant & Meade moved their Hd. Qrs. out on the Richmond road, about 1½ miles beyond Salem Church, or Haas Stores, and went into camp.[36] All day there was very hard fighting along the line, and especially in the centre late in the afternoon & evening. We advanced our lines and took some prisoners. The line was formed by the 5th Corps (Warren) on the left, 9th (Burnside) left centre, 2nd (Hancock) right centre & 6th (Wright) on the right. Maj. Gen. "Baldy" Smith from the Peninsula connected with and reported to Meade. We have now communication with the North by way of White House on the York River.

During the next day, Tuesday [May 31], we lay in the same place. Some fighting along the lines.

———

May 31st. Tuesday. We remained in this place, beyond Salem Church, during the day and night. This is the ground over which the Cavalry had such a hard fight the other day against Infantry and the ground and trees mark the struggle. We had to

bury a good many dead rebs around here. Our valises came up for the first time dur-
ing the campaign.

———

June 1st Wednesday. About 8 AM Hd. Qrs. started again on the march, and moved about 5 miles over to the left front. During the afternoon and evening, there was some very hard fighting, in which our left moved forward some distance, 18th Corps (Smith) on the left, 6th left centre, 5th centre, 9th right centre & 2nd on the right.[37]

June 2nd Thursday. Very warm & terribly dusty. At daybreak Wetherill & I, with 100 men, went out to the front, got 500 prisoners (the result of last night's fight) and took them to the rear, where the prisoners are always collected previous to being sent north. The dust was suffocating, and we had a very long march. Hard fighting during the day & skirmishing all night.[38] Hd. Qrs., during the day, moved to this place, and we have remained here since.

On June 3d Friday, without breaking camp, Gens. Grant & Meade & staffs, with our regiment as escort shortly after daybreak, went up to 6th Corps Hd. Qrs., about ½ mile from Cold Harbor, to personally superintend the battle. An advance was ordered for the whole line, which it did in fine style. We captured a line of breastworks & 8 pieces of artillery, but the enemy opening on our troops from enfilading batteries, compelled us to return to our first position. The fighting was very hard all day. Our loss during the day was estimated at 6000 in all. The Generals remained in this place all day, and our regiment was kept busy getting prisoners from the front, and driving up infantry stragglers, examining the wounded so as not to let any skulkers pass, etc. Nearly all day shell and solid shot were wizzing all around us at Hd. Qrs. in the field. I was out in front on duty several times. If you look at Lloyd's map, at the lower part of Hanover County, and compare this sketch, you can gain some idea of how we are laying.[39]

June 4th, (Saty.) There was fighting all along the line. Out on duty nearly all day....

———

June 4th. Saturday. Early in the morning Maj. Walsh, Capt. Wetherill, Lieut.
Ward and I were sent out for the purpose of driving up all the stragglers from beyond
the heavy trains (3 miles off on the White House road) up to Hd. Qrs. We changed
our bivouac to a more camp-like form.

———

This is a summary of the events of the past week. Yesterday was exactly one month from the time the campaign opened, and there has been scarcely a day in which the army has not been fighting. We are laying in position in front of Richmond, but the enemy have not yet fallen back to the celebrated defenses of the city, and there will have to be some terrible fighting to get in. Our supplies now come from the "White House," on the York River, by means of wagons.

We are getting along very well. Carter & I had a grand addition to our tough beef & hard tack for dinner yesterday, in the shape of peas, the first I've eaten for two years. An old negro came up to me the other day with a peck of peas for which he wanted $5.00!! or $3.00 for a half peck. I told him I would give the comparative value in green backs but he was too ignorant to know the difference. Our cook, however, gave him about 20 cts. worth of coffee & sugar for the peck, and the old "dark" was glad enough to get it. We have not tasted tender beef or fresh bread or potatoes for a month, and, in the money line, a poorer set of rascals you never saw, with over 3 mos. pay due us.

We occasionally see a paper, and every one is filled with some ridiculous story about Grant—such as the words he says to "his boys" about his going to take Richmond, that the army has never been handled rightly till now, etc. None of these stories are true. If they were, the army would have no respect for him, and as for the enthusiasm displayed towards him, I, who see him every day, never have seen it. Meade does all the fighting here, and Grant gets all the credit. By this I don't mean anything disrespectful towards Grant, who is indeed a fine officer, but merely wish to contradict the statements of the press, who are trying to make a fool of him. How persons in the army do laugh at them! But anything in the nonsensical line will do for penny-a-liners.[40]

I suppose, now, you are all crazy about the Sanitary Fair, like everyone else.[41] Frank Wetherill is well, also his brother the Col., whose regiment has been in the thick of the fight.[42] I enclose a photograph for my collection of Capt. Wm. Baughman, Co "E," of "ours." . . .

Camp, Hd. Qrs. Army of the Potomac
near Charles City Court House
June 14th, 1864

Dear Mother:

Since I last wrote, on Sunday June 5th, I have been unable to write, as, just as I was on the point of doing so, orders to move came. We have shifted our quarters considerably since my last, dated Cold Harbor, and are now on the James River.

The army lay in line of battle for 10 days in all, the left pickets being at Bottom's Bridge and Old Church being the right. The 1st & 2nd Divn. Cavy. Corps were on the extreme right at Newcastle on the Pamunkey R., but about the 6th started on a raid, and to join Gen. Hunter at Charlottesville.[43] We had considerable hard fighting along the line.

On June 3rd there was a grand attack along the line, in which, in most places, we were successful, but the enemy opened on our troops from enfilading batteries wherever we took their works, rendering them untenable. At dark our line remained the same; our loss was between 5000 and 6000. Again on Sunday 5th, just before dark, the reb's made a feint upon Gen. Gibbon's Divn. of the 6th Corps and attacked Birney's Divn. of the 2nd Corps, charging his works in mass, but were driven back splendidly, & with great slaughter. With the exception of the pickets having a go at each other at nearly every hour of day & night, everything was quiet, the Great Moguls maturing their plans and preparing "something big."[44]

———

Meticulous to a fault in documenting his daily activities in his letters, Rawle uncharacteristically left a six-day gap, from June 6 to June 11, in his correspondence. His diary entries provide the details of his experiences during this time.

———

June 6th. Monday. Early in the morning Frank Wetherill and I took a ride out to the front to see how things are going on. Everything looks as if we were going into a siege and get the Rebs out by digging. We went to see his brother, Lt. Col. of the 82nd P.V. He has lost half his regiment and has just been relieved for a few hours from the front line. Our right, from the centre, has swung back, for better protection of the trains I suppose. Maj. Walsh, Lt. Galloway, Lt. Carter and I, with 75 men (Co.'s C, H and ½ of L were detailed for Pro. Guard back at the wagon trains, so we moved back there and went into camp, near the X Roads of Cold Harbor and White House Road and Old Church and Bottom's Bridge roads. I suppose we will be here for some time for the purpose of preventing straggling and protecting property in rear of the army. In the morning I went out towards New Castle.[45] Our 9th Corps has swung round to Old Church, and the 1st and 3rd Divisions of Cavalry are beyond it. Gen. Sheridan's Hd. Qrs. are at New Castle.

June 7th. Tuesday. Major Walsh, in command of the detachment Pro. Guard, requested me to act as Battalion Adjutant. Nothing much going on. In the afternoon I took a ride out to the front to see what was going on. There was some pretty brisk cannonading going on, but everything remained the same. The Cavalry Corps is concentrating at New Castle with eight days rations, it is supposed for another raid. From all appearances the siege of Richmond has commenced.

June 8th. Wednesday. Fine Weather. We are pleasantly situated back here, near Parsley's Mill, nothing much to do except patrolling the country from White House and in the direction of Old Church and Bottom's Bridge.[46] *As my watch was out of order I sent it home per mail, but I never expect to see it again.*

June 9th. Thursday. Very warm and close. Everything pretty quiet today. Some firing along the lines during the day. The Richmond & West Point R.R. is being repaired, and is finished nearly to Summit Station, a blind most probably to the enemy.

June 10th. Friday. Very pleasant weather. Several parties of marauders have been assaulting safeguards and pillaging, and we went out after them, arresting about two dozen.

June 11th. Saturday. Pleasant weather but terribly dusty. About 2 P.M. we were relieved from duty in rear. . . . We returned to the regiment at Hd. Qrs. near Cold Harbor. In the evening Potter and I went over to Hd. Qrs. and saw Capt. Cadwalader and Major Biddle. We had a treat in the shape of ice cream made here. . . . Our Cavalry Corps has gone on a raid to Charlottesville where Hunter is (he relieved Sigel). A movement in the direction of the James River is projected, but is considered to be a very delicate move.

———

"I find now, after more than thirty days of trial," Grant wrote to Halleck soon after Cold Harbor, "that the enemy deems it of the first importance to run no risks with the armies they now have. They act purely on the defensive, behind breast works, or feebly on the defensive immediately in front of them and where in case of repulse they can instantly retire behind them."[47] With this reality in mind, Grant vacated his lines near Cold Harbor on June 12–13 and, as Rawle predicted, moved south to the James River, which the Army of the Potomac crossed between the fourteenth and the eighteenth. His plan was to bypass Richmond and seize the strategic rail center of Petersburg, twenty-two miles south of the Confederate capital. The capture of that city, seated at the juncture of five railway lines and a vital cog in Confederate supply and communications, would hasten the fall of Richmond, render Lee's position untenable, and, Grant hoped, force the Confederate commander out from any prepared defenses, where he could be brought to battle on more advantageous terrain.

Grant stole a march on his adversary when he left Cold Harbor. (Lee learned soon after they departed that the Northerners were gone but was uncertain where they were headed.) As Union troops crossed the James and approached Petersburg, only 4,200 Southerners garrisoned the city.[48] Unfortunately for the Federals, leadership was lacking at the point of the attack. Although an assault on June 16 broke through the city's outer defenses, the Northerners failed to forcefully press the advantage they had gained, allowing Lee's infantry time to march south from Cold Harbor and occupy the trenches ringing the eastern and southern outskirts of the Cockade City. In a situation that required initiative and leaders at the front who would "act with vigor and promptness," remarked a Federal brigadier general, the local commanders instead proceeded "methodically and cautiously."[49]

Less than two weeks after they arrived in front of Petersburg, Rawle and a detachment of the 3rd Pennsylvania received a break from their usual responsibilities when sent east into neighboring Prince George's County to safeguard Southern citizens and their property, scout for deserters, and pick up stragglers. The Pennsylvanians remained there, enjoying the light duty and the fruits of the countryside, for nearly a month.

———

On Sunday June 12th, after a Regimental Mounted Inspection by Gen. Patrick, the old gentleman called up the officers and complimented them on the general satisfaction the regiment had given. He stated that Col. McIntosh had applied to Gen. Meade in person to have the regiment sent to his brigade in Wilson's Divn. of Cavy. (3d), but that his request was denied, as its presence here (notwithstanding the laurels such a regiment would necessarily gain in the Cavalry Corps), was indispensable to the service for performing the delicate duties at Hd. Qtrs.[50]

At 3 PM on the same day Hd. Qtrs. left Cold Harbor—5th Corps in advance, for another case of "flank by the left" on a large scale, crossed the Richmond & York River Rail Road at Dispatch Station, and camped for the night at Moody's Cross Roads on the Richmond & Williamsburg Stage road.[51]

On June 13th Monday, (yesterday), at 6 AM Hd. Qrs. resumed the march. Our regiment, with Gen. Patrick, took a longer road, to avoid the crowded state of the main roads, as the army is on the march. From [Moody's] X roads, we went via Emman's Church and the residence of the late President Tyler (where, in the gardens, in Virginia style, his family are buried), struck the main column again at Long Bridge on the Chickahominy River, which luckily was rather low, and not very swampy, crossed on pontoons and joined Gens. Grant and Meade near there.[52]

When near St. Mary's Church, our regiment, with Gen. Meade's personal escort of the 1st Mass. Cavy. took the advance, ahead of the 2nd Corps, and with some signal officers, took the straight road to Wilcox's Wharf on the James River, below Harrison's Landing, arriving there at 3.20 PM, and communicated with Gen. Butler's forces by signaling to the opposite bank. We were the first troops to reach the James River, and it was a pleasant sight to see a real river & gunboats, etc. On arriving there, we threw out pickets towards Harrison's Landing & Charles City C.H. until Gen. Meade came up, followed by the 2nd Corps, which took up a position parallel, almost, to the river. Hd. Qrs. were established near Charles City Court House, in a very nice place.

This country along the river is the most fertile part of Virginia, the garden spot of the state, good crops, pretty country. We have travelled over most of the country of McClellan's Peninsular Campaign. The 5th Corps connected with the 2nd Corps. The 6th & 9th came up in rear of us, crossing the Chickahominy at

Provost Marshal General of the Army of the Potomac Brig. Gen. Marsena Patrick and staff. Patrick, seated at center, regarded the 3rd Pennsylvania highly and was probably responsible for their retention at army headquarters. The officer seated on the porch bench to the left, his arm behind a post, is Lt. John Vernou Bouvier, the great-grandfather of First Lady Jacqueline Bouvier Kennedy. (Courtesy Prints and Photographs Division, Library of Congress)

Jones' Bridge, I believe. Baldy Smith's 18th Corps shipped at White House for City Point, I suppose. It is supposed that this army will ship for City Point or some place on the river bank of the James R., in a few days, to join Butler. This morning Grant crossed per boat to pay Butler a visit at Bermuda Hundred. Such [is] the condition of affairs. . . .

8 PM—I have just been down to the river. Tried to lay pontoon bridges but the river too deep & wide. The army is crossing in several columns to the other bank of the James. On to Richmond!!!

Camp, Hd. Qrs. Army of the Potomac
in front of Petersburg, Va.
June 21st, 1864

Dear Mother:

I was unable to write my regular Sunday letter, owing to a case of picket on hand at the time, resulting from a <u>spat</u> between Gens. Meade & Warren, it is said. I last wrote to you from Charles City Court House on the 14th, telling you that the army was just crossing the James River. The 2nd Corps crossed on that day from Wilcox's Wharf to Wind Mill Point, in ferry boats, as the engineers could not lay pontoons. All that day, & until late in the next, they tried to pontoon across about a half mile above Fort Powhatan, and at last succeeded, and during the night of the 15th, the 9th Corps crossed and some of the train. On this day, Hd. Qrs. were on the banks of the river, and on the morning of the 16th, at 8 AM, we crossed the pontoon bridge. During last night I had my best horse stolen, a fine chestnut sorrel.

June 15th. Wednesday. Fine day. . . . Out driving stragglers and arresting marauders outside the lines during the day.

The pontoon bridge was 700 ft. long, in 70 feet of water, anchored to schooners to steady it.[53] After we crossed, without stopping, we marched in a S.W. by W. direction about 21 miles, and arrived in front of, and in sight of, the city of Petersburg (1½ m. off).

June 16th. Thursday. . . . Marched in S.W. by W. direction, following 9th Corps. The stragglers have burned, pillaged and stolen almost everything along the route, the worst corps in the army.[54] About 5 P.M. we arrived within sight of Petersburg

(1½ miles). . . . The enemy in the hollow around the town are digging like beavers. . . . Hd. Qrs. camped for the night about two miles from the City, between the City Point and Weldon R.R.'s.

————

The 18th Corps (Baldy Smith) having shipped from White House & landed at City Point arrived here last night and immediately charged a splendidly built and very strong line of redoubts & earthworks, taking the defenders entirely by surprise & captured them with cannon, colors & prisoners, the positions commanding the town.[55]

June 17th Friday. More works, artillery & prisoners. Town shelled, hard fighting. Recd. Lilly's letter of 10th.

————

June 17th. Friday. . . . A battalion of the regiment was out in front during the day and one man wounded in the leg, Burns Co. "L," who died after amputation.[56]

————

June 18th Saty. At 8 AM our regiment was ordered out to report to Gen. Warren, whose corps has the left of the line. After laying near his Hd. Qrs. for a couple of hours under artillery fire, a regiment of Col. McIntosh's brigade of Wilson's Cavy. Divn. reported, thereby relieving us. Gen. Warren told Col. Jones that he might report back to Gen. Meade, being relieved. Gen. M. said that he believed he commanded this army and knew what to do with his cavalry, so he ordered Col. Jones out again to reinforce the other regiment, & take command of the whole.[57]

It is believed that the original plan was, that the whole line was to advance on the enemy's position, our regiment being on the left of the 5th Corps, but that Warren had failed to obey orders, thereby preventing our regiment from being cut to pieces, and Gen. Meade, who is sometimes very crusty, gave the above hit to Warren. The result of it was, that we lay out in the sun, and under artillery fire, on Col. Avery's Farm, supporting the line of pickets on the left for 2 nights & 3 days (much to the disgust & indignation of Gen. Patrick, who thinks the world of "his cavalry"), until last evening, when we returned to camp.[58]

Our base of supplies now is City Point on the James River, and our line of battle, including Gen. Butler's line (whose Hd. Qrs. are at Bermuda Hundreds), runs from the James River, crossing the Appomattox River somewhere near Port Walthall on the right to a point about a mile south of the Petersburg & Norfolk RR. There has been hard fighting ever since we arrived here.

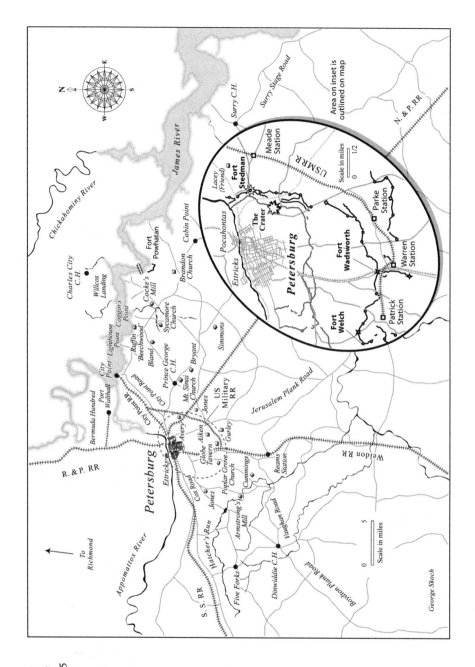

Operations near
Petersburg, June
1864–March 1865

It seems very marvelous that Grant did not, immediately upon arriving here, push on and take the town before Lee's army had time to come up. Prisoners state that when we arrived here we could have taken the whole concern with one Division, Lee having been outgeneraled and not knowing where we were.[59] It is rumored that another important maneuver is up, so I suppose Grant expects to do more by strategy than in any other manner. He likes the rebs to attack us, but he can't make them resort to strategy. Such appears to be his way of doing business. . . . I hear grand accounts of the Sanitary Fair. Tell Lottie to send me full accounts of it. I send for my collection a vignette of Lt. Ward.

———

June 19th. Sunday. Fine day. Very warm. We lay in the same place all day, as main picket reserve. The picket line is about seven or eight miles long. The enemy have fortified very strongly and Lee has a very large force in front. It seems very strange that Grant and Meade did not push on when we first came in front of Petersburg. Prisoners say we could have pushed clear through the town, but I suppose we will give the Rebs another dose of "strategy." Hard fighting going on all day, and the Cohorn mortars played during the night; very pretty to look at. The country around here is pretty open, and by going out a little distance we could see the greater part of both lines. A Flag of Truce was sent in by Gen. Meade in the afternoon, and for a while it was quiet.

June 20th. Monday. Very warm. Out on picket reserve all day. In the afternoon with a party of men I was ordered out to scout the roads and country on our left rear, and communicate with patrols from Col. McIntosh's Brigade of Wilson's Divn. Cavy. which covers the rear of the army. Lively artillery firing during the afternoon, of which we got our share. About 8 P.M. we were relieved and ordered back to camp, having been out three days and two nights, all for a spat between Meade and Warren.

June 21st. Tuesday. Fine day. In camp all day. To all appearances, the siege of Petersburg has commenced, heavy siege guns having come up. Received . . . a copy of the Poem (anonymous) "The Days of '63," written by my mother for the benefit of the Sanitary Fair. It is a beautiful work.

———

Hd. Qrs. Army of the Potomac
Jones' Farm, in front of Petersburg, Va.
June 26th, 1864

Dear Mother:

. . . We are still in front of Petersburg, nothing much having been gained since I wrote last Tuesday. On Wednesday [June 22], we threw our left out more beyond the Jerusalem Plank Road. As all the cavalry are off on another "bust," our regiment marched, deployed as skirmishers to protect the extreme left flank, and we had a rough time, and tho', by accident, we at one time got between our and the enemy's lines of battle, we got out with the loss of only one man wounded in the spur.[60] That day we camped where we now are, in a wretched, heaven-forsaken sand hole, with wretched water, and that very scarce. We have to take our horses nearly two miles to water, and to dig holes in the ground about 15 ft. deep to get drinking water, and even that is very bad. If we stay here long we will all get sick.

The dry weather has made the roads into a fearful state, the fine powdery dust being so thick that sometimes it is very difficult to see the man along side of you. It is very hard, after a march, to tell our men from the rebs, they being veritable "greybacks," our faces, eyes, beards & clothes being all of one color. Imagine the sensation. In the last few days the heat, in addition to all this, has been fearful, and I have had a good chance of testifying to it.[61]

On Friday [June 24], at 4.30 A.M., Maj. Walsh, 4 other officers & 100 men were ordered out to hunt up some guerillas who had cut the telegraph wire; if possible, in one day, to go to Surry C.H. and returning the next, to collect all the stragglers & deserters on the way. We marched steadily for 28 miles in the broiling sun and suffocating dust, reaching Cabin Point at 4.30 P.M. On arriving here (which place was still 15 miles from Surry CH) we found that a party of cavy. from Fort Powhatan had gone on just before on the same goosechase, and as our horses were exceedingly jaded, we bivouacked for the night.

The next day [June 25] by marching hard for 10 hours, we got back to camp before sunset, carrying out all our orders, but with nary guerillas of course. It was, if possible, warmer than the day before.

———

June 25th. Saturday. Exceedingly hot and dusty. Started on the march back at 5 A.M., the party from Fort Powhatan having done all that was necessary. I drew a topographical map of the Stage Road at the request of Maj. Walsh, scale 1 mile equals 1 inch. . . . [G]ot into camp about 6 P.M.

———

There has been fighting more or less every day, but as it has been too ovenlike to leave my tent to get the "chin" I have no news. . . .

———

> Hd. Qrs. Army of the Potomac, in front
> of Petersburg, Va., June 27th, 1864

Dear Mother:

I wrote yesterday and also sent photographs of the officers & men of our company. . . . Be careful in opening the roll of photographs that you don't bend them. . . . The "C" Compy. photograph is in front of my tent. My picture is not good, it is front of the Company, to the right of the centre of the picture as you look at it. All of the others are good. . . .

———

June 27th. Monday. In camp all day. Nothing much going on, one of the quietest days along the lines we have had yet. We received the large 6 x 7 group photographs taken last April at Brandy Station. I sent one of the officers groups to Clem. B. Barclay and one to mother, and also one of "C" Co. They are both very fine pictures. A very welcome and refreshing thunderstorm in the afternoon.

———

> Camp, Detachment Pro. Guard
> near Cox's Mill's, Pr. George Co., Va.[62]
> July 2d, 1864

Dear Mother:

. . . As you see, the date of my letter is changed. On June 28th, Lieut. Carter & I, with "C" Company and part of "A" Co., in all numbering 54 men, were sent out to this point to establish a camp to patrol the country, protect property and arrest stragglers and deserters from our army.

———

June 28th. Tuesday. Very pleasant weather. At 5 A.M. . . . we started out via Prince George Court House on the Surry Stage Road, arrived at Dr. Strong's place, "The Gleed," about 1 P.M. and camped around the house. . . . The camp is very near Paulding's Creek and in a very pleasant situation. We expect to remain here for some time.

June 29th. Wednesday. Fine day. Everything pretty quiet. During the afternoon and evening Gregg's Division of Cavalry passed on towards Prince George Court House. I saw Capts. Treichel and Potter who called up to see us, also other friends. The other day the division was attacked by vastly superior forces and was driven back with heavy loss. Capt. Phillips of Gen. Gregg's staff killed, Col. Covide, it is feared, mortally wounded and a prisoner.[63]

June 30th. Thursday. Splendid day. In the morning I took up a scout with a few

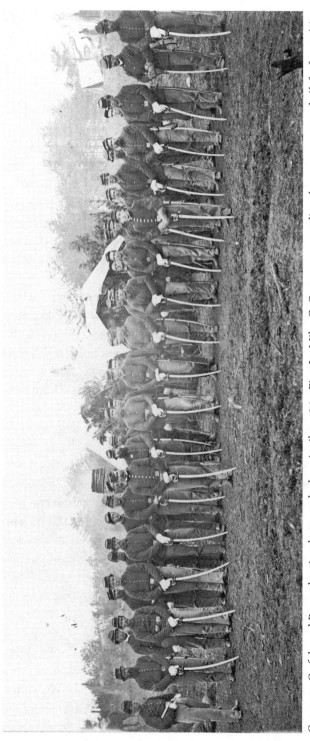

Company C of the 3rd Pennsylvania, photographed on April 15, 1864. First Lt. Miles G. Carter, commanding the company, stands (*left of center*) in front of the enlisted men; 2nd Lt. William Brooke Rawle stands (*right of center*) in front of the men. All of the soldiers in the photograph are identified in a caption within the *History of the Third Pennsylvania Cavalry*. Those pictured who are mentioned by Rawle in his letters include his first sergeant, former Regular Army cavalryman John J. Brandon (*second from left*); Quartermaster Sgt. Jacob Hartenstine (*far right*); Pvt. James Montgomery, the heavily bearded man in the front rank of the enlisted men (just behind Carter); and Pvt. William Boyle, the first soldier in the rear rank on the right (*fourth from right*). Boyle died while in the service in 1864. (Courtesy Prints and Photographs Division, Library of Congress)

men to hunt up stragglers. They have formed themselves into gangs under leaders and live on the country by stealing, pillaging, etc. We got 15 during the day.

———

We are about 17 miles from Hd. Qrs., Army of the Potomac, on the Surry Stage Road, on Powell's Creek, about 5 miles from Fort Powhatan and 3 miles from the James River. This country is full of deserters from our army, who hide in the woods and plunder all around the country. Some of them steal clothes from citizens, make for our lines at Norfolk and state that they are Union refugees. Our duty is to arrest as many of these as possible. We are comparatively isolated from the rest of the army, there being no troops within 4 or 5 miles of us. Our camp now is on the lawn of the house of the Rev. Mr. Woodward who, like almost everyone else, abandoned it when the army came here. It is completely torn to pieces, furniture smashed, books stolen, papers torn up, clothes torn into shreds, etc. This is the case everywhere.

At present we are living gloriously. The few inhabitants around here, to whom we have furnished safeguards, supply us with the necessaries; we giving them coffee, sugar and other "Commissaries." For example, our soldiers dinner today consisted of fried chicken, fresh potatoes, squash, cucumbers, beets, fresh butter & biscuits, also honey. We have a cow, which we picked up on the road & which supplies us with fresh milk. Ain't that glorious? To be sure, we could have none of this if we were with the Regiment.

Of the general news & progress of the siege of Petersburg you know as much as we do, from the papers. Having occasion to go to Cabin Point yesterday [July 1], I came upon what remains of Gen. Wilson's Divn. of Cavalry at that point. They have just returned from an extensive raid on the Richmond & Danville R.R. I saw Gen. Wilson on business, who gave me a full account of the raid. They marched 400 miles in 10 days, destroyed 31 miles of the R. & D. R.R., also Burkesville Junct., fighting the whole time against overwhelming numbers, was completely surrounded, cut his way through, losing all his artillery, burned his wagons and came back utterly used up, starved and quite demoralized. Col. McIntosh's Brigade lost 1000 men. Many now reported missing will come in, as the country is full of his stragglers. . . .[64]

———

July 2nd. Saturday. In the morning our Pro. Guard detachment changed camp, about a mile on the City Point Road, to the abandoned place of Rev. Woodward. We did this as the camp on Dr. Strong's was too much exposed. We are now behind a swampy creek, with the bridge ready to tear up if necessary.

———

Camp, Detachment Provost Guard, 3d Pa. Cavy.
near Cocke's Mills, Pr. George Co., Va.
July 6th, 1864

Dear Lottie:

. . . Carter and I, with our 54 men, are still back here having a quiet, but pretty good, time, which, in the army, means plenty of good things to eat. We live on the farmers and slaves around here who are glad enough to exchange chickens and different kinds of vegitables for coffee, sugar, flour, etc., and we have our two cows, and drink nothing but milk. Last but not least we have an ice house, full, and very good water. None of these luxuries could we have at Hd. Qrs., which is camped in a low, woody, dusty, warm place, with very little water, and that got from a swamp by digging holes in the ground.

Last Sunday [July 3] a couple of rebs, most probably guerillas, captured a safeguard which we had placed at a gentleman's house near here. Safeguards should be respected as a flag of truce, as they are placed for the protection of property and no advantage is gained by the service. Last night we recd. an order from Hd. Qrs. to make a full report upon the matter, to be sent to the Rebel Authorities. His release is to be demanded from them.[65]

Having some business on July 4th at Gen. Sheridan's Hd. Qrs., at Light House Point on the James River about 6 miles from here, I took advantage of it by going to see Capt. Will White of the 6th Pa. Cavy. They have just returned from a long raid and are completely used up. All the Cavalry is in like condition & are now getting a few day's rest. Will White got through very well. His regiment lost 160 men & 8 or 9 officers. Charlie Coxe is with his regiment, having got over his wound. Charlie Leiper was only slightly, but painfully wounded in [the] foot. . . .[66] "Hark the trumpet (bugle) calls to duty," or, in other words, I must go to "stables."

———

July 5th. Tuesday. Fine day. Warm. We are sadly in want of rain. The whole country is dried up and the crops (what are left) are spoilt.

———

Rawle's letter of July 9, 1864, was captured. In its place he supplied transcriptions from his diary in a subsequent letter home to cover the missing timeframe. He remained on detached service near Cocke's Mills, Prince George County.

———

Thursday July 7th, 1864. Very warm. A thimbleful of rain in the afternoon. Flies terrible. Everything quiet. No news from the front. . . .

Friday July 8th, 1864. Excessively warm. Almost eaten up by flies. In afternoon an order came from Army Hd. Qrs. to remove all safe guards—they not being respected by the enemy.[67] Recd. papers of the 6th. Account of sinking of the "Kearsarge." Also a threatened raid across the Potomac. Twelve thousand 100-day men called out by the Governor of Pennsylvania.[68]

Saturday July 9th, 1864. Very warm. Nothing new going on. The Cavalry near here are doing a good deal of damage, and we arrest a good many.

Camp, Detachment, Pro. Gd. Army of the Potomac
Near Cocke's Mills, Pr. Geo. Co., Va.
July 13th, 1864 Wednesday

Dear Lilly:

. . . We are still back here having a pretty good time. We go over to bathe on the fine beach by the James River, about 1½ miles from here. Also, we fish every day in the Creek (Powell's) near here, and have "catfish & coffee" every day. About 1½ miles from here is the Army Cattle Herd, where we have 3 companies as guard. Capt. Frank Wetherill is there. Their camp is around a beautiful house and grounds of Mr. Ruffin, the man who fired the first shot at Fort Sumpter. The house is on an elevation, and at the bottom of the hill is the James River and a fine beach. It overlooks the river and is a superb place.[69] The river here is about as wide as the Delaware at Phila.

There is nothing much (outside of the <u>digging</u> routine of a siege) going on in front. The 6th Corps have left for Baltimore to attend to the Reb invasion. We are mining in front of the 9th Corps, and if <u>Jonny</u> don't look out he will get "lifted."[70] The Rebs (according to the latest I have heard, 10th), appear to be playing the mischief up in Maryland. I hope they won't interfere with our mails. Grant won't leave here, I don't think, for Washington, or anything else, just now.

For the first time, we are beginning to receive advantages from the Sanitary Commission, in the shape of 2 lemons & a bottle of Jamacen Rum, with which we have been indulging in Milk Punch, Egg flip, etc. [during] this warm weather. Some persons can get wines & all kinds of things in abundance, while others get nothing. Influence is everything. In some cases regiments have had delicacies issued at the rate of 6 nutmegs to the regiment, ½ an onion to a man, etc. which is ridiculous. It gives them a taste and no more. It is getting dark, so I must close.

———

July 15th. Friday. Three men, Corp. Bickley Co. "L," Privates York "L" and Smith "C" were gobbled by guerillas this side of Prince George Court House.[71] They were out on patrol. . . .

July 16th. Saturday. Early in the morning I started with an orderly to pay a visit at the Regiment. . . . Saw the officers, including Capt. Miller lately returned from Recruiting service. Dined with Col. Jones and Maj. Walsh and the Doctors. . . . Yesterday two men of the 72nd N.Y. were hung for ravishing a lady near here.[72]

———

Camp, Det. Pro. Gd. A of P
Near Cocke's Mill's. Pr. Geo., Va.
July 17th, '64 Sunday

Dear Mother:

Owing to the Rebs having paid Maryland and the District of Columbia another visit, we have received no mail for six days, but expect a "rouser" tomorrow. The last letter I rec'd from home was Lilly's of the 8th. I wrote to her on the 13th. My letter of [the] 9th probably was captured near Gunpowder Br. on the 11th, if you have not recd. it.

I was up at Hd. Qrs. yesterday. Word had been recd. that the Rebs had recrossed the Potomac at Edward's Ferry. It was said that Grant was very angry at their getting off so easily.[73]

Nothing much is going on in front. We are digging like beavers. The mining in front of the 9th Corps has been very seriously impeded by the mines filling with water. It seems no secret, as it is talked of openly, so I suppose my information is not contraband. In my opinion, it seems one of the only chances left to us to take the position. The object in the mining is to blow up a very strong line of works erected on a strong position.

There is some talk that the army will recross the James, but no rumors of the kind are to be relied upon. We will have a hard job (if indeed we ever can) to take Richmond from this quarter.

We are still back in the rear, as you see. The Cavalry now have a picket line outside of us, so we are comparatively safe. The guerillas trouble our patrols sometimes. We have lost 4 men captured. . . .

———

July 17th. Sunday. In the morning I took a patrol out to scour the country between the Petersburg & City Point Roads. Arrested a 5th N.Y. Cavalryman for ravishing a pretty mulatto girl at "Blands." . . .

July 18th. Monday. This morning the pickets at Sycamore Church were troubled by this party of guerillas around here, killing a lieutenant and wounding several men (1st N.H. Cav.).[74] *I got a fine blooded Virginia mare the other day, with foal, and I determined to try to make something out of her. She bore a colt this evening, which I took away from her (to improve her). She has a large grass belly, owing to running loose for a long time, which I hope to get off of her. This small stock, "Sand-snipes" as we call them, are very tough and will stand any quantity of work.*

———

> Camp, Detach. Pro. Gd., A of P
> Simmon's Farm, Pr. Geo., Va.
> July 20th, 1864

Dear Lottie:

I recd. Mother's letter of the 10th and yours of the 14th both on 18th—the first mail we recd. for 6 days, during the Invasion. How scared you all were at the rebs. I suppose [Uncle] W.H.R. went out with the "milish." You think they act so badly when they pay Maryland & Penna a visit. If you could only see how the stragglers of <u>our</u> army behave, you would think nothing of the Reb doings. To see the ravages committed by our troops often makes me disgusted with the army and with the cause. To be sure, this is not done by the <u>army.</u> We are hanging men very often for such offenses. In any army of course there must be a proportion of rascals, and ours has its share. These are mostly men who have lately enlisted for the bounty, and entered the service hoping to get through the war without being in a battle. . . .

We are as poor as Job's turkeys—no money anywhere and no prospect of getting any. U[ncle] S[am] owes me more than $500, and here I am without even a postage stamp. I will soon have to <u>draw on my bankers,</u> i.e. beg from home.

At last we have had a taste of rain. Yesterday it rained nearly all day, and it looks as if we were going to have a shower this afternoon. The suffering from the drought has been very great. What with the suffocating dust and the scarcity of water (and that even very bad when we <u>could</u> get it), existence has been a bore. . . .[75]

Nothing much seems to be going on. Last night and afternoon there was some very hard fighting in front, but I have not yet found what was up. The "Commissions" [the US Christian and the Sanitary] do not furnish very good paper. This is about all I can beg, steal or borrow.

———

> Camp, Det. Pro. Gd., A of P
> near Cocke's Mills, Pr. Geo., Va.
> July 23rd, 1864, Saty.

Dear Mother:

. . . You ask if we don't feel very lonely where we are. Ward is here now, and the cattle guard battalion of our regiment is only about 1½ miles off. Our duty is not hard now. We amuse ourselves by fishing, sailing and bathing on Powell's Creek and the James River. Books <u>would</u> be very acceptable, but these are very scarce. I am now reading "Bleak House."[76]

In Lilly's letter she wanted to impress me with the magnitude of the Rebel force in Maryland, and said that it took "<u>two hours!</u>" to pass one place. What would she think if she had to sit for at least <u>10 days</u> to see the whole Army of the Potomac pass one given spot, trains and all, marching day & night?

So Frank Wetherill has been writing home in a disconsolate tone? He is very eager to get out of the service. We all have the blues more or less. The term of service of the regiment expires on Aug. 26th. Some of the company's terms are up already. We then don't know what will become of us, or what officers are to be retained in the service. There is much discontent among us on account of our not being promoted to existing vacancies. Gov. Curtin some time ago issued an order that promotions should not be made except in companies, and not by seniority. Therefore I have to wait till Capt. Price & Lieut. Carter of my company get out of the service before I can get up, whereas a low contemptible sergeant can be promoted in "I" Co. over my head as 1st Lieut.[77]

We prefer to let things remain as they are, rather than comply with Gov.'s orders, so with a few exceptions there has been no changes since I joined the regiment. Otherwise I would not be far off from a Captain now. Every time an officer is promoted, he is remustered for the term of 3 yrs., consequently the Government can keep whatever officers it wants in the service.

When the main Regiment is discharged next month there will be left about 400 men in all, principally recruits, whose term will not expire. There is some talk of the regiment's going to Washington about that time to reorganize, i.e. to be dismounted, consolidated with another skeleton regiment, and probably sent into the field again dismounted, to act as infantry. Now, if that happens I will not be able to stand it. Having my 3 horses always ready I never think of walking 300 yds. Consequently, my feet are in no condition to stand a march, and up I go.

Again it is said that the Government will not allow officers to take their own private horses out of the service, but will keep them and pay the government price, $160, for them. Also that the government is going to charge $12 per month for each U.S. horse an officer rides. What with sugar at 25 cts. pr. lb. & other <u>commissaries</u> at proportional prices—$25 pr. month taken from an officer's pay for his groom, $24 pr. month for his horses, etc. what are we to do? We won't be able to get along. But there is no use in troubling ourselves. We are all right at this moment, and let the future look out for itself. That is the only way to get along in the army.[78] I would never have mentioned the subject had you not heard of it through F[rank] W[etherill].

On top of all these miseries, imagine our not having a cent in the whole mess, nor any prospect of getting any, with 5 months' pay due us. "Sic transit gloria arma [Thus passes away the glory of arms]."

Don't you worry yourself about me, however. "My faithful pipe," and Sanitary tobacco help me drive dull care away, and altogether I am about the most contented man in the Regiment, as far as one could judge from the amount of grumbling—that soldier's sole privilege. . . .

——

July 24th. Sunday. Orders to be ready to join the Regiment at short notice. Many surmises as to our future fate. Capt. Hess received his commission as major. . . . Col McIntosh is trying to get the Regiment to Penna. to recruit, wanting to keep his commission as colonel, as he has been recommended as Brig. Genl. Hard rain and blow all night. About 3 A.M. the tent and bowers of evergreen were all blown down and a change of base was safely effected into the house in a damp condition.

July 25th. Monday. Fine day. Cool. . . . In the evening some whiskey got into the Company and O[rderly] Sgt. Brandon, who out of liquor is the best O.S. in the Regiment (an old 5th U.S. Cavalry soldier), and one or two others got troublesome, and then mutinous. After a little trouble he was arrested, put into the Guard House and had to be gagged.[79]

July 26th. Tuesday. Fine day. Nothing much going on. Expect to move up to Hd. Qrs. tomorrow. Col. McIntosh of "ours" has got his star and is now a Brig. Gen. The second from our regiment.

CHAPTER SIX

Operations near Petersburg

July 27–November 4, 1864

From a military perspective, the opposing lines at Petersburg had remained mostly static since Rawle had been sent on detached service in late June. With the exception of localized skirmishing and sharpshooting, which claimed the lives of dozens of soldiers on both sides every day, no major combat operations occurred. Each army had remained occupied, however, improving and strengthening their entrenchments, fieldworks, and fortifications. As Rawle notes in his July 13 letter, Pennsylvania coalminers in the IX Corps had also been busy throughout the month, constructing the framework for a massive, powder-filled mine reaching under a section of the Confederate earthworks.

Historian Earl Hess has usefully grouped and numbered the major offensives undertaken by Grant and Meade in front of Petersburg. The "First Offensive" entailed the initial attacks against the city covering June 15–18, while the "Second Offensive," June 22–23, represented the first of numerous attempts to disrupt and cut off Confederate supply lines into the city from the south and west. In addition to attempting to prevent Lee from sending reinforcements to Georgia, Grant's "Third Offensive," which began on July 26, envisioned Sheridan's Cavalry Corps moving north of Richmond and cutting one of the capital's key supply lines, the Virginia Central Railroad. Concurrently, Hancock's II Corps would also move north of the James to attack the city. These initiatives against Richmond, known collectively as the First Battle of Deep Bottom, were both unsuccessful, yet they succeeded in compelling Lee to send most of his infantry away from Petersburg to meet these threats. Learning that the Rebel lines had been weakened, Grant saw in Burnside's mine the opportunity to breach the Southern fieldworks.[1]

The comparatively soft duty that Rawle and his detachment had enjoyed since June 28 came to an end on July 27, when they were ordered to return to the main body of the 3rd Pennsylvania, stationed at Meade's headquarters near Petersburg. Significant organizational changes were in the offing within the regiment. The three-year enlistments of the original officers and men were set to expire in late August, requiring a new organization formed from the reenlisted veterans and newer members. As a result of the consolidation that took place, Rawle was assigned to a position within the newly constituted veteran battalion that, while important, he found distasteful. The duty was only temporary, though, and his mildly wounded pride was healed when the depleted ranks of the 3rd Pennsylvania were replenished with recruits—and Rawle rewarded with promotion.

The initial enthusiasm that had attended the movements of the armies of the North during May and June waned in July as overall casualties rose to unprecedented levels and decisive victories seemed out of reach. Some in the Army of the Potomac grew despondent, wondering privately whether victory could ever be won. "This most unequalled campaign," mused a Massachusetts officer, "and its entire failure, thus far, to accomplish its main object; has begun to tell on us all. The men are getting to look on a fight as useless butchery and altogether their morale is not what it was."[2]

———

Head Qrs., Army of the Potomac
July 27th, 1864

Dear Mother:

As an organization, the 3d Penna. Cavalry is no more. Today decided our fate. The term of service of the Regiment expires on Aug. 26th, and all the men who are to be discharged, with most of the officers, went this morning to City Point to ship for Washington, where they are to remain for the remainder of their term.

The "Veterans" and recruits and all those whose term does not expire then have been formed into a battalion of 3 companies, and the following officers picked out to remain with them:

Compy. A. Capt. Stillé, Lieut. Beaton, Lieut. Gregg
Compy. B. Capt. Treichel, Lieuts. Carter & Brooke [Rawle]
Compy. M. Capt. Hess, Lieuts. Potter & Ward

Major Walsh is to command the battalion. Lieut. Gregg was only promoted from Sergeant two days ago. I am detailed as battalion Qr. Master & Comm[issary], a job which I hate like everything. The responsibility is very great, and I know nothing about the Department. Everything seems so gloomy, all of the other of-

A retouched photo of Irish native James W. Walsh. Walsh had served in the Regiment of Mounted Rifles before the war and was originally commissioned as captain of Company I of the 3rd Pennsylvania in January 1862. He would eventually rise to lieutenant colonel and lead the veteran battalion of the 3rd from its formation until the end of the war. Rawle held Walsh in high esteem. (From Regimental History Committee, *History of the Third Pennsylvania Cavalry* [1905])

ficers having left us, Wetherill, Vernou, all. Unless the Regiment is recruited up, they will be discharged. In a short time more I would have been promoted to 1st Lieut. in the Regt., as my Capt., Price, is to be appointed Major in the Ins[pector] Gen[erals] Dept., but the skeleton companies have been consolidated and there is no prospect of my being anything but what I am. Small encouragement to serve nearly three years as 2nd Lieut.

Before the rest of the Regiment left Hd. Qrs., Gen. Patrick made a speech stating that he was so sorry to lose them and complimented us very highly, stating that no Regiment, Regular or Volunteer, had ever given such satisfaction as ours had. Gen. Patrick thinks the world of Maj. Walsh, and is going to keep our battalion with him still at Hd. Qrs.

Very early this morning we left our Camp, Detachment Provost Guard, A of P near Cocke's Mills and rejoined the Regiment. The battalion numbers in all 247 men I believe, on paper, but one half that number for duty will be a large estimate. . . .

Camp, Battn. 3d Pa Cavy.
Hd. Qrs. Army of Potomac
July 31st, 1864 Sunday

Dear Mother:

. . . I wrote on the 27th, the day the "3d" went home to Washington, to tell you of my fate and future prospects.

Gen. McIntosh just got his star a day or two before. He had an order in his pocket relieving us from duty at Hd. Qrs., as he wanted us with him to keep him in his position as Colonel. Gen. Patrick did not want to lose us, so when McIntosh was promoted, all his interests in having the Regiment with him were gone.[3] When the Regiment went to Washington, Maj. Walsh's battalion of Vet's & Recruits were detailed for permanent duty at Gen. Patrick's, so here I am still.

I am acting Quarter Master and Commisy. of the battalion, the officers present here are Maj. Walsh, Capts. Hess & Stillé, Lts. Carter, Potter (Act. Adj.), Ward, Gregg (just promoted from O[rderly] S[ergeant] Compy. A), Brooke [Rawle] (AQM). I was very sad to part with the others, especially Wetherill.

The siege of Petersburg is progressing very slowly. All day and night we have artillery and infantry firing, but only desultory. Early yesterday morning (2 AM) [July 30] Hd. Qrs. was up and the troops under arms, in case of emergency. Our battalion with Gen. Patrick went out with Gen. Meade to Gen. Burnside's Hd. Qrs. where Gen. Grant was. About 4.15 AM a terrific cannonading opened and shortly after the mine under a fort, the key of the enemy's strong position, was touched off, and up went the fort most beautifully. At the same moment a charge was made all along the line, under cover of a very heavy artillery fire.

The 1st line of works was gallantly taken, and then the 2nd in like manner with the exception of the works attacked by the nigger Divn. (4th, 9th Corps). The black rascals tumbled over the works, and when the rebs rallied, the negroes, four times their number, tumbled back again in the most clumsy style imaginable, and ran like cowards. Their white officers stood upon the works, trying to make the niggers follow, but <u>no go,</u> and they were shot down like sheep.[4] This important position being lost, the rest of the line had to fall back, and this grand movement was a failure. I don't know how much (if any) we hold of the 1st line. So, all for the cowardly niggers, we lost upwards of 2000 men, one of the best planned maneuvres of the campaign, and much trouble and expense for no purpose. The indignation against the niggers is very great. Notwithstanding what the papers say, they are thought very poorly of through[out] the army.[5]

Part of the Cavalry Corps passed on their way to the left of the army yesterday. They have been with the 2nd Corps across the James for a few days, and took 3 colors and some prisoners.[6] I saw Will White, Coxe and others. All very well.

We are suffering intensely from [the] heat, and the water is very bad. It is hard to sleep at night between the heat and confounded mortar batteries about a mile off, the reports of which nearly bounce you out of bed. Do you remember Smyser of our class at college? I met him yesterday while out looking at the fight. He is now an Asst. Surgeon in 2nd Divn. 9th Corps. . . .[7]

> Camp, Battn. 3d. Pa. Cavy.
> Hd. Qrs. Army of Potomac
> In front of Petersburg, Va.,
> Aug. 4th, 1864

Dear Lilly:

. . . I have not recd. any letters since yours, as the Regiment proper has gone to Washington, and the mail goes to it. Those who went with the Regiment thought they had the joke on us, but almost immediately on their arrival there, they were remounted & equipped and sent into Penna. & Maryland after the Rebs, so the tables have turned.[8]

Nothing much is going on here now. The heat is terrible, as also the flies, and existence is almost a bore. We have the usual amount of artillery & musket firing going on continuously, and something big appears to be up. But "farther deponent sayish not." Some big bug will go up the spout for the lamentable failure of Saturday. A Court of Inquiry is sitting to investigate it. I hope it won't be Meade who has worked the Army of the Potomac better than anyone else. One thing is certain—it was not the troops of the old A of P which acted so badly in the assault. If we had only had some of our own Veterans there, we would not be where we are now, and for such a terrible blunder somebody must suffer. Hancock's 2nd Corps and Torbert's & Gregg's Cavy. Divns. had crossed the James River and drawn a very large part of the Reb army away from our front, which was the design of the diversion, and it is certain that we only had 3 Divns. in front of us on Saturday. Such a splendid opportunity we never had before, and will not have again, and it was lost.[9]

Gen. Sheridan with Torbert's Divn. of Cavalry have shipped for Washington. Sheridan is to take command of the Department of the Susquehanna while the Rebs pay their 2nd visit of the Campaign to Md. & Pa. . . .[10]

Camp Battn. 3d. Pa. Cavy. Hd. Qrs. A of P
In front of Petersburg, Va., Aug. 7th, 1864

Dear Mother:

. . . I write in a state of <u>toast.</u> The heat is terrible and has been so without inter-mission. We have not had any rain for weeks, and we are very nearly done <u>brown.</u>

. . . Nothing much is going on. On Friday Afternoon [August 5] the Rebs undertook to show their skill in mining in front of [the] 18th Corps. They under-took to blow up a fort but it appears that they must have become <u>discombober-ated,</u> as they instead blew up the ground near the pickets, not having dug far enough. They also made a feeble charge which was repulsed.[11]

I have just finished reading "Doctor Antonio" which somehow got out of some Virginia family library.[12] . . . Most of the Cavalry Corps, Torbert's and Wil-son's Divisions, have gone up to help you in Penna. & Maryland. We have a guest here, Lieut. Commander of a Gunboat on the James River, who has paid us a visit to "the front" to see the great Siege operations in front of Petersburg.[13] It is so hot that I will have to close.

—

August 9th. Tuesday. Very warm. . . . Lieut. Carter and I had considerable trou-ble owing to my not giving in to a whim of his uncontrollable temper, and Ward and I shifted our quarters. He tried to do some very ungentlemanly things, such as taking away all U.S. property in my use belonging to the Company, but as I was supported by Maj. Walsh and all the officers he had to give up.

—

Camp, Battn. 3d. Pa. Cavy. Hd. Qrs. Army of Potomac
In front of Petersburg, Va., Aug. 12th, 1864

Dear Lottie:

. . . While I am writing, pretty heavy firing is going on along the line. A con-founded heavy mortar battery about 1 mile from here is banging away, and every minute or two pretty nearly bounces me out of my seat. All last night and all today they have kept it up, and we could get little or no sleep. This done to cover movements.

Today information came that a large force has left our front, and is marching for Maryland, and the 2nd Corps marched off in a great hurry, and are shipping as fast as it can. There are rumors of other Corps going soon, and if so most prob-ably Gen. Meade will go with them, and us with him. For myself, I would like a campaign in Maryland or Penna. very much, but I fear its effect on our cause.[14] I doubt if anything can be done here. Judge Allison and Mr. Hanna of the Phila. Bar are paying a visit. I asked them this morning about their opinion of things here generally, and they said they saw now "why the Army of the Potomac don't move."

It is a very fine thing to witness the immense operations of this army in siege. All the engineering skill known is brought into play, and it would remind you of the siege of Sebastopol in the "Interpreter."[15] From the distance, you would see a plain all cut up by earthworks, but scarcely a moving object, but going close up to it, the work that has been done and is doing is marvelous. We can go to within a very few rods of the enemy's lines without his seeing us, by means of the "covered ways," "parallels," "saps," etc. All the quarters of the men along the line have "bomb proofs," and they don't in the least mind a big shell lighting in the middle of their camps now. The men have a good deal of fun in the trenches, making their pipes into mortars, throwing balls all the way to the enemy, etc. On the picket line a great deal of sharpness is exhibited in the way they get their antagonists to show, and then picking them off.[16]

It is a beautiful sight to go out into the trenches of a "quiet night" and see the opposing mortar batteries play. From the blast of the gun, the large shells can plainly be seen by their fuse, until they burst in the works. They look, when many are playing, like a Fourth of July fireworks exhibition. . . . They look like so many rockets.[17]

We had a terrific explosion at City Point Landing the other day. Most probably it was the most terrific that ever took place. The whole place is torn to pieces. Ward, who was at Grant's Hd. Qrs. at the time, within a few rods of the place, describes it as terrific. He was in a group, and five shells burst in among them. He was struck on the leg with fragments and knocked over, but only slightly bruised. At this distance, 8 miles, I felt the shock as much as if there had been a very hard clap of thunder right near me.[18]

We are having a very dry spell, and are suffering much from the terrific heat. Our battalion does the same work as the Regiment did. By the bye, I see that Collis' 3d Penna. Cavalry has distinguished itself. Collis, the conceited jackanapes,[19] puts his name in the paper whenever he can. He writes for the Philadelphia Inquirer.

I have succeeded in placing hors du combat a miniature specimen of our companions here, in the shape of a mosquito, which for curiosity I have measured—4 inches from tip to tip. . . .

Camp, Battn. 3d. Pa. Cavy. Hd. Qrs. A of P
In front of Petersburg, Va.
Aug. 15th, 1864

Dear Mother:

. . . I generally receive your letters two days after they are written, but don't see why it takes five for mine to reach you. I recd. on Saturday a letter from Grandma, dated 9th, in which she said that she had been scared sick, thinking I was blown up in the mine.

Nothing much is going on here, the centre of interest of the whole country. We have been having terribly hot weather, but last night we had a pretty good rain storm the first for many weeks. This evening again we had a regular pour.

On Aug. 12th the 2nd Corps, which had been in reserve for some time, recd. orders to move, went in quick time to City Point, shipped and sailed down the river, supposing that they were going to Washington. After dark however they turned about, went up the river, disembarked on the North bank of the James beyond Butler's right, and have been fighting with very good success, as that corps always does. It was a blind, and succeeded admirably. There are rumors of Hancock's doing some big things there.[20]

While I am writing, the people out in front are banging away. Very often in the evening we ride out to the line of hills overlooking the town to see the mortar shelling, which is beautiful. Excuse the brevity.

———

August 15th. Monday. A glorious rain last evening, and also this afternoon, which was gladly received after such a long spell of hot dry weather.[21]

August 16th. Tuesday. Warm. Got requisitions for ammunition and ordnance stores approved by Lieut. John R. Edie, Chief Ordnance Officer, A. of P.; went up with a wagon to City Point and drew stores from Lieut. Morris Shaff, Depot Ord. Offr.; also turned in five unserviceable horses to Depot of Repairs, Capt. E. J. Strang, Q.M., U.S.A.[22] *Dined with the 5th U.S. Cavy. officers, Gen. Grant's escort at Hd. Qrs. Armies of the U.S. on City Point, and returned in afternoon.*

August 17th. Wednesday. Very warm. Rain in evening. Issued ammunition and ordnance.

August 18th. Thursday. Cloudy, warm. In the morning, as I had business at City Point, Lieut. Potter and I rode down together. Called to see Capt. Chas Treichel at 2nd Cav. Divn. Hospital. He is very sick and expects to go home in a day or two. Called also at Cavy. Corps Hospital, saw Lt. Col. Janeway of 1st N.J. Cavy. lately wounded in hand.[23]

———

Camp Battn. 3d Pa. Cavy., Hd. Qrs. A of P
In front of Petersburg, Va.
Aug. 20th, 1864

Dear Mother:

. . . I have been very busy all this week at my Q.M. duties, so that I have been unable to write before.

Last evening our Pay Master paid us a visit, and, what was much more acceptable, 4 month's pay. If I can, I will send to you $245 per Adams Express, directed to care of Wm. H. Rawle. $34.50 is for Hoyt for a coat ordered in my name for Carter, bill enclosed. Please pay Uncle WHR $10.50 for a draft I drew on him April 23d, when I was very hard up. . . . If I ever should get as hard up as I have been during this campaign, I will have to be able to draw upon myself, and not on a certain friend of ours.

Thanks for the puff about the "Bloody Third." I had not seen it before. It's a shame they did not mention the gallant veterans who remain, and the officers who were selected from the whole Regiment to lead them on to Victory or Death, etc., etc.

We have been having some wet weather this week, which was very acceptable. We were beginning to suffer from want of water, which is very scarce around here, and our wells were rapidly giving out.

We have been having some movements about lately among the corps. Hancock went over to the right and afterwards Warren to the left, where he destroyed the Weldon RR, and is holding his position. I don't think "Jonny" is so strong in front of us now, and fear that he has sent a good many other Jonnies up towards your part of the country. This is only my idea.[24]

Having some business down at City Point the other day, Potter . . . and I went on the Sanitary Commn. boat and had a very good dinner. I did not know before that they kept a table for soldiers who were there pro temp., gratis of course. Another blessing of the Insanitary. . . . I have just finished "Cecil Dreeme" by Winthrop, very good.[25] It's getting late, so adieu!

———

August 20th. Saturday. Rainy. Got "Jenkins" for servant, lately with Capt. Treichel.

———

Camp Battn. 3d Pa. Cavy., Hd. Qrs. A of P
In front of Petersburg, Va.
Aug. 24th, 1864

Dear Lilly:

. . . On Monday I went down to City Point and expressed to [Mother], care of WHR, $245. This is the first money I have been able to save, and I don't know but that I will have to draw on it some day. I would not have been able to save even that, if we had been paid regularly, since, having no money, we had to starve almost at times, which is a cheap way of living. I have paid off some $150 of debts, etc. and now don't owe a cent in the world.

Nothing much going on. Gen. Warren still holds his position on the Weldon RR, I believe. Gen. Averell we hear is a Major Genl., at which we are highly rejoiced—the 3d star for the 3d Pa Cavy.[26]

———

August 25th. Thursday. Warm. Went down to City Point. . . . [D]rew of Capt. Strang 8 Cavalry horses, and some horse medicine from Capt. H. B. Blood.[27] Dined on board the Sanitary Commission boat, came home, found that the battalion and rest of Household Brigade had gone out, towards the left. Hard fighting out there all day. No particulars. P.S. The enemy in force broke our picket line yesterday, and today Mott's Division, 2nd Corps, with part of our Battalion in advance, went out to establish communication. There was some terrific fighting. Barlow's Divn. 2nd Corps broke, Hancock rushed in front of his men and rallied them. In all we got the worst of it, losing 2 batteries in 2nd Corps, one of them Sleeper's. Capt. S. had gone to the rear wounded before that. This happened near Reams Station. We lost one line of breastworks.[28]

———

Camp Battn. 3d Pa. Cavy., Hd. Qrs. A.P.
Aug. 29th, 1864

Dear Mother:

The glorious 29th passed without anything extraordinary happening with the exception of a mild addition to our midday feed in the shape of watermellons at $1.50 a piece, sweet potatoes at $1.25 pr. half peck and some canned stuff.[29] . . . I recd. Lottie's and your letter of the 24th, with the cravat all right, and Lilly's of the 26th today. I also recd. this evening a pair of stockings, I suppose from you, only about 3 times too large. Some patriot will like to have them tho! The cravat is very lovely, and proportionally delicate, as I found out when I first put it on, and tore it in half. I fixed it up though and it is as nice as ever. I'm afraid I will not be able to wear it more than 2 or 3 times, as our starching and ironing facilities are not the best here "in the trenches." . . .

We hear that the Regiment, officers and men, have been mustered out. Galloway, a very amusing fellow, as soon as he gets into his "city," writes a very abusive letter to know "why the Army of the Potomac don't move?"

I have just returned from an evening ride to the front to see "a quiet night in the trenches." Hearing that the City was to be shelled at 7.20 this Eveng., Potter & I rode out and witnessed a beautiful site, but a few mortar shells coming rather unpleasantly near, we retired in good order. They are banging away everlastingly while I write, but from here, we may laugh at them.

Last evening I recd. a letter from S. W. Pettit, who is now a Lieut. in a 100 day Regt., 196th P.V., on duty at Chicago, Ill.[30] We have received over a hundred recruits for the Battalion within the last 24 hours—for a wonder a pretty good lot of men. More "food for powder." . . .[31]

Tell Sallie that, in return for wishing to send me a peach for a present, I would like to send in return a specimen of Virginia fruit which grows wild about here in the shape of a beautiful 12 pounder ball, which I use to keep papers together now on my table. It is a very pretty specimen, but the P.O., I fear, would not send it for me.

Camp Battn. 3d Pa. Cavy., Hd. Qrs. A of P

Sept. 1st, 1864

Dear Lilly:

It is your turn for a letter, as Lottie is as usual irregular. I recd. Mother's letter of the 29th last evening. I have been very busy today, as yesterday was the last of the month, and my monthly returns for Qr. Master's Prop[erty] and Clothing, Camp & Garrison Equipage are due.

Nothing much is going on. At Hd. Qrs. yesterday I heard that they are building a Rail Road to connect the City Point RR with the Norfolk RR.[32] That looks either very much like a move, or like a winter camp near here. If the latter, when it is completed, we will probably remain here until the railroad is completed, and then move more to the left, and operate better against the enemy's communications between Richmond and the South and South West.

Within the last 2 or 3 days we have recd. over 100 recruits. All of the officers and men of the Regiment were mustered out of the service were here. So "Verny" [Vernou] is blustering at Long Branch with his pretty little wife, and making himself out to be a <u>brave</u> man. You want two letters a week, so must take them as they are.

[P.S.] Please put this photograph of Lieut. Richardson of Collis' Zouaves in my album.[33]

Camp Battn. 3d Pa. Cavy.
Hd. Qrs. A of P near Petersburg
Sept. 4th 1864

Dear Mother:

   . . . Nothing much is going on to change the dull monotony of the siege. This afternoon, as one of my horses was getting pretty wild (his name is Satan, a dark bay), I rode out to the front to see things generally and to take some of the exuberance out of him. I went to the nearest part of our line to the City, from which place we can see the people walking about. It was very quiet along the line so I had a pleasant ride. The new RR is being built rapidly. We will remain here a good while I guess. Gen. Meade is home on leave, and Mrs. Genl. Grant is down here.

   The Regiment, except our Battn., was mustered out of service, officers & men, and there is much wire-pulling going on between Col. Jones & Major Robinson, which, if successful, will not do any good to our Battalion. May they never come back!

Camp Battn. 3d Pa. Cavy. Hd. Qrs. A of P
In front of Petersburg, Va.
Sept. 8th 1864

Dear Mother:

   . . . There is nothing much going on here, the new RR is completed for some distance beyond the Norfolk RR and runs out to our position on the left.

   On Sunday Eveng. [September 4] the confirmation of the taking of Atlanta, Ga. came with some particulars, and by Genl. Grant's orders, as soon as Sunday was past and Monday commencing (i.e. about 1 AM) we opened a terrific cannonade all along the line. All the bands commenced playing and the men cheering, which succeeded perfectly in keeping us awake.[34]

   Having some business connected with my Q.Mship, I went down to City Point yesterday. I met Lieut. Farley of the Ordnance Dept. in charge of the Ord. Depot there. He seems not very well pleased, to say the least of it, at having to leave his comfortable quarters at Alleghany City, and his pretty little, newly married wife (Fannie Brinley) for this. . . .[35]

Maj. Oliver Ormsby Gregg Robinson. (Courtesy Civil War Collection, US Army Heritage and Education Center, Military History Institute, Carlisle, PA)

Camp Battn. 3d Pa. Cavy. Hd. Qrs. A P
In front of Petersburg, Va.
Sunday Eveng. Sept. 11th, 1864

Dear Lottie:

. . . As you see we are still "In the trenches," and, at present, with little prospect of getting farther. Everything is hopeful though. We are getting convalescents and recruits for the Army every day, and Grant expects 50,000 more men, I believe. I suppose we will try to get into the "Cockade City" before dead winter sets in, and winter around it.

If we "ever get in" young lady, and everything goes on well, that is to say if some fatherly old gentleman relation of some of us, with & in charge of a bevy of our charming wives and sweethearts should get it into their heads to come to the "glorious Front," and we get comfortable quarters at the St. Charles, or some other house, how, young lady, would you like to join it? This was done last winter at Warrenton by a party of young ladies, sisters of Ward, Potter & the Miss Carpenter, under charge of Mr. Carpenter of Germantown, and they had a glorious time.

Unless such things <u>do</u> happen however, I would not advocate any such proceeding. (Miss Annie Criswell, with the Gov's wife and daughters, were with the army on a visit last winter also). You could have then plenty of horseback riding, and what is more, see the "sacred soil," the glorious Army of the Potomac, and the grandest siege in the history of the world! I don't suppose however that our maternal will permit any such thing. Yes, the "grandest siege in the history of the world" is not using too strong language. It is a glorious sight to behold such an army "in the trenches."

Our line now runs from somewhere near Dutch Gap on the James River, on the right, to Reams Station on the Weldon RR on the left. Our position is said to be impregnable by the best engineers, and the enemy's equally as strong. From an old rebel work, on a hill where Gen. Birney, Comdg. 10th Corps, has his Hd. Qrs., we have a splendid view of the city, and a beautiful place it is. But to get a still better view we take advantage of a little quiet, ride out a little beyond this hill along the City Point RR where it runs into the city, dismount and walk out to the picket lines on the RR. With my glasses I can distinctly see the people walking the streets, etc., and it makes us think "will we ever get in?"

Each army has a strong picket line, with the main army in close supporting distance. Every man on picket has his own little gabion and breastwork, and all sorts of devices are made use of by the antagonists (every man has his own) to bring his "friend on the other side" to expose himself, and then they pop away.

Some scenes are very amusing. During the night, sometimes, they will make a figure of a man, dress him in uniform, put a musket across his arms and stand him up; attached to his hand, which works on a pivot, they fasten wires. They then wait "till daylight doth appear." As soon as the rebs can make out this man, standing here so unconcernedly, they pop away at him. The men at the wires pull his head in the direction of the man who fires. After a while the rebs get firing lively, and our men take advantage of their exposing themselves and give them a pop in return.

At first, there was much more firing than now. When the new pickets came out, which had to be done always at the very darkest part of the night, the first thing a man did was to take his spoon out and dig away to make a snug nest for himself. He then would set to work scientifically to find out where his particular antagonist lay. He would hold his hat on his gun and move it gently, just as if he were digging away. Presently there would be a pop and down goes his hat with a hole through it. He would be on the watch to see where his man lay, and then again use his devices to get him to expose himself.

The men used to amuse themselves by making miniature mortars out of their pipes, and sending miniature little balls over into the enemy's lines. Many other amusing incidents happen among the pickets. Now there is a much better feeling between the pickets, and "swops" are frequent. This is only among the white troops, tho! Where the negro troops occupy the line, they are banging away unendingly, as at the present moment. We often get Richmond papers of that same day, both by the intercourse of the pickets and by the deserters, who come in every day.

Along the line every tent has its bomb-proof, for protection against the enemy's shells, which are continually flying about. These bomb proofs are caves, dug underground with small apertures, and as soon as the shells begin to fly about regardlessly, in the men pop and are safe. Every available place, artificial or natural, is bristling with heavy guns and mortars.

We hold the Weldon RR at and about Reams Statn., but the enemy use this all important road beyond our position, and still get their supplies from that quarter by teaming around our line. The other day Gregg at a gallop rode in between the Reb Cavalry and infantry, expecting to capture one of their trains, but he was a little too early, or too late, and had to come back, at a gallop also, as the Reb infantry moved around in force to intercept him.

The new RR, which runs a short distance from here, is completed, and runs as far as the Weldon RR, where we are now expecting a Field Depot. In front of here, the Road is plainly visible to the enemy, and they bang away at every train, sometimes hitting them, and sometimes sending their shells and shot among our camps here. When every train passes we look out for them.[36]

Now haven't you had enough of a letter for one night? I would ruin the San[itary] Commission at this rate, and with a bad pen it is hard work writing. . . .

———

September 13th. Tuesday. Fine day. Took a ride out to 10th Corps lines in the evening and made a visit to Col. Counselman of the 1st Md. Cavy. (dismounted) in the trenches.[37]

September 14th. Wednesday. Fine Day. . . . Everybody seems to be going into Autumn quarters. It is supposed that Grant will try to get Petersburg before winter. The Rebs still continue to throw shells and Whitworth bolts at the R.R. Cars, and they occasionally give us a taste of their gentle reminders. Meade was very mad at finding the R.R. was built in front and not in rear of his Hd. Qrs., while he was at home. Some talk of its being changed.

———

Camp Bttn. 3d Pa. Cavy. Hd. Qrs. AP
Sept. 15th, 1864

Dear Mother:

. . . There is nothing going on outside of the usual course of events. The officers of our regiment are busy at work administering the Oath of Allegiance to all persons inside of our lines, according to Gen. Grant's orders. Those who will not take it are to be sent, free of charge, either to Washington or into the enemy's lines, as they desire.[38]

The officers of our Regiment who went home are, a great many of them, endeavoring to get into the service again, principally the State service. We hear that Col. Jones has authority to raise a regiment, as also Lieut. Galloway. Cauffman is to raise a squadron of Cavalry. . . . [39]

Camp Battn. 3d. Pa. Cavy. Hd. Qrs. A of P
Before Petersburg, Va.
Sept. 18th, 1864 Sunday Eveng.

Dear Mother:

. . . We are still in the same place, all rumors to our having moved across the James notwithstanding. Some people around here are building Winter Quarters, and at City Point they have orders so to do, but the impression is that we will try to get Petersburg before wintering. If so we will have to move.

On Friday [September 16] we had a little "divarshin" to change the monotony of things generally. Doubtless you have heard me speak of the Army Cattle Herd near Cocke's Mills. Until the Regiment went home we had a battn. there doing Guard duty, but when the change took place, a squadron of the 13th Pa. Cavy. relieved us. At daybreak 3 Brigades of Rebel Cavalry and one of infantry broke the picket line there, capturing and knocking the mischief out of the 1st Dist. of Columbia Cavy., on picket, attacked the Cattle Herd, and captured the whole of it, 2500 head.

The squadron of the 13th Pa. Cavy. made a good fight, but of course were overpowered. They then made a diversion upon Pr. Geo. C.H. and City Point, but only to gain time. Kautz's Divn. & Gregg's Divn. of Cavalry and some infantry started in pursuit, Gregg endeavoring to head them off. Our Battn. also started out and scoured the country from Jordan's Pt. to C.H. The pursuit did not commence till 8 AM, consequently they got a good start on us. So we did not succeed in retaking them. It was a great mistake in having the Cattle Herd where it was, on Jordan's Pt. on the James. An attack was feared at City Point, and everything was ready for them, gunboats in position, etc. but they were a little too wise. . . .[40]

I bought a set of chess men at City Point the other day, and we non-poker players amuse ourselves in that way at odd times. McClellan stock is very low in the army since his acceptance of Vallandingham Platform, and Lincoln stock up proportionately. I never thought George B. would forsake his friends that way. . . .

———

September 20th. Tuesday. Fine day. Two more companies were organized to-day, "C" & "F," and Lieuts. Potter and Carter recommended to the Governor for Captaincies, myself, Ward, and Gregg for 1st Lieutenants and Sergts. Humphries, Ewing, Frazer and Hayden for 2nd Lieutenancies.[41] There are 45 more recruits assigned temporarily to different companies, until 37 more come, when another company will be organized, for me as Captain, I suppose. . . .

September 21st. Wednesday. Fine Day. . . . Lieut. Carter assumed command of his new Co. "C," and I of "B" to see to the rights of my Company. I am still Q.M. and only nominally in command of "B." Lieut. Carter and I, who have been together for a long time, notwithstanding his extreme selfishness, could not part without another of our numerous rows; consequently we had it hot and heavy. Ward and I concluded to split partnership entirely and are going to run a new mess of our own.

———

Camp Battn. 3d Pa. Cavy.
Before Petersburg, Va., Sep. 22nd, 1864

Dear Mother:

. . . As far as we can tell, the feeling, in politics, is against McClellan, owing to his having something to do with the Chicago Platform. Tho' partial to McClellan personally, I think that a change would be prejudicial to the good of the cause. Consequently if I take advantage of my right of "exercising the election franchise," as all the Penna troops are allowed to vote, I don't know yet whether I will or not. I don't like much the idea of soldiers meddling with politics.[42]

Tell Uncle Wm. that I don't think that I am indebted to the Government, but I am responsible for property fully to the amount he mentioned, $500,000. I am very careful about my papers and returns, always making them out myself and not relying upon my clerk, thereby having them done to my satisfaction. Every officer that was mustered out was in trouble, as they had to have certificates from the Ordnance and Q.M. Depts. that they were not indebted to the U.S. Some can't get any pay at all. In the Ord. Dept. especially they are very strict, and we are caught up often for losing the smallest screw. A company commander of Cavalry is responsible for U.S. Propy. to the amount of $30,000 or $40,000 at least, and it is not at all dishonorable to be what you would call defaulting. . . .

McIntosh distinguished himself up in the Valley. We hear that he has lost his leg, a dear price for his Brigadier's star. Nothing much going on. Yesterday at 7 AM by Grant's order a salute of 100 shotted guns was fired from the batteries along the line in honor of the victory in the Valley. It kicked up a good muss. . . .[43]

———

Camp Battn. 3d Pa. Cavy.
Before Petersburg, Va.
Sept. 25th, 1864 Sunday Eveng.

Dear Lottie:

. . . Nothing much going on at present, except for the visit of the Pay Masters. Ours has not appeared.

There is something up. Butler, on the right, has been banging away pretty hard, and different corps and divisions are changing positions. All Quarter Masters are ordered to have nothing superfluous on hand, and everything indicated the opening of the Fall campaign. We can't go very far, unless we recross the James, which is not probable. I suppose we will try to take the Enemy's position, by either flank.

Monday Eveng. I was interrupted last eveng. . . . Our Pay Master will pay us tomorrow for July & August. Ain't this new income tax a humbug? I hear they are going to tax us at 5 p[er] c[ent] for the last 18 months but I don't know about it. . . .[44]

Camp before Petersburg, Va.
Sept. 28th Eveng.

Dear Mother:

I have just recd. your letter of the 25th. We were paid off yesterday, and today sent $150.00 pr Adams Expr. Receipt enclosed herein. I fear I will soon have to call on you for some of this money, as I have run some $20 short, in sending money home for my men, consequently it will come out of my pocket. The coupon notes I don't understand. All I know about them is that they are of a very clumsy size.

Considerable fighting is going on tonight. The whole army has orders to be in readiness to move at 4 AM, and these Hd. Qrs. at 6. We are going to have a stiff old battle tomorrow. It will have to be the decision whether we are to have Petersburg this winter or not. The rebs have sent 2 divisions from our front, consequently Grant wants to give them a tug. Our orders to move are most probably for the purpose of following up if the line is broken. No one knew anything about the stir until after dark. I think the main attack will be on the right and the right centre. I will write as soon as possible.

An undated wartime photograph of William Brooke Rawle. (From Regimental History Committee, *History of the Third Pennsylvania Cavalry* [1905])

Head Qrs. Hancock's (2nd) Corps A of P
Before Petersburg, Va.
Oct. 3d, 1864

Dear Lottie:

. . . You seem to be greatly scared about my saying I did not feel very well the other day. It turned out to be nothing, though I myself thought I was going to have bilious fever. I had a little attack of it, but was getting better, and sleeping in my overcoat out in the open air last night made me much better. . . .

I wrote to Mother on Wednesday [September 28], stating that we expected to move next morning. Hd. Qrs. was in readiness to move all day and night until yesterday (Sunday) to the Gurley House, somewhere between the Jerusalem Plank Road and the Weldon RR. But not so with us. On account of the combined movements on both flanks, all the troops had to be taken, as also Kautz's Cavy., which protected the rear of the Army, consequently the "Household Brigade" had to get into their fighting duds and go out there to bleed for their country. Our regiment is still doing picket duty at and around Prince George CH.

Yesterday when Hd. Qrs. moved I (being a demoralized Quarter Master) was ordered to take my train out to the Regiment. Last night I parked about ¾ of a mile in rear of it, barricaded myself, and had a strong camp guard of teamsters, blacksmiths, etc. for my protection. The guerillas troubled our pickets a good deal, but not me.

This morning I had to go to Gen. Hancock's Hd. Qrs. and also Gen. Gibbon's, of 2nd Corps, for ammunition, and I had a considerable talk with them both at Gibbon's Hd. Qrs. The regiment is now, "<u>pro temp</u>," during the "Emergency" under the orders of Gen. Hancock. As a wagon train is a rather lumberly thing to do picket with, I moved this afternoon to this place, where I will await further orders, or until the Regiment is relieved. Gen. Hancock's Hd. Qrs. are <u>near</u> the crossing of the Norfolk RR and the new City Point RR.

I am unable as yet to get any definite intelligence from the flanks. On Sept. 30th, our pickets on the right were in sight of Richmond. The movement was very successful. On the left where the hardest fighting was, we drove the enemy. Gregg's Divn. has had some terrific fighting, having been attacked by Hampton in force, but he (Gregg) knocked the "slathers" out of him. I have just received a report, but it cannot be vouched for, that we have advanced so far on the left that our left is on the upper Appomattox, and that we hold the South Side RR, the one we have been wishing most to get, and the most important one the Rebs have. I don't believe the report, but give it for what it is worth.[45]

On Wednesday I wrote to mother enclosing a receipt for $150, sent per Adams Express. Tell her to pay Hoyt a bill of $37.75 for a coat he made for Dr. Durant, and for which he paid me. I recd. the caps on Friday. They were exactly what I wanted. I have not heard from the 6th Penna. Cavy. since it was mustered out of service. Charley Leiper, Carrie tells me, is Major in command of the Vet Battn. Has Will White left the service? When I saw him last he was desirous of leaving it. I feel very tired so must close.

Camp 3d Pa. Cavy. Hd. Qrs. A of P
Before Petersburg, Va. near
the Gurley House[46]
Oct. 6th, 1864

Dear Mother:

Allow me to congratulate you on the promotion of your dutiful son. Today I was mustered in as 1st Lieutenant of Compy. "B." We all have recd. a "highest." Carter and Potter are Captains, Ward and myself 1st Lieutenants, and Sergeants Frazer, Humphries, Hayden and Ewing are 2nd Lieutenants.

Nothing much is going on. Our regiment has been on picket for 6 days, during the Emergency, and was relieved yesterday, returning to these Hd. Qrs., which we found about 4 miles from our old camp, about ¾ of a mile from the junction of the Weldon RR and City Point RR. We have advanced our line here a little during the late battle. Butler still holds his position on Chaffin's Bluff, about 6 miles from Richmond on the right. . . .

I have recd. the caps and they are the envy and admiration of all. They are pronounced decidedly "nobby." They are for Lts. Gregg, Ward and myself. . . . I am Acting Quarter Master, and consequently not very belligerent, but as I never entered the army to keep shop, I hope soon to get out of it, but how, more hereafter, if all goes well. . . . We're not in Richmond quite yet, and, to all intents and purposes, as far off as ever.

As my commission is a valuable document, and one I don't wish to lose, I send it enclosed, to put with my first one, to be kept safely. The army is strong for Lincoln. McClellan stock is low, very low. I do not yet know whether I will vote or not. . . .

———

October 6th. Thursday. . . . Major Walsh told me today that he was going to organize a company for me and asked what letter I wished. I chose "D." . . .

October 7th. Friday. . . . I chose from the unassigned recruits, by ballot, 82 men for my Company.

October 9th. Sunday. Organized my Company today. Put Sergt. Woods (late a Captain commanding 69 Regt. P.V.) as Orderly Sergt.[47] Material very good for a Company. Put it in camp in rear of Regiment.

———

Camp Battn. 3d Pa. Cavy.
Near Parke's St. Before Petersburg, Va.[48]
Oct. 10th, 1864

Dear Mother:

. . . We are encamped about a half a mile from the City Point and Army RR, but as it is not a very nice place, we have been expecting Hd. Qrs. to move beyond the Weldon RR. A negro brigade of Ferrero's was camped here before we came, and consequently it was a filthy hole, but we have improved it greatly. . . .

The men who are appointed to superintend the voting of the Penna Soldiers came here today, with Poll books, etc. and copies of the acts relative to the matter, and if we only knew who were running for the county offices, we company commanders would have a hard job of it tomorrow. But neither do I care or know who wants to get the position of senior cook to the junior clerk of the Coroner or Sheriff. The Presidential election takes place next month sometime, and then we may expect some work. McClellan stock is very low in the army.[49]

We are having very cold nights now, and an extra blanket is very acceptable. I have nothing much to write about. Oh, by the bye, please send over by mail a copy of "Kautz's Manual for the Company Clerk." They are to be had at T. B. Peterson's.[50]

Camp Battn. 3d Pa. Cavy.
Hd. Qrs. A of P, near Eakin [Aiken's] House
Before Petersburg, Va.
Sat. Oct. 15th, 1864

Dear Mother:

I have not written to you since Monday, as I have been rather busy, I having both the Quarter Master Department and my new company, "D" to attend to.

I recd. your letter of Oct. 9th on Thursday. I am very glad indeed that you have recovered from your indisposition. Don't be alarmed about me as I am all "O.K." For a few days I thought I was going to have a nasty little old <u>sick,</u> but I got better as soon as we began to rough it a little more than usual. I had a little attack of jaundice, and for a while was as yellow as my shoulder straps. Dr. Durant thanks you much for your offer, and says that he will take good care of your boy for you.

Who tells you that the 3d Pa. Cavy. will be taken into the Regular Army? Every Regiment says the same thing. To be sure our Regiment, it has been declared by those competent to judge, is the very best in the United States service, the Regulars not being excepted. To be sure we are often called the "3d Regulars."[51] I don't think any Regiments, as organizations, will be taken into the Regular Army, but there will have to be a reconstruction, reorganization and increase in it, and I would then, if all goes well, like to be transferred to it with my rank. If nothing turns up to prevent me, or change my mind, I want to see this war out. It seems to be the opinion that the Rebs are about used up. Well, so they have been for the last 3 years, but they manage to keep us at bay pretty well notwithstanding.

Four or five days ago it was rumored that Grant expected to be in Richmond in 2 weeks, but as yet there are no signs of it. I believe that the 6th and 19th Corps are expected soon, and if pushed suddenly on our right we may "get in."

There is nothing much going on. I have been busy all day fixing up my tent, and making myself comfortable for these cold nights and mornings, that is to say, having a floor laid and a brick chimney built. We may have to move soon, and it may be all to no purpose but, "Dum vivimus" is the best motto for a soldier.[52]

The election in the army went off very quietly. None of us officers bothered ourselves about it, but let the men manage it among themselves. Capt. Stillé returned from 20 days sick leave yesterday.

I don't like bothering you so much, but I can't do them for myself down here, so must ask you to do a few things for me. Please order at Hoyt's for me a fine dark blue beaver vest, double breasted (for cold weather) the two rows of 7 buttons each fine <u>raised</u> cavalry buttons, very narrow standing collar, the vest to be made according to my measure of Feb. 11th last. Also please [buy] at Lambert's two more English fatigue caps, No. 6⅞ and 7⅛. The one of 7⅛ I want for myself to be of fine dark blue cloth, the side to be of leather or other stiffening, not pasteboard which breaks badly. To be trimmed with black braid in every respect like the others you got, except for the braid on top to be gilt and 2 braids. The one of 6⅞ to be just like those you got for me last. Please send all these things by mail as soon as possible, and take the "wherewithal" you have from mine. Excuse the trouble I give you.

———

Oct. 17th. Monday. I am kept pretty busy now. Drill twice a day, besides attending to Q.M., Commissary and Ordnance Departments of the Regiment.

Oct. 18th. Tuesday. In the morning Dr. Durant and I went down to City Point on the R.R. I went down to attend to several things, especially to get Gen. Ingalls approval of a requisition for 54 horses. His A.A.G. would not give it to me, as all horses had been ordered to be supplied to Gen. Gregg, but me and the General had a talk and he approved it and ordered Capt. Strang to let me have the first lot he received.

———

Camp Battn. 3d Pa. Cavy. Hd. Qrs. A of P
near Aiken's House, Before Petersburg, Va.
Oct. 19th, 1864

Dear Lilly:

I received your letter last evening, on returning from a journey to City Point, whither business of various kinds had called me. I call it a journey, for we now go on the Army RR, and not on horseback as formerly, because it is about 16 miles. Until lately it was about as much as a man's life was worth to ride on the breakneck concern, & almost every train ran off or smashed up or got shelled by the enemy, but now they have fixed things better, and have built high earthworks where the RR was exposed to the enemy's fire.

For a while we expected a grand move upon the arrival of the 6th & 19th Corps, but this evening I hear that the 6th has been ordered back.[53] We are fixed up pretty comfortably now, with floors & fireplaces in our tents. The nights here are very cold at this season of the year.

I am very busy now, and deeply mixed up with red tape, drawing horses for remounts, ordnance & ordnance stores, Clothing, Camp & Garrison Equipage, Quarter Masters Stores, etc. besides having my company to attend to, which keeps me pretty busy. . . .

Nothing much is going on here. There is a very unusual quietness along the lines. The Secretary of War and a lot of other big bugs paid us a visit here a few days ago.[54] I have nothing to fill a second letter during one week with, as everything is so dull.

Camp, Hd. Qrs. Army of Potomac
Before Petersburg, Va.
Oct. 24th, 1864

Dear Mother:

. . . I recd. your letter of the 20th yesterday morning. I recd. the copy of Kautz's "Company Clerk" and am very much obliged. All these things I ask you to get for me I want you to pay for out of the money I sent home. Of course I expect you to break the notes. What in the world is the use of my getting any money if I can't spend it? I don't want to be under any obligations to WHR and would prefer your taking one of my notes. I have not a cent to spare, as things cost tremendously here. Dr. Durant paid me his bill to Hoyt, and as otherwise I would have had to send home for money. I took it, and told you to pay the bill out of my money. I did not calculate enclosing any when I sent home part of my last pay. I will try hereafter to send home $50 per month, but I doubt if I can. What do you think of paying $8.00 for a pair of gauntlets and the same for a pair of shoulder straps? Butter .80 per lb., sweet potatoes 6 cts apiece, etc. . . .

You know I always had some difficulty in hearing, but it is now no worse than formerly. About this time of year only, I am troubled with the old running at the ear. My eyes have improved wonderfully since I made a practice of not using spectacles. When I want to see anything at a distance I use my field glasses, which I have conveniently attached at my belt.

Aunt Juliet is greatly mistaken in thinking, because the soldiers won't as a general thing vote for McClellan, that there is unfairness in the matter. McClellan has no show whatsoever in the army now.

Nothing much is going on, but it is rumored that a general movement will take place in a few days. Sheridan, "Cavalry Sheridan," is doing well up in the valley. My old classmate at college Harvey Fisher is very near us with his Regt. (Lang. Wistar's). He is a 1st Lieut.[55]

Oh, by the bye, part of the insides of my revolver are out of order, and of course I must fix it myself. Please get for me from Krider's, NE cor. 2nd & Walnut, a dog & spring exactly the size of the enclosed. It is part of the arrangement that makes the cylinder work. Tell him to let you have a good strong one, and please send it to me as soon as possible. It is for the Manhattan fire arm Co.'s pistol, 5 inch barrel, 5 chambers cal. 36 (same as Colt's Navy Pistol).

———

Sheridan's triumphs in the Valley and Sherman's capture of Atlanta in early September had alleviated much of the pressure that had been building on the Lincoln administration for battlefield victories and effectively squelched any momentum that McClellan and the Peace Democrats had gained in the presidential race. Nonetheless, with an eye toward bolstering Lincoln's chances in the coming election, Grant launched his Sixth Offensive—which in its design and objective was similar to the Fifth Offensive—on October 27, less than two weeks before the vote.

On the Petersburg front, soldiers from three different corps plus Gregg's cavalry division would move west and attempt to sever two key Southern supply lines, the Boydton Plank Road and the South Side Railroad. Simultaneously east of Richmond, Butler and the Army of the James would launch a secondary attack intended to prevent reinforcements from being sent to aid the Petersburg defenders. That Grant and Meade had high hopes for this attack is evidenced by the fact that they committed over 45,000 men against the Petersburg defenders alone. The IX Corps was to push out along the Confederate right, which was protecting the Boydton Plank Road, followed by the V and II Corps, which were to extend to their left, pivoting on the IX and sweeping around to the west and north. Gregg's troopers would cover the far left flank of these forces. The 3rd Pennsylvania briefly manned trenches abandoned by the infantry; acted as escorts for Grant and Meade, who accompanied the movement; scouted in advance of the V Corps during the early stages of the offensive; and later acted as rear guard to drive up stragglers at the close of the brief campaign.[56]

———

> Camp Battn. 3d. Pa. Cavy. Hd. Qrs. A of P
> near Aiken's House
> Oct. 29th, 1864

Dear Mother:

Since I last wrote to you on Monday we have had a campaign, short but by no means sweet, consequently I have not been able to write.

Early on Wednesday morning [October 26] we recd. orders to move, everything sent to the rear, all the wagons going to City Point, & Hd. Qrs. taking nothing but a few spring wagons. Hd. Qrs. moved to Poplar Grove Church, near the left of our line, and bivouacked for the night.[57] Before daybreak of Thursday (27th), the 2nd & 5th Corps started out, with 4 days rations, for one of Grant's old left flank movements. Our regiment, dismounted, the 114th P.V. & 68th P.V., i.e. the "Household Brigade" were ordered to occupy the line of works forming the left of the line.

About 12 M. our Regiment was ordered to report to Gen. Warren, I suppose to advance on the left flank of the 5th Corps, until the 2nd Corps, which moved by a back road, should connect with it. We escorted Gens. Grant & Meade, who, I suppose, went to hunt up the 2nd Corps, but on arriving on the left of the 5th Corps, we found that the 2nd had already made connection. This was about 2 miles beyond the crossing of the telegraph road over Hatcher's Creek [Run]. We had driven the enemy this far, about 8 miles, until they were found in large force behind strong works.

We then returned with the Generals to the "Armstrong House" near the [Run], where Gen. Meade's Hd. Qrs. were for the night, Gen. Grant going back to City Point, & Capts. Stillé & Carter, with their companies, being sent out to picket in rear, on the Vaughn Road, and the left of the 2nd Corps which formed a horse shoe.[58] We passed a very rough night of it, as it poured very hard, and our led horses did not come up till midnight. I went to sleep under a small shelter tent with 2 fence rails for a bed, and a cup of water and a pipe for my dinner & supper.

Friday the 28th was a beautiful day. Finding that the enemy had anticipated us, the army, early in the morning, began to fall back. The 2 remaining companies, Hess's & mine (I having sent my wagons to the rear went out with my company), remained near the bridge on Hatcher's Run supporting our pickets. Our orders were to wait until the 2nd & 5th Corps had fallen back, and then follow in rear of the 2nd Corps, driving up all stragglers. Both Corps crossed the bridge (on the Telegraph Road), the 5th first, which took the direct road running into our line of works, and the 2nd Corps moving by a wood road running from the Telegraph Road near the run to the Vaughn Road, about ¾ of a mile off, which ran parallel with it.

Both columns of infantry were about a mile beyond us, we being left in the extreme rear, when Carter's pickets beyond the bridge were driven in and immediately charged by a brigade of splendid rebel cavalry in column. Stillé was at the junction of the Vaughn and Wood roads. Hess was immediately ordered up to support Carter, and I [was ordered] to throw out a strong skirmish line to protect his left flank. They charged us so quickly and in such force that I recd. orders almost immediately to fall back on the 2nd Corps on the Vaughn Road.[59] I gave the order to "Rally on the reserve" at a gallop, when a strong skirmish line of dismounted cavalry appeared 100 yds. before me, which immediately charged with their demoniacal yell. According to orders I fell back at a trot & joined Capt. Stillé, at the junction of the roads, who had not yet been attacked. We then fell back on the infantry, driving up the stragglers and helping the wounded along, the two other companies, Carter's & Hess's, following the 5th Corps, we being cut off from them.

When our column had fallen back about 2 miles, we still in rear, we met 2 regiments of Gregg's Divn. going out to picket. They afterwards had a skirmish. Very luckily, we got in all right, and waited at the "Yellow House," on the Weldon RR, where the [rail]roads met, while the rest of the regiment came up.[60] On their part, they had a considerable skirmish, as also the infantry on which they fell back.

Carter had his horse badly wounded, and one man of "M" slightly wounded. We returned to our old camp near the "Aiken House," which we had left, never expecting to see it again.[61]

Gen. Gregg during the movement had a pretty lively fight, and his new brigade (3rd) consisting of new troops were pretty badly scattered. In the expedition we took about 900 prisoners but lost the same number, and had to leave most of our wounded behind, as very few ambulances were taken along.[62] Altogether the movement was a failure. I saw, several days before the movement took place, a statement in a Richmond paper that we were going to make that movement, and consequently they were prepared for it.

So our campaign, which was to lower the price of gold and increase the enthusiasm for Lincoln and discourage the McClellanism, was unsuccessful. We were all very glad to get back to our chimneys.

On Tuesday I recd. the two English fatigue caps. They are so much admired that most probably I will have to send for more. Please don't forget to send the spring for my revolver. It is not exactly a kind of purchase to ask a lady to make, but I have no one else to ask to get it. I want it very badly, as my pistol won't work, which circumstance, with having a company consisting entirely of new recruits, is not very well adapted to give one much confidence in a fight.

[P.S.] 9 PM

Merely to prevent mistakes, as I don't wish to end our correspondence, please direct hereafter to "Captain" Wm. Rawle Brooke!!! I have this moment received my commission as Captain of Co. "D." You may have wondered at my commanding a company and being Q.M. also, but I did the first to look out for my own interests. . . .

Camp Battn. 3d Pa. Cavy.
Oct. 30th, 1864

Dear Mother:

I wrote to you yesterday about our late expedition, and in a postscript said that I had that moment received my commission as Captain of Co. "D." It came just after I had closed & posted the letter, but I had just time to get it back & tell you.

Please take the enclosed 1st Lieut's shoulder straps to Lamberti's and have them made into a Captain's, that is, have the additional bar on each end put on, exactly like the other, which means that the wearer is a big Cavalry Captain. Please send them to me as soon as possible as it will save me $6 or $8.

Everything is lovely, and there is a prospect of our staying "in statu quo" for some time.

Camp 3d Pa. Cav. Hd. Qrs. A of P

Nov. 4th, 1864

Dear Mother:

I have just received your letter of Nov. 1st, 1864, and also a copy of "Maurice Tiernay," which I am very glad indeed to get, but was it intended for Maurice Dering by the author of Guy Livingston? I hear that he has written another book and have been trying to find out the name in order to send for it. He is one of my favorite authors and I have bought about half a dozen copies of "Barren Honour" down here. It is the only one of his books I have ever seen the Hd. Qrs. newspaper man have. I got a copy of Thackeray's "Irish Sketch Book" there, and am now reading it, that is when I get the time.[63]

The vest came all right on Saty. Eveng. and is much admired. Carter, 5 minutes before I recd. it, said that it was foolish to get a double breasted one, but no sooner had he seen it than he offered me $15 cash for it, and bothered me until I wrote to Hoyt to send one exactly like it. I never get anything but he must have one exactly like it, so we always dress exactly alike. Don't think it is all dressing down here. I suppose you do, as I have sent for so many things for myself and others, but we always keep our fighting clothes ready, and when we don them there is nothing very dandyish about us. When we turn out for Inspection, Review, Parades, etc. however, you would say that the U.S. army is much better organized than the English from "Vere Egerton's" accounts of "Ropsley" and others.[64] The dress suit I got last February has been so little worn that it looks perfectly new, notwithstanding the numerous knocks and tumbles my not very extensive "transportation" has received.

I have also recd. the pistol spring which works to a T. My fellow officers laughed heartily at the idea of sending part of my pistol to a lady to have fixed, but I have no one else to ask.

Many thanks for the congratulations. We have had several changes in the Reg't. Maj. Walsh is now Lieut. Colonel, Capt. Hess, Major and Ward & I Captains. I have no Lieutenants in my Company of 93 men, and am very hard worked. We have no non-commissioned officers we can promote, as very few make good officers. We have had several examples of fine Sergeants being spoiled by making them officers. Col. Walsh is very particular about whom he has for his officers, and if anyone don't suit, he will soon get him out of the Reg't. He wants some of our citizen friends to accept commissions, but we know of none. He says that the citizen appointments have made such fine officers, and indeed have given the name to the "Third Cavalry," that his ideas have changed a great deal. Indeed all the officers he selected from the Reg't. to remain with him were outsiders except one, who was only commissioned a day or two before, and had to be kept. . . .[65]

There is not any news. We are mostly building log huts, although we don't expect to winter exactly <u>here,</u> but "dum vivemus—suppose we be comfortable." I suppose you think that a canvas roof and comfort are incompatible, but a person's ideas alter materially when he "goes for a sojer." I wonder if Uncle Wm. has changed his mind regarding me since I've come into the army, and risen about as high as I or anyone else can expect? You know I never was good for anything. Ask without letting him know I said anything about it.

Write soon. The Lt. Col. has just come in for our nightly game of <u>checkers,</u> so I must close.

CHAPTER SEVEN

Winter at Petersburg

November 6, 1864–March 11, 1865

The cold air of early November portended the onset of a change in seasons, prompting the soldiers gathered around Petersburg to prepare winter quarters. The presidential election was foremost in the minds of many, and while sympathetic in spirit to McClellan and the Democrats, Rawle would have to decide whether their platform merited his support.

With active combat operations waning, the energies of the men of the 3rd Pennsylvania were directed to intelligence gathering; escorting prisoners to Washington, DC; and scouting expeditions that took them across the James River and over the old Peninsula Campaign battlefields southeast of Richmond. Much to his satisfaction, Rawle was relieved of his onerous position as regimental quartermaster and returned to company command, first with Company D at Meade's headquarters and later with Company B, assigned to Grant's headquarters at City Point. Adding to his contentment, Rawle was able to see his family in Philadelphia twice during this time: the first trip home was a furtive, unauthorized absence, while the second visit was sanctioned through regular channels.

Militarily, the four and a half months between November 1864 and mid-March 1865 were far less eventful than the first four and a half months the armies had spent confronting each other at Petersburg. Grant, however, continually sought opportunities to restrict the flow of supplies into the Cockade City. The early December Hicksford Raid—which devolved into a nasty affair punctuated by murder, arson, and pillage—and the Seventh Offensive in early February allowed the Federal general in chief to tighten his grip on Petersburg. Desertions among the Southerners increased as the winter progressed, further sapping Lee's already understrength Army of Northern Virginia, while on the other side of the ledger, the Army of the

Potomac added thousands of one-year recruits and gained over 16,000 veterans when the VI Corps returned from the Shenandoah Valley in December.

———

Camp 3d Pa. Cavy. H Qrs. AP
Nov. 7th, 1864
Monday Eve

Dear Lottie:

... With this letter I send some old copies of the "Petersburg Express" which may be a curiosity to you. So you went to Peterson's and read "Maurice Tiernay" for "M. Dering" and sent it to me. I was just wanting a book and if you would send me the latter (which I wish you would) I will have <u>two</u> books, quite a library in the army. Down here, as soon as you read a book, you give it to someone else to read, and that is the last seen of it. But I will keep the book very quietly if you send it to me. I recd. the vest from Hoyt all right. I wish you would send the shoulder straps on as soon as possible.

Tell Lilly that I am no longer a demoralized Quarter Master; also no wonder that she could not find "Eakin's Court House," there is no such place that I know of. The Aiken House is just opposite to Hd. Qrs., and is where a family of Aiken's live. Last night [November 6] I paid them a visit decidedly disagreeable to both

The Aiken House near Petersburg, which Rawle searched on November 6, 1864. (Courtesy Prints and Photographs Division, Library of Congress)

parties. Being "Officer of the Day," I recd. orders from the Provost Marshall General to perform a strictly secret and very delicate duty, viz, to search the house from roof to cellar, and also the persons of the inhabitants, consisting of one elderly lady and six young ones, some of them very pretty. They are suspected of carrying on a correspondence with the enemy, and of giving them information of our late move in time for them to be ready for us.

I, with one of the best of Gen. Patrick's scouts, searched every nook and corner of the house, putting all the inhabitants in one room under guard, and I read every document in the house. Think of my having to go through all of the young ladies' love letters, etc. and examining their persons ("go away man, you make me blush") for treasonable documents. Isn't that romantic now? . . . I would have given up 6 months pay rather than do it, but orders must be obeyed. I took the old lady around with me to see that nothing was taken or disturbed except some <u>billy duxes</u> which I quietly put into my pocket.[1] I was at it till midnight, when I left, leaving a guard there to keep them under surveillance.[2]

I have a nice day's job for tomorrow. Some copperheads, election men, have been through the Reg't, quietly, and the McClellan feeling is very strong, so tomorrow I will have to challenge every vote in the company, 96 men. . . .[3]

Camp 3d Pa. Cavy.
Nov. 12th, 1864
Eveng.

Dear Mother:

Last evening I received your letter of [the] 8th, and Lottie's of [the] 9th enclosing the shoulder straps, which have been spoilt by some careless person, being covered with ink. I recd. also the copy of Maurice Dering, which I have just finished. I like it immensely, as, indeed, I do all works by the same author.[4] I am afraid I will not be able to keep it very long, as I have promised to lend it to everyone. Books, like tobacco, in the army, are common property. . . .

The election in camp [on November 8] passed off very quietly—no disturbances whatever. I was presiding judge of the election in my company. I accepted the nomination as I knew they were strong for McClellan and I heard rumors of illegalities at the October elections, and I did not want that to be said this time. It was the most <u>democratic</u> (in the sense we use the word, i.e. without discipline) thing I ever did, coming in so close contact with my men off duty. My company, composed in great part of Schuylkill & York County men, miners, etc. went for McClellan 42 to 14. The Regiment went for McClellan by about [an] 80[-vote] majority, I'm very sorry to say. All the officers however voted for Lincoln, which shows well for the discipline of the Regiment, that is, that officers and men never have the slightest familiarity between them. The army however went for Lincoln, strong. I of course voted for "old Abe" because I think the administration should be upheld at all hazzards. When anyone attempts anything he ought to carry it through. It is the only way to succeed in the army.

———

November 8th. Tuesday. Election Day for President of the U.S. The Pennsylvania and New York soldiers were allowed to vote, and though canvassing was prohibited there were a good many commissioners and party agents down here. To prevent any fraud I was elected one of the three Judges of "D" Co. I voted for Lincoln and Johnson, my first vote, but the Company, mostly being York and Schuylkill County men, went for McClellan, and carried the polls 14 to 42. The Regiment went for Mc-Clellan on account of the many recruits. Jerry McKibbin of Philadelphia, a strong Democrat, was down as a commissioner, and to prevent his electioneering we kept him here at the 3rd until he was pretty tight, and he remained all day.[5] It is supposed the Army will go for Lincoln by about 2500 majority.[6]

———

Poor old "Pickaxe" is no longer in my possession. He became almost blind from some eye disease, and when going fast would stumble very badly—once or twice falling on his head and nearly breaking my neck. He never could see a ditch or fence, and consequently would not jump, so I was under the necessity (after keeping him for several months, for the sake of his past services, to try and cure him, but he got no better), to reduce him to the ranks and give him to someone less ambitious.

I have now the two finest horses in the Regiment, a thoroughbred Virginia mare named "Carrie!," a splendid animal and for which several times I have been offered $250, and a fine little dark brown, tough, sinewy, close set horse, "Satan," a very devil in temper. I have been lately giving him only half feed of grain, to keep his spirits down a little, but he is very fiery. Unless my nerve is <u>very</u> steady, I don't attempt to mount him. He will stand on his hind legs, walk several steps, then jump high off the ground and come down on his fore legs (called "buck-ing") several times in succession. He is very hard to ride at first, but when he is mastered will behave beautifully. Ward last night wanted to try him, & as he was a stranger, Mr. Satan tried hard to unhorse him, but as Ward is a splendid rider, it was <u>no go,</u> so he got the bit in his teeth and ran off with him, jumping high fences & everything in his way.

My dear Mother, don't be alarmed about my company loving me too much, from any acts of kindness or familiarity of mine. The strictest discipline is used

in this Regiment, and the slightest infraction of orders or Regulations is immediately punished in the most summary manner. The more severe and unrelenting
a commanding officer is, the more his men think of him, and very often, if you
cut a man down with your sabre, he afterwards will think the more of you for it,
and I am by no means the most lax among the officers as regards discipline. Our
Reg't now being composed in great part of men who have enlisted for the Bounties alone, we show them little mercy in their short comings.[7]

Capt. Ward, who has been in command of the Detachment of our Reg't on
duty at Gen. Grant's Hd. Qrs. at City Point, returned on Wednesday, and as we
are "bunkies" we immediately set about fixing up our establishment. Among the
York County men I have a couple of very good rough carpenters. I had a log house
built, 10 x 14 feet, covered and lined with shelter tents, and a large brick chimney &
fireplace in it, made from the ruins of some <u>palatial</u> Virginia mansion, and a board
floor. When Ward came we pitched his wall tent and fly up in rear, and opened a
door between them, and put our bunks in it, and have our desks, tables, etc. in the
front one, as follows:

Consequently, we have the most luxuriant mansion around the country. We
have it surrounded with evergreens, for fear Gen. Meade might see it, and turn us

Rawle's drawing of his winter quarters, near the Aiken House outside Petersburg, from
his letter of November 12, 1864. (Courtesy The Civil War Museum of Philadelphia and
the Abraham Lincoln Foundation of The Union League of Philadelphia)

out and take possession himself. We have recd. no orders about going into winter quarters, but we have all fixed up nevertheless, for "<u>dum vivimus</u> suppose we do it." There is some talk of moving Hd. Qrs. in a few days, before going into winter qrs., which we must do soon. Grant says that he will have to drill the army all winter before it is good for anything, there being so many recruits, etc. in it now.

And now after eating an apple costing 8 cts! I will smoke a fragrant (?) cigar costing 15 cts, put on my Sanitary Commission slippers, put my feet over the fireplace, sit in my easy (?) chair and—wonder "why the Army of the Potomac don't move."

> Camp 3d Pa. Cavy.
> Hd. Qrs. A of P
> Nov. 16th, 1864

. . . Everybody is fixing up winter quarters around here, altho' we have recd. no orders so to do. Most probably Hd. Qrs. will be nearer City Point for the winter. It is reported that Grant will be in Washington this winter, and that Meade will have command of all the "Armies Operating against Richmond," subsequently he will have to move more to the right. Gen. Hancock is going North to recruit his Corps, and Maj. Gen. Humphries, Meade's Chief of Staff, will have command of the 2nd Corps.[8]

There will be much sickness in the army this winter, on the left here. The Reb papers say they have got us exactly where they want, where the malaria can kill off our army.

We are very comfortably fixed up. Indeed Ward & I have the most comfortably fixed up "shebang" around here, and tastefully decorated. Between the log house & wall tent, we have a door & have it curtained with our company Guidons, our arms, spurs, riding whips, gauntlets, etc. hanging up on either side.

During our late movement I picked up the enclosed Rebel order (inducing all foreigners to desert our army) which they scatter around where our men can get them in case they fall back. It is a Curiosity.[9]

———

November 17th. Thursday. Nothing much going on. 50 more 1 year recruits. Sherman has cut loose from Atlanta, but where he is going no one knows, most probably to Charleston, S.C. or Savannah, Ga. . . .

November 19th. Saturday. Rainy. Fixing up my old Q.M. papers still. I have had all the forage I received and a good deal more invoiced to me, and it swells out my return considerably. The Officers held examinations of the most worthy non-com. officers for promotion. We are very hard up and will have to take in some very ignorant men.

November 20th. Sunday. Officer of the Day. Rain all day. Still at my papers. Examination of non. com. officers still going on. I had occasion to pay another visit to the Aiken House but not quite so disagreeable a one as the last. Some of my Hd. Qrs. friends dragged me in and introduced me to the ladies.

———

Camp 3d Pa. Cavy.
Hd. Qrs. A of P
Nov. 22nd, 1864
Monday[Tuesday] Eveng.

Dear Mother:

It has been one steady pour for the last three days, and the mud is fearful, and I take the opportunity of squaring up my Quarter Master's Propy., making my last returns for about $75,000 worth of Government property, for which I, until lately, was responsible. I have almost closed my accounts.

This afternoon I had occasion to go down to Gen. Gregg's Hd. Qrs. on business with Capt. Charlie Treichel, and it was about all "Satan" & I could do to get there, on account of the mud. It has been very quiet about here for some days. A move was anticipated before settling into Winter Quarters, but I suppose this rain will prevent it, or at any rate delay it, for the army would be sure to "stick in the mud" for at least two weeks to come.

Did you see an account, very exaggerated to be sure, of my searching the "Aiken House" in the papers? My name was not mentioned, thanks for that, but it reflected upon me indirectly as no correct account of it could have got about except through me, and I did not tell anyone about it.

I am reading "Maurice Dering" for the second time. It always requires two or three readings of the works of its author before they can be appreciated properly. How do you manage to get along with the prices of things? Down here it is all we can do to make ends meet. I'm afraid I must go without a new coat this winter, and who ever heard of an officer stinting himself? Now my pay will be about $27 a month more, but that is not much, at present rates. It is a terrific shame that the pay of officers is not raised. That of enlisted men is, and our pay proportionally is only ⅓ of what an officer's was before the war, as then they were always paid in gold.

It's raining like the blazes, and I'm mighty glad to have a roof over me, though it is only a canvas one, and leaks a good deal, but "who wouldn't leave his little farm and go for a sojer?"

———

November 25th. Friday. Received my detail to go to Washington with prisoners. Went down to City Point on 7.44 A.M. train. Got 63 prisoners there, got on the mail boat "Dictator," started at 12 M. A magnificent day, and had a pleasant trip, arriving at Fortress Monroe before sunset. The accommodations on board the boat were good and state rooms comfortable. We were on the trip all night, sailing up the Chesapeake Bay and Potomac River.

November 26th. Saturday. We arrived in Alexandria before daybreak. I sent the Sergeant in charge with prisoners to Camp Distribution,[10] *and I went on to Washington, where we arrived at daybreak. I went to the "Metropolitan," where I got cleaned up, breakfasted, then drew two month's pay ($224.50) from Maj. Latham for September and October. Attended then to some business, got some army photographs at Brady's, called to see Mr. Clinton Lloyd . . . at the Capitol, went with him home, saw his wife, dined there, had buttons changed on my coat (I had borrowed pantaloons from Ward), got a shawl from Clinton Lloyd, and started for Philadelphia on a "French," where I arrived at 3.45 A.M.*

———

Rawle sent a telegram from Washington, DC, on November 26 notifying his family that he would be home at 3:00 A.M. on the twenty-seventh. Based on the fact that he went to great lengths to disguise the fact that he was a soldier and describes this trip home as "French" leave, Rawle was absent without leave during this time. He spent less than three days with his family, journeying back on the evening of November 29.

———

Camp 3d Pa. Cavy.
Dec. 4th, 1864
Sunday Eveng.

Dear Mother:

As you see, I am all right, back in camp. After my short visit to you "on a French" leaving on Tuesday night [November 29], I arrived in Washington before daylight on Wednesday. After breakfast at "Kirkwood's," I went to Cousin Lottie Lloyd's. I attended to some business and left for "the Front" at 3 PM in the mail boat "[James T.] Brady." The weather was delicious, and the trip down the Potomac delightful. We were all night going down the river and Chesapeake, and arrived at Fortress Monroe about 8.30 AM on Thursday, which was another superb day. The bay was swarming, almost, with wild ducks. We saw the mast of the pirate "Florida" sticking out of water where she had been lying when I passed her going up. To prevent having to give her up, which was probable, she was sunk, of course by accident.[11] The trip up the James was delightful.

We arrived at City Point about 4 PM (Thursday) and, per Army RR, I got to camp all right about 7.30 PM. Found everything right, with the exception of not being able to find anything at all in my house, it being in what Ward calls "good order." Next day, after I had set the house to rights, Ward protested that <u>he</u> couldn't find any of <u>his</u> things. Of course my company, having been six days without an officer, was fast going to destruction, and I had to knock things (not to say men) around considerably. . . .

Nothing much is going on. Gregg did a very good thing the other day, destroying an immense amount of property at Stony Creek Station on the Weldon RR, from which place the Rebs have their supplies, etc. around our left.[12] Everything seems as if we were going to winter here, but there are as yet no orders upon the subject. Gen. Meade & staff are fixing up pretty extensively. We are having glorious weather, and the inhabitants around this part of the country say that when they have this kind of weather until the 3d of December, it is pretty certain that it will continue throughout the month. If so, look out, somebody will get his mother's monkey into a scrape. . . . In Washington, I bought a copy of "Guy Livingston," and I am reading it, for about the tenth time, with extreme gusto.[13]

———

December 5th. Monday. Magnificent day. In afternoon we had Regimental drill. I commanded the second squadron, my first time on drill as squadron commander. . . .

December 6th. Tuesday. Magnificent day. Detailed for special duty. With a squad of 10 men I went around to visit all the houses from our left to beyond Prince George Court House, where we have safeguards from this portion of the regiment. It was about a ride of 30 miles, starting at Guard Mount and arriving in camp around dark. Had a very pleasant time, calling on several young ladies, etc.

December 7th. Wednesday. Rainy, clear in evening. I had to go out to Widow Bryant's, near Mount Sinai Church. I had one orderly and met Lieut. Ewing with two. I had orders not to go out with less than 100 men if the Cavalry picket line had been withdrawn. I could not find out for certain whether the pickets were there or not until I got almost out to the place. We concluded to go up at a gallop. I did not dismount, but had the ladies out in the rain, got through some questioning and then dashed off again, coming back by Prince George Court House. The house of Mrs. Bryant is on the cavalry picket line, and when it is withdrawn it is frequented by scouts and gueril-

las. If we had come back as we went, by the Quaker Road, we surely would have been
caught; it was a ride of about 25 miles, mostly at a gallop. . . .

———

Notwithstanding Gregg's successful raid against the Weldon Railroad at Stony
Creek Station on December 1, Lee's ongoing ability to secure supplies by a combi-
nation of rail and wagon transport continued to confound Grant. Accordingly, he
planned another strike in that direction designed to minimize the flow of provender. The VI Corps had recently returned from the Shenandoah Valley to Meade's
army, freeing up troops for the effort. On December 7, in a movement that became
known as the Hicksford Raid, Warren's V Corps, preceded by Gregg's cavalry and
supplemented by a II Corps division, headed south along the Jerusalem Plank
Road to the Meherrin River to destroy as much of the track of the Weldon Railroad
as they could. Grant hoped that Lee would send troops to counter the move. Rawle
and the 3rd Pennsylvania were initially sent to support infantry probing for weak
points that might result in the Southern lines southwest of Petersburg.[14]

———

Dec. 10th, 1864

Dear Mother:

We have just returned from a rough job without anything to eat or any sleep,
and are ordered out with 4 days rations, I don't know where to. Will write as soon
as possible.

Ward went home this morning on 30 days leave. He was slightly wounded
yesterday. Good bye, yours thoroughly tired and disgusted. . . .

[P.S.] I'm all right. Don't be anxious.

Camp 3d Pa. Cavy. Hd. Qrs. Army of Potomac
Dec. 13th, 1864

Dear Mother:

We have been having a decidedly rough time lately. On Saturday night [De-
cember 10] we came into camp for a couple of hours only, and I wrote you a few
lines, not to be alarmed; that, so far, I was all right, altho' Ward was wounded. I
did not have time to go into particulars.

During Dec. 4th & 5th, most of the 6th Corps arrived, relieved the 5th, which
massed in rear for some expedition. On Tuesday & Wednesday [December 6
and 7] I had some duty to perform, and rode each day 35 miles, which was a bad

preparation for hard work. On Wednesy. 7th the 5th Corps and Gregg's Cavalry Division started and got as far as Stony Creek without trouble.

About 3 PM of Thursday [December 8] orders came for the Regiment to report to Col. Kerwin of the 13th Pa. Cav. at Gen. Gregg's late Hd. Qrs., with 2 days rations & forage.[15] The 13th Pa. Cav. & 6th Ohio Cav. had been left behind by Gregg. About 5 PM we started, 13th in advance, out the Weldon RR and Vaughn Road. We drove in the Rebel cavalry pickets about ¾ of a mile outside of our line, and drove them about 2 miles to Hatcher's Run. Here we found infantry strongly posted in earthworks on the other bank of the creek, and we could not cross. After skirmishing with them for some time we withdrew with the loss of 7 wounded. We returned to camp about 10 PM but soon recd. orders to report to Col. Kerwin again at 4 AM tomorrow.[16]

Dec. 9th Friday. Weather very cold & blustering. Reported to Col. Kerwin at 4 AM. Shortly after daylight we again started out. Gen. Miles' Division of 2nd Corps went with us. We started out with light saddles, i.e. no forage or rations. We took the same road—cavalry in advance, drove in Reb pickets, again to Hatcher's Run, and finding that we could not dislodge them, the Infantry came up. The 13th Pa. & 6th Ohio went to the right of the Vaughn Road to Armstrong's Mills where we had had a skirmish on Oct. 28th.

Capt. Ward's squadron was ordered to take a road running in rear, and past the Cumming's House, running down to an old mill and wretched mud hole of a ford, the bridge having been destroyed by the enemy when we drove them in. Ward's

Rawle's good friend George S. L. Ward of Philadelphia. He and Ward joined the 3rd at the same time. Ward served from May 1863 until the end of the war in Company M, rising to its captaincy in October 1864. He was wounded during the fighting along the Vaughn Road near Petersburg in December 1864. Ward and Rawle shared living quarters during the winter of 1864–65. (From Regimental History Committee, *History of the Third Pennsylvania Cavalry* [1905])

orders were to charge across, take the position, and hold it. The road down was very bad, the ford still worse, and the rebel infantry held strong works on the other bank, and their sharpshooters were posted in a house. Before they knew where they were, Ward was hit in the left side, and Coyle of M Co., one of the bravest men that ever drew the breath of life, mortally wounded in the abdomen.[17] On the position of affairs being reported, my squadron was ordered down, and Col. Walsh was ordered to cross. But we found it impossible. We remained here protecting the right flank and holding the position for about 2 hours.

The infantry effected a crossing below the Vaughn Road, and a party came down on the other bank, and flanked out the party in front of us. Our two squadrons shortly after scouted all the roads in front, while Capt. Stillé's squadron and the 13th Pa. Cav. drove the enemy out the Vaughn Road steadily for about 6 miles to the Military Road, and cut the telegraph. We struck the Vaughn Road at the Cavalry outpost and reported to Gen. Miles' Hd. Qrs. at the Cummings House. I was sent out to picket the right. It was a bitter cold night, raining, sleeting & freezing, and we had no forage, rations, tents, blankets or anything.

Dec. 10th Saty. Very cold. No forage or rations, and an infantry General in command. These Infantry Generals, when they get a few cavalrymen into their hands, think themselves big bugs, but they are elephants in their hands as far as using them properly. Our battalion scouted out the Vaughn Road, driving in the Reb pickets about 4 miles, when we found another strong line of pickets. We then withdrew. This was to cover the falling back of the expedition. We had just turned and our line had just commenced to fall back when the Reb cavalry and infantry in force succeeded in crossing at Armstrong's Mills, and moved down the creek pressing the infantry closely. We were dismounted and thrown across the Creek at the lower ford into the Rebel works. This was to hold the position until the rest of the line could go back. When we recd. orders to fall back the Reb cavalry was in our front, and to gain time for the men to mount up we tore up the bridge and then got back just in time. For the second time today we were within an ace of being cut off.

The Cavalry, under Col. Kerwin, recd. orders to report to Gen. Miles immediately. We returned to camp but merely to get supper, feed our horses, get 4 days rations and 3 days forage. We started out again, well worn out, in two hours. All that night we lay in a field in the cold rain and mud, waiting for ammunition from City Point, and about an hour before daybreak [December 11] started out on the Jerusalem Plank Road. Two Divisions of 9th Corps were ahead of us, not having had time to wait for us. Gen. Potter (Bishop's son) in command.[18]

About 12 M. we came up with the Infantry, just as we made connection with the 5th Corps on the Nottaway River. The object in our going out there was to help the 5th Corps and Gregg's Cavy. out of the scrape. But they did not need us. The 5th Corps had destroyed 20 miles of the Weldon RR and Gregg had gone 15 miles beyond, to Bellfield.[19] Gen. Gregg was wrathy when he found us out there to help him out, and sent us back to camp, where we arrived about midnight after a march that day of over 30 miles. On the way back via Jerusalem Plank Road, every house was burnt to the ground, magnificent mansions as well as negro huts. Some say it was done by order, as the bodies of several artillerymen were found in one of them, murdered by guerillas.[20]

Ward started home with a 30 days leave in his pocket on Saturday morning. About half the regiment is sick, many officers having frozen feet, noses, etc. I am all right, with the exception of having my face swollen up with fever blisters, and slight aching in my bones. It was one of the roughest trips I ever experienced, marching all day and laying out in the bitter, bitter cold rain with no cover and nothing to eat for ourselves or our horses. The sufferings were intense. But now we are back in our comfortable quarters again, and, for the most part, as happy as Kings. . . .

> Camp Third Pa. Cavy.
> Hd. Qrs. Army of Potomac
> Dec. 18th, 1864
> Sunday Eveng.

Dear Mother:

. . . I wrote you a long letter on Tuesday, upon our return from our very rough trip, to say I was all right. It was one of the hardest tours of duty I ever experienced, and some of us have not recovered from the effects yet, but being half frozen to death, the other half starved to death, and one more half worked to death, don't have any effect on my fortunate (or unfortunate) constitution, and I feel better for it.

Nothing much is going on. Hd. Qrs. seems to be fixing up for a winter camp. No orders have yet been issued for granting leaves, and I don't know whether they intend to or not. It will be hard if they don't let us have a week or so, after the hardest campaign of the war.

A lot of commissions came this evening, mostly for sergeants. Charlie Treichel's as Major also has come. By order of the Secretary of War, . . . I have been transferred to Company "B," Treichel taking Co. "D." It is an old company, and consequently preferable to a new one. Col. Walsh wished his old officers to have the old companies. "B" Company is my old company, and is stationed at Gen. Grant's Hd. Qrs. at City Point, and I expect to move down there about New Year's, not sooner, as I want to transfer and receive property at the close of 4th Quarter 1864.

We have recd. glorious news from Sherman and Thomas. A salute of 100 guns was fired this morning at daybreak, in honor thereof.[21] I have not heard from Ward since he left for home, but I suppose he is getting along all right. . . . Tell [Lottie] to eat a double amount of roast turkey and cranberry sauce on Xmas for me, as I will have to have my eternal tough beef steak. Don't forget the box, by all that's holy, nor the slippers either. Put in the box if you have time a good book or two—paper covered novels of the best tho! Merry Christmas to all. . . .

———

December 22nd. Thursday. Fine Day. Cold. At request of Col. Walsh I went down to City Point on business with him with Bvt. Maj. Gen. Ingalls, Q.M. Genl., with ordnance officer and Maj. Starr, commanding dismounted camp near Light House Point. Could not get through with all my business, so stayed with Capt. Carter. Made arrangements about moving down at the end of the month.

———

Camp Bat 3d Pa. Cavy.
Xmas Eve, 1864

Dear Mother:

I suppose that you are all enjoying yourselves now, while I am writing. A Merry Christmas! I recd. your note, enclosing the Adams Expr. Co's receipt for the box, but I'm afraid I will not have the turkey, etc. for my Xmas dinner. But I hope, at any rate, that it won't be delayed long.

We have glorious news, at any rate. Gen. Grant telegraphed to Gen. Meade, late last night, that a telegraph operator had just deserted, coming direct from Richmond into Butler's lines, bringing intelligence that Savannah had unconditionally surrendered to Sherman, with from 15 to 18,000 men under Hardie, that our fleet was off Wilmington, N.C. & Fort Fisher taken by our troops, and that Jeff. Davis was very ill. Today it is reported that the Reb pickets have called across that he is dead, but he has already been killed so often that we don't rely upon the report. . . .[22]

. . . Nothing much is going on, but a good spell of cold weather. I expect to move down to City Point in a few days. Lieut. Frank C. Grugan, late of 114th PV (Collis' Zouaves) has been transferred to our Regiment, and is Acting Adjutant. I used to go to school with him at Hare's.[23] He is a very clever fellow, and a thorough gentleman. He is living with me. He has been living in Europe for several years previous to the war. . . .[24]

No order has yet been issued granting leaves, and I doubt if they will do it for some time, as something may turn up. Think what a glorious time we are going to have tomorrow. We will celebrate Xmas by—having no Inspection or Dress Parade!! I must close with a "Merry Christmas and Happy New Year" to all.

———

December 25th. Sunday. A Merry Christmas indeed! Nothing much going on. Some whiskey of course got into the regiment and I had to put one of my men in shackles and prefer charges enough to kill him several times. In the evening a dispatch came from Genl. Grant, stating that Genl. Sherman had sent to President Lincoln a Christmas gift in the shape of a dispatch announcing the capture of Savannah.

December 31st. Saturday. Rainy and sleety. Lt. Frazer moved up here and was mustered with "D" Co. I moved down with all my duds in 12:44 P.M. train and was mustered with "B" Co. at City Point.

About 1½ hours before "Reveille" this morning the enemy made a break into the picket line in front of Hd. Qrs., and came within a few hundred yards of our camp and attacked the infantry, setting up a big "Ky-y-y." The long roll beat among the "doughboys" and "to arms" in our camp, and we were out in line in a few moments time. They were soon driven off, having captured about 30 pickets.[25]

———

Hd. Qrs. Armies Opp. Against Richmond
City Point, Va.
Jany. 1st, 1865

Dear Mother:

As you see now I have moved down to Gen. Grant's Hd. Qrs. at City Point. Altho' transferred to "B" Co. by the War Department some time since, I did not come down sooner, but waited until the end of the 4th Qr. 1864 to prevent the trouble of making out more than one set of property accountability returns. There are 3 companies down here, "B," "C" & "F," Capt. Carter commanding the Post. Gen. Patrick is here, and Capt. Potter is on his staff. We are fixed up very nicely here, on a bluff overlooking the James River and the fleets. This, being the base of operations and supplies, is a very busy place, and is getting to be quite a considerable town—canvas & frame. Our men have very comfortable quarters built, and, what is a great advantage, we get plenty of forage for the horses. The men have a great deal of work to do, and we are kept busy. Carter was so lonely by himself that I consented to live with him, and we are fixed up very comfortably in houses, one with two rooms and one for a dining room. To be sure, the houses are only canvas ones, but they are very comfortable with a rousing fireplace in each. . . .

No orders granting leaves of absence. Can't you get [Uncle] WHR to write me a short business letter requesting my immediate presence to attend to that important legal business? I can get a leave then. I think that case of Brooke vs. Smithrobinsonjones will be coming up soon. It would have to be written by him as family lawyer, as I would have to enclose it in my application. For anything of that kind, the powers that be will grant a leave. It is generally thought that no order granting furloughs will be issued, as then it would be necessary to do the same for the enlisted men, which would be prejudicial to the good of the service. Meade is now home on furlough. If you want to see me for 15 days this winter, just do as directed above.

You ask if my having "B" Company makes me next to senior captain. No; the captains rank—Stillé, Potter, Carter, Brooke [Rawle], Ward, etc. I am by no means a Major yet. . . . I got a letter from Ward the other day; he is getting along very well. . . .

Camp, Detmt. 3d Pa. Cavy.
City Point, Va., Jan. 4th, 1865

Dear Mother:

The Xmas box arrived all safe today, and my friends had a glorious dinner. The delay of two weeks in arriving here was occasioned by the Potomac being frozen up, and no vessels could come down. Indeed, we came very near being without forage in the Army. The storehouses here were entirely emptied, and for over a day we had no grain for our horses.

Nothing was spoiled in the box. The turkey, ham & tongue were delicious, as also the sugar plums, cake, etc. The canned milk I will keep till needed, as we now have a splendid cow, which gives 6 qts. a day. So we have milk toast, <u>cream</u> and milk for both meals. We have breakfast at 9 AM and dinner at 5 PM. Very high toned, isn't it? We find it economical to have but 2 meals a day; besides, it gives us an appetite, a great desideratum in the army. It is a great thing to be able to enjoy our coarse, and often unpalatable food.

I don't know how officers in the army are to get along with the present pay, and the high prices of everything. We are allowed $36 per mo. for rations, but [it] costs us from $45 to $60. Our servants cost us about $30 more, and with clothes at such high prices, the enormous rates of sutler's charges, tobacco from $2 to $2.50 per lb., etc. we don't know what to do. A great many petitions have gone in to Congress to increase the pay, and it is said they are going to increase the commutation for a ration from .30 cts to .60 cts, which will give us $72 per mo. for "grub." I was always very careful of my clothes, which have lasted very well, and I now wear government clothes—of course nicely altered by tailors—consequently I will have to spend little or nothing for such things this winter. Speaking of clothes, my underclothes have pretty nearly played out. I wish you would order at Scott's, or some place where they will be made well and strongly, some what are called "hickory" shirts, that is of small blue check cotton (?) like workmen wear. . . .

No news. Dutch Gap was blown up on New Year's Day, but came down again from where it started, and consequently it was a failure. . . .[26]

———

January 5th. Thursday. In the morning I went out to make arrangements to have the Prince George County Poor House moved away. It is out on the Cavalry picket line near Zion Church and Surrey Stage Road. . . .

January 6th. Friday. Rainy. I have had built a shed stable for my horses. "Carrie" and "Satan" are comfortable now.

———

Camp Detm. 3d Pa. Cavy. City Point, Va.
Jan. 8th, 1865 Eveng.

Dear Mother:

. . . This afternoon I had a pleasant visit from Dr. Dalton, in ch'ge of Genl. Hospital, A of P, who brought with him Darley, the artist. Mr. Darley has been down here about two weeks on a visit to the army, and returns home tomorrow. He came over here to take a sketch of some rebel deserters.[27]

Carter has gone up to Baltimore on duty, and I am, for a week, holding the responsible position of "Chief of Cavalry Provost Marshall General's Department, Armies operating against Richmond."

Nothing much is going on. No signs of leave granting, which is eagerly desired here, you may be assured. . . .

———

January 8th. Sunday. By order of Genl. Patrick I sent Lieut. Ludwig and 15 men to Washington to escort some prisoners. As this time very good men were required he called on "his own cavalry."

January 9th. Monday. Took a ride around in the morning, visiting the vedettes and patrols. I placed Lieut. Humphries under arrest on account of disorderly conduct and conduct unbecoming an officer and a gentleman.

January 10th. Tuesday. Preferred charges against Lieut. G. G. Humphries, Co. "F"—five charges. This by order of Col. Walsh. He will be knocked higher than a kite.[28]

———

Camp Detm. 3d Pa. Cav.
City Point, Va.
Jan. 14th, 65

Dear Mother:

. . . There are more peace rumors flying about. We are getting a great many deserters now. They say that they are very hard up in the Rebel army, and on half rations. I have never put any confidence in these reports until lately. Those in Provost Marshall Department here are the ones to know the truth of such statements, and now we are beginning to believe them.[29]

I have been in command of the Detachment here for a week past, but Carter returned from Washington & Baltimore today. I'm afraid I must decline your offer of good things—Blancmange and Curds & Whey, etc. would not agree with me. My taste has become so depraved of late that if I eat anything <u>rich</u> I lose my appetite for nearly a week. . . .

I am busy fixing up my returns of ordnance & ordnance stores, Quarter Masters Property and Clothing, Camp and Garrison Equipage for the 4th Quarter 1864. If you come across any good books in mailable form I would like some. I read "Guy Livingston" & "Maurice Dearing" over and over again.

Camp Detm. 3d Pa. Cav.
City Point, Va.
Jan. 18th, 1865

Dear Mother:

. . . I had a very pleasant trip yesterday. I recd. orders from Bvt. Brig, Gen. Sharpe, Chief of the Secret Service, to proceed with 23 of my men, and three scouts on a very important expedition connected with the secret service department, the character of which, of course, I am not at liberty to divulge.[30] We crossed the James River on a steamboat, horses and all, at 1 PM yesterday (17th), landed at Harrison's Landing, and travelled the country near the Chickahominy, returning by Malvern Hill to Haxall's Landing, where the steamboat was waiting for us, and got back to camp about 3 AM this morning.[31] I send you some Richmond papers, as a curiosity; take good care of them.

News arrived yesterday of the fall of Fort Fisher, and the good tidings connected with it. Yesterday I saw the Richmond papers of the same day, in which was published that news. They said that of course they had now lost their last port, but it was to be looked at in light of a blessing to the country, as they would now be thrown upon their own resources, and it would encourage manufactures, etc.!!! What a fortunate disposition they have, in looking at every disaster as a blessing to them. . . .

                                                Camp Detm. 3d Pa. Cav. City Point, Va.
                                                                    Jan. 23d, 1865

Dear Mother:

I have delayed writing until I should receive the bundle expressed to me. I recd. it today. The shirts are the exact thing, and the stuff much superior to the exact thing I wanted. If I should want any more I will get them when I go home on leave of absence, which, if all goes well, I hope to be in a couple of weeks.

I intend taking my "valley de sham" [his servant] with me to Philadelphia to give him a little holiday also. Jenkins is a nice, clean good looking darkey, and won't be any trouble. Can you have some place for him to sleep? Up in the 4th story front room if nowhere else. It will be a good deal of expense to me to have him along, but he is a good servant and I don't want to lose him. You need not concern yourself about the addition to the family. . . .

We have been having a pretty steady rain for two or three days, and the roads are in fearful condition. I had to ride some six miles this morning, which I did at a gallop, and I came in, horse and all, in a decided state of "splash." Mitchell, my groom, said, "Oh Capting, and ya wouldn't know Satan wi' the mud that's on him!" I have Satan tamed down considerably now. I can now go in his stable without a certainty of getting my brains knocked out. "Carrie" is very well, and when I go to see her, she puts her delicate head to my cheek to be petted. "Pickaxe" is now in Capt. Carter's service, and is so fat that he can hardly walk. He has recovered from the affection of the eyes which he had, and is ready to splash the mud in the faces of some more rebs.

Lilly's former friend, Septima Levy, now Mrs. General Collis, is down here at City Point with her husband. I often see her riding, sometimes with only an orderly. I must say that I don't like to see it much. She looks very well. . . .[32]

I have finished and sent in to the Departments my return of C[amp], C[lothing] & G[arrison] E[quipage], Q.M. Property, and Ordnance & Ordnance Stores for 4th Quarter 1864, which is a great deal off my mind, I assure you. . . .

                                                                City Point, Va.
                                                                 Jan. 29th, 1865

Dear Mother:

. . . I send you another Richmond almanac, which I recd. per "underground railway" the other day. On [the] 26th I wrote to Uncle Stephen H. B[rooke] sending him a copy of the Richmond Dispatch of the 25th.[33] I was over in the Chickahominy country again the other day on another scout. I got some splendid smoking tobacco from Richmond the other day.

I wrote to you on Monday [January 23]. That night the rebel gunboats tried to come down to City Point, and came pretty near getting down. We blew one of them up and sent the other one back.[34] But for [a] blunder by one of our Monitors we would have captured them. All the troops at City Point were out under arms. When Gen. Patrick was asked whether he wanted "his cavalry" as he calls us, to charge the gunboats, there was such a laugh that he protested that, if they should ever get down here, he would let us take care of ourselves.

————

January 24th. Tuesday. Very cold. I was sent out with 22 men and some scouts across the James River again. Landed at Harrison's Landing, went over near the Chickahominy on secret service, and returned by Haxall's Landing, getting back to camp by 1 P.M.

————

On Friday [January 27] all the troops of the Post were out to witness the execution by hanging of a deserter, which, to say the least of it, was not the pleasantest sight in the world.[35] We have been having some bitterly cold weather here lately. This morning [January 29] the James River (as wide as the Delaware at Phila) was frozen across here, but the high tide broke it up. We are afraid of having our supplies cut off again. . . .

————

January 31st. Tuesday. All the troops at the Front are under marching orders, but that don't affect us.

————

Rawle received his anticipated leave of absence and left City Point on the mail boat *Cornelius Vanderbilt* on February 3. "Accommodations wretched," he complained in his diary. Because the Potomac was clogged with ice, the ship docked in Annapolis on February 4. Rawle went on to Washington, where he drew $271, representing two months' pay; had lunch at Gautier's, a fashionable capital establishment; and arrived home at midnight on February 4. He visited his family in Philadelphia (without his servant, Jenkins) until February 18, when he began his trip back to the army. His mother and sisters were loath to see him go back to Virginia. "The only reason I dislike coming home," he wrote in his diary upon his return to the army, "is the leaving them again so soon; they all take on to such a ridiculous degree."

During Rawle's time away, Grant initiated his Seventh Offensive, which involved an attempt to further encircle Petersburg and cut off supply routes from the south and west. The Battle of Hatcher's Run was fought on February 5–7 as the Federals tried again to wrest control of the Boydton Plank Road from the Rebels. Though the move fell short of its goal, Grant was able to extend his lines an additional four miles and interdict the Vaughn Road south of Hatcher's Run, thus permitting unopposed crossings of the stream during future offensives.[36]

———

Camp Detm. 3d Pa. Cav.
City Point, Va.
Feb. 21st, 1865

Dear Mother:

I arrived here all right yesterday (Monday). We left Phila at 11:15 PM, on Saturday, arrived in Washington about 7 AM Sunday. Pemberton came with me.[37] We tried to get a pass for him to the front but could not, as it was Sunday, so we went to church. As Pemberton could not come down with me, & as I was behind time, I left him in Washington, starting for Annapolis, Md. at 3 PM. After a good deal of trouble in that wretched place (such a thing as an omnibus or carriage was never heard of there), I got off in the "City Point" steamer at 7 PM. We made very good time, arriving at Fortress Monroe at daybreak of Monday. There were very few on the boat, so we were very comfortable.[38]

We left Fortress Monroe at 8 AM and arrived at City Point at 2.30 PM, making remarkably good time. The trip up the river was very pleasant. There were on board some rebel officers going up to be exchanged, among them Brig. Gen. Alb. Johnson, who was shot through both eyes and is totally blind. Also a brother of the rebel Genl. Morgan of great repute. They were a very gentlemanly and good set of fellows.[39]

I expected Pemberton down today but he did not come. Capt. Carter is going on Leave of Absence for 15 days, tomorrow, which will leave me in command here. I caught a most abominable cold the night I left home, but thanks to Dr. Mitchell, it has almost gone.

There is nothing going on here of any interest. It is reported that the rebs have evacuated Charleston. They seem to me much bothered about Sherman. He appears to be making his way up in this direction. We are receiving a great many men from the North, convalescents, recruits, etc. at the rate of about 3,000 a day, which will considerably strengthen our army for the Spring Campaign. I have a good deal to do tonight so <u>adieux.</u>

Hd. Qrs. Detmt. Third Pa. Cav.

City Point, Va., Mch. 1, 1865

My dear Mother:

. . . I wrote to you this daybreak, and intended to write to you on Sunday evening [February 26] again, but my day of rest (?) was broken into in a most unmerciful manner. Lieut. Pemberton had reported to me for duty that morng., and we had just returned from a lengthy ride when orders came from Genl. Grant for me to report immediately with all my available command, with 3 days rations & forage, to Capt. Mason of the 5th US Cavy., Gen. Grant's escort.[40] I reported to him at 2 PM with 125 men & Lt. Pemberton. Capt. Mason had 50 men & 2 officers and the whole command embarked on 2 large steamships, crossed, landed at Harrison's Landing, fed our horses, got something to eat, and at dark started out with 2 scouts to scour the country along the Chickahominy after a considerable party of Rebel cavalry who were reported to be about. We reached Nance's shops, between Long bridges & St. Mary's Church, about 1 AM, and lay there till daybreak, having thrown out a strong picket force.

Early Monday morning [February 27] we started out, separating the party—I going to the left, striking White Oak Swamp and going down the Chickahominy to Long Bridge, where I met Capt. Mason. We picked up some Rebels who claimed to be deserters. We separated again, taking roads, meeting again between St. Mary's Church and Charles City Court House, went thro' the C.H. and took the River Road thro' McClellan's old camps to Harrison's Landing, where we arrived about dark, having marched steadily since we started, with the exception of about 4 hours, about 60 miles, scouring the country thoroughly. Owing to some delay in getting transports, we did not arrive in Camp until 10 PM.

Deserters are crowding in, 150 a day. It is rumored that the Rebs are evacuating Petersburg. If so, Grant will be greatly disappointed, for he wants to hold Lee here, and fight the whole thing out on this line, after he & Lee have both consolidated their armies. Won't there be some stinging old squabbling this spring?

Some deserters brought in today told a cock & bull story about Lee consolidating, making a rush for Washington (he having the inside track), getting inside the works, declaring himself Dictator, and playing the mischief generally.

I see all the Rebel Richmond papers of the same day by 2 o'clock every day, at Grant's Hd. Qrs. There is nothing much in them. They are not allowed to publish any military news, and are rather despondent. . . .

City Point, Va.
March 7th, 1865

Dear Lottie:

. . . I did not write on Sunday, as Col. Walsh came down and spent the night with me, and in the evening we went round to see our friends at Gen. Grant's Hd. Qrs. at the 5th U.S. Cav, 4th & 11th U.S. Infy., Lt. Farley and others, which kept us up to the "wee sma' hours."

I recd. a letter from Carrie & Sophie [Heberton] today. They were in Washington and wrote to expect them down here in a few days. Hon. J K Moorhead & family, and Carrie & Sophie are coming down to Fortress Monroe and City Point, in a steamer offered them by Secy. Stanton.[41] They will only stay part of a day if they ever <u>do</u> get here. I did not get up to Washington as Capt. Carter is away on leave, and either he or I have to be here the whole time.

Strange to say, the cork mattress which Grandma sent to me shortly after the battle of Gettysburg arrived here very unexpectedly the other day. It has been a considerable time in getting down here—only 20 months. It is a wonder it ever <u>did</u> arrive, from the direction on it. The "Lt. Wm. Rawle" were decidedly on a case of straggle, and the "Brooke" seemed to have no connection with the rest of the name whatsoever. It will be very nice for the coming campaign, if indeed I can get transportation for it. I have not yet had a chance of calling on Col. Horace Porter, but will do so as soon as I can.[42]

There is something big in the wind. A large fleet of gunboats and monitors is going up the James River, troops changing position, earthworks being leveled, others thrown up, so in a few days look out for news from this quarter. We have been having very rainy weather lately, the mud is 2 and 3 feet deep around here, where there is much travel. Something must be done to cooperate with Sherman. We recd. news of Sheridan's good luck yesterday. There was an old joke that "the early bird had got his <u>Phill</u>" but now I think the "Phill" was too much for that "<u>beast</u>" they call the bird.[43]

Mr. Pemberton is living with me. He is a fine fellow. He is 11 years older than I am, tho' I am his Comdg. officer. He is a relation of ours, and we have many a talk about mutual friends & relations.

Beyond the Post-works the roads are pretty good, and Capt. Potter and I took a ride to Broadway Landing on the Appomattox. It is a beautiful place. My mare is getting along finely, and is in such good order & high spirits that she runs away with me almost every time I take her out. I have another pet now, in the shape of a <u>cat,</u> which sleeps on my pillow at night. I had to get it as the rats and mice trouble us very much. They often run over our beds and pillows at night, which is not the pleasantest thing in the world.

———

March 9th. Thursday. Clear during the day and rain again at night. I went over to Gen. Grant's to see my father's cousin, Col. Horace Porter, Ordnance Department, of Gen. Grant's staff. Despatch received from Sheridan at Staunton; had completely routed Early's command in the Valley and Gen. E. had to flee to the mountains; many guns and trains captured.

———

City Point, Va.

Mch. 11th, 1865

Dear Mother:

I feel <u>awfully</u> blue. Yesterday was, without exception, the pleasantest day I ever spent in the army.

I was out at the execution of a deserter,[44] when an orderly brought out a note from Col. Horace Porter, telling me that the "River Queen" had arrived with the expected party. I came in at a fast gallop, went on board, covered with mud (the roads are fearful), and who should be there but Carrie and Sophie Heberton, Mary Moorhead and a party of ladies and gentlemen with Gen. Moorhead at the head. Gen. Grant was on board and received the party. We all got into a special car on the 12.30 train and went to Genl. Meade's Hd. Qrs., arriving at Parke's Stn. all right, with the exception that a car in front of us fell over the embankment. At the station, several ambulances were waiting, and we went over to Genl. Meade's Hd. Qrs. He received the party and we got into the ambulances again and rode over to the left, with Genl. M and staff.

We went out to Fort Welsh, on the very front line of battle, from which place we could distinctly see the two picket lines and the rebel camps, which was only a half mile distant.[45] The party got up on the parapets and took a good view of "our friends on the other side." Luckily for the ladies there was no firing along the line. We then went to see Genl. Meade review a division of the 6th Corps, and then went to Patrick Stn. where the special train awaited us.[46] The ladies got a good taste of riding in ambulances. They are very springy and the roads are full of ruts and mostly corduroyed. The principal object is not to retain the seat, but to prevent running your head through the <u>top.</u> The party, on arriving at City Point, went back to the boat, and I went up to get some supper and to dress.

About 8.30 PM I went down to the boat again with Lieut. Andy Pemberton. The 4th Infy. Band was there, along with Gen. Grant and staff, Gen. Ord and other officers.[47] We danced, promenaded on deck, etc. and had a good time generally. The "River Queen" is a magnificently furnished boat—it belonging to the Department of State. At midnight we took a moonlight walk around Gen. Grant's Hd. Qrs., and showed the girls how us poor fellows suffer down here in winter quarters. We then bid the party good bye. They left during the night for Fortress Monroe and Washington. It was without exception the pleasantest day I ever spent in the army, and it cheered us up <u>muchly,</u> but the reaction is fearful. Pemberton & I have had a fearful fit of the blues. As he says "Angels visits, few and far between." I'm afraid if they had stayed longer some officers would have lost their hearts. It is such an immense thing to see ladies down here, especially lady <u>friends,</u> that we appreciated this visit greatly, to what extent "words is wanting to tell what."

I did not get off to Washington. Carter returned yesterday, and I expect, if all goes right, to go up tomorrow. I want to get there before the opera goes, to take my last look at civilization before the opening of the Campaign.

Nothing much is going on. We have been having a great deal of rain, and the roads are in a fearful condition. Of course we cannot do anything until they dry up. . . .

CHAPTER EIGHT

The Fall of Petersburg and
the Appomattox Campaign

March 12–May 15, 1865

"The war seems to be moving on with irresistible grandeur," an officer of African American troops in the Army of the James near Richmond had written in a mid-February letter. "Its progress is like the motions of planets, almost imperceptible, but steady and sure. . . . The power that opposes us is just as steadily crumbling away. One by one its cities, its arsenals, its railroads, its armies are slipping from its grasp." An artilleryman before Petersburg agreed: "Everything during the winter had betokened a rapid wasting away of the so-called Confederacy, and we felt the end to be near."[1] The indiscernible progress that the infantry officer recognized would soon tangibly manifest itself, bringing about the end that the cannoneer sensed was not far off.

The Federals in the trenches were not the only ones who foresaw a close to the war, as all but the most ardent Confederates were aware that the rebellion was reaching a tipping point.[2] Sherman was moving north almost at will through the Carolinas, and it was but a matter of time before he would reach Virginia. Sheridan had returned to Petersburg from the Valley on March 26 with 10,000 hardened, veteran cavalrymen, tearing up the Virginia Central Railroad as he came.

Despite the momentum clearly shifting in favor of the North, Grant was concerned that Lee and his soldiers would slip away and move south.[3] Lee, acutely aware that as the Army of the Potomac continued to extend its lines to the south and west the position of his own Army of Northern Virginia would become untenable, decided to preemptively strike. In the predawn hours of March 25, over 11,000 Confederates of Maj. Gen. John B. Gordon's Second Corps attacked the IX Corps positions east of Petersburg at Fort Stedman. Lee hoped that his attack might reach the Union supply base at City Point and, with the Federals in disarray, buy him the time needed to vacate the Petersburg lines—as Grant feared—in order to unite with Johnston's army in North Carolina. Despite initial success, the Southern attack failed, costing Lee more than 2,500 irreplaceable veterans. In the balance it provided the Army of the Potomac, which had pursued the retreating Southerners and captured their picket line, an advantageous position from which to launch subsequent assaults against the Petersburg defenses.[4]

———

> Hd. Qrs. Army of the Potomac
> Mch. 19th, 1865
> Sunday Eveng.

Dear Mother:

Please take notice that my address is changed again. One day this week (Sunday 12th) I went up to Washington in charge of a lot of rebel and other prisoners; arrived there on Monday at 9.30; Went on the "Collyer," the fastest boat on the line and it was running on time.[5] I met Cousin Lottie Lloyd in the street, and at her earnest and very kind invitation I stayed at her house. Sophie Heberton was there and we had a very pleasant time, driving all about and around Washington, visiting all the public buildings, going to the German Opera, etc.

———

March 14. Tuesday. In the morning I attended to some business. Went to [the] War Department for Carter, then to [the] Ordnance Department, had my Ordnance accounts squared up at the 2nd Auditors, then to Maj. Rochester's; drew $249.60 for Jany. and Feby. (minus $10. per month responsibility from my full pay by mistake).

March 15. Wednesday. Mrs. L, S and I took a drive out through Georgetown, crossed the Potomac by the Aqueduct, went all over Arlington, late belonging to Reb. Gen. R. E. Lee, now used as a National Cemetery for soldiers, then out to Camp Distribution, paid a visit and home over the Long Bridge.

March 16. Thursday. Regular March day. Very windy. Attended to some business in the morning. Bought a pair of light cavalry boots at Burns', 9th and Penna. Ave., for $18 and sent my others home.

———

I stayed there until yesterday, Saturday [March 18], when I left for the "Front" at 3 PM on the "Brady." We arrived at City Point at 2.30 today, when I found that our Detachment at City Point had been relieved by the 1st Mass and had reported to the Regiment. I found a good many other changes there.

A regular military post has been organized at City Point, and the 114th & 68th P.V. have been sent there.[6] I went on to this place, where I found my company all right, altho' to be sure, I lost some company property in the removal.

There is something <u>big</u> up. All sutlers are ordered to the rear, and officers have been ordered to reduce their baggage to the smallest limits. I will have to send my Company desk, papers, etc. to the rear tomorrow. I suppose there will be a move in a few days. Grant, I presume, is watching Lee, to pounce on him the moment he moves to clear out, which we expect daily, therefor he has his army under light marching orders.

———

March 19th. Sunday. . . . Bvt. Brig. Gen. G. N. Macy is Provost Marshal General Army of the Potomac, and the 3rd and 11th U.S. Infantry are now at Hd. Qrs.[7]

March 20th. Monday. Much Ordnance and Quarter Master Property had to be left under guard at the old Detachment camp, belonging to "B," "C" and "F" Companies, and I went down to City Point to turn it all in. I worked very hard all day. Lunched with Gen. Patrick's mess with Capt. Potter and returned to the Regiment at Hd. Qrs.

March 21st. Tuesday. Officer of the Day. Rainy; very hard storm during the night.

March 22nd. Wednesday. Fine day but very windy. We had squadron drill. I had "B," "E" and "M" Cos. It was very windy and I came back hoarse. A difficulty has arrived respecting the ranking of Ward and myself, as we were mustered as 2nd Lt., 1st Lt. and Capt. on same days, and I rank him by commission as 2nd Lieut., while his commission dates mine as Captain. It is a very delicate difference. Col. Walsh made application for a decision in the case, in order to arrange the squadrons.

———

Camp 3d Pa. Cav.
Hd. Qrs. A of P, Mch. 23d, 65
Thursday

Dear Mother:

. . . While in Washington, I sent by express a pair of boots which were a little worn, as I got a new pair which suited me better costing $18. Rather heavy, ain't it? Please keep the old ones. I also sent $100, from which please take $50 which I owe you, and add the other to the nest egg. I send the receipt. Lieut. Ludwig, my 2nd Lieut., took home for me a pair of pantaloons such as are bought by officers for $4.75.[8] Did you get them? If so, please keep them until I want them. I wear government clothes nearly all together now. I believe the bill increasing our pay has passed, tho' as yet we have recd. no benefits therefrom.

Today a large party of ladies and gentlemen came down on a visit to Genl. Meade. Among the party were Mrs. Genl. Meade, Miss Maggie [Meade] (& necessarily Willie Wharton), Col. Jim Biddle & wife, Mrs. Hard Norris, Misses Fannie & Annie Cadwalader, Morton Henry and wife and others. It was one of the most windy days I ever saw, and the whole party went out to see a review of the 2nd Corps. Some of the ladies rode with the staff, and the rest in ambulances. The wind blew so that down came all their hair apparatus, waterfalls, rats & everything else.[9] The party returned to the boat in the eveng., and tomorrow they will visit the Army of the James. If the weather is fine they will come here again day after tomorrow. I was out riding and met the party, but steered shy of it. There were too many stars about, and all together it was a little too ranky.[10]

I wrote you Sunday telling you of the change in our affairs. Our det'ment is now with the Regiment. The troops composing the Hd. Qrs. brigade now are all regulars except our Regiment, and are a magnificent body of men. Our brigade guard mounts are beautiful. There was a good deal of discussion about our Regiment relative to changing. Genl. Patrick, whose pets we are, wanted us very badly, but Genl. Meade said he could not do without us, and as Gen. Macy, Pro. Mar. Gen. A of P said the same thing, Gen. Patrick said that altogether we would do much more service here; so here we remain.

The army is under marching orders, leaves & furloughs stopped, sutlers, etc. & extra baggage sent away, and we are ready at a moment's notice to pitch into Lee as soon as he evacuates, which he is expected to do daily. . . .

———

March 24th. Friday. Still in readiness to move, ready to pounce on Lee the moment he evacuates, which is expected daily.

———

Camp "Stumps"[11]
Hd. Qrs. A of P, Mch. 26th, 65

Dear Mother:

. . . We have given our camp the above euphonious name from the multitude of stumps in it, among which it is very dangerous to walk in the dark. I wrote the other day telling you of the change in our location from City Point to these Hd. Qrs.

I am Brigade Officer of the Day, and I am sitting up (it is midnight) in order to make the "Grand Rounds" after 12 AM to see that the Hd. Qrs. camps are all right & Genl. Meade safe. Altho' expecting to move every day, we are still in the old place. Night before last [March 25] the Rebels broke into our lines near Meade's Stn. directly in front of Petersburg, and came near making a big thing of it, but

"Camp Stumps," the camp of the 3rd Pennsylvania near Petersburg during the winter of 1864–65. (Courtesy Prints and Photographs Division, Library of Congress)

we succeeded in retaking all we lost, and about 2,000 prisoners. Of course the "Provisional Brigade" was out in support in the afternoon.

———

March 25th. Saturday. Shortly after reveille the Provisional Brigade was ordered out, as the Rebels had broken through our lines near Meade's Station in front of Petersburg. They almost got to Hd. Qrs. 1st Division 9th Corps, Lacey House, and came near making a big thing of it, but we re-captured Fort Steadman and our lines, and took 2000 prisoners, with a total loss of 800 men in all. We had to escort these up, and did not get anything to eat until 1 P.M. . . .

———

Mr. & Mrs. Lincoln came here, and with Gens. Grant & Meade went out to a review, and witnessed another very pretty fight of the 2nd Corps, in which we captured some works and 1,000 more prisoners.[12]

The pickets have been very lively vigilant after the surprise, and are keeping up a lively firing along the lines, especially about Fort Hell. I hear that Gen. Sheridan is expected here tonight, and we expect big things before many days have passed.[13]

I have just returned from my "Grand Rounds," and "the country is safe." It is very late and I am very tired so please content yourself with a short letter. . . .

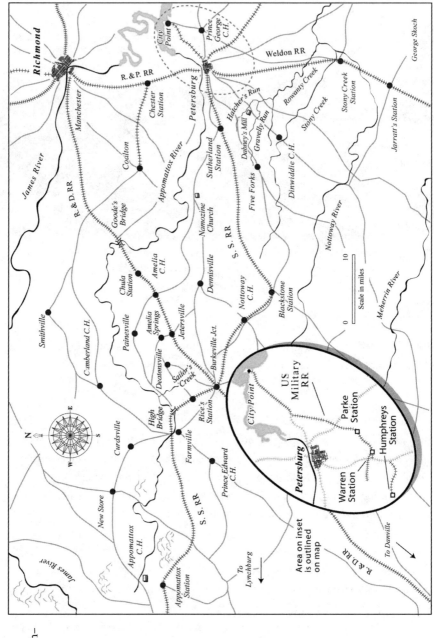

The Appomattox
Campaign, March–
April 1865

Camp Hd. Qrs. Army of Potomac
near Gravelly Run, Va.
March 31st, 1865

Dear Mother:

I have returned to my writing with pencil on scraps of paper, or, in other words, the "Campaign of 1865" has opened. I wrote to you Sunday from our last camp near Parke's Station. For some time we had had orders to be in readiness to move at a moment's notice. On Sunday night [March 26] Gen. Sheridan arrived with his Cavalry Corps at Point of Rocks, and on Monday at Hancock Station. On Tuesday we recd. orders to move at daylight the next morng.

———

March 28th. Tuesday. Orders to move early tomorrow morning. The 24th and 10th Corps, Army of the James came up; also Gen. Sherman on a visit to Gens. Grant and Meade for cooperation. I suppose we will move out to the far left, to cooperate with Sherman's army and open more lines of approach to him.[14]

———

Prior to the attack on Fort Stedman, Grant had been planning his Eighth Offensive. Beginning on March 29, Sheridan and the cavalry would swing out to the south and west from the Petersburg lines with the goal of severing two of Lee's remaining supply lines, the South Side Railroad, which entered Petersburg from the west, and the Richmond & Danville Railroad, which angled in to the capital from the southwest. Soldiers from the Army of the James had moved into the lines near Petersburg, replacing II and V Corps troops of the Army of the Potomac who moved out in support of Sheridan. Once in position, the infantry would move up the Boydton Plank Road, Warren's V Corps connecting with Sheridan's right, while Humphreys's II Corps extended the line from Warren's right.[15] Lee, Grant hoped, would be forced to vacate his fortifications and fight the Federals on open ground, where the numerical superiority of the Northerners could be used to their advantage.

———

[March 29.] (Wednesday) We broke camp, Gen. Grant and staff came up, and we started out with the "Great Moguls"—4 days rations in haversacks, 4 of forage and 8 days in wagons. Portions of the Army of the James came to occupy our former lines, and the 2nd, 5th and I believe the 10th Corps moved out to the left by parallel roads and established a line of battle (driving the enemy's pickets parallel with the South Side Rail Road, and North of the Vaughn (or Dinwiddie C.H.)

Road. Hd. Qrs. were established near this road where it crossed a small creek called Gravelly Run.[16] That night, just as is usual in all our moves out here, Gen. Warren of 5th Corps called for Cavalry, and ours being the nearest and most convenient, Frazer's & my squadrons, under Major Hess, went out and established a picket line from the Junction of two roads towards Stony Creek on the left and Dinwiddie Court House on the right. It rained all night, and our pickets being very much troubled, we had to stand to horse all night.

This was on the extreme left of the infantry lines, but Sheridan, with Crook com'ding Gregg's old Divn., and Kautz's late Divn., comprising all the Cavalry of the Armies operating against Richmond, was out around Dinwiddie C.H on the left of & 4 miles to the left of our infantry lines. We had an extremely rough night of it—soaked through, it raining too hard to keep a fire and a cold wind blowing.[17]

We were relieved the next day [March 30] (yesterday) by Capts. Stillé & Carter, and returned to camp in the same place where it was left.

——

March 30th. Thursday. . . . Great humbugging on account of being under an Infantry General. . . . Raining hard day and night and we will surely stick in the mud; roads fearful. Considerable musketry firing on right of our new line, which connects with our old one. Our new line runs parallel with the South Side R.R., North of the Vaughn Road, and extending West of Dinwiddie Court House. Gen. Sheridan, with part of his staff and a small escort, came in through my line. They did not hear the picket's challenge, who tried to fire on them, but their caps snapped and they were driven in to the reserve. The party looked like Rebs, having india rubber coats on and grey blankets in front of their saddles.[18]

——

It rained all yesterday also, so I was still in a pleasant state of "damp." It has cleared off temporarily today (12 M) [March 31], and, while I write, they are fighting like the old Harry. All goes well so far. I believe that all except the Virginia troops have been withdrawn from the front, they being left here because they would not fight except on their own soil and there they <u>do</u> fight magnificently. Today we are issuing 3 days rations, making 4 from tonight. Gen. Sherman was up here to see Gens. Grant & Meade on Tuesday [March 28], and I suppose this movement is to cooperate with him, and give him more avenues of approach. . . .[19]

On picket Apr. 1st, 1865.

I closed my letter [of March 31] suddenly as I had to go out to the 5th Corps line on duty. The rebels made a terrific charge on that part of the line, and down our line some distance. [We] lost very severely, but regained the ground in a fine countercharge. During the day Gen. Sheridan had a very hard fight some-where near Dinwiddie C.H., and was very roughly handled—in other words, he was badly whipped—by cavalry & infantry. The ground around this part of the country is very miry, and he tried to make a magnificent Cavalry charge, but his horses foundered, and he was badly cut up. They have not got Early to fight now. I have recd. no particulars yet.[20]

———

March 31st. Friday. . . . The roads are perfectly fearful, trains moving to issue three days rations, teams stalled, wagons upset etc. every few yards. One of the worst cases of "stick in the mud" the army was ever in. Out along 5th Corps line in afternoon on duty. Horses floundering in the mud every few yards.

———

This morning [April 1], before daybreak, the Rebels made a heavy charge on our right but were gallantly repulsed. . . .

We came out this morning to relieve Capts. Stillé & Carter. So far it is much easier work here than if <u>we</u> were relieved, as otherwise we have a good deal of marching to do. The roads are perfectly fearful, as bad as when Burnside stuck in the mud—miry and swampy—every few yards you can see a team stalled, wagons upset, etc. Words can't describe the state we are in. If it had not been for the bad weather, a good deal would have been done. Today is clear, & we pray it may con-tinue so. Write regularly, & I will try to do the same. Hd. Qrs. moved to Dabney's Mills. . . .[21]

On the march, Jetersville Stn.
on the Richmond & Danville RR[22]
April 6th, 1865

Dear Mother:

Of course by this time you have all the glorious news, & know <u>more</u> of it than we do. Richmond & Petersburg in our possession, & Lee retreating—we after him as hard as we can go.

I wrote to you on April 1st while on picket during our movement on the South Side RR. The day previously Sheridan with his cavalry was very badly handled near Dinwiddie C.H., and on April 1st, the 5th Corps, under Griffin (Warren being relieved), was sent to report to him. They routed the enemy, took 4,000 prisoners and carried the South Side RR. It was a glorious victory, the grandest the Army of the Potomac ever saw, and all credit was due to Gen. Meade. Gens.

Grant & Meade had a difference about the mode of attack, Gen. G wishing to attack all along the line simultaneously while Meade protested against it and wished to attack in mass at several places. Grant gave in to Meade & it was a glorious success. A large number of prisoners, guns etc. captured. The Rebel army in full retreat & our troops following closely.[23]

———

April 2nd. Sunday. Hard fighting all along the line. We were ordered back to Hd. Qrs. near Dabney's Mills in the morning. An attack was made in mass at several points along the line, with perfect success, carrying the enemy's works and cutting the South Side in several places. . . . Rebel army in rapid retreat. Our troops following. Assisted in escorting prisoners to Warren Station, and then camped with my company at Humphrey's Station near Hatcher's Run.[24]

———

Lee now had lost his main supply artery, the South Side Railroad; seen his fortifications protecting Petersburg overrun; and had suffered over 5,000 casualties on the fateful day of April 2. He was faced with no other alternative except to attempt to escape with the remainder of his army to the west. "It is absolutely necessary," he informed government officials, "that we abandon our position tonight or run the risk of being cut off in the morning."[25] The Southern forces protecting Petersburg and Richmond withdrew on the night of April 2–3, heading west from the beleaguered cities to rendezvous at Amelia Court House, where supplies would be waiting. From there Lee planned to march for Danville, Virginia, heading for what he hoped would be a junction with General Johnston's Army of Tennessee in North Carolina.[26]

———

April 3d. [Monday.] Early in the morning our troops entered and took possession of Petersburg & Richmond. Of course, as I always expected, we saw nothing of Richmond, the Army of the James taking it. Our Regiment rode through Petersburg with our colors flying with Gens. Grant & Meade. Our Regt. acted as Provost Guard of the town, went through the tobacco factories & got as much as we could possibly carry along. I also got this note paper there. . . . I also got a copy of the last Petersburg Express published. From the advertisements, it seems they expected nothing like being at the hands of the Yankees so soon. The "Cockade City" was evidently once a beautiful place, but now part of it is battered to pieces by our shells, and the other part is sadly in need of repairs, like the whole country indeed. We did not stay long in the place, however. We moved out and Hd. Qrs.

for the night were at Sutherland's Station on the South Side RR. Our army, and part of Gen. Ord's, started out following up very closely the cavalry in advance.

———

April 3rd. . . . Plenty of women in the part of town uninjured. Our men went through several tobacco factories and I got a lot of very fine. Could have had hogsheads of it. Destroyed lots of applejack, etc. . . . Petersburg was a beautiful place. . . . Severe fighting near Namozine Church.[27] *Now for a run of it to head off Lee!*

———

April 4th Tuesday. Started on the march at daybreak, out the Namozine Road, and camped for the night near Dennisville. Roads blockaded up with troops, wagons, etc., roads very bad yet. Cavalry fighting in front.[28]

April 5th Wednesday. Hd. Qrs. started on the march about 9 AM. As Gen. Meade was unwell he rode in his ambulance, so we did not have to travel so hard. About 4 PM we came up with the Cavalry near this place [Jetersville]. The Cavalry struck the enemy's left flank, captured a large train of wagons. Our old brigade made a magnificent charge capturing 10 guns, 5 of which were celebrated Armstrong guns, a present from some people in England and, it is said, the only battery of its kind in this country. They took many prisoners, mules, etc. but lost very severely, among the number a good many friends of mine whom you don't know.[29] I saw Col. Charlie Leiper, now full Col. of 6th Pa. Cav. By the bye Charlie Coxe is Major in the same Regt. . . . Our rations & forage are out, and I had very little to eat, I assure you.

Apr. 6th Thursday. The Cavalry started out again this morning; there was some fighting in front but we appear to be driving the enemy. Thanks to Maj. J R Coxe we got something to eat today. Our trains are far in rear. We are expecting to move forward every moment, & I hear there is a mail going off today, so I write. . . . We are rushing the rebs like the old Harry, and giving them fits whenever they make a stand. I don't know when or where we are going to stop. I suppose they aim taking to the mountain country. There are some beautiful military combinations in progress—Thomas, Stoneman, Sherman, Hancock & Grant. I think we are near the last ditch now.

Camp in the Field
near Appomattox C.H., Va.
4 miles from Appomattox C.H.
Apr. 10, 1865

Dear Mother:

During a halt on the march while Gens. Grant and Meade were holding a conference at Jetersville on the Richmond and Danville RR on April 6th I wrote to you telling you of the glorious successes of our army, the occupation of Richmond and Petersburg, the retreat of Gen. Lee & his army, and our rapid pursuit. The letter did not leave my hands for 2 or 3 days after that date, but I had no time to write any more. Now I have still more glorious news, but by this time you know all about it. Yesterday afternoon at 4 PM Gen. Lee surrendered his army to Gen. Grant. We are now waiting I believe for all his detachments to come in, in order to go through all the formalities. As soon as he sent in word that he would surrender, a salute of 100 guns was fired, all the bands commenced playing, and a tremendous cheer went up through the whole army. Such rejoicing I never saw before. We know not the particulars of the surrender yet.

After I wrote to you on the 6th, we moved past the Amelia Springs, and camped about 6 miles West of them. On that day our troops captured miles of the Rebel Wagon train, Gen. Ewell and several other General officers, & 12,000 prisoners, many pieces of artillery, etc.[30]

On April 7th we marched to High Bridge on the Appomattox River, over which we had drawn the enemy and occupied the other bank, a very strong position. Hd. Qrs. for the night were Rice's Station on the South Side RR. Yesterday and today there was some terrific fighting. The country was covered with dead and wounded, captured artillery, the debris of a retreating army, wagons, ambulances, etc. which in our rapid march we had to leave behind us. This paper which I am writing upon was captured in Gen. Ewell's Hd. Qr. train.[31]

———

April 7th. Friday. We started out on the march about 8 A.M. I was in rear driving up stragglers and foraging for corn, etc. For miles along the road the Rebel trains captured by our troops were burning, the woods full of dead and wounded. . . . We have driven Lee across the Appomattox and hold the other bank. Hd. Qrs. for the night were at Rice's Station on the South Side R.R. Hd. Qrs. during the day were at High Bridge on the Appomattox River. Rice's Station is 8 miles West of Burkesville [Burkeville] Junction and 62 [miles west] of Petersburg and Richmond. Saw the New York Herald of the 4th. The whole North crazy over the glorious news.[32]

———

Shortly after daybreak of April 8th, we again started on the march along the S.S. RR to Farmville, quite a town for Virginia, then into Buckingham County, near no particular place, where we encamped. Marching and detail work has pulled our Regiment down almost to nothing. During the day Gen. Lee sent in a flag of truce and considerable correspondence passed between he and Genl. Grant. Sheridan with the Cavalry & 24th & 25th Corps were fighting in the enemy's right rear.[33]

———

April 8th. Saturday. . . . Marching and detail work very hard. Have not now as large a squadron as my Company when we started out.

———

April 9th Sunday. We marched out on the Lynchburg Road about 5 miles beyond New Stores—with Gen. Meade—to the extreme front of our lines, where Gen. Grant and Lee were in consultation, the result of which I have already given you.[34] Gen. Sheridan with his command got between Lee & Lynchburg, and the only way to get out was through an impassible swamp.

———

April 9th. Sunday. Palm Sunday indeed! Started on the march early into Appomattox County; went with Gen. Meade to the extreme advance on the Lynchburg Road, where a conference was going on between Grant and Lee, regarding terms of surrender. The Rebel army is laying along the road around Appomattox Court House. All the arrangements were made for a surrender by 2 P.M., a salute of 100 guns fired, all bands playing and the whole army cheering. The most glorious day of the Potomac Army's most glorious campaign. From 8,000 to 12,000 men in the Rebel Army of Northern Virginia is estimated at—all that is left.[35]

———

I have not the slightest idea what we are to do now. We have several smaller armies to fix up yet, and it may be some time before we have peace. At any rate I think we have the last ditch. For the first time during the Campaign we have a prospect of a day in camp, although it is only a temporary one and the weather is cold and rainy. We have been having a pretty rough time of it lately.

While we were in Petersburg on April 3d 1st Lieut. Coleman Hall Watts of Carlisle, Pa. reported to me for my company. He is a fine fellow and well connected, as from his name. He is a nephew of Henry M. Watts, Esq. of Philada. and is acquainted with some of my relations.[36] I have now a 1st & 2nd Lieut. in my company.

We have very little communication with civilization. The latest paper I have seen is of April 4th. From all accounts the North has gone crazy over the successes of our Army. I have not heard from home since Lilly's letter of 31st of March.

> On the march
> Farmville, Pr. Edward Co., Va.
> April 12, 1865

I could not get that letter off sooner. [April 10]. After I wrote the first part of this letter I took a ride all through the Rebel army. It was laying along the Lynchburg Road as far as Appomattox Court House where Genl. Lee's Hd. Qrs. were. After the formalities of the surrender were through with, Gens. Grant & Lee started for Richmond, most probably on the way to see the President, in regards to peace. The rebels for the most part were very glad at the prospect of peace, while a good many were very blue and still very hopeful of their cause. All their arms & colors were stacked, and though contrary to the strictest orders, the Yanks & rebs were in each other's camps as intimate as possible. I called to see Frank Rawle, Major in the Louisiana Brigade, but he had just left camp. I left my pasteboard for him.[37] Mord Lewis' Regiment, Brigade or Division was not to be found. Everyone told me at present it was stationed at Point Lookout, Md.!!![38]

———

Rawle wrote the following account of his experiences on April 10 sometime after the war for inclusion in the regimental history of the 3rd Pennsylvania.

> . . . I determined to try to find a relative of my own who was Major and Quartermaster on the staff of the Louisiana Brigade. Accordingly, I directed my orderly bugler to get a grain sack and fill it with what little pork and hard tack, coffee and sugar were available. He was then to follow me. He was a mere boy—small, smooth-faced and pink-cheeked, with a bugle slung over his shoulder shining bright as gold and riding a white pony, while I myself, a beardless youngster, would not have been taken to be much older myself. With my orderly following, I cantered out the Lynchburg Road, right in the face of the rebel army, until stopped by a party of "gray backs" on the skirmish line, who informed me that their orders were positive not to allow any Yankees—officers or men—to pass into their camps. I accordingly rode back a short distance, and then struck across country to the left to a point beyond the rebel lines, made a wide detour, and, avoiding other obstructionists, arrived unmolested and unchallenged at the Court House, near which lay the remnants of Lee's army.

After inquiring the whereabouts of the Louisiana Brigade, and visiting the McLean House, where General Lee had on the previous day formally surrendered his army to General Grant, I started off, rode through the Confederate army, found the brigade headquarters I was in search of, learned that the major, my rebel cousin, was in our own lines searching for me, left my card for him with the bag of provender, and chatted a while with the other officers of the staff. I found them glum, indeed rather surly, notwithstanding the good things I had brought with me. This was not the case, I found, with the enlisted men—at least many of those to whom I talked were polite, cordial and in good spirits at the prospect of returning home to their families, now that the war was practically at an end.

I then started for home by the Lynchburg Road, which I had endeavored to pass along a few hours before. It was now dusk, and as I did not yet feel quite comfortable about being in the midst of the Confederate army with only my bugler boy by me, I rode along at a clipping gait. The guards at the outpost called to me to halt and raised their pieces. Consigning them, in words of frequent use in our army vocabulary, to a warmer place, I waved my hand in farewell, put spurs to my horse, and rode on. They did not fire, and we got back to camp in safety.

As soon as I dismounted I was given to understand that what I had done was in disobedience of orders and rather risky, and that I had better keep quiet about it, else I should get into trouble in consequence.[39]

———

Grant allowed all officers to keep their arms & horses. Sheridan with the 9th & 24th Corps gone to Danville. We started out again yesterday morning [April 11] at daybreak, backwards, having accomplished much more than was hoped for. The 5th Corps I believe are to escort the Rebel army to Burkeville Junction, where they will be paroled & sent to their homes when a guerilla warfare of magnificent proportions will be commenced.

We marched 28 miles on terrible roads to this place, where we encamped last night. The army is moving back to Burkeville Junction when I suppose we will lay and rest and watch Johns[t]on, whose men I hear are deserting rapidly. The Regt. has moved on with Hd. Qrs. and I with my squadron are left here as Provost Guard of this town until the 6th & 2nd Corps have passed through. This is the most celebrated tobacco country of Va and I have a lot of it. We all have as much as we can carry. . . .

———

April 13th. Thursday. Started with my squadron on the march at 8 A.M., took the road North of the Appomattox to avoid the troops and trains, crossed again at High

Bridge and halted to rest and call on Miss Jennie R. near Rice's Station. Arrived at Burkeville Junction, near which place Army Hd. Qrs. were, at 3:30 P.M. A wretched country, swampy and no bottom to the land. Our cars running to the junction. The country full of paroled Rebels making their way home. . . .

April 14th. Friday. In the Morning General Head Quarters and all troops connected with it moved camp a few hundred yards, to some more solid ground.

———

Camp 3d Pa. Ca.
Hd. Qrs. A. of P.
Burkeville Junction, Va.
April 15, 1865

Dear Mother:

I have just returned from a long march from Farmville, where I had been left behind with my squadron. Upon my arrival at camp I found your letter of the 3rd. Along the march I have written to you, but have not been able to mail the letter I enclose.

You need not be alarmed about me. I am all right, and there is no force of rebs in this part of the country now. The rebel Army of Northern Virginia is being paroled, and the men sent home. The country is full of forlorn grey backs wending their way in every direction.

I am very tired and have just got my valise for the first time during the campaign and I must perform my lavations and put on a clean "hickory."

Camp 3d Pa. Cav., Hd. Qrs. A of P
Burkeville Junction, Va.
Easter Sunday, April 16, 65

Dear Mother:

. . . Yesterday I recd. your letter of the 10th, in which you seemed joyed over the news of Lee's surrender. Frank Wetherill was wrong when he told the girls that our Regiment was with Sheridan. We were, as usual, on escort duty at Genl. Meade's Hd. Qrs., and saw everything.

Gen. Meade recd. a telegram yesterday that President Lincoln, Secretary Seward & son had been assassinated. We could hardly credit it, especially since some guerillas had been troubling our communications by the South Side RR, tearing up the track, etc. I sincerely hope that there is no truth in the report. We can't well spare Lincoln now, especially since Johnson is Vice President.

You seem to be very anxious about me. I wish you would not worry yourself so. We are laying still, resting from the extremely hard work of this short but very decisive Campaign. . . . I wrote you an outline of the Campaign in my last letters.

I must close, as "Dress Parade" will sound in a few minutes. We celebrate Sunday by Inspection for Morning Service, and Dress Parade for the evening. . . . Is this not a fine quality of tinted paper? It was once a rebel's but now has come into the possession of Uncle Sam. . . .

———

April 16th. Easter Sunday. Inspection in morning, Dress Parade in evening. A telegram was received at Head Quarters confirming the report of the assassination, that President Lincoln was shot though the head at "Ford's" on Friday evening and died at 7:22 A.M. yesterday; that Mr. Seward will live but not his son. J. Wilkes Booth, son of Edwin Booth, is the murderer of the President. He has been in communication with the South for some time.

———

Camp 3d Pa. Cav., Hd. Qrs. A of P
Burkeville Junction, Va.
April 26th, 1865

Dear Mother:

I was unable to write any regular Sunday letter as I was away from camp on duty for several days. The last letter I wrote you was on April 16th.

———

April 17th. Monday. Clear. Presentation at Gen. Meade's of all the Rebel flags captured by the 6th Corps. The captors take them to Washington with 30 days leave. Took a ride in the evening with Lieut. Grugan.

April 18th. Tuesday. Relieved Capt. Carter as Officer of the Day, he having received a leave of absence for ten days to visit his home, Richmond, where he has not been for several years. The Regiment being ordered out on light duty, and I being senior Captain present with the Regiment (Capt. Stille being on Provost Marshal duty at City Point) I was put in command. . . .

———

Wednesday [April 19] was set aside in honor of Pres. Lincoln, as he was buried on that day.[40] Salutes were fired, etc., and no work was done.

On Thursday [April 20] Capt. Ward returned to the Regiment. After his recovery from his wound he was on <u>soft</u> duty in Harrisburg & Philadelphia, and has been having a good time for the last four months.

———

April 20. Thursday. Official news received at Head Quarters of the surrender of Gen. Johnston to Gen. Sherman. No particulars. . . .[41]

———

On Friday the 21st I was ordered out with a party of men to Prince Edward Court House, about 20 miles from here, to look after stragglers, negroes and confederate soldiers who have been marauding, pillaging and robbing everyone indiscriminately. Pr. Edward is called the "<u>Queen</u>" County of the State on account of its society. The 5th Corps and the Cavalry had passed through the C.H. during the pursuit of Lee's Army, and completely <u>went through</u> the whole concern. Nearly all the livestock, corn, fowls and everything to eat had been stolen, and the people were almost starving.[42] I went to see a good many gentlemen owning thousands of acres and hundreds of negroes who had not a cent in the world, and who did not know actually what they should do for breakfast next morning.

———

April 21st. Friday. . . . Started out at about 1 and arrived at the Court House by dark. Well received by the inhabitants, took supper with a gentleman and cantoned my men in an old tavern.

———

About a mile from the C.H. is Hampden Sidney College and Theological Inst. There are some very pleasant gentlemen among the faculty and I had several very pleasant visits there.

———

April 22nd. Saturday. Magnificent weather. Took a ride around the country to get the "lay" of the land. The depredations committed by our army, principally by stragglers, is terrible. . . . I called on Dr. Smith and faculty at Hampden Sydney College, about one mile from the Court House and dined with Dr. Smith. The county is celebrated for its society.

April 23rd. Sunday. Magnificent day. The country seems to be pretty well cleaned out of marauders. I have only succeeded in catching three. Called to see several gentlemen. Mr. A. D. Dickinson of the State Senate, a very wealthy and kind hearted gentleman, is left without a cent.[43] *Such is the case with almost everyone.*

April 24th. Monday. Fine day. Took a ride with Capt. Atwell, late of Rebel Gen. Heath's staff, and made some very pleasant calls.[44]

April 25th. Tuesday. Fine day. Warm. As my rations run up tonight, and I have no means of getting more from the country, I started back this morning with my party, four prisoners and Capt. Atwell, a clever gentleman, who wishes to go North. I sent the party by Sand River Church, but Capt. A. and I, with two orderlies, rode by way of Rice's Station. Reached camp near Burkeville Junction around 5 P.M. Found a considerable mail, including a good many letters from anxious wives and mothers, etc., which are a great bother to me.

———

My stay of 5 days at the C.H. was very pleasant, but it would have been much more so had there been more to eat, and more forage for my horses. There are a great many paroled prisoners about. It seems very strange to be able to ride about with only one orderly through the thickest woods without any apprehension of danger.

The slave owners about here fear their own slaves as much as anything else. They have little enough to eat, in all conscience, and would be very glad for their negroes to leave them, but they will not. Many of the black men have got it into their heads that they are now free, and can therefore live and do nothing. A good many of them join with bands of stragglers and do a great deal of pillaging—even going so far as to rob and burn the houses of their masters. The majority of the white people are wishing for us to drive the negroes away.

Measures are being taken to put all the Railroads of Va. into running order. The 6th Corps has gone out to Danville, the 5th Corps guarding the S.S. RR, and the 2nd Corps is left here, the 9th being sent to Washington. Things look now very much as if the Rebellion had something the matter with it. I begin to think the war is over at last. . . . My mail now consists principally of letters from wives, sisters, mothers and such of men of my company, asking for information regarding them after the late battles. I am bothered a great deal with them. I get about one private letter a week now—you people must write more.

———

April 26th. Wednesday. Not well last night, but better this morning. Sent to Capt. Schuyler a written report of my expedition to Prince Edward Court House.

April 27th. Thursday. Officer of the Day. Very fine weather. A dispatch came to Gen. Meade about 3 P.M. that Baker's men had killed Booth near Port Royal, Va., and that Harold, his accomplice, had been captured.

April 28th. Friday. News arrived that Rebel Gen. Johns[t]on had surrendered to Gen. Grant, who went down to North Carolina after him, upon the same terms as

Gen. Lee. Gen Sherman took too much on himself in arranging terms with Johns[t]on, much more indeed than Grant had a right to do. Sherman has "gone up" in public estimation.

The Rebellion is pretty well played out by now, there being no organized force this side of [the] Mississippi.

April 29th. Saturday. Nothing much going on. The fact that we have no enemy in front of us can hardly be realized.

—

Camp 3d Pa. Cav., Hd. Qrs. A of P
Burkeville Junction, Va.
May 1st, 1865

My Dear Lottie:

. . . We break camp tomorrow and move back to Richmond. I believe that Hd. Qrs. Army of the Potomac are to be at Alexandria, and that we are to march there via Fredericksburg. Very probably, however, our Regiment may be left at Richmond with Gen. Patrick, who thinks everything of us, and always wishes us to be with him. I don't care much what we do. Everything looks as if they are going to disband the armies. We have the pleasing intelligence that the Treasury Department has ordered that no officers be paid unless all their accounts with the government have been settled up. As far as I know at present, I am pretty near square, with the exception of my returns for this year, but such is by no means the case for everyone. An Act of Congress will have to be passed to free officers from a great deal of their responsibility.

I suspect before the summer is over we will all be [private] citizens. They may keep the Cavalry on, however, for some time to come. I know that if they muster us out of service, as is always the case, we will have such a trouble to get certificates of non-indebtedness in order to draw our pay that, but the time we <u>do</u> get it, we will have spent as much or more than the pay itself amounts to, what with going to Washington, stopping there, employing clerks etc. It is a very great satisfaction for serving your country! As if we would steal from the government several thousand dollars' worth of property!

Wherever we go, I am very glad to get out of this wretched place. What with the swampy water to drink and boggy ground to live upon, I have succeeded, now that the war is over, in getting a little case of "fever & ague" for the first time since I have been in the army. I am off duty, but I will be all right again before long. . . .

The officers of our Regiment look as if they were going to their own funerals, with a long piece of crape on the left arms, and another on their sabre hilts in memory of the President, by order of the War Department. We just got our crape today. . . .

Camp 3d Pa. Cav.
Richmond, Va.
May 5th, 1865

Dear Mother:

Here we are at last, which we have been trying to get for four long years, in Richmond. . . . Gen. Meade and staff went down to Richmond by Rail on [the] 1st, and early on the 2nd the Head Quarter troops and trains started on the march, all under the command of Gen. Macy, Pro. Mar. Genl. A of P. The weather was magnificent and roads in excellent condition, wide and neither muddy nor dusty, and very shady for the most part, country beautiful.

On Tuesday [May 2] marched 23 miles and camped on Richmond & Danville RR about 2 m. W. of Chula Stn.

On Wednesday [May 3] marched about 20 miles and camped near Swift Creek, having pontooned and crossed the Appomattox at Goode's Bridge. Our camp was 13 m. from Richmond.

On Thursday May 4th, on the march again, arrived at Manchester, a suburb of Richmond, at 10 AM and crossed into Richmond at 12 M. As soon as we arrived there the Regiment was ordered to report to Gen. Patrick for duty. Gens. Meade and Macy were terribly angry when they heard of it. Meade told Patrick "that he never would have got the better of him in getting the Third Cavalry if he had only been here earlier." Gen. Halleck commands the Department, and Genl. Patrick is his Provost Marshal General. The 2nd Pa. Cav. took our place with Genl. Macy. We are all very glad to get back with old Gen. Patrick; he thinks "the world and all" of the 3d.

I met Capt. Carter of ours yesterday. He lives here (or rather, he used to, and his family do now) and is on leave of absence to see his family, having been away from home 7 yrs. We took a ride together all through the town. Richmond is beautifully situated on 7 hills (overlooking the James River), from which fine views of the river and country are to be had. "Shakoe" and "Church" Hills are the fashionable parts of the city.[45] We passed by Castle Thunder and Libby Prison, which latter is a low three-storied brick warehouse on the wharves. Major Turner, who had charge of the prison while our officers were confined there, and who treated them so shamefully, is now there himself, kept in close confinement and hard treatment. At first officers were allowed to go see him, but one punched his head so that Capt. Potter of our Regt., who has charge of the Institution, had to lock him up, and not let anyone see him.[46]

We also rode to see Jeff. Davis' house, the C.S. and Va. State Capitol and most places of interest. Fully one third of the city is in ruins, Early having fired it and the four bridges across the James on leaving the city, and there are now two pontoon bridges connecting the city with Manchester.[47] We met a good many young ladies promenading the streets, many of them pulling down their veils, turning up their noses and walking as if every step they took was upon the neck of a Yankee.

We are encamped on Union Hill, in a sunny place, very hot and very dirty. We expect in a few days to go into barracks in town here. We muchly like the idea of staying here. We are detached entirely from the Army of the Potomac, and are now at Gen. Halleck's Hd. Qrs. He commands the Dep'ment of Va. Hd. Qrs. A of P starts tomorrow morning for Washington by land, via Fredericksburg. We prefer being here at Richmond to being at Alexandria, which is a wretched place. . . .

Camp Winder
Richmond, Va.
May 9th, 1865

Dear Mother:

. . . We remained encamped on Union Hill until this morning, when our Regiment moved out to this place. This is called the "Winder Hospital" and consists of a good many wooden, white-washed buildings 28 paces long by 10 wide, and as dirty as can be. We have occupied 20 of these buildings, separated from the rest of the hospital, having one company of men to a building, thus occupying 8 of them, and each company has one building for stables. The officers have one of the buildings which is divided into 8 rooms. . . .[48]

The southern people are unfortunately the laziest and dirtiest creatures on the earth, and such a filthy place for a hospital I never saw. Actually I am afraid to go to bed tonight on account of the bed bugs which fill the quarters by the millions. I had a bed made today after having all the boards scalded with hot water, and then scrubbed. I filled every crack and joint with mercurial ointment, and painted it over the legs to prevent the beasts from climbing up. They are such sharp creatures I fear they will climb exactly over the bed, on the ceiling, and drop. . . . People around here say they get used to them, however. . . .

The glorious old Army of the Potomac passed through the streets of Richmond on Saturday [May 6], and was reviewed by Gen. Halleck. It was a glorious sight. They were "homeward bound," with their faces turned directly for Washington. Sherman's army passes through tomorrow, going in the same direction. . . . We are left here, as also the 4th, 11th & 14th US Infantry and will be kept in the service some time I think, and will not be present at the Grand Review of the Armies of the United States at Washington.

Camp 3rd Pa. Cav.
Richmond, Va
May 15th, 1865

My dear Mother:

. . . On Wednesday [May 10] we were ordered out in parade order, mounted, early in the morning as Gen. Sherman's Army was to have passed through the City "Homeward Bound," but it was postponed, and we were reviewed over in Manchester by Genl. Patrick for the benefit of some Northern young ladies visiting the City.

That same eveng. I was ordered to report to Genl. Patrick for Special duty, and next morning I started out with half a dozen picked men and horses on secret service. Marched out by Mechanicsville, over the Cold Harbor Battle ground to "Old Church," crossed the Pamunkey at Piping Tree Ferry (which ferry consisted of a raft polled across the river by an aged negro), went to King William C.H. then up the Matapony River to near "Aylett's" where I was overtaken by darkness and a tremendous thunderstorm.

Spent the night at a house and, in the saddle by daylight crossed the Matapony at Dunkirk Ferry and went to the residence of Mr. Wm. Boulware near Newtown, and arrested him as a State prisoner by order of the Secretary of War. He is a strong rebel and is a gentleman of high standing. He was minister to Naples under Pres. Pearce.[49] I brought him back to Richmond by way of Dunkirk and Newcastle Ferries, Old Church & Mechanicsville, arriving in Richmond at about 8 PM, making the march of about 80 miles in 2 days. The evening before I started out, Carter came back from a similar expedition with Hon. R. M. T. Hunter, a very eminent man and a member of the C.S. Senate.[50] I suppose we will have a good deal of this to do in bringing the big guns of the Confederacy to a settlement of their accounts.

Last evening [May 14] Grugan & I were taking a ride through Richmond when news arrived of the capture of Jeff Davis. I hope they will stretch him. As Pemberton & I were riding thro' town the other afternoon we met several of our Philadelphia young ladies on a visit here. The ladies of Richmond seem to be getting over their aversion to our officers. They won't wear so many thick veils and have a little more pleasing expression on their faces. The change so far is barely perceptible but there is one nonetheless. I suppose they find there is not a sufficient number of young gentlemen left for them, and are open to approaches from a few "Mudsills." It don't bother me much as I have neither time nor inclination to seek their good graces. . . .

EPILOGUE

The Civil War had ended, and the last vestiges of Confederate forces still in the field would surrender by the end of May 1865. As part of the provost marshal's contingent assigned to occupy Richmond, however, duties remained for the 3rd Pennsylvania to perform and endless amounts of paperwork for its officers and clerks to process. "Tremendous muster rolls and fixing up of all accounts and books are wasting us away," Rawle complained.

The quiet that accompanied peace afforded the opportunity for reflection, allowing the young officer to ponder his future. While completing personnel forms in late May, Rawle was perplexed when the final question asked for his occupation: "I puzzled over the last for a long time, undetermined whether to put down a vagrant, student or lawyer, and determined upon the last."[1]

Ten officers who had served with the 3rd Pennsylvania would eventually accept Regular Army commissions, a prospect that, at this time, was appealing to Rawle. "In everything but age I am 10 years older than the day I entered the service," he wrote to his family, "and if I stay 5 or 10 more in the service it will have as much effect on me as 3 times that much in citizens life." He went on to add, "I think I have left my seat vacant at the head of your table for a sufficient time for you to become accustomed to the sight of <u>not</u> seeing me there."[2]

By an order from the War Department dated May 8, 1865, many of the battle-thinned regiments of the Army of the Potomac whose terms of enlistment had not expired were slated to be consolidated with other units in order to bring them close to full strength. Men whose terms of service were to expire before October 1 would be discharged, and all volunteer cavalry remaining after these discharges "will be immediately consolidated into complete, maximum regimental organizations." The order further directed that organizations would be consolidated only with those from the same state. Rumors were rife throughout May that the 3rd Pennsylvania, with its eight undersized companies, would be absorbed by a larger regiment.[3]

The provost marshal responsibilities undertaken by the 3rd Pennsylvania after it moved to Richmond soon proved tiresome. Rawle wrote that the regiment was acting as "a sort of military street police." These routine duties, combined with the heat ("perfectly enervating," he called it), the quality of rations, and the irregularity of their wages were not conducive to harmony. Writing to his mother on May 19, the young lieutenant expressed his dissatisfaction:

> Our position here is by no means a sinecure. We are on duty 2 out of 3 days, and that in the hot sun of the streets of Richmond. You may say that is not hard work for $5.50 per diem, but we consider it so, taking prices into consideration, which are fearful. Altho' my pay amounts to that, I have not had a cent of money in my pockets for 2 weeks, nor has anyone in the mess. We are stranded high and dry. We live a hand to mouth existence, eating principally fish, which we get for a few cents a piece. We are living on the bounty of our negro servants, who are able at present to buy their masters, heart and soul. I find it economical to live on nothing, that is one satisfaction.

The enlisted men of the 3rd were growing restless too. On May 21 Rawle was dismayed to learn that two soldiers of his company (one a first sergeant) had deserted, taking with them several of the best horses in the command.[4]

The monotony of provost marshal duty in the former Confederate capital was interrupted on May 24, when Rawle was ordered to take four men and travel to Farmville to arrest Richard McCulloh, a civilian employee of the Confederate Nitre and Mining Bureau who had been implicated in plots to burn Northern cities. McCulloh, a Baltimore native and an expert in the use of chemicals and explosives, had abruptly resigned his teaching position at New York's Columbia College in the fall of 1863, traveled to Richmond, and offered his services to the Confederacy. The War Department had ordered his arrest, Rawle wrote, because "some correspondence of his relating to the adaptability of Greek Fire to burning shipping, etc. was found . . . and that he had something to do with manufacturing torpedoes, etc."[5]

Trains had not yet begun to run west out of Richmond, so the lieutenant and his party rode south to Petersburg to board cars on the South Side Railroad, which was still serviceable. After taking lunch at Jarret's Hotel, Rawle spent the afternoon riding through the Cockade City "and along the lines of earthworks to Forts 'Hell' and 'Damnation,' the opposing forts, Federal and Confederate, on the Jerusalem Plank Road."

The party camped for the night in the Petersburg suburbs and the next morning, May 25, loaded their horses aboard a boxcar and headed out on the South Side Railroad, which Rawle described as "the most rickety concern imaginable." Disembarking at Burkeville Junction, the group rode through Rice's Station and arrived in Farmville at nightfall. After a rainy night spent in a barn with his men,

Rawle initiated his search for the professor the next morning "but found no Mr. McC, nor any traces newer than 7 mos. old. I found that he had most probably left for Europe during last December."[6] As a result of accidents along the railroad and strong spring rains that threatened to wash away bridges along the route, it took the Pennsylvanians several days to return to Richmond.

Not long after his arrival back in camp, Rawle learned that the rumors regarding the consolidation of the regiment were true. The eight undersized companies of the 3rd Pennsylvania Cavalry would be combined into four full companies to form a battalion of the 5th Pennsylvania Cavalry, which was also stationed at Richmond. The relationship between the men of the two Pennsylvania units would prove to be contentious. Like the 3rd, the 5th Pennsylvania had also been raised principally in Philadelphia in 1861, had served near the capital in late 1861 and early 1862, and was sent to the Virginia Peninsula in May 1862. But any similarities between the two regiments ended there. The 5th was a predominately German American regiment that also contained a sizeable contingent of Irish Americans. More importantly to the men of the 3rd, the war service of the 5th was very different, and far less distinguished, than their own.

After arriving on the Peninsula in May 1862, the 5th Pennsylvania (with the exception of two of its companies) was assigned not to fight with the Army of the Potomac, which was then advancing against Richmond, but to occupy Williamsburg and perform garrison duty. The regiment would remain there long after McClellan and his army had sailed north, campaigning on the periphery of the main action for much of the war. Relegated as it was to the backwater of the conflict, the 5th had few chances to distinguish itself; when these infrequent opportunities did present themselves, the Pennsylvanians invariably failed to rise to the challenge. In September 1862 the 5th lost its state flag and one hundred men after a surprise attack on its camp by Rebel cavalry under Wade Hampton. In the spring of 1863, while positioned near Yorktown, the regiment's camp was attacked again—twice—by Confederate cavalry; in each instance the enemy broke the 5th's picket line, burned portions of its camp, and destroyed various amounts of equipment and supplies. Following more skirmishes and further outpost duty, the 5th garrisoned Norfolk in September 1863, remaining there until the spring of 1864, when it was transferred to the cavalry of the Army of the James.

As part of that army, the 5th participated in the disastrous Wilson-Kautz Raid in late June. During its eight-day expedition, the regiment again lost its state colors to the Rebels and suffered the loss of between two and three hundred men, most of whom were taken prisoner. The only historian who ever ventured to write about the 5th Pennsylvania Cavalry, Edward Longacre, concluded that the unit "achieved a record of failures, defeats, setbacks and disasters probably unequalled by any other regiment."[7]

That the 5th had suffered the humiliating distinction of having lost its colors—a symbol of immeasurable significance to Civil War soldiers—not once but twice was known by the men of the 3rd Pennsylvania. When combined with any inherent prejudices they may have entertained toward recent immigrants, it made the prospect of becoming part of the 5th disagreeable to the Army of the Potomac veterans. Unsurprisingly, discipline in that unit was lax compared with the 3rd (a "democratic regiment," is how Rawle disapprovingly referred to the 5th in a letter). The officers of the 5th were "a class of men with which I don't care to be thrown," declared Rawle. "I will be sorry," he added, echoing the sentiments of the enlisted men of his regiment, "to have to take the '3' off my cap."[8]

On June 5 the order directing that the 3rd Pennsylvania consolidate its existing eight partial companies down to four full companies of 100 men each arrived. The 3rd Pennsylvania Cavalry ceased to exist when these companies became part of the 5th Pennsylvania.[9] Over the ensuing few weeks, the dissatisfaction of the newly consolidated enlisted men, now a part of what they considered a mediocre regiment, would grow and, when compounded by the intense heat, the poor rations, and the irregular pay of which Rawle had complained, would lead to an action that would have severe consequences for many of the former 3rd Pennsylvanians.

Two weeks after his transfer to the 5th, Captain Rawle was sent on another expedition, this time to locate currency and other personal property that had been confiscated from captured US officers held in Richmond's Libby Prison. Just prior to the fall of the Confederate capital, this money and a box containing the valuables had been sent west by rail. Federal authorities had learned that the box was at Greensboro, North Carolina.[10]

Rawle and a sergeant of his company set out from Richmond on the morning of June 18, traveling on the Richmond & Danville Railroad. It was not, according to him, an enjoyable journey. "The roads have been turned over to the R.R. companies," he recounted to his mother in a letter written several days later, "and, like the whole Confederacy, have gone to the mischief." The train moved at a glacial eight miles an hour, and at the crossing of the Appomattox River, the passengers were compelled to walk across the bridge and board another train waiting on the other side, as the trestle was thought too weak to support the cars. "We started out with 14 cars all heavily loaded with rebels just released from Northern prisons," he continued, "but by the time we reached Danville, . . . we had only three, having shed them along the road at places where the grading was heavy, the leaky engines not being able to pull them. The car I was in had to be left because the truck box caught fire whenever the train moved, and I had to ride all night on top of a box car crowded with filthy rebels, which threatened to break through every moment."[11]

The next day Rawle journeyed from Danville to Greensboro on the Piedmont Railroad. Arriving in Greensboro, he "put up at a mean tavern for the night" and then located the box he had been sent to secure. This container, he noted in his diary, "belonged to Capt. Morfitt, late A.Q.M., C.S.A., now confined in Libby Prison. The box contained papers and accounts relative to property taken from Federal Officers who had been confined in Libby. The box had been broken into and robbed of a lot of watches, pocketbooks, etc."[12]

The "mean tavern" in Greensboro was lacking in basic comforts: "a more wretched place I never saw in my life. Nothing to eat but bacon and biscuit, with some wretched coffee, only enough plates for 10 to eat at table at the same time and only 6 spoons. . . . The beds consisted of dirty mattresses without sheets; the rooms had no furniture in them; there were only three basins in the house, and of course I had no show at any of them, as some ladies stopped there for the night thro' necessity and they had the use of them. And with all this they had the impudence to charge $4 per day board."[13]

On the morning of June 20, Rawle traveled back to Danville and checked in at the Tunstall Hotel on Craghead Street, which, he complained, was "only one degree better" than the tavern in Greensboro. There he met with Rev. George W. Dame, a New Hampshire–born local clergyman who had ministered to Union captives held in the prisons in that city. Reverend Dame gave him $2,980, "which I suppose had also been taken from officers of ours in the hands of the Rebels."[14] Two days later, after turning over the box and currency to the provost marshal general of Richmond, he was back in the camp of the 5th Pennsylvania, which had relocated to a site on the Nine Mile Road, two miles outside of downtown and just inside the fortifications.

The initial discord that had characterized relations between members of the the two regiments had not ameliorated during the time Rawle was gone, and the officers and men of the former 3rd continued to perpetuate the divide—in both a physical and psychological way—between the groups. In the new camp they occupied, the battalion of four formerly 3rd companies occupied a site separated from the rest of the regiment by a ravine and a high fence; as a consequence, wrote Rawle, "we keep very much to ourselves."[15]

Social intercourse between the two factions was also limited. "The officers . . . seem to be very uncivil, and I know nothing of them at all, being acquainted with but one or two. None of us are very eager for the acquaintance," wrote Captain Rawle. "As we joined the 5th, the officers should have to a certain extent treated us as their guests when we came here," he told his mother, "but instead of trying to act like gentlemen, they paid no attention to us. We have nothing much to do with them except on duty." Writing on June 23, he boasted, "We had a Regimental Dress Parade this evening, and our battalion of four companies . . . took the shine off the rest of the Regiment."[16]

The routine of camp and garrison life went on, but the repetitive and tiring nature of military-police duties combined with the mountain of paperwork he had to process depressed the young captain. "I have the 'Blues' terribly," Rawle wrote in June. "We have been hard at work at every spare moment settling up the books, accounts and papers of our Companies to send them to the War Department. It has been an awful job as they were very backward, we having no chance of keeping them regularly, sometimes not seeing them for months at a time while in Campaign."[17]

According to Rawle's diary and letters, his interactions with residents of the former Confederate capital during his time there were almost nonexistent. "I have not been inside of a Richmond dwelling yet," he had informed his mother in May, "neither have I spoken one word to any of the belles or any of the sex, & how bashful I am!" Later in the month he related, "I have not yet granted the extreme pleasure of my acquaintance to any of the Richmond girls, nor is there much prospect of it."[18]

On the afternoon of July 11, after having spent the morning serving on general-court-martial duty, Rawle returned to the camp of the 5th Pennsylvania and learned that the majority of the enlisted men from the 3rd had mutinied, refusing to attend drill or perform other duties. The captain explained their motivations: "There has been a very great dissatisfaction on these four companies . . . about being consolidated with the 5th Pa. Cav., which was, until recently, a very inferior Regiment. They did not like to serve in a regiment which had lost the only two sets of colors it had. They were much displeased at losing the no. '3'; they have not been paid for more than six months and the rations which the Government issues to them now that the war is over are far worse than those they got in campaign."[19]

The officers of the former 3rd, in what Rawle believed was a considerable concession, had gone "so far as to <u>ask</u> the men to comply with their orders and gave them until tomorrow morning to decide." Later that day, at dress parade, the captain made a short speech to the men, enjoining them to reconsider their course. "Men who had served through the war, and had not a blot on their records, were engaged in this," he recorded incredulously.

When "Boots and Saddles" sounded, calling the men to drill the next morning, most of the men from the 3rd held firm and stayed in their tents. Although sympathetic to their plight, the officers had no choice but to discipline their wayward charges. "No words were wasted on the matter," wrote Rawle, "but all the mutinying non-commissioned officers and the ring leaders were marched off to

Castle Thunder," a former Confederate prison for Union enlisted men. "About half of each Company said they would go too, so they were marched off also. They are to be confined on bread and water, at labor, and then Court Martialed."[20]

Only twenty-four men out of ninety were left in Rawle's company after the mutineers were imprisoned. Although those who remained served faithfully ("the men left behind never did better"), the captain could not help but vent his frustration at the consequences of the revolt: "All our trouble in bringing our Companies to such a splendid state of discipline has been thrown away, and I am afraid we will never have such control of the men as formerly." The mutineers remained incarcerated for a week, performing hard labor and subsisting on prison fare, which finally broke them. "The men came back thoroughly disgusted with the place," Rawle recorded on July 18, "and changed their minds about a good many matters & things. . . . They seem very penitent, having had a terribly rough time, and have made up their minds to obey their officers in everything hereafter."[21]

Rumors that the regiment would be ordered north grew stronger during the month, and on July 31 the War Department directed that the 5th Pennsylvania Cavalry be mustered out of the service. "I expect before many days to be a respectable citizen once more, and doff the well-worn blue," Rawle happily informed his family.[22]

The ensuing week was spent "fixing up our books, papers and accounts" and settling other personal matters. Rawle gave one of his favorite horses, Satan, to a fellow captain, Miles Carter (a native of the Richmond area); sold a stallion colt for fifty dollars ("the price horses are bringing here"); but could not bear to part with Carrie, a thoroughbred mare that he determined to take home, along with another gray horse he owned. By August 5, the regiment had turned in all of the government horses and equipment. On the afternoon of August 8, the men of the 5th Pennsylvania boarded transports in Richmond and steamed down the James River. The ships docked at Fortress Monroe at the tip of the Virginia Peninsula at daylight on the ninth and pushed off again near midday, arriving near the Philadelphia Navy Yard at 8 P.M. the following day.

Early in the morning of August 11, the men of the 5th Pennsylvania, including those from the 3rd, landed in the city at Vine Street Wharf. "There were a good many Dutch people to receive the 5th," Rawle noted in his diary, "and some of our friends to receive us." His mother had been summering at their home in the Chester County countryside but journeyed to their Philadelphia residence to greet her son. "He looks very well," she recounted to her own mother soon after, "brown & sunburnt, with a beard, which he will shave off clean, as it does not become him." She continued: "In regards to his plans, nothing is settled as yet. He has a great leaning to the Regular Army, but does not know whether he will be able to enter it. . . . [H]e will take a little rest at home, and then see what he will do."[23]

The returned cavalrymen who lived near the city were allowed the privilege of staying at their homes until formally paid and discharged provided that they report to Philadelphia's Camp Cadwalader (located near Girard College) every day at 8:30 A.M. Spending his first night in Philadelphia at his house, Captain Rawle dutifully reported the next day and turned in his ordnance, complaining that he "had a good deal of trouble" with the task "as everyone was drunk."[24] Over the next ten days, Rawle went through the motions attendant to separating from the army. On August 15 the enlisted men from the old 3rd Pennsylvania were paid off and discharged. One week later, in the final entry in his diary, Rawle recorded that he was paid off and received his discharge, backdated to August 7.

Within a few months of his return to Philadelphia, William Brooke Rawle began the study of law under the tutelage of his uncle Henry, but the possibility of further service in the army continued to interest him. He had told his mother while stationed in Richmond in June that he had decided that he would try for a regular commission "so I will never regret not having done it."[25] While the process took longer than he likely anticipated, Rawle would, in October 1866, be appointed a second lieutenant in the 7th US Cavalry, his commission backdated to July 28, 1866, the date the regiment was established. By that time, however, whatever enticements an army career had held for the young man at the close of the war had waned; he declined the position one month after it was tendered.

Nevertheless, several military laurels remained in his future. In December 1867 the former provost marshal general of the Army of the Potomac, Maj. Gen. Marsena Patrick, wrote to Gen. Ulysses S. Grant in support of a brevet promotion for Rawle and his friend and fellow officer in the 3rd George S. L. Ward. Calling the 3rd Pennsylvania "the best cavalry regiment that ever served with me," Patrick recalled that the "gallantry and whole conduct" of Rawle and Ward "merited special notice." Also writing in support of Rawle, Maj. Gen. George Meade endorsed Patrick's recommendation, stating that "from personal knowledge, I take pleasure in concurring in Gen. Patrick's letter." On October 14, 1868, Rawle received brevet promotion to major "for gallant and meritorious service in the Battle of Hatcher's Run, Va., December 9, 1864, to date from March 13, 1865," and to lieutenant colonel "for gallant and meritorious service in the campaign terminating in Lee's surrender in 1865, to date from April 9, 1865."[26]

NOTES

INTRODUCTION

1. There has been robust debate about the nature of Stuart's assignment opposite the right flank of the Army of the Potomac at Gettysburg. Some, including William Brooke Rawle, believe that Stuart was there to coordinate his attack on July 3 with the Pickett-Pettigrew-Trimble charge against Cemetery Ridge, rush in behind the main Union line, and obstruct their lines of supply and retreat. National Park Service markers on the East Cavalry Field battlefield interpret Stuart's intentions this way. Eric Wittenberg has tackled the controversy ably in his study of the cavalry fighting on July 3. His opinion, which I share, is that Stuart's objectives were far more limited: He was to secure the Confederate left and would ambush the Union cavalry on the right under Brig. Gen. David Gregg if the opportunity presented itself. For a thorough discussion of Stuart's role, see Wittenberg, *Protecting the Flank at Gettysburg*, 138–57. For a view that supports the theory that Stuart sought to coordinate his attack with the assault against Cemetery Ridge, see Carhart, *Lost Triumph*, esp. chaps. 13–15.

2. F. Rawle, *William Brooke Rawle*, 4.

3. William Brooke Rawle (hereafter referred to in the notes as WBR) to Dr. William P. Henry, Oct. 31, 1911, copy bound into WBR Diary, Foundations of the Union League of Philadelphia, typescript. In this letter WBR recorded Miller's reply to his suggestion to attack: "I have been ordered to hold this position at all hazards but if you will back me up if I am court-martialed for disobedience of orders I will order a charge."

4. Miller, "Cavalry Battle near Gettysburg," *Battles and Leaders* 3:404.

5. Lewis, "Presentation of Portrait of Colonel William Brooke Rawle," 127.

6. F. Rawle, *William Brooke Rawle*, 5. Another account referred to Charles Brooke as a "brilliant young member of the Philadelphia Bar." Lewis, "Presentation of Portrait of Colonel William Brooke Rawle," 126.

7. Reuther, "Descendants of John Brooke," 18, http://www.kennedyreuther.com/barlow/brooke_report.pdf (accessed Nov. 28, 2016).

8. Jordan, *Colonial and Revolutionary Families of Philadelphia*, 1:156.

9. Information on WBR's ancestors in the foregoing paragraph was extracted from notes contained in the introduction, background notes, and abstract to the William Brooke Rawle Papers, Historical Society of Pennsylvania.

10. William Henry Rawle (1823–89), WBR's uncle and known as Henry, graduated from the University of Pennsylvania in 1841, passed the bar two years later, and had a notable career as an attorney. He authored several books on title law and contracts and also served as a director of the Philadelphia Library Company. Henry would serve in a thirty-day militia company during the Antietam Campaign and as quartermaster sergeant of a thirty-day artillery company (Landis's Battery) during the Gettysburg Campaign. He was also an original member of Philadelphia's Union League.

WBR's last name is shown as "Rawle Brooke," or simply "Brooke," in Regimental History Committee, *History of the Third Pennsylvania Cavalry*. Because he made a point to change the order of his name two years after the war and was known by his reordered last name for most of his life, I have chosen to refer to him as William Brooke Rawle (or simply Rawle) instead of William Rawle Brooke.

11. WBR attended Episcopal Academy of Pennsylvania and Faire's Classical Institute before matriculating as a member of the class of 1863. Lewis, "Presentation of Portrait of Colonel William Brooke Rawle," 127, 133.

12. WBR's commission as second lieutenant was dated December 18, 1862. He was mustered in at that rank when he reported for duty on May 16, 1863.

13. Regimental History Committee, *Third Pennsylvania*, 5–9, 16.

14. Brig. Gen. George Stoneman, then serving as chief of cavalry, sent a note to Colonel Young on September 11, 1861, congratulating him for "having put the first regiment of cavalry in the field." Regimental History Committee, *Third Pennsylvania*, 9.

15. Young was a native Kentuckian who had served in Mexico under Col. Edward Baker, an ally and friend of Lincoln's whose death at Ball's Bluff in October 1861 created a sensation in the North. Young had also participated in William Walker's forays into Central America in the 1850s. At war's outbreak, he was an attorney in Mount Pulaski, Illinois. "He was accustomed to making frequent speeches to the men, promising what valorous deeds he would perform," remembered a member of the 3rd Pennsylvania. Young spent approximately two months in the service but even then incurred substantial personal expenses attendant to the recruiting and equipping of his regiment. He petitioned Congress unsuccessfully for reimbursement several times after the war, notably in 1880, when he submitted, without any corroborating documentation, a $64,000 claim. Basler, *Collected Works of Abraham Lincoln*, 1:453; *Constitution and By-Laws of Company H*, 16; Senate Committee on Military Affairs, *Report*, 51st Cong., 2nd sess., 1891, S. Rpt. 1965, 1–6. Pennsylvania adopted the practice of numbering the volunteer infantry and cavalry regiments raised within its borders in the order they were accepted for service. Thus, because it was not recognized by the state until October 1861, the numerical designation assigned to the 3rd Pennsylvania Cavalry was the sixtieth regiment, although this number was almost never used and rarely referred to.

16. Throughout this book, I will usually refer to the 3rd Pennsylvania Cavalry as either the "3rd Pennsylvania" or simply the "3rd." There was no "3rd Pennsylvania Infantry" (although the 3rd Pennsylvania Reserves—the thirty-second regiment of infantry raised—shared a similar numerical designation), so this should not engender any confusion.

17. Averell later related that "the amount of patient and persistent hard work required to convert twelve hundred untrained citizens, unaccustomed to the care of a horse or to his use under a saddle, and wholly inexperienced in the use of arms, into the semblance of a cavalry regiment in six months is known only to those who have done it." Regimental History Committee, *Third Pennsylvania*, 55.

18. F. Hess, "First Cavalry Battle at Kelly's Ford, Va." 6; Regimental History Committee, *Third Pennsylvania*, 17, 22–25, 27–28. One major, seven company commanders, and two surgeons were among those who left the 3rd. In the early months after he assumed command, Averell held an evening school for the officers, conducted mounted drills, and put his men "through sabre exercises and everything else that went with cavalry training in that day. He had a large hospital tent with wooden floor, fireplace and a blackboard. At the latter he was a master hand, sketching and illustrating his points readily. The school work did the officers much good." Edmonds, *Owen Edmonds*, 15. For remarks on the thoroughness of the 3rd Pennsylvania's training under Averell's supervision, see Starr, *Union Cavalry*, 1:243.

19. Egle, *Life and Times of Andrew Gregg Curtin*, 418–19.

20. "A large proportion of vacancies were satisfactorily filled," recalled Averell, "by the promotion of young gentlemen from the noncommissioned officers of the regiment. These promotions encouraged a gratifying emulation in discipline and efficiency, the effects of which were felt and seen in the ranks." Eckert and Amato, *Ten Years in the Saddle,* 341.

21. Speese, *Story of Companies H, A, and C,* 15. Andrew J. Speese, who served as a corporal in the 3rd Pennsylvania, was an embittered man whose resentment toward many of the regiment's officers deepened in the decades after the war.

22. *Constitution and By-laws of Company H,* 18.

23. "The tyranny of most of the officers—their total disregard of the rights of the enlisted soldiers . . . —had such a discouraging effect, that less than one hundred men were induced to re-enter the service." *Constitution and By-Laws of Company H,* 54. This comment was penned by Andrew Speese, who as previously noted had an axe to grind. Despite the source, there is undoubtedly some truth in his statement.

24. For perspective, Maj. Gen. George B. McClellan had at his disposal some 145 infantry regiments during the Seven Days' Battles (June 25–July 1, 1862). In addition to the eight complete cavalry regiments, sixteen assorted companies from five other cavalry regiments also served with McClellan's forces. The 3rd Pennsylvania, the first cavalry regiment to land on the Peninsula, led the advance of the Army of the Potomac to Big Bethel, Virginia, on March 28. For most of the campaign, the regiment was attached to the III Corps. Starr, *Union Cavalry,* 1:263; Longacre, *Lincoln's Cavalrymen,* 68–69.

25. Apart from several accidental deaths, the regiment recorded losses of six killed, three wounded, and three captured, all occurring during the Seven Days' Battles. Regimental History Committee, *Third Pennsylvania,* 82–85.

26. Eckert and Amato, *Ten Years in the Saddle,* 356.

27. Maj. Gen. Wesley Merritt, quoted in Starr, *Union Cavalry,* 1:241. As the various companies of the 3rd Pennsylvania arrived in Washington, DC, in July 1861, they were dispatched to serve with infantry brigades. The regiment was not reunited until Averell assumed command three months later. Regimental History Committee, *Third Pennsylvania,* 10–11.

28. Alfred Pleasonton to Randolph B. Marcy, Sept. 17, 1862, quoted in Longacre, *Lincoln's Cavalrymen,* 105. Pleasonton would rise to command the Army of the Potomac's cavalry for a time in 1863. The man to whom he criticized McClellan, Randolph Marcy, was McClellan's father-in-law and serving as his chief of staff.

29. McClellan quoted in Wittenberg, *Union Cavalry Comes of Age,* 3. A vedette is a mounted sentry. Averell remembered that in the prewar army it was a widely accepted fact that it took three years to make a cavalryman. Regimental History Committee, *Third Pennsylvania,* 55.

30. Though the weapons were limited in range compared with traditional long arms, many Union cavalry regiments were equipped with carbines (originally single-shot models, but later in the conflict transitioning to repeating varieties), which multiplied the volume of their fire and gave them the ability to contend against infantry, where the most skilled soldiers could manage only three shots per minute. In a circular written to his cavalry division in March 1863, Averell instructed that the carbine "is intended to strike the enemy at a distance of from 50 to 500 yards, and should be the weapon used most by skirmishers and men fighting on foot. A cavalry man [*sic*] on foot, who can use a carbine and six shooter skillfully, taking advantage of cover, is formidable." Averell Circular to the 2nd Cavalry Division, Mar. 12, 1863, WBR Letters, Foundations of the Union League of Philadelphia. "During the Civil War," wrote Averell in later years, "a skirmish line of dismounted cavalry, armed with the Spencer magazine-rifle, often stood off and sometimes drove an equal or stronger line of infantry." Eckert and Amato, *Ten Years in the Saddle,* 327. A good overview of the weaponry used by Union cavalrymen is in Longacre, *Lincoln's Cavalrymen,* 40–45.

31. Eckert and Amato, *Ten Years in the Saddle*, 328.

32. Nevins, *Diary of Battle*, 115; Acken, *Service with the Signal Corps*, 145; Gienapp and Gienapp, *Civil War Diary of Gideon Welles*, 75. The fact that Stuart was able to conduct his second raid almost completely unmolested, penetrate Northern soil, and cause the loss of hundreds of thousands of dollars of property left Union soldiers and civilians embarrassed and disheartened. For more Northern reactions to the October raid, see Gray and Ropes, *War Letters*, 5; and Cassedy, *Dear Friends at Home*, 172–73.

33. Regimental History Committee, *Third Pennsylvania*, 116–17. The regiment was severely understrength at this time, due principally to the lack of healthy horseflesh, and many of its members were at the "dismounted camp" awaiting fresh mounts. During the Battle of Antietam, one company of the 3rd counted only twenty-four men present for duty; other companies were likely in a similar plight. Two battalions of the 1st Massachusetts Cavalry had been ordered to Washington from South Carolina to serve with the Army of the Potomac in August, but the sea journey had gone hard on their horses, which continued to break down throughout the fall. In late October 450 out of the 600 troopers of that regiment were in Washington trying to secure serviceable mounts. Crowninshield, *First Regiment of Massachusetts Cavalry*, 83–84.

34. Regimental History Committee, *Third Pennsylvania*, 123–24, 128–29.

35. Averell wrote that Captain Johnson "brought disgrace and shame upon his regiment, the brigade to which it belonged and our cavalry service into disrepute." US War Department, *War of the Rebellion*, ser. 1, 19:14 (cited hereafter as *OR*; unless otherwise noted, all citations are to series 1).

36. *OR* 19:13–14; Regimental History Committee, *Third Pennsylvania*, 158, 172–73.

37. Letterman reported to Hooker on April 21 that the "favorable state of the health of the army" was attributable to the issuance of fresh bread and fresh vegetables to the troops, which had commenced on February 1. These had eradicated the symptoms of scurvy that in January "had begun to assume a serious aspect." For Letterman's summary of the effectiveness of his efforts, see *OR* 25(2):239–40.

38. Hennessy, "We Shall Make Richmond Howl," 9–11.

39. Wittenberg, *Union Cavalry Comes of Age*, 13–27, 62.

40. Longacre, *Lincoln's Cavalrymen*, 126.

41. Griffin, *Three Years a Soldier*, 122. A sampling of cavalrymen's reactions to Hooker's changes is in Wittenberg, *Union Cavalry Comes of Age*, 31.

42. These quotes and my condensed summary of the action are assembled from a comprehensive recounting of the event in Wittenberg, *Union Cavalry Comes of Age*, 49–62.

43. F. Hess, "First Cavalry Battle at Kelly's Ford," 12.

44. *OR* 25(2):244.

45. Starr, *Union Cavalry*, 1:351–63. Averell had, in fact, been following the most recent orders that Stoneman, his immediate superior, had given him, a detail that Hooker overlooked. His division actively campaigned for six of the eighteen days they were out before ordered to Chancellorsville. During that time, they captured a few supplies and thirty-one prisoners, losing one man killed and four wounded, a meager result for a force that size. "This army will never be able to accomplish its mission under commanders who . . . display so little zeal and devotion to the performance of their duties," Hooker would later write regarding Averell's effort. *OR* 25(1):1073.

46. Bigelow, *Campaign of Chancellorsville*, 459; Starr, *Union Cavalry*, 1:365; Tobie, *First Maine Cavalry*, 144.

47. In British Army fashion, the troops attached to Army of the Potomac headquarters sometimes referred to themselves as the "Household Brigade." Elite, highly trained troops were traditionally assigned to guard royalty, to include members of the royal household, resulting in the terminology.

48. Regimental History Committee, *Third Pennsylvania*, 409–10. Provost Marshal General Brig. Gen. Marsena Patrick became particularly devoted to the men of the 3rd and was likely responsible for their retention at headquarters.

49. Gause, *Four Years with Five Armies*, 223.

50. Regimental History Committee, *Third Pennsylvania*, 455.

51. "On account of the temporary absence for brief periods, from time to time, of the two divisions of the Cavalry Corps, our battalion was often called upon to perform sterner duties than those which usually fell to the lot of the 'Household Brigade.' At such times advance-guard duties, scouting, skirmishing for information and position and opening and maintaining communications between separated corps or divisions, fell to our lot." Regimental History Committee, *Third Pennsylvania*, 473–74.

52. Wongsrichanalai, *Northern Character*, 9, 16, 251. By way of comparison, 31 percent of males in the United States age eighteen to twenty four were attending college in 2000. US Census Bureau, *Census Atlas of the United States*, 2007, https://www.census.gov/population/www/cen2000/censusatlas/pdf/10_Education.pdf, p. 159 (accessed Nov. 4, 2017).

53. Bledsoe, *Citizen-Officers*, 65–66.

54. This quotation is taken from WBR's letter of June 17, 1865, other key elements of which are incorporated into the epilogue but is itself not included in this volume.

55. Gallagher, *Union War*, 34.

56. Wongsrichanalai, *Northern Character*, 4, 62. Although Wongsrichanalai's study is focused solely on collegiate New Englanders, there is little reason to doubt that their core beliefs and traits were markedly different than WBR's or other Philadelphians of similar education and social standing.

57. Sutherland, *Savage Conflict*, 52.

58. On at least one occasion, during skirmishing on the evening of July 2, 1863, along Brinkerhoff's Ridge east of Gettysburg, WBR faced his cousin in the 2nd Virginia Infantry on the battlefield, though both were almost certainly unaware of this at the time.

59. Hess, *Union Soldier in Battle*, 14.

60. French for "memories of service."

61. Frank A. O'Reilly, lead historian at Fredericksburg and Spotsylvania National Military Park and the author of a comprehensive work on the Fredericksburg Campaign, had possession of WBR's original diaries for a time in the late 1970s or early 1980s, when he was quite young. A family that learned of his budding interest in the Civil War had given them to him as a gift, along with WBR's Civil War Veteran's medal, Society of the Army of the Potomac medal, and Sheridan Cavalry medal. O'Reilly selflessly tried to donate the items to the Civil War Library and Museum of Philadelphia—which held WBR's letters and typescript diary—not long after receiving them and was offered a tax break in return. A tax break was unappealing to someone his age ("I was a kid! I didn't pay taxes"), so he generously offered the deduction to the family who had given him the materials. Suddenly aware that there might be some monetary value associated with the diaries and medals, the family reclaimed them; what happened to them after that remains unknown. O'Reilly distinctly recalls that some of the "private matters" that WBR excised for his typescript diary included many references to girls he was interested in and notes about his correspondence with them, some of which he had attempted to erase or obscure. It is unknown whether the original diaries and medals given to O'Reilly were originally a part of the museum's collections. Frank A. O'Reilly, email to the editor, Nov. 30, 2016, in editor's possession.

62. F. Rawle, *William Brooke Rawle*, 5–6.

63. See Bates, *History of Pennsylvania Volunteers*, 2:360–68.

64. WBR to Capt. J. E. Barr, June 29, 1893, Brooke Rawle Papers, Historical Society of Pennsylvania, Philadelphia (cited hereafter as HSP).

65. WBR's postwar Gettysburg-related correspondence is part of the holdings of the Historical Society of Pennsylvania. His communications with former Confederate officers is polite and collegial, even when they failed to agree on certain aspects of the action. After an exchange of letters disputing which side retained possession of the Rummel Barn, a key landmark on the East Cavalry Battlefield, after the fighting was over, Maj. H. B. McClellan, one of Stuart's former staff officers, wrote to WBR, "Can't we get the Union and Confederate cavalry together on the field . . . and work out a narrative to which we can all subscribe?" H. B. McClellan to WBR, Apr. 8, 1886, Rawle Papers, HSP.

66. WBR to My Dear Sir, Oct. 8, 1890, Rawle Papers, HSP. "With Gregg in the Gettysburg Campaign" is an overview of the movements of David Gregg's division between June 27 and July 16, 1863, with special attention given to the participation of the Purnell Legion of cavalry and William Rank's section of the 3rd Pennsylvania Heavy Artillery. It only gives passing mention of the cavalry fighting on July 2–3.

67. WBR to Capt. J. E. Barr, June 29, 1893, Rawle Papers, HSP.

68. A group of reenactors, or living historians, Civil War Historical Impressions, restored the flagpole and rededicated it during a Remembrance Day ceremony in November 2014.

69. Wittenberg, *Protecting the Flank at Gettysburg*, 171.

70. Through my tenure on its board of governors, I became familiar with the archival holdings of the Civil War Library and Museum (as the Military Order museum was then known) in the late 1980s and was able to view the cartes-de-visite albums assembled by WBR. At that time approximately 70–80 percent of the images were missing. On many of his photographs, WBR ink stamped the reverse side with his name and address, denoting his ownership of the image, and it is assumed that many of these, now in private hands, are adorned with this identifying mark. I have one such carte-de-visite, purchased from a reputable dealer several years ago.

71. WBR to Cecil Battine, Feb. 21, 1908, Rawle Papers, HSP.

1. BRANDY STATION AND THE GETTYSBURG CAMPAIGN

1. Wittenberg, *Union Cavalry Comes of Age*, 187–89.

2. In relation to rank, it is important to note that, in the case of numerous officers who served in the 3rd Pennsylvania, their date of commission differed from their date of mustering in—i.e., the date they reported for duty with the regiment. The commissions of WBR and Davis dated from December 16, 1862, while Ward's dated from April 1, 1863; all three were mustered in together on May 16, 1863. WBR's good friend Ellwood "Ned" Davis (1844–63) left school following his junior year at the University of Pennsylvania to accept his commission in the 3rd Pennsylvania. George Silver Luttrell Ward (1841–1901) would be promoted to first lieutenant on October 5, 1864, and to captain on the thirty-first. Ward left the service after the war ended in 1865, but the next year he accepted a commission in the regular infantry, retiring as a captain in 1891. Regimental History Committee, *Third Pennsylvania*, 568, 572, 574; Heitman, *Historical Register and Dictionary of the United States Army*, 1:1001.

3. This paragraph was written by WBR as part of the introduction to the typed copy of his diary, which he prepared in 1898.

4. The most fashionable hotel in Washington, DC, and the epicenter of political intrigue and gossip in the capital in the nineteenth century, the Willard Hotel is located at the northwest corner of Fourteenth Street NW and Pennsylvania Avenue NW.

5. A descendant of one of Philadelphia's oldest families, WBR's friend George Emlen would serve in Landis's Battery, a ninety-day artillery company, during the Gettysburg Campaign.

6. *The Interpreter* was a novel by George Whyte-Melville, a Scotsman who served in the British Army during the Crimean War (1853–56). Messire's was a hotel located in Pera (Constantinople) and is described in the book as "a well known rendezvous . . . where congregate all that have any connexion with the mother country; a place where every rumor is to be heard, with its latest embellishments." Before appearing in book form in 1858, the work garnered notice in the United States when it was published serially in *Littell's Living Age* magazine in 1857.

7. Son of a career army officer killed during the Mexican War (1846–48), Col. John B. McIntosh (1829–88) had served as a midshipman in the US Navy during that earlier conflict. He left the navy in 1850. McIntosh was commissioned as a second lieutenant in the 2nd US Cavalry in June 1861, transferred to the 5th US Cavalry two months later (where he was promoted to first lieutenant), and was appointed colonel of the 3rd Pennsylvania on November 15, 1862. The men who served under him held him in high esteem: "We have found in him a polished gentleman, a strict disciplinarian and an earnest Soldier," wrote a group of his officers on January 24, 1864, in supporting his promotion. "His intrepidity, and the masterly manner in which he handles a Brigade and his coolness in action excite universal admiration." Heitman, *Historical Register and Dictionary of the United States Army*, 1:669; Regimental History Committee, *Third Pennsylvania*, 172, 562; Letters Received by Commission Branch, US National Archives, at Fold3.com, https://www.fold3.com/image/303493714 (accessed Nov. 4, 2017, membership required).

8. Troopers from the Cavalry Corps who had lost their horses, whether due to fatigue, illness, death, or wounds, were sent to the Dismounted Camp at Dumfries, Virginia, to await new mounts. The camp was at this time commanded by Maj. Claude White of the 3rd Pennsylvania. Regimental History Committee, *Third Pennsylvania*, 236, 241.

9. Edward Miles Heyl (1844–95) had left the University of Pennsylvania to join the 3rd Pennsylvania in August 1861, serving as quartermaster sergeant and first sergeant of Company E until commissioned as a second lieutenant in September 1862. Promoted to first lieutenant in May 1863, Heyl became captain of Company M on May 2, 1864, and mustered out of the service with the original members of the regiment that August. He reentered the military after the war, but his Regular Army career was controversial. Commissioned in the African American 9th US Cavalry in 1866, it soon became apparent that Heyl was a racist of the first degree (he named his horse after a derogatory slang term for African Americans), supplementing his prejudices with a violent, sometimes alcohol-fueled temper. His boorish, physically abusive behavior toward his men eventually precipitated a mutiny in the 9th, during which an officer and an enlisted man of the regiment were killed. In 1869 he was severely wounded (and later promoted) for gallant and meritorious service while fighting Native Americans in Texas. Two years later, in October 1871, during a skirmish against Native Americans at Rio Blanco, Texas, Heyl was accused of fleeing from the fight with twelve of his men, leaving a fellow officer and five troopers to face a superior force of attacking Comanches alone; the abandoned officer called his actions "rank, white livered" cowardice. These discreditable episodes notwithstanding, Heyl would rise to the rank of colonel and inspector general of the army in 1889. Regimental History Committee, *Third Pennsylvania*, 562; Kenner, *Buffalo Soldiers and Officers of the Ninth Cavalry*, 72–80; Carter, *Tragedies of Canon Blanco*, 25–30, 34–42, 64–71; Heitman, *Historical Register and Dictionary of the United States Army*, 1:527.

10. Henry Winsor (alternately spelled Windsor) had served with the 6th Pennsylvania Cavalry (also known as Rush's Lancers) since October 1861, working his way up from enlisted man to captain of Company G by May 1863. He later served at headquarters of the 1st Cavalry Division and mustered out of the service due to disability in August 1864. The environs of Hartwood Church, located approximately ten miles northwest of Fredericksburg,

had proven to be a fruitful hunting ground for Confederate cavalrymen seeking Union prisoners. Pickets of the 3rd Pennsylvania had been surprised and captured there on November 28, 1862, and again on February 25, 1863. In the November incident, seventy-seven men and five officers were captured; the captain who commanded that detachment was dismissed from the service. Gracey, *Annals of the Sixth Pennsylvania Cavalry,* 310–11; Regimental History Committee, *Third Pennsylvania,* 172–77; 188–92; OR 21:13–14.

11. Great-grandson of Robert Morris, a financier of the American Revolution and signer of the Declaration of Independence, University of Pennsylvania graduate Robert Morris Jr. (1837–63) had mustered in as major of the 6th Pennsylvania in October 1861 and served at that rank until his capture at Brandy Station in June 1863. Charles L. Leiper was originally the first lieutenant of Company C of the 6th. He would be promoted to captain, major, lieutenant colonel, and finally to colonel and command of the Lancers in March 1865, breveted to the rank of brigadier general at war's end. William White, a University of Pennsylvania graduate, had served in a three-month regiment in 1861 before joining the Lancers as second lieutenant of Company D in November 1862. Advanced to first lieutenant in November 1863, he was promoted to become captain of Company H in April 1864 and mustered out in October of that year. Wittenberg, *Rush's Lancers,* 6; Gracey, *Annals of the Sixth Pennsylvania Cavalry,* 311–12; Bates, *History of Pennsylvania Volunteers,* 2:753, 761, 780.

12. Civil War cavalry units utilized distinctive bugle calls, both in camp and while on the march, to convey orders and instructions to their men. In this instance, WBR notes that he received his mother's letter at "Water Call," which typically took place around midmorning while in camp, and that he read it at "Stable Call," directing the cavalrymen to feed and care for their mounts, which occurred twice during a day, early in the morning and again at approximately 4:30 in the afternoon. When not actively campaigning, the principal bugle calls employed were "Reveille" (before sunrise), "Stable Call" and "Sick Call" at 6:30 AM, "Orderly Call" at 7:15 AM, "Breakfast" at 7:30 AM, "Watering" at 8:30 AM, "Guard Mount" at 8:30 AM, "Drill" at 9:30 AM, "Recall" at 10:30 AM, "Drill" (again) at 11:00 AM, "Recall" at noon, "Dinner" at 12:30 PM, "Drill" at 2:00 PM, "Recall" at 3:00 PM, "Stable Call" (again) at 3:00 PM, "Retreat" and "Dress Parade" at fifteen minutes before sunset, "Tattoo" (lights out) at 9:00 PM, and "Taps" at 9:30 PM. Stephen Starr notes that calls could vary from regiment to regiment and that weather, time of year, and other extenuating circumstances could change their number and frequency. Crowninshield, *First Regiment of Massachusetts Cavalry,* 296–97; Allen, *Down in Dixie,* 172; Starr, *Union Cavalry,* 1:190.

13. Charles Alexander Vernou (1843–1919) was appointed second lieutenant in the 3rd Pennsylvania from civilian life on April 18, 1862, and served for less than three months before his honorable discharge on July 8. He reentered the 3rd as second lieutenant of Company F on May 9, 1863, serving until he was again honorably discharged in August 1864. In February 1865 he joined the 6th Pennsylvania Cavalry as first lieutenant and was promoted to captain of Company D on March 22, 1865. After the war Vernou would serve for thirty-one years in the Regular Army, rising to major and chief quartermaster of volunteers during the Spanish-American War (1898). Regimental History Committee, *Third Pennsylvania,* 563–64; Bates, *History of Pennsylvania Volunteers,* 2:763.

14. The "good Sergeant" and Methodist minister was Sgt. Joel Rammel of Company B. WBR has more to say about Rammel later.

15. A close friend of WBR's, Frank D. Wetherill (1839–1922) had joined the 3rd Pennsylvania as a second lieutenant of Philadelphia-raised Company F on February 17, 1862. Promoted to first lieutenant of Company K six months later, he became the captain of Company F on May 1, 1863, which he led until mustered out with the original members of the regiment in August 1864. Wetherill's son, born in 1874, read law under WBR's tutelage in the 1890s. Originally a sergeant, E. Willard Warren assumed the second lieutenancy of Company C

on September 13, 1862, and was promoted to first lieutenant of Company E on May 21, 1863, serving at that rank until his muster out in August 1864. Wetherill, Warren, and Lt. Franklin C. Davis (Company D) were among over 150 Federals captured near Hartwood Church on February 25, 1863. Warren had the misfortune of also being captured there in November 1862 and had just returned to the 3rd Pennsylvania from Richmond's Libby Prison before being taken again. Bates, *History of Pennsylvania Volunteers,* 2:386; Regimental History Committee, *Third Pennsylvania,* 188, 568, 570–71; *OR* 25(1):25.

16. Union cavalry regiments were led by a colonel, seconded by a lieutenant colonel, and comprised, almost without exception, twelve companies (although prior to mid-1862 some regiments contained more) lettered successively A through L (there was no Company J). Each company was commanded by a captain, supported by a first and second lieutenant, and on paper contained 100 men. A regiment's companies were grouped into three battalions, each led by a major. A squadron was a subdivision of the battalion and consisted of two companies.

17. Lt. Col. Edward S. Jones of Philadelphia (1818–86) was originally the captain of Company C. He was promoted to lieutenant colonel in November 1862 and served in that capacity until mustered out in August 1864. WBR comments on Jones in later letters. Regimental History Committee, *Third Pennsylvania,* 566–67.

18. The first commander of the Army of the Potomac's Cavalry Corps, Maj. Gen. George Stoneman of New York (1822–94), an 1842 West Point graduate, had taken a medical leave of absence on May 20. General Hooker, displeased with what he perceived as the empty results delivered by his horsemen during the recent Chancellorsville Campaign, soon after relieved and replaced him with Brig. Gen. Alfred Pleasonton.

19. George W. Pepper had been commissioned as second lieutenant of the 6th's Company H in October 1862; he resigned on May 22, 1863, due to his arm injury, resulting from a fall off his horse. Gracey, *Annals of the Sixth Pennsylvania Cavalry,* 121.

20. WBR employed a succession of servants, including men detailed from the enlisted ranks of the 3rd as well as African Americans, during his time in the service. "The officers," explained a Massachusetts cavalry captain, "were compelled to have non-enlisted men for servants—by the way, almost an impossibility to obtain. These servants, frequently negroes, marched with the baggage animals of the brigade, and with the officers' led horses, and few were good servants. . . . Those servants who were smart would usually manage to beg, borrow, buy or steal something for the officer's dinner during the day's march. They got to be called 'strikers,' and there was a great rivalry among them in getting food and little articles of luxury." Crowninshield, *First Regiment of Massachusetts Cavalry,* 298.

21. WBR noted in a later addition to this letter that he was mistaken regarding McIntosh having attended West Point.

22. Appointed to the 3rd Pennsylvania from the Regular Army, Oliver Ormsby Gregg Robinson of Pittsburgh was originally the captain of Company G. He was promoted to major to date from November 1862 and served at that rank until his muster out in August 1864. He would enter the Regular Army in December 1864, serving as a private and sergeant in the 1st US Cavalry until commissioned in the 2nd US Cavalry in March 1865. Robinson mustered out of the army in 1870 as a captain. William Redwood Price (1836–81) had been commissioned second lieutenant of Company D of the 3rd Pennsylvania in January 1862. Promoted to first lieutenant to date from March 1862, he moved into a staff position as regimental commissary in January 1863 (advancing later, as WBR notes, to a similar position on the brigade staff) and was made captain of WBR's Company C that May. Honorably discharged from the regiment in August 1864, he was promoted to major and acting assistant adjutant general on the staff of Maj. Gen. William Averell that same month, attaining the brevet rank of brigadier general for his war service. Entering the Regular Army, Price served as major

of the 8th US Cavalry and lieutenant colonel of the 6th US Cavalry and would be cited for bravery in combat against Native Americans in 1868. Originally a sergeant in Company L of the 3rd Pennsylvania, Samuel Boyer was promoted to second lieutenant of Company D in September 1862 and to first lieutenant of Company C that December. He was promoted to regimental quartermaster on May 1, 1863, and served on the regimental staff until he left the service in August 1864. Asst. Surg. Henry J. Durant joined the regiment in November 1861 and had been promoted from hospital steward to his current position at an unspecified date. One of the longest-serving members of the 3rd, he mustered out of the service in August 1865. Regimental History Committee, *Third Pennsylvania*, 563, 566; Heitman, *Historical Register and Dictionary of the United States Army*, 1:839.

23. Miles G. Carter (b. 1836), a slaveowner who hailed from Henrico County, Virginia, had served as an enlisted soldier in the 5th US Cavalry since August 1858. He was commissioned in the 3rd Pennsylvania to date from December 1862, joining the regiment as first lieutenant of Company C in May 1863. He would assume the captaincy of Company C in October 1864 and lead it until mustered out in July 1865. Because of his familiarity with the countryside east of Richmond, Provost Marshal General Patrick would press Carter into service as a guide during the operations near the Confederate capital during the summer of 1864. "He is a Loyal Virginian," Patrick would write in February 1865 on a recommendation in support of Carter receiving a Regular Army commission, "& has lost . . . all his property by espousing the right." Regimental History Committee, *Third Pennsylvania*, 568–69; Sparks, *Inside Lincoln's Army*, 385.

24. Col. John Irvin Gregg (1826–92), a veteran of the Mexican War and cousin of 3rd Cavalry Division commander David Gregg, had recently been promoted from command of his regiment, the 16th Pennsylvania Cavalry, to lead the 2nd Brigade of the 2nd Division of the Cavalry Corps; the 2nd Division was commanded by French native Col. Alfred N. Duffié (1833–80) of the 1st Rhode Island Cavalry. John Gregg would develop into a polished horse soldier, finishing the war as a brevet major general, while Duffié, who proved to be a poor choice for divisional command, would find himself demoted back to command of his regiment by mid-June. Alexander C. M. Pennington of New Jersey (1838–1917), an 1860 graduate of West Point, at this time commanded Battery M of the 2nd US Artillery. Despite his youth, Pennington was considered one of the best horse-artillery battery commanders in the army.

25. Harrison L. Newhall (1843–1918) had been commissioned as second lieutenant of Company B of the 3rd Pennsylvania on October 4, 1862. He was one of three brothers from a Mayflower-descended Philadelphia family serving in the army at this time. He was promoted to adjutant of the regiment on May 1, 1863, and was honorably discharged in March 1864. His brother Walter was the captain of Company A of the 3rd (see note 36 below), while another brother, Frederic, a captain with the 6th Pennsylvania Cavalry, was serving as the acting assistant inspector general of the Cavalry Corps. Regimental History Committee, *Third Pennsylvania*, 566–69; Gracey, *Annals of the Sixth Pennsylvania Cavalry*, 215–16.

26. This was Berea Church, located on the Warrenton Road northwest of Fredericksburg and roughly midway between that city and Hartwood Church. *OR Atlas*, plate 39, map 2.

27. Originally a first sergeant in Cumberland County–raised Company H, David M. Gilmore (1840–1900) was promoted to second lieutenant of Company A on April 2, 1862; to first lieutenant of Company M in August; and finally to captain of Company D on May 1, 1863. Gilmore was seriously wounded while fighting Confederate guerillas in January 1864 and mustered out of the service at the expiration of his three-year term of service that August. Regimental History Committee, *Third Pennsylvania*, 385, 566–67, 570–71, 574–75, 599.

28. Maj. Gen. George Gordon Meade of Philadelphia (1815–72), an 1835 West Point graduate, was at this time the commander of the Army of the Potomac's V Corps but would soon rise to command of the army, a position he held through the end of the war. WBR was

friendly with his son, George Jr., who at this time was serving as an officer with the 6th Pennsylvania Cavalry.

29. William H. Horstmann and Son (also known as Horstmann Brothers and Company) had been founded in Philadelphia in 1816 and was one of the most well-known military outfitters in the North, supplying uniforms, flags, swords, and other equipment to Federal soldiers. Sauers, *Guide to Civil War Philadelphia*, 8, 95–96.

30. Maj. Gen. James Ewell Brown "Jeb" Stuart (1831–64) was the capable leader of the Army of Northern Virginia's cavalry, but he was not present during this action. Partisans under the command of Maj. John S. Mosby had derailed and burned a Federal supply train near Catlett's Station on the Orange and Alexandria Railroad, but no bridges were destroyed. See O'Neill, *Chasing Jeb Stuart and John Mosby*, 196–201.

31. Although it courses roughly parallel to the Orange & Alexandria Railroad, Elk Run lies several miles southwest of the rail bed. WBR may have been referring to either Licking Run, which intersects the railroad several miles below Warrenton Junction (modern-day Calverton), or Owl Run, which crosses the tracks nearly at the junction itself.

32. Three days before his strike at Catlett's Station, Mosby had received what was described as a "mountain howitzer" to supplement his firepower; this gun was captured by Federal cavalry who pursued the Rebel raiders after their destruction of the train. Again, no bridges were burned. O'Neill, *Chasing Jeb Stuart and John Mosby*, 196, 201–2.

33. *OR* 27(3):5.

34. *OR* 27(3):27.

35. Sulphur Springs on the Rappahannock River, also referred to in various accounts as Warrenton Sulphur Springs, White Sulphur Springs, Warrenton White Sulphur Springs, and Fauquier Springs.

36. Walter S. Newhall (1841–63) of Philadelphia, a son of the aforementioned Newhall family, packed a wealth of experiences into his twenty-two years of life. An internationally renowned prewar cricket player, he was the brother of the adjutant of the 3rd Pennsylvania, Harrison Newhall, and had served in the early months of the war under Maj. Gen. John C. Frémont in Missouri. When Frémont was relieved of his command, Newhall returned east; was commissioned first lieutenant of Company G of the 3rd on January 24, 1862; and was promoted to captain of Company A five months later. He also served as acting assistant adjutant general of the 1st Brigade of the 2nd Division of the Cavalry Corps. Newhall was seriously wounded at Gettysburg but returned to duty after several months of recuperation. William E. Miller (1836–1919), a native of West Hill, Pennsylvania, entered the 3rd as the second lieutenant of Cumberland County–raised Company H in August 1861 and was promoted to captain of the company on March 8, 1863. Miller mustered out of the service in August 1864; in the postwar years he was awarded the Medal of Honor for his services at Gettysburg on July 3. "No one in the whole regiment was more respected and beloved, both by the officers and men," WBR would write of Miller years after the war. "He was almost adored by . . . his company, and they would follow him anywhere." Wister, *Walter S. Newhall*, 2–22, 33–51; Regimental History Committee, *Third Pennsylvania*, 572–73, 566–67; Rawle, *Refutation*, 9.

37. Hooker had relieved Averell of command on May 4, mistakenly believing that the cavalryman had failed to execute orders Hooker had issued attendant to Stoneman's Raid. Colonel McIntosh was, as WBR correctly relates, incensed at the treatment of Averell and his subsequent relief. Though he made known his intent to resign his commission in protest, McIntosh never did. For an explanation of the incident, see Wittenberg, *Union Cavalry Comes of Age*, 188–90.

38. The trooper killed accidentally was Pvt. Eli Hartenstine of Company C; he had mustered in on August 1, 1861. His brother, Jacob, had enlisted the same day; promoted to corporal in February 1862 and later that year to quartermaster sergeant, Jacob mustered out of the

service in August 1864. Dr. Theodore T. Tate of Gettysburg had mustered in only five days before this incident. He served with the 3rd until his honorable discharge on August 24, 1864. Regimental History Committee, *Third Pennsylvania*, 267, 566, 586–87.

39. Warrenton Sulphur Springs was located on the Rappahannock River some six miles southwest of Warrenton. Famed for the purported recuperative powers of the sulfurous water that bubbled up from its natural springs, the sprawling hotel could accommodate eight hundred guests. Many of the structures burned as a result of an artillery duel that took place on the property in the early stages of the Second Manassas Campaign in August 1862. "What remains of this once magnificent structure," wrote a Federal surgeon in the autumn of 1863, "is only calculated to fill the mind with sadness at the desolating destruction of war." Greiner, Coryell, and Smither, *Surgeon's Civil War*, 145. For good descriptions of the grounds and ruins of the resort, see Hays, *Under the Red Patch*, 206–9; and Griffin, *Three Years a Soldier*, 118–19.

40. The infantry force of 1,500 men at Kelly's Ford was made up of picked regiments from the I, II, and VI Corps, commanded by Brig. Gen. David A Russell. They had driven off the Southern pickets along the river in the early morning hours.

41. Brig. Gen. John Buford commanded the 1st Division of the Cavalry Corps during the fight, along with his own regular-cavalry brigade. He was to cross the Rappahannock at Beverly Ford and advance to Brandy Station on the Orange & Alexandria Railroad. Six miles to the south, at Kelly's Ford, Brig. Gen. David Gregg commanded both his own 2nd Division and Colonel Duffié's 3rd Division, which contained the 3rd Pennsylvania. Gregg was to cross at Kelly's Ford, the 2nd Division then to link up with Buford at Brandy Station. As the plan went, the combined force would advance toward Culpeper, where Stuart's cavalry was believed concentrated. Gregg, *Second Cavalry Division*, 5.

42. While the bulk of the serious fighting during the Battle of Brandy Station took place northeast of the railroad station and in the vicinity of Fleetwood Hill (where Buford's 1st and Gregg's 2nd Divisions concentrated their efforts), Pleasonton had ordered Duffié's 3rd Division—and the 3rd Pennsylvania—to advance west from Kelly's Ford toward Stevensburg, five miles south of Brandy Station. From that point, Duffié could either cut off Stuart's cavalry in the event the Rebels were forced to retreat or cover the left flank of the planned Northern advance on Culpeper. After reaching Stevensburg and pivoting north, a small group of Confederate cavalry impeded the colonel's advance, and additional orders received from Gregg—dictating that he halt at Stevensburg and open communication with the troops at Brandy Station—then essentially pinned him in place. Wittenberg, *Union Cavalry Comes of Age*, 255, 296.

43. After halting for much of the day in the vicinity of Stevensburg, Duffié received orders from David Gregg to join the 3rd Division, then heavily engaged near Brandy Station. Instead of brushing an inferior Confederate force aside and advancing on a direct northerly route to the aid of his fellow horsemen, Duffié backpedaled toward Kelly's Ford, then struck a byway leading north, which slowed his arrival at Fleetwood Hill and prevented him from reinforcing General Gregg in a timely manner. Col. John Gregg's brigade, with the 3rd Pennsylvania, was left near Stevensburg to confront the remaining Rebels but eventually broke off contact and followed the balance of the division to the vicinity of Brandy Station, also arriving too late to have any effect on the fighting there. Duffié's entire division of over 1,600 men lost but 29. John Gregg's 2nd Brigade lost only 4 men captured and 1 wounded, while the 3rd Pennsylvania suffered no losses. Wittenberg, *Union Cavalry Comes of Age*, 299, 300–303.

44. University of Pennsylvania graduate Capt. Charles Cadwalader (1839–1907) had served as an officer in the 6th Pennsylvania Cavalry until late 1862. In March 1863 he secured a position as an aide on the staff of General Hooker and later served on the staff of his successor as Army of the Potomac commander, General Meade. Cadwalader's half sister, Mary, who died in 1861, had been married to WBR's uncle, Henry. Gracey, *Annals of the Sixth Pennsylvania Cavalry*, 304–5.

45. The *Official Records* list the 6th Pennsylvania's losses at the Battle of Brandy Station as 5 killed, 25 wounded, and 78 missing or captured, for a total of 108. Major Morris of the Lancers was taken prisoner after his horse was shot and rolled over him; he died in Richmond's Libby Prison two months later. Capt. Charles Davis of Company F was killed during a charge by his regiment and the 2nd US Cavalry late in the afternoon. Adj. Rudulph Ellis was wounded but recovered and rejoined the 6th, was promoted to captain in April 1864, and later served on the staff of Brig. Gen. Alfred T. A. Torbert. WBR's friend Leiper was, as noted, prostrated by a saber cut to the head, though he had, recalled one of the regiment's majors, "fought like a Turk with pistol and sabre, and was surrounded and disarmed, but still stuck to his horse and striking with his fists finally broke away and escaped." Second Lt. Thompson Lennig of Company M had enlisted in the 6th Pennsylvania in September 1862 and was commissioned in November. Captured at Brandy Station, as WBR relates, he spent the succeeding nine months in Richmond's Libby Prison. Exchanged in March 1864, he resigned in April due to ill health resulting from his prison experience. The four regular regiments brigaded with the Lancers (the 1st, 2nd, 5th, and 6th US Cavalry) reported 3 officers killed, 9 officers wounded, and 8 officers missing or captured. *OR* 27(1):169; Wittenberg, *Rush's Lancers*, 112, 116; Gracey, *Annals of the Sixth Pennsylvania Cavalry*, 167, 312.

46. H. B. McClellan to WBR, Aug. 20, 1885, Rawle Papers, HSP; McClellan, *Life and Campaigns of Major General J. E. B. Stuart,* 294; Gregg, "Union Cavalry at Gettysburg," 376.

47. Wittenberg, *Union Cavalry Comes of Age,* 311.

48. *OR* 27(1):34–35.

49. Since the formation of the Cavalry Corps in February 1863, the 3rd Pennsylvania had served in the 2nd Brigade of the 2nd Division. At Brandy Station the 2nd Division was commanded by Colonel Duffié and the 2nd Brigade by Colonel Gregg. Col. Percy Wyndham had led a brigade in the 3rd Division but was badly wounded at Brandy Station, where Duffié had proven that division command was beyond the scope of his talents. In a reshuffle that took place soon after, the 3rd Division was combined incorporated into the 2nd Division and placed under the command of General Gregg, while the 1st Division, with the permanent addition of the regular brigade, went to General Buford. The 3rd Pennsylvania remained in the 2nd Division but became part of the newly expanded division's 1st Brigade, which was initially commanded by Col. John P. Taylor of the 1st Pennsylvania Cavalry (in the wounded Wyndham's stead) but who was replaced on June 24 by Colonel McIntosh. Later in the month a third division, commanded by recently promoted Brig. Gen. Judson Kilpatrick, was added back to the Cavalry Corps.

50. Confederate cavalry under Brig. Gen. Albert Jenkins, scouting in advance of Lt. Gen. Richard Ewell's corps, had reached Chambersburg, Pennsylvania, on the evening of June 15. It is somewhat remarkable that WRB was aware of the event within twenty-four hours of its occurrence.

51. The advance of Gregg's division was led by Kilpatrick's brigade. Late in the day on June 17, as the horsemen moved west through Aldie toward the gaps of the Blue Ridge, they were confronted by pickets from Col. Thomas Munford's Virginia cavalry brigade. Both forces became fully engaged, and the fighting continuing until dark, resulting in losses of approximately 120 for the Rebels and over 300 for Kilpatrick. The 1st Massachusetts Cavalry was hit particularly hard, losing half of its 300 men during the battle. WBR's statement that two artillery pieces were captured is untrue. *OR* 27(1): 952–53; Crowninshield, *First Regiment of Massachusetts Cavalry,* 143–53.

52. The exposed remains of hastily buried casualties from the Battles of First Manassas in July 1861 and Second Manassas in August 1862 were often remarked upon by soldiers who subsequently ventured near the scene of the fighting. "I will tell you one sight I saw at Bull Run in crossing over the old battlefield," wrote a Vermont infantrymen in October

1863. "I saw the bones of many of our unburied men some so poorly covered that the dirt had washed from their bones, skulls, toes, and bones of the different parts of the body lying about uncovered." An Ohioan who passed through the battlefield en route to Gettysburg recorded similar sights: "Bony knees, long toes and grinning skulls are to be seen in all directions." Young, *Voices from the Attic*, 223; Wilbur S. Nye, ed., *The Valiant Hours, by Thomas Francis Galwey, Eighth Ohio Volunteer Infantry* (Harrisburg, PA: Stackpole, 1961), 91–92. For more comments on the ghoulish sights witnessed near Manassas, see Survivor's Association, *History of the Corn Exchange Regiment*, 331–32; Regimental Association, *Under the Maltese Cross*, 157; Hyndman, *History of a Cavalry Company*, 180–81; and Macnamara, *History of the Ninth Regiment Massachusetts Volunteer Infantry*, 348–49.

53. Charles Brinton Coxe (1843–73) was an 1862 graduate of the University of Pennsylvania and a nephew of former Army of the Potomac commander George McClellan. He was at this time serving as second lieutenant in Company M of the 6th Pennsylvania Cavalry. Advanced to first lieutenant of Company L and captain of Company K in 1864, he was promoted to major in March 1865. Wittenberg, *Rush's Lancers*, 66, 205; Gracey, *Annals of the Sixth Pennsylvania Cavalry*, 314.

54. Colonel Duffié had recently suffered the misfortune of having been demoted from command of the 2nd Division, which at Brandy Station comprised six regiments in two brigades and an artillery battery, down to command of his regiment, the 1st Rhode Island Cavalry. On June 17 he and his Rhode Islanders had been ordered on what historian Edward Longacre has rightly called a suicide mission (Cavalry Corps chief Pleasonton disliked Duffié—and almost all foreign-born officers—intensely and deliberately sent the Frenchman and his regiment into harm's way) when they were detached from their brigade and sent to scout northwest from Manassas through Thoroughfare Gap, placing them squarely behind Confederate lines. After a few brushes with Rebel scouts, Duffié and the Rhode Islanders retreated north to Middleburg, there pushing aside a small Rebel force that included Jeb Stuart. The Confederate cavalry commander returned several hours later, heavily reinforced, and nearly wiped out the regiment, killing, wounding, or capturing nearly two-thirds of the approximately 280 Federals engaged. See Longacre, *Lincoln's Cavalrymen*, 167–68; and Denison, *Sabres and Spurs*, 232–42.

55. Pvt. James Montgomery of Philadelphia-raised Company C had enlisted in August 1861. He served his three-year term and reenlisted as a veteran volunteer in August 1864. Regimental History Committee, *Third Pennsylvania*, 588.

56. The striker mentioned by WBR was likely Pvt. William H. F. Ward, who served for three years in Company C. Abel Wright of New York was commissioned as second lieutenant of Company G in December 1861; he was promoted to first lieutenant of Company M on March 24, 1862; to adjutant on September 17; and to captain of Company K on May 1, 1863. He mustered out with the original members of the regiment in August 1864. Regimental History Committee, *Third Pennsylvania*, 566–67, 572–75, 589.

57. "As the officers were expected to keep their men in column, and were as tired and sleepy as the men," remembered a captain in the 3rd Pennsylvania, "they had to resort to every expedient to keep awake. When nearing Westminster it was discovered that part of our line on the left was not up. A halt was ordered; investigation found all the men and horses of a battery fast asleep; the troops in front had moved forward while that portion in the rear of the battery was asleep." Gilmore, "With General Gregg at Gettysburg," 100–101.

58. A rare mistake by WBR. Manchester is in Carroll County, Maryland, nine miles northeast of Westminster and five miles south of the Pennsylvania border. Hampstead lies four and a half miles south of Manchester.

59. Later in the war, when the Army of the Potomac was campaigning on Southern soil, the mounts that had worn down and become unserviceable were not as fortunate as those that

gave out during the Gettysburg Campaign. On the march into Pennsylvania, broken-down horses were usually relieved of their saddles and equipment and then set free; during the 1864 campaign in Virginia, they were killed. "This was done," explained a doctor with the 6th Ohio Cavalry, "to prevent their falling into the hands of the enemy. For this purpose there was always a rear guard, and when the disabled horses fell back, they were immediately shot. On a very hot day during a terrible march I remember counting some forty-five horses that had been thus disposed of along a course of less than five miles." At the close of the Seven Days' Battles in 1862, many horses that had given out also were shot, their bodies cast into the James River. Rockwell, *Rambling Recollections*, 154; Longacre, *Lincoln's Cavalrymen*, 94–95.

60. The eleven-mile march from Manchester, Maryland, to Hanover, Pennsylvania, was well remembered in the regiment. "Horses by scores fell from exhaustion along the road. The route in rear of the column toward the last presented a motley appearance. Officers and men, begrimed past recognition, tramped along on foot, leading their worn-out horses to save their strength, well knowing how much depended on it. Dismounted cavalrymen, whose horses had fallen dead or dying, straggled along, some carrying their saddles and bridles in hopes of being able to beg, borrow, buy or help themselves to fresh mounts, others without anything but their arms." Postwar, WBR recalled that in order to save the strength of his mount, he was compelled to walk most of the way between Manchester and Hanover, leading his horse by its bridle. One officer estimated that the 3rd Pennsylvania lost seventy-two horses during the advance to Gettysburg. Regimental History Committee, *Third Pennsylvania*, 266; Rawle, *Refutation*, 27; Gilmore, "With General Gregg at Gettysburg," 100.

61. On June 30 Stuart's cavalry attacked the tail end of Kilpatrick's 3rd Division as it was moving north through Hanover, Pennsylvania. Newly promoted Brig. Gen. Elon J. Farnsworth turned his brigade south and pushed the Rebels back through the town. A seesaw fight then ensued until dusk, when Stuart broke off contact and moved east toward York. The fight at Hanover further delayed his attempt to unite with the main body of the Army of Northern Virginia. Longacre, *Cavalry at Gettysburg*, 173–78.

62. The 3rd Pennsylvania had been resting near the intersection of the Low Dutch and Hanover Roads since their arrival from Hanover in the early afternoon; many sought shelter from the intense heat. Sometime after 6:00 P.M. they were ordered to advance toward Gettysburg to support a picket line of the 10th New York Cavalry then under attack from Confederates intent on securing their army's left flank preparatory to an infantry assault against the Union right on Culp's Hill. Moving west on the Hanover Road, the 3rd formed line behind Cress' Run (north of the road), pushing two squadrons of the regiment (including Capt. William Miller's, in which WBR was serving) across the stream and up onto the spur of Brinkerhoff's Ridge, where the stone wall was located. Capt. William D. Rank's two-gun section of Battery H, 3rd Pennsylvania Heavy Artillery (equipped with three-inch ordnance rifles) loaded and fired from the middle of the road, slowing the rush of the 2nd Virginia Infantry's attempt to reach the wall before the Federals; supplemental fire from the cavalry skirmishers eventually drove the Rebels back. In his diary WBR states that the race for the "stone fence" took place at about 7:00 P.M. and that the regiment remained in line of battle until 9:45 P.M., when they withdrew. The presence of the Federals along the Hanover Road forced Confederate general Allegheny Johnson, who was readying the assault against Culp's Hill, to draw off a brigade of his infantry to help meet this threat, and weakening the forces available to strike the Federal XII Corps. Regimental History Committee, *Third Pennsylvania*, 267–69; Rawle, *Gregg's Cavalry Fight at Gettysburg*, 7–8; OR 27(2):518. For an excellent account of this action, see Pfanz, *Gettysburg: Culp's Hill & Cemetery Hill*, 158–67.

63. Hugh Judson Kilpatrick of New Jersey (1836–81), an 1861 graduate of West Point, had recently assumed command of the newly formed 3rd Division, composed of troops formerly commanded by Brig. Gen. Julius Stahel. Famously called a "hell of a damned fool" by Wil-

liam T. Sherman, under whom he served later in the war, Kilpatrick was a self-serving glory hunter who failed to command the respect of many of the men who served under him because they felt he had little regard for their lives. "Kilpatrick is a brave injudicious boy," wrote Charles Francis Adams of the 1st Massachusetts Cavalry after Gettysburg, "much given to blowing and who will surely come to grief." Ford, *Cycle of Adams Letters,* 2:44–45.

64. Fifteen years later, in a letter to his former squadron commander, WBR would recall: "I remember lying in the clover field perfectly and while we were grazing the fearful Artillery firing along Cemetery Ridge took place and we could distinctly see it. Do you remember seeing the rebel ammunition wagon explode?" WBR to William E. Miller, June 12, 1878, Robert L. Brake Collection, US Army Heritage and Education Center, Carlisle, PA.

65. The other regiment was the 1st New Jersey Cavalry.

66. In a postwar notation to this letter, WBR states: "Capt. Miller & I were the only officers of the squadron present. Capt. Walter S. Newhall's squadron (of which I was the only officer present) and Capt. Miller's squadron (of which he was the only officer present) were consolidated together temporarily under his (Miller's) command." Miller, Rawle, and their men were at this time located on the edge of a belt of woods that ran north of the Lott House.

67. It was only a single regiment of Brig. Gen. George Armstrong Custer's brigade, the 1st Michigan, and not Custer's entire brigade which met the onslaught of regiments from the brigades of Col. John Chambliss, Brig. Gen. Fitzhugh Lee and Brig. Gen. Wade Hampton. Capt. Miller, stationed in the Lott woods, was without orders, but the heavy column of Confederate cavalry, exposing its flank as it charged from right to left in front of his position, was too tempting a target. Additionally, noted Miller, "we soon discovered that Stuart was too heavy for Custer, and unless some diversion was made, all would be lost." WBR suggested to Miller that they close up the squadron preparatory to a movement, and when Miller asked the young lieutenant if he would stand by him if he ordered a charge, WBR replied, "I will stick to you, Captain, till hell freezes over." WBR would later estimate that the distance between his position at the edge of Lott's Woods and the flank of the Rebel column was between one hundred and two hundred yards, and that when it was time to go in he ordered "Front into line, draw sabres, charge!" without taking time to form up because he had fallen behind the other elements of Capt. Miller's squadron who had already begun to advance. Regimental History Committee, *Third Pennsylvania,* 306–7; WBR to John P. Nicholson, Rawle Papers, HSP; Rawle, *Refutation,* 29. In 1906, a year after the regimental history of the 3rd was published, Andrew J. Speese, who served as a corporal in Company H, published a vitriolic pamphlet addressed to the governor of Pennsylvania and the president of the Historical Society of Pennsylvania. In it he attacked the veracity of the contents of the regimental history—omitting that he was a member of the committee that published it—and vehemently disputed the sequence of events surrounding the charge at Gettysburg. Speese's contention was that the men of his company undertook to charge the Rebel cavalrymen on their own, without any orders from Capt. Miller, and attempted (mostly unsuccessfully) to pick apart the account of the action contained in the Third's history, referring to parts of it as "the veriest rot," and "beyond credence." He concluded the twenty-three page diatribe by advising the governor to recoup the funds that had been set aside by the legislature for the publishing of the history from WBR, and directed the president of the Historical Society (where WBR was serving as vice president) to have WBR "officially brought to book and exposed, to serve as an example to future writers of pseudo history." As I have mentioned in the notes to the introduction, Speese was a man with a chip on his soldier who did not hesitate to engage in published ad hominem attacks against former officers of the Third, who he was especially resentful of. In the years after the war Speese had become a successful businessman, and managed to convince his contemporaries outside of the Third to refer to him as "Captain" Speese, even though he never rose above the rank of corporal. WBR did not

let Speese's unsupported attacks go unchallenged, and he assembled but never published his own lengthy refutation dismantling most of Speese's assertions not long after the pamphlet appeared. See Speese, *Story of Companies H, A, and C;* Rawle, *Refutation.*

68. "While my Sergeant was forming my platoon," WBR wrote to Capt. Miller in 1878, "I rode back to see if in a short distance I could get through or over the fence but finding I could not, I had (I think if there was one) the fence in front of me torn down. I went through and made for the rear of your squadron which was about starting. The field I had to go through was ploughed up & my poor played out horse could hardly get through it. However with my 15 or so men (I had lost several during the firing) I did my best to catch up to you but as you went in the rebs appeared to turn. The two columns were being jammed together by the fence. The men in the rear still coming on, and the head of the rebel & our column spread out to right and left and the head of the rebel column seemed to fray at the edges and the current like an eddy seemed running back. As I got up the current of rebs on the outside swept me along with it, still trying to get in closer, but at one time I found myself surrounded and 3 or 4 rebs devoting themselves to calling me bad names and demanding my surrender. I then tried to make my way out again with little success until two of the regiment worked themselves up to me and together we worked ourselves out with one of the rebs whom we captured, and by the time we got clear, the whole rebel column was sweeping back to the rear. With the few men I could get together I rode over to the battery (Randol's) where I thought I could find some of the regiment. . . ." To a British author in 1908, WBR related: "Having command of the left (the rear wing in moving in column) of Capt. Miller's squadron, I was cut off in the charge from the larger portion of it by the swarms of retreating Confederates, who began to fall back just as we struck their flank, and was surrounded by them with a few of my men, and was swept along with the current. We were charging with drawn sabres. My revolver was out of order, and as a Confederate was endeavoring to take me prisoner, though beyond sabre reach, I dropped my sabre, letting it hang by the sabre-knot from my wrist, and drew my pistol from my right boot leg, where I always carried it in a scrimmage, and tried to fire at him. But my pistol would not "cock," and with some perfervid language I threw it violently in my would-be captor's face, which blinded him and enabled me to get past him in cutting my way over to the right to Lott's woods, whence we had started our flanking charge." In 1897, Capt. Miller would be awarded the Medal of Honor for his actions at Gettysburg on July 3. WBR to William E. Miller, June 12, 1878, Brake Collection, US Army Heritage and Education Center; WBR to Cecil Battine, Feb. 21, 1908, Rawle Papers, HSP.

69. The bracketed words are a postwar addition by WBR.

70. During the final charge of Stuart's brigades, the 3rd Pennsylvania squadrons of Capt. Charles Treichel and Capt. William W. Rogers were posted in a hollow to the left of the Federal line (and on the right flank of the onrushing Rebels, who passed along their front from left to right) and, along with Company A of the Purnell Legion (Maryland cavalry), were ordered to charge the flank of the attacking Southerners. The Pennsylvanians and Marylanders (one officer recalled that the men of the Purnell Legion were "huddled up and confused" prior to the charge), accompanied by Captain Newhall of the 3rd, who was serving on the brigade staff and had delivered the order directing the charge, made a beeline for Wade Hampton's color guard, intent on capturing the general's flags. Treichel's arm was broken by a gunshot, and he was temporarily taken prisoner but escaped; his wound would keep him away from the regiment for three months. Captain Rogers (1832–90) of Bucks County, Pennsylvania, who had enlisted in Company B of the 3rd in July 1861 and was promoted through the ranks (assuming the captaincy of Company L on May 1, 1863), was shot through the chest and shoulder, as WBR relates. Despite the severity of these injuries, he returned to the 3rd on September 28. (He would transfer to the Veteran Reserve Corps in February 1864 and

later served in the Regular Army from 1867 to 1889, retiring as a captain.) Captain Newhall had a singular experience. As he bore down upon the Confederate color bearer, the Rebel dipped the staff of the flag parallel to the ground, spearing Newhall in the face with the tip. The force of the blow tore open the captain's cheek and shattered his jaw, knocking him out. Newhall would make his way home to Philadelphia after several days and returned to duty in early September. First Lt. Howard Edmonds (1840–1916) of Pottsville, Pennsylvania, who had been serving as first lieutenant of Company L since joining the 3rd in August 1861, had been wounded earlier in the war at Fredericksburg and was shot twice through the body and dazed by a saber blow to the head during the fighting at Gettysburg. His wounds precluded a return to active duty in the field, but he would serve on court-martial duty in Washington until mustered out in August 1864. Losses in the 3rd were comparatively light (and lower than WBR believed), with none killed, two enlisted men mortally wounded, and six officers wounded. Three additional enlisted men were wounded (one of whom was taken prisoner), and two others were captured. The total loss was 13 men out of 394 carried into the fight. Wittenberg, *Protecting the Flank at Gettysburg*, 101–2; Wister, *Walter S. Newhall*, 111–15; Regimental History Committee, *Third Pennsylvania*, 159, 258, 315, 563, 574–75; Gilmore, "With General Gregg at Gettysburg," 101; Edmonds, *Owen Edmonds*, 60, 63.

71. In actuality, the Confederates lost a total of 20,451 men at Gettysburg, including 4,150 captured or missing. Losses in the Army of the Potomac were slightly higher, with total casualties between 22,000 and 24,000, including 5,365 captured or missing. Guelzo, *Gettysburg*, 444–45. There are numerous examples during this time of troops of the Army of Potomac being told that McClellan had been restored to command. See, for example, James, *Memories*, 36–37; Acken, *Inside the Army of the Potomac*, 298; and George D. Bisbee, "Three Years a Volunteer Soldier," in *War Papers Read before the Commandery of the State of Maine, Military Order of the Loyal Legion of the United States*, vol. 4 (Portland, ME: LeFavor Tower, 1903), 125. The 22nd Massachusetts of the V Corps was told that McClellan, again in command, had arrived near Gettysburg with 60,000 fresh troops. The news, one of the men recalled, "fell dead on our ears. What a year before might have been most joyful intelligence to many (but not all) of the rank and file now called forth little or no enthusiasm in the thoroughly seasoned, much marched, but badly handled and worse fought veterans of the Army of the Potomac." Another V Corps soldier recorded that, on the night of June 30, it was announced to his regiment that McClellan had replaced General in Chief Henry Halleck, "and the wild cheers that broke from the men as the news communicated from regiment to regiment resounded along the various roads on which the army was moving well into the night." An officer of the 3rd Pennsylvania posited, "The McClellan legend in the Army of the Potomac, lasted a long time and was slow in dying out." Carter, *Four Brothers in Blue*, 298–99; Hennessy, *Fighting with the Eighteenth Massachusetts*, 171–72; Edmonds, *Owen Edmonds*, 56.

72. WBR added, in a postwar postscript, that the thirty men he led on this mission brought twenty-five wagons and were "fired on by a squadron of rebel cavalry who were drawn up across the road."

73. The 3rd Pennsylvania picketed the area to the south and west of the Round Tops, initially posting their reserve near Plum Run at the Slyder farmhouse. "The house was being used as a field hospital," the regimental historians recorded, "and was filled with wounded upon whom the surgeons were engaged in their revolting work. As fast as the men died their bodies were taken out of the house and into the rain and left there temporarily. The scene was so painful and sickening to us that we determined to remain with the picket reserve out in the pitiless downpour of rain." A staff officer who was nearby recalled: "I will never forget that night. It was raining hard and so dark that we were compelled to use lanterns to move the dead and dying out of the way, fearing our horses would crush them under their feet. The

moans of the dying were horrible. Sometimes I imagine I can still hear their voices ringing in my ears. It was awful!" Regimental History Committee, *Third Pennsylvania*, 322–23; Thomas, "Some Personal Reminiscences," 14.

74. *OR* 27(1):967.

75. Horace Binney III (1840–81) of Philadelphia had entered the service as the second lieutenant of Company B of the 118th Pennsylvania in August 1862 and would spend most of his war on the staff of Brig. Gen. Thomas Neill of the VI Corps. Binney's grandfather Horace, a former congressman, was one of the most well-known lawyers in the United States, and his family was among the wealthiest in Philadelphia. Binney would eventually be promoted to captain and be breveted major at war's end. Survivor's Association, *History of the Corn Exchange Regiment*, 688, 694.

76. Philadelphia-raised Landis's Independent Battery of Light Artillery had been mustered in "for the emergency" that the invasion of Pennsylvania occasioned on June 27; its 108 members included WBR's uncle, Henry (referred to by his first name in this letter), a sergeant in the unit. The battery saw light action against Confederate cavalry near Camp Hill, Pennsylvania, on June 30 and at Carlisle the following day. They mustered out on July 30, 1863. George Emlen, William Winsor (older brother of Captain Winsor of the 6th Pennsylvania Cavalry; see note 10 above), John B. Thayer, and John C. Biddle were all serving as privates in the battery. Taylor, *Philadelphia in the Civil War*, 248. During an artillery duel on July 1 near Carlisle, Pvt. C. Stuart Patterson, "a young gentleman . . . noted for his agreeable refined manners," had four fingers of his right hand severed by an enemy shell. An account of Patterson's experiences and wounding is in Wingate, *History of the Twenty-Second Regiment of the National Guard of the State of New York*, 214–19.

77. McIntosh's 1st Brigade was relieved from its attachment to the VI Corps on July 12, rejoining the remainder of Gregg's division when it reached Boonsboro. Regimental History Committee, *Third Pennsylvania*, 324.

78. WBR added a handwritten notation to his diary explaining that his servant "ran away with the property, fearing to return to Virginia, having escaped from slavery."

79. When orders for this movement across the Potomac arrived, Union commanders believed that Lee was still north of the river near Williamsport; Gregg's cavalry was thus sent to try to capture his trains and sever his lines of communication. But the Army of Northern Virginia had, in fact, crossed the Potomac on the night of July 13–14, effectively ending the Gettysburg Campaign. *OR* 27(1):959.

80. General Gregg had moved his cavalry division from Bolivar Heights at Harpers Ferry north to Shepherdstown on July 15 and, after establishing camp for the night, sent pickets west out Winchester Pike to guard his position. On the morning of the sixteenth, the Confederate cavalry brigades of Fitzhugh Lee and Chambliss attacked these pickets and pushed them back up the road to Shepherdstown. Gregg dispatched reinforcements, and the two sides battled throughout the day. In the course of the action, he sent portions of McIntosh's brigade, including the 3rd Pennsylvania, to shore up the left of the Federal line, which straddled Winchester Pike. Sunset brought an end to the action, with losses on each side of approximately 100 men. Gregg tried to return to Harpers Ferry by the same road he had advanced upon on the fifteenth but found it in possession of the Southerners. He eventually located an alternate route and moved his command south. Trout, *After Gettysburg*, 18–22; WBR to Pennock Huey, Nov. 30, 1883, Rawle Papers, HSP.

81. As noted earlier, WBR had left the University of Pennsylvania as soon as he completed his senior year studies. His Class of 1863 had formally graduated on July 3.

2. FIGHTING MOSBY AND THE PARTISANS

1. Regimental History Committee, *Third Pennsylvania*, 329. For remarks by other members of the Cavalry Corps on the difficulties encountered during this time, see Denison, *Sabres and Spurs*, 277, 281; and Griffin, *Three Years a Soldier*, 121–22. Brigade commander Col. John Gregg complained: "The enemy are becoming troublesome along our entire line, and I do not see how they are to be chastised, as the great advantage they possess over our troops renders it easy for them to escape. I cannot make a single movement that is not known at Sperryville before it reaches Amissville." *OR* 29(1):89.

2. Vestal's Gap (also known as Keyes or Keys Gap) of the Blue Ridge Mountains is located approximately four and a half miles south of Harpers Ferry. Heading northwest from Loudoun County to Jefferson County, the Charles Town Pike (present-day Virginia Route 9) passed through the gap and led to Key's Ford (also known as Keyes Ferry), located on the Shenandoah River several miles south of Harpers Ferry. *Map of Loudoun County, Virginia,* 1854, Library of Congress, https://www.loc.gov/item/2012589658/.

3. Henderson, *Road to Bristoe Station,* 20–33.

4. William Baughman (1829–1909), a married father of four, entered the 3rd as the first lieutenant of Cumberland County–raised Company H in August 1861. He had been promoted to the captaincy of Company E on May 1, 1863, and served as such until the expiration of his three-year term of service in August 1864. Regimental History Committee, *Third Pennsylvania,* 570, 572.

5. Robert T. Beaton had enlisted in Philadelphia-raised Company A of the 3rd in July 1861, serving as quartermaster sergeant and first sergeant until his promotion to second lieutenant of Company G on May 1, 1863. He was promoted to first lieutenant on April 16, 1864, but was not mustered at that rank, likely due to a shortage of men in the company. He was discharged in August 1864 with many of the original three-year members of the regiment. Albert Bradbury served as corporal and first sergeant in Philadelphia-raised Company M. While a sergeant, he was captured near Hartwood Church in November 1862 and spent six months as a prisoner. Upon his return to the regiment, he was promoted to second lieutenant of Company D, mustering out at that rank in August 1864. Regimental History Committee, *Third Pennsylvania,* 181–82, 570–71, 572, 578, 609.

6. Originally a sergeant in Cumberland County–raised Company H, William H. Bricker was promoted to first sergeant of his company on April 2, 1862, and to second lieutenant of Company B on May 1, 1863. He would be captured—as WBR details shortly—and held a prisoner until his parole on December 10, 1864. Regimental History Committee, *Third Pennsylvania,* 568–69.

7. WBR has previously mentioned Sgt. Joel G. Rammel of Company B. Rammel had been wounded at Gettysburg during the close combat on July 3. Parrying a saber blow from an "immense, long haired, swarthy rebel," Rammel's sword was mangled and a finger laid open to the bone. He would be promoted from sergeant to chaplain in March 1864 and mustered out of the 3rd that August. Chaplain Moses Hoge Hunter (1814–99), a native of Virginia, was an Episcopalian minister who held degrees from Yale and Princeton and had superintended a boys' school near Detroit, Michigan, prior to the outbreak of the war. Appointed chaplain of the 3rd on November 29, 1861, he served for just under two years, resigning in early November 1863. WBR's uncle on his father's side, William Herbert Norris (1814–80), was an Episcopalian minister who led churches in Carlisle, Pennsylvania, and Woodbury, New Jersey. His son, William L., was killed at Antietam while serving with the 4th New York Infantry. Regimental History Committee, *Third Pennsylvania,* 303–4, 583; Charles Elihu Slocum, *History of the Slocums, Slocumbs, and Slocombs of America,* 2 vols. (Defiance, OH: by

the author, 1908), 2:439; Bates, *History of Pennsylvania Volunteers*, 2:369; *Obituary Records of Graduates of Yale College, Deceased from June 1870 to June 1880* (New Haven, CT: Tuttle, Morehouse, and Taylor, 1880), 399.

8. "Spons" is an abbreviation of the word "spondulix," a slang term for money; "phiz," an altered abbreviation of "physiognomy," is a slang expression referring to an individual's head or face.

9. James Heslet had mustered in as first sergeant of Philadelphia-raised Company K of the 3rd Pennsylvania in August 1861. He was promoted to second lieutenant of the company on April 20, 1863, and was captured on November 29, during the Mine Run Campaign. He was honorably discharged on March 11, 1864. Regimental History Committee, *Third Pennsylvania*, 372–73, 574–75, 603.

10. Pvt. Lewis Hummel was an original member of Schuylkill County–raised Company L. He served for three years with the regiment and mustered out of the service in August 1864. Durne remains unidentified. Regimental History Committee, *Third Pennsylvania*, 607.

11. The oldest house of worship in Culpeper County, Oak Shade Church, now known as Little Fork Episcopal Church, is situated at the intersection of modern Virginia Routes 624 and 726 near Rixeyville, nine miles north of Culpeper. The current structure, which is the same one WBR comments on, was completed in 1776 and was predated by two earlier buildings, both of which had burned down.

12. WBR noted in his diary entry for August 13 that the Rebels across the Rappahannock belonged to the 7th Virginia Cavalry.

13. Maj. John Adams Sabin of Vermont served from 1862 to 1866 as an additional paymaster of volunteers. Heitman, *Historical Register and Dictionary of the United States Army*, 1:856.

14. As a second lieutenant of cavalry, WBR's monthly pay was $112.40.

15. Barber's (also called Barbee's) Cross Roads was located due west of the Bull Run Mountains and twelve miles northwest of Warrenton. It is known today as the town of Hume, Virginia.

16. Orderly Sgt. Daniel Jones of Schuylkill County's Company L had been commissioned (but not mustered) as second lieutenant of his company in August 1862. He died as a prisoner of war in Richmond on December 30, 1863. The other two Company L men taken remain unknown. Regimental History Committee, *Third Pennsylvania*, 574–75.

17. WBR's cousin, William Kelty Ingersoll (1843–88), a native of Vicksburg, Mississippi, had entered the University of Pennsylvania in 1860 but left during his freshman year and enlisted in the Confederate army. He was captured at Vicksburg. In a letter written soon after, he characterized his sufferings during the siege of the city as "very severe," noting that he was "reduced to eat[ing] mule & horse flesh." *Semi-Centennial Register of the Members of Phi Kappa Sigma Fraternity . . . 1850 to 1900* (Philadelphia: Avil Printing, 1900), 16; Jonathan W. White, ed., *A Philadelphia Perspective: The Civil War Diary of Sidney George Fisher* (New York: Fordham University Press, 2007), 200.

18. The 6th Ohio had been ambushed on September 1 near Barbee's Cross Roads, losing one man killed, five men wounded, and twenty-five captured. *OR* 29(1):91.

19. Col. Horace B. Sargent (1821–1908) of the 1st Massachusetts Cavalry voiced his frustration with the local population in a report issued at this time:

> Tonight I might, perhaps, report that there is not an armed rebel within the circuit of country that the colonel commanding expects me to clear. Tomorrow the woods may be full of them. A policy of extermination alone can achieve the end expected. . . . The people here all have sons or brothers in the cavalry. The mountains are full of men whose statements are fair, and whom nothing but infantry can capture and the Dry Tor-

tugas control. . . . I can clear this country with fire and sword, and no mortal can do it in any other way. The attempt to discriminate nicely between the just and the unjust is fatal to our safety; every house is a vedette post, and every hill a picket and signal station.

OR 29(1):90.

20. McIntosh's brigade had been sent to scout the area around Middleburg, Virginia, on September 10 but found nothing of importance. The cavalrymen returned the following day. *OR* 29(1):104.

21. WBR recorded in his diary that his horse had been injured by a pistol ball, indicative of the close combat he experienced. WBR Diary, Sept. 6, 1863, transcript.

22. The men captured were Pvt. John W. Artley of Company B; Pvt. Henry Martin of Company H, who would die as a prisoner in Richmond on March 6, 1864; and Pvt. Alfred C. Titus of Company B, who would die at Augusta, Georgia, while being transferred to Andersonville Prison in 1864. An account of this incident by Artley is in Regimental History Committee, *Third Pennsylvania*, 535–36.

23. "After the affair," wrote WBR in his diary, "I was told by an old negro woman, living in a house in the neighborhood, that the rebel party was a company of Moseby's men numbering 48 under Lieut. Mountjoy." WBR Diary, Sept. 6, 1863, transcript. Richard Montjoy, a twenty-three-year-old native of Mississippi, was one of Mosby's most trusted subordinates.

24. Capt. Jacob Lee Englebert had entered the 3rd Pennsylvania as a private in Philadelphia-raised Company B in July 1861. Promoted to sergeant in the company, he was advanced to the regimental staff as battalion quartermaster sergeant; soon after, in November, he was commissioned as second lieutenant in Company E. Promoted to first lieutenant of Company G at an unspecified date, he was promoted to the captaincy of Company G to date from May 1, 1863, serving in the 3rd until his muster out in August 1864. Englebert was slightly wounded during the Mine Run Campaign. He received the brevet ranks of major, lieutenant colonel, and colonel in the omnibus promotions of March 1865, giving him the distinction of having been promoted through more grades than any other member of the regiment. Regimental History Committee, *Third Pennsylvania*, 369, 570–71, 572–73, 576, 584.

25. Newhall quoted in Longacre, *Lincoln's Cavalrymen*, 224; *OR* 29(2):201.

26. The 3rd Pennsylvania, occupying a position north of the Rapidan River near Rapidan Station, was exchanging skirmish fire with elements of Maj. Gens. Henry Heth's and Richard Anderson's divisions of Lt. Gen. A. P. Hill's corps. The Southerners occupied fortifications south of the river while maintaining a position on the north side to protect the railroad bridge. Henderson, *Road to Bristoe Station*, 44–45.

27. WBR requested "a winter sack [coat] . . . lined warmly for winter, 3 or 4 yards of 1/16 inch india rubber flat braid, two silver plated cross sabres [insignia]—City Troop pattern—and two [number] '3's of proportionate size, . . . also if possible 2 bundles of 14½ paper collars."

28. The Cavalry Corps had received 1,000 fresh mounts on the fifteenth. WBR would name his horse, which presumably came from this shipment, Little Mac. Trout, *After Gettysburg*, 136.

29. This was Bristoe Station, a stop on the Orange & Alexandria Railroad between Manassas Junction and Catlett's Station. Many correspondents in the Army of the Potomac mimicked WBR's misspelling of the location (which I have corrected in future mentions). Today the settlement is known as Bristow.

30. After learning of the strength of the Confederate positions across the Rapidan, Meade sent Buford's and Kilpatrick's divisions to probe along the river for possible avenues of advance beyond Lee's left. Trout, *After Gettysburg*, 156.

31. John Minor Botts (1802–69), a Virginia Unionist and former congressman, lived with his family on a sprawling estate, known as Auburn, several miles northwest of Brandy Station.

"He is a fat man, with a mild blue eye," observed one of Meade's aides, "and his clothing seemed to show the world had gone hard with him." Botts had been held under arrest in Richmond for nearly two months in early 1862, and despite his political sympathies, he hosted high-ranking officers from both sides at his house during the war. Not every Union soldier shared WBR's high opinion of him. A Maine soldier whose regiment was encamped near Auburn during the winter of 1863–64 found Botts to be an "unmitigated fraud" because of his constant complaints to Meade about soldiers appropriating his wood for their fires. Another wrote, "The soldiers have never had the same respect for Botts that army commanders appear to entertain; and no tears are shed over the losses that are said to make the irate old Virginian more crusty than ever." Lowe, *Meade's Army,* 39; Houghton, *Campaigns of the Seventeenth Maine,* 152; Locke, *Story of the Regiment,* 291. A very good article-length discussion of Botts is in Hennessy, "Scourge of the Confederacy," 32–40, 75–77.

32. Meade had been ordered by the administration to send the XI and XII Corps (numbering between 17,000 and 23,000 men) to reinforce Rosecrans in Tennessee after the latter's defeat at the Battle of Chickamauga on September 19–20; WBR mistook the retirement of these two corps for a retreat. The XI Corps had been guarding the line of the Orange & Alexandria Railroad and was replaced by Gregg's cavalrymen.

33. Had there been such a term in the mid-nineteenth-century vernacular equivalent to a modern-day "running joke," WBR's cork mattress and his attempts to retrieve it would have fit the description. The mattress was given to him by his grandmother before he joined the regiment, and as noted in his first letter home, he had sent it back to his mother soon after leaving Philadelphia because it was too clumsy to carry. Mentions of the mattress and his efforts to secure it appear periodically throughout his future correspondence.

34. This is a puzzling comment, especially since WBR was on intimate terms with many officers of the 6th and should have been more familiar with their combat record. The Lancers had been heavily engaged up to this point in the war, most notably at Brandy Station, where they lost eight officers and 100 enlisted men—the largest loss of any Federal regiment that day—afterward detached from the army on August 15 and sent to Washington to refit. As further proof of the hardships they had faced, the regiment had counted 600 officers and men in their ranks in April 1862; as these Pennsylvanians settled in around the capital sixteen months later, fewer than 160 troopers remained. Wittenberg, *Rush's Lancers,* 115, 146.

35. Maj. Samuel Chester Staples of Massachusetts, an 1856 Amherst College graduate, had been appointed an additional paymaster of volunteers in mid-September 1862, serving in that position until his muster out in July 1866. Heitman, *Historical Register and Dictionary of the United States Army,* 1:916.

36. *Marmion* (1808) and *Lady of the Lake* (1810) are epic poems written by Sir Walter Scott.

37. Pennsylvania governor Andrew Curtin would win reelection in the October polling by a margin of 15,000 votes. Hesseltine, *Lincoln and the War Governors,* 326–29, 336.

38. WBR noted in a postscript that, although this letter was mailed immediately upon completing it, his family did not receive it until March 1865, seventeen months after it was sent.

39. A member of the 1st New Jersey Cavalry noted at this time that with respect to provisions, Gregg's cavalrymen were "rolling in the lap of luxury. From every part of the surrounding country negroes flocked into camp, bringing milk, eggs, poultry, sheep and vegetables for sale; and the paymaster having made his welcome visit, everyone was able abundantly to supply his mess." Pyne, *First New Jersey Cavalry,* 172.

40. The newspaper report stated that Bricker had been dismissed "for neglect of duty in not taking proper precautions for the safety of a scouting party under his command, thereby causing it to be surprised and himself captured." *Philadelphia Inquirer,* Oct. 1, 1863. Bricker eventually succeeded in having his dismissal reversed and received an honorable discharge in January 1865.

3. BRISTOE STATION AND MINE RUN

1. Regimental History Committee, *Third Pennsylvania*, 344–51.

2. Brig. Gen. Henry L. Eustis commanded the 2nd Brigade of Brig. Gen. Henry D. Terry's 2nd Division of the VI Corps.

3. The fragment of the flag WBR sent home is still attached to this letter.

4. Brentsville is approximately three miles to the southeast of Bristoe Station (modern-day Bristow).

5. On the afternoon of October 14, A. P. Hill, commanding Lee's Third Corps, spied what he believed were the rear elements of Meade's army crossing Broad Run near Bristoe Station and ordered an attack. Unknown to Hill, Maj. Gen. Gouverneur Warren's II Corps was trailing behind the troops he had seen, and Warren discretely secreted his men behind the raised embankment of the Orange & Alexandria Railroad near the station. As the Confederates advanced across the open fields west of Bristoe to attack the Federals moving off, they were surprised and severely punished by fire from artillery and infantry of the II Corps. Hill lost over 1,300 men, while Warren lost 548. WBR reported the echoes from this fight.

6. "Leaving Captain Walsh and his small regiment, greatly reduced in numbers, alone to look after the safety of the wagons, General Buford, notwithstanding that they had not all yet crossed Bull Run, and that a large number of them were stalled in the bottom, took his command, or the greater part of it, over to the other side." Regimental History Committee, *Third Pennsylvania*, 346.

7. An original member of Company F, 1st Sgt. Charles Dodwell, "one of the most efficient non-commissioned officers of the regiment," had been promoted from corporal sometime in 1862, after the company's then–first sergeant had deserted. Captain Wetherill commanded Company F, in which Sergeant Dodwell and Lieutenant Davis served. Dodwell, Wetherill recalled, "was cut in half with a cannon ball." Another officer of the 3rd wrote that the shot that struck the sergeant was "so close to Lieutenant Brooke [Rawle's] body that by the merest chance there was only one instead of two casualties to report." Of WBR's close friend Elwood Davis, Wetherill remembered that he "left me singing to go on the skirmish line and was killed as soon as he got on the line. Davis was new. It was almost his first fight. He would have made a fine officer, intelligent and without fear." Francis Dring Wetherill memoir, US Army Heritage and Education Center; Regimental History Committee, *Third Pennsylvania*, 354.

8. Pvt. Joseph C. Kern had mustered in to Philadelphia-raised Company B in July 1861. Official returns from the fight list the 3rd's losses as three killed, seven wounded, and four missing. Regimental History Committee, *Third Pennsylvania*, 337, 593, 584; OR 29(1):359.

9. Lieutenant Davis had joined the 3rd at the same time as WBR, and they had attended the University of Pennsylvania together. He "was an exceedingly tall, slender handsome lad, but eighteen years of age, though he looked somewhat older. Belonging to a wealthy family, he unselfishly left a home of luxurious comfort to serve his country." Taken ill with fever during the Gettysburg Campaign, Davis had only been back with the regiment for eighteen days before he was killed. Regimental History Committee, *Third Pennsylvania*, 355–56.

10. Originally the first sergeant of Company B, Charles C. V. Vandegrift had been commissioned as second lieutenant in Company A to date from December 27, 1862. He was honorably discharged on September 15, 1864. Regimental History Committee, *Third Pennsylvania*, 568–69.

11. First Lt. George A. Heberton was originally the second lieutenant of Company K of the 110th Pennsylvania Infantry. Promoted to first lieutenant on March 10, 1863, he was discharged in December 1864. WBR notes that the lieutenant was serving as acting inspector general on Brig. Gen. Thomas A. Rowley's staff at this time. Heberton had been cited by the general for his promptitude and energy during the Battle of Chancellorsville. Bates, *History of Pennsylvania Volunteers*, 3:1009; OR 25(1):291.

12. The semi-anonymous author of the article, almost certainly Maj. Myron H. Beaumont of the 1st New Jersey Cavalry, wrote that during the cavalry fight on the third day at Gettysburg, the 3rd Pennsylvania "worked with us as skirmishers, and kept pace with us well. After a while word was sent to the General that our ammunition was giving out, and some other regiments were sent to relieve us. It was a curious fact that they [the Pennsylvanians] could not be got up to the point where our men were standing. Their officers formed them behind a fence several hundred yards in our rear, and then we were ordered to fall back behind them. This gave the enemy a chance, which he was quick to take advantage of. Across the space thus left free he charged a brigade." "Something Like Campaigning," *Harper's Weekly,* Oct. 17, 1863. The 1st New Jersey's regimental history also makes note of the fact that the 3rd Pennsylvania's skirmishers would not initially advance to support them. See Pyne, *First New Jersey Cavalry,* 165. Beaumont may not have been an entirely reliable source, however, based on comments by some of the men who served under him. One officer wrote that the major "had the habit of being able to get away often from the regiment and of avoiding the harder part of the service, especially the battles." Rea, *War Record and Personal Experiences of Walter Raleigh Robbins,* 106.

13. Pvt. William Boyle of Philadelphia-raised Company C was part of the original complement of the 3rd, enlisting in August 1861. He reenlisted as a veteran volunteer and was promoted to bugler on August 1, 1864, but died at City Point, Virginia, on September 9. Regimental History Committee, *Third Pennsylvania,* 586.

14. *The Antiquary,* a novel by Sir Walter Scott, was published in 1816.

15. Ohio-born Lt. Thomas L. Haydn (1835–81) was later promoted to captain and major. He would be wounded while fighting with the VI Corps in the Shenandoah Valley in 1864 and received a brevet promotion to lieutenant colonel just after the war's end. The Classical Institute of Dr. John W. Faires, where Haydn had taught WBR, was a college preparatory school located in Philadelphia at Thirteenth and Spruce Streets.

16. "The Rebs made a dash along the Waterloo and Warrenton Pike, coming in at Carter's Church and gobbled some of the vedettes along the road, re-crossing at Waterloo." WBR Diary, Nov. 2, 1863, transcript.

17. Captain Horner, ostensibly of the 13th Virginia Cavalry, remains unidentified. There was a Capt. George W. Horner serving with the 2nd Virginia Cavalry at this time, but it is impossible to determine if this is the officer in question. This conversation, according to WBR's diary transcript, took place on November 4.

18. First Sgt. Thomas J. Wier was originally the quartermaster sergeant of Washington, DC–raised Company D. While the nature of his alleged offense is unclear, Wier was captured sixteen days after this hearing, which likely prevented a resolution of his case. Exchanged at an undetermined date, he mustered out of the service in June 1865. Regimental History Committee, *Third Pennsylvania,* 589.

19. WBR had joined this mess, consisting of Capt. James W. Walsh, Captain Wetherill, Lieutenant Carter, and Lieutenant Heyl, on October 18.

20. Lee had retreated south of the Rappahannock River after the fighting at Bristoe Station but had left a stronghold on the northern bank at Rappahannock Station, where the Orange & Alexandria Railroad crossed the river. Meade contemplated a move against Fredericksburg until Major General Halleck declared unacceptable any maneuver that involved changing either his base of operations or his line of communications. Meade then determined to clear Lee from his positions along and below the Rappahannock. What WBR reported were the reverberations of a successful assault by General Russell's division of the VI Corps, partially supported by the V Corps, against the bridgehead at Rappahannock Station. Confederate casualties exceeded 1,600 men; losses in the V and VI Corps were just over 400. Humphreys, *From Gettysburg to the Rapidan,* 36–37, 42–45.

21. *OR* 29(2):443.

22. The three fords mentioned by WBR were all crossings of the Rappahannock roughly midway between White Sulphur Springs to the north and Rappahannock Station to the south. From north to south, Fox's Ford was closest to the springs, several miles below it was Font's Ford (also known as Lee's Ford—WBR spells it phonetically), and farthest south was Freeman's Ford, which had figured prominently in the early stages of the Second Manassas Campaign. The editor is indebted to Clark B. "Bud" Hall of Culpeper, Virginia, for helping him make sense of WBR's misspelling and locate Font's Ford.

23. The disgraced soldiers, both from Philadelphia-raised Company C, were Pvts. Edward Garrison and James Lewis. A horse artilleryman who witnessed the ceremony agreed with WBR's assessment: "They looked very comical with one half their heads bald, and what hair they had was quite long. One was quite a young man and of light complexion, the other darker and much older. The younger one seemed to take his punishment much more to heart than the other." Regimental History Committee, *Third Pennsylvania*, 587; Griffin, *Three Years a Soldier*, 152.

24. Sgt. Daniel W. Whaler of Company H had been promoted to first sergeant on June 14, 1863. He mustered out with the original members of the 3rd Pennsylvania in August 1864. Sgt. Beatty Lyons of Company A left the 3rd in February 1864, accepting a commission as second lieutenant in Company H of the 20th Pennsylvania Cavalry, in which he served until discharged in January 1865. As the 3rd had disengaged from the fighting on the night of the fifteenth and resumed their retrograde movement, the two sergeants, "without asking permission, walked out to the spot leading a horse, coolly picked up the body [of Lieutenant Davis], placed it across the saddle, and came back into the line uninjured. The enemy, doubtless observing the brave act, refrained from firing upon them." The regimental history of the 3rd relates that a different soldier, Sgt. John C. Wagner of Company H, accompanied Whaler on the mission to retrieve Davis's remains. Regimental History Committee, *Third Pennsylvania*, 355, 578, 599; Bates, *History of Pennsylvania Volunteers*, 5:65.

25. *Devereux* is a novel written by Edward Bulwer-Lytton and published in 1829.

26. In a wartime postscript to this correspondence, WBR writes: "I gave this letter to the mail carrier, but as our communications were cut off, it cd. not be sent off. The mail was captured by the Rebels in their attack upon the Regt at Parker's Store on Nov. 29, and was found by one of the men on returning to the ground, minus envelope, photographs, etc., just as you see it."

27. In a letter written to his family after he returned to camp, Captain Newhall of the 3rd, who was serving on the brigade staff, related (and seems to have magnified) his role in the fighting on November 27.

At 11 o'clock A.M. my advance drove in the enemy's pickets and first line of skirmishers near Mount [New] Hope Church. Here the enemy's line was strengthened and it became necessary to dismount three of my squadrons in order to dislodge him from a thicket of pine trees and the Rail Road where he was strongly posted. This duty was well done by two squadrons of the 3rd Penna. Cavalry and one of the 1st Mass. Cavalry. During the charge of this woody country the enemy used grape & canister without effect. A section of Martin's 6th N.Y. Battery opened on the guns, and the squadrons mentioned having been reinforced they drove the enemy from his cover, charged across the open space beyond and occupied the edge of the opposite wood, putting to flight several squadrons of Rebel Cavalry. The enemy now advanced his Infantry and in ten minutes my line was heavily pressed. With the exception of the supporting Regiment (6th Ohio), and a few minor supports, the ground being impractical for Cavalry, I threw my entire command, dismounted, against the enemy, repulsed his charge, took his positions and captured thirty-four Infantrymen, including a Captain, with their arms, etc., besides killing & wounding a large number. During this time the enemy answered with artillery from three positions, keeping Martin's Battery actively engaged. . . . My line was engaged until 4½ P.M., when, my ammunition giving out, I was relieved by the Infantry of the 5th Corps.

Walter S. Newhall to Mother, Dec. 5, 1863, Walter S. Newhall Correspondence and Diary, Newhall Family Papers, HSP.

28. John W. Kester (b. ca. 1838–42, d. 1904) had spent a year with WBR at the University of Pennsylvania in 1859–60 before leaving school to work in his family's apothecary business. He had served in the three-month militia earlier in the war and was commissioned as a captain in the 1st New Jersey Cavalry in December 1861. Earlier in November 1863, Kester had been relieved from duty on the staff of General Gregg and promoted to lieutenant colonel; this was the first time he had commanded the 1st New Jersey in action (there was no colonel serving with the regiment). Peter Penn Gaskell (b. 1843), a direct descendant of William Penn, was the captain of Company F of the 1st New Jersey Cavalry, and served on the staff of General Buford. In February 1864 he was appointed major of the African American 2nd Louisiana Cavalry, which he served in until September 1864. Pyne, *First New Jersey Cavalry,* 196; Kester, *Cavalryman in Blue,* 1–3, 101–3; Jenkins, *Family of William Penn,* 226.

29. Four men of the 3rd were killed and sixteen were wounded, two of whom later died. Regimental History Committee, *Third Pennsylvania,* 363.

30. WBR wrote in his diary on November 29 that while he was cut off from the regiment and serving with General Gregg, "three brigades [of the enemy] charged the 3rd Pa. and the 1st Mass., who were dismounted, part of the command unsaddled, grooming. They killed and wounded and captured a good many, but many of the latter escaped." Later that day an artilleryman at Wilderness Tavern saw the Keystone State troopers returning from this encounter: "The 3rd Penna. Cavalry were badly cut up. They came in about noon with their horses and selves all bespattered with mud. They had run their horses all the way." Griffin, *Three Years a Soldier,* 157.

31. Butler D. Price (1845–1919) was the son of the commander of the 2nd Pennsylvania Cavalry, Col. Richard Butler Price. The younger Price had been commissioned as a second lieutenant in the regiment's Company E in October 1861 (he was sixteen at the time), then promoted to first lieutenant in November 1862 and to captain of the company in February 1864. He mustered out upon the expiration of his term of service in January 1865. Butler Price then enjoyed a lengthy postwar career in the Regular Army, attaining the rank of brigadier general before his retirement in 1905. Bates, *History of Pennsylvania Volunteers,* 2:338; Heitman, *Historical Register and Dictionary of the United States Army,* 1:806.

32. Prior to the Rebel cavalry attack that surprised the 1st Massachusetts and 3rd Pennsylvania on November 29, a group of Bay State officers were gathered under a tree near Parker's Store, shucking corn. With them was a young African American servant named Tom Chisholm. Following the attack, which scattered the men, the troopers regained the ground they had lost but found Chisholm's body hanging from the tree where he and the officers had been sitting. Inside Parker's Store they also discovered the bodies of three Union soldiers who had been shot through the head execution style. These were sick or wounded men who had gathered inside the building to await ambulance transportation. Crowninshield, *First Regiment of Massachusetts Cavalry,* 186–87.

33. "The Rebs got our mess kits and so we had to get along the best we could, cooking our meat on sticks, to help the darkies." WBR Diary, Nov. 30, 1863, transcript.

34. This is a reference to the strong Southern positions looming behind Mine Run, which, according to many of the infantrymen who would have had to assault them, were among the

most formidable they had ever seen. "They were composed of logs built six feet high," wrote a New Jersey lieutenant colonel who reconnoitered the ground over which the attack would have taken place, "and in front [were] fallen trees with the limbs sharpened and extending some fifty feet in front. . . . I came back through the woods with a heavy heart, feeling confident I would lose two thirds of my men." Many of the Federals were resigned to their fate: "I doubt that if on any similar occasion in the experience of the regiment," wrote a III Corps soldier, "so many valuables, addresses and messages to friends were given to the chaplain as there were on that cold winter morning at Mine Run." Recalled one veteran in the V Corps, who had survived, among other battles, the Wheatfield at Gettysburg, "I had faced many dangers, had been under fire many times, but never felt, as I did then, that death stared me in the face." Major General Warren, commander of the II Corps, recognized that the undertaking would likely result in disaster and called off the attack. Longacre, *To Gettysburg and Beyond,* 166; Marbaker, *History of the Eleventh New Jersey Volunteers,* 143; James, *Memories,* 45. An excellent description of the obstacles faced by the Federals at Mine Run is in Greiner, Coryell, and Smither, *Surgeon's Civil War,* 160.

4. WINTER AT WARRENTON

1. Hennessy, *Fighting with the Eighteenth Massachusetts,* 222. "I tell you how it is Louisa," wrote a VI Corps surgeon to his wife, "if Meade ever did a noble act in his life, it was when he concluded *not* to fight Lee in his strong hold upon the banks of Mine Run at a temperature of the weather far, far below freezing." Greiner, Coryell, and Smither, *Surgeon's Civil War,* 160.

2. Pyne, *First New Jersey Cavalry,* 211. A member of the 1st Pennsylvania Cavalry, writing later in 1864, recalled that the duties assigned to the regiment during the winter of 1863–64 were "the most constant, exhausting service it has ever performed." Lloyd, *History of the First Reg't Pennsylvania Reserve Cavalry,* 85.

3. "The pay of line officers," noted an officer of the 1st Massachusetts Cavalry, "was at this time much reduced by charging $54 a month for an enlisted man as a servant, and it was difficult, sometimes impossible, to get any other; while embarrassing stoppages from the inspector's department, for various reasons, sadly reduced the pay." Crowninshield, *First Regiment of Massachusetts Cavalry,* 199. The $54 per month charged of the Massachusetts officer is twice as much as WBR records he was charged.

4. WBR added a handwritten note in his diary transcript at this time: "December 13th, while out riding on some duty, my horse reared and fell back on me, his head being jerked up by an unseen military telegraph wire sagging from one tree to another, but owing to the deep mud I was not hurt, though the pommel of my saddle struck me in the middle of my stomach, just below my chest, without injury to me, as I thought at the time, but 47 1/3 years afterwards, on April 11, 1911, I was operated on at the Pennsylvania Hospital by Dr. LeConte as a private patient for a slight hernia which developed there in my declining years."

5. Lieutenant Colonel Jones's culpability in the events that led to the surprise of the 3rd Pennsylvania and 1st Massachusetts Cavalry on November 27 would do little to enhance his reputation. During the Overland Campaign, a squad of the 1st Massachusetts was detailed for picket duty under Jones, who, "I regret to say," wrote Charles Francis Adams, commander of the Bay State men, "is the unfortunate old woman who got us into our scrape at Parker's Store last autumn, and I have little confidence in him." Ford, *Cycle of Adams Letters,* 2:151.

6. German-born Rev. Otto S. Barten (1831–97) served as rector of St. James Episcopalian Church during the Civil War. In December 1865 he transferred to Christ Church in Norfolk, Virginia, and in the course of his ministry there provided spiritual counsel to former Confederate president Jefferson Davis, who was being held in nearby Fortress Monroe. A Pennsylvania

officer who attended services at St. James in the fall of 1863 remarked that Barten "prayed for all Civil Magistrates and for wounded Soldiers but was very cautious not to say anything objectionable." James Cornell Biddle to Wife, Oct. 25, 1863, James C. Biddle Papers, HSP.

7. This resident of Warrenton, WBR elaborated in his diary on December 15, was Annie Lucas, who was accompanied by her cousin, Mary Horner. The women had approached the 3rd Pennsylvania's vedettes, and, WBR remembered,

> begged me most imploringly to let them outside the picket line to go to a house half a mile distant to procure eggs for egg nog. Of course I could not allow it. I had a delightful conversation for about 1½ hours with them. They were terribly secesh and most aristocratic; knew many of my Philada. and army friends. They would not under any circumstances let me know their names, but, accidentally, within half an hour, I found out names, addresses and everything. Some of us shortly after took a dash out to the house after one of Moseby's Lieuts., Mountjoy and a man, but could not capture them. We, however, got some eggs which I sent in to Miss Lucas by an orderly, with a small note. She was astonished at my finding her out so soon, but sent back a pretty little note of acceptance. This may be an opening into Warrenton society if we remain here this winter, should I desire to push it, which however is very hot secesh, and very aristocratic.

WBR had experienced a prior run in with Montjoy, on September 6, while scouting on the Salem Road near Warrenton. Wounded and captured earlier in the war, Montjoy was promoted to captain in Mosby's 43rd Virginia Battalion in March 1864 and was killed in a skirmish near Leesburg, Virginia, on November 27. In a peculiarly ironic twist, Annie Lucas, who WBR spent over an hour talking to (and who was likely, unknown to the young officer, trying to glean intelligence from him) was engaged to Montjoy. Wert, *Mosby's Rangers*, 122, 151–52, 257.

8. A captain in the 1st Massachusetts Cavalry wrote that his regiment considered it their fortune to spend considerable time picketing in and around Warrenton in the fall of 1863, noting that the hamlet was "famous for its pretty girls, who did not fail to tell wonderful stories of the Confederate troopers, predicting attacks upon us, and the discomfiture which they said was always the result of an engagement with their Virginia heroes." Another 3rd Pennsylvania officer offered a different perspective: "We appear to have settled down for winter quarters, much to the delight of the citizens hereabouts, who look forward to innumerable and jolly raids by their favorite cut-throat, Mr. Mosby." Crowninshield, *First Regiment of Massachusetts Cavalry*, 189; Walter S. Newhall to Mother, Dec. 13, 1863, Walter S. Newhall Papers, HSP.

9. Newhall was very highly regarded both within the 3rd Pennsylvania and throughout the 2nd Division of the Cavalry Corps. It was widely reported that he died, as WBR relates, when his horse fell midway through the crossing of a swollen tributary of the Rappahannock, pinning Newhall underneath and drowning him. In a letter written thirty-four years later, WBR provided more details. Newhall, he wrote, "was always well-mounted, and the horse 'Tim Whiffler' he was riding was the race winner of the Corps." The captain and his orderly crossed the railroad bridge at Rappahannock Station and were moving along a corduroy road that traversed a stretch of swamp when they found the road blocked by teams. "Newhall jumped his horse from off the road to one side of it, and he had not gone far when his horse became mired in a quicksand and rolled over on him, and before he became extricated he was suffocated in the mud." Clement Biddle Barclay, who had helped WBR secure his commission in the 3rd, brought Newhall's remains to Philadelphia for burial. Expressions of regret over his death were issued by high-ranking officers, including Maj. Gen. Winfield Hancock and Brigadier General Averell; one of the officers of the 3rd, Alexander Vernou, would later name his son after the

deceased officer. Wister, *Walter S. Newhall*, 134, 136–38; WBR to William B. Harrison, Dec. 6, 1899, Rawle Papers, HSP; *Philadelphia Inquirer*, Dec. 21, 1863, 4.

10. Over the preceding sixteen months, John Buford had developed into one of the most skilled cavalry officers in the Federal service, particularly distinguishing himself at Gettysburg, where on July 1 he checked the Rebel advance into town until infantry reinforcements arrived. Worn down by exertion and typhoid fever, the general's untimely death on December 16 was universally mourned by the Army of the Potomac. Buford was remembered by a trooper who fought under him as "that noble man too great to seek for glory, . . . the perfect type of an honest and true soldier." Fox, *New York at Gettysburg*, 3:1134.

11. "Helmet and pulse warmers" may refer to a knit smoking or sleeping cap and gloves.

12. Nicknamed the "Black Horse Cavalry," the 4th Virginia Cavalry's ten companies were, in fact, each raised from ten different counties of Virginia. Company H, nicknamed the "Black Horse Troop," was populated by citizens from Fauquier County, many of whom were residents of Warrenton. Four officers who served as colonel of the regiment during the war (Beverly Robertson, William Payne, Williams C. Wickham, and South Carolina–native Stephen D. Lee) were promoted to general-officer rank.

13. WBR was unknowingly critical of his mother, who, he added in a postscript, he later learned was the author of the eight-stanza Newhall tribute. The poem is reprinted in Regimental History Committee, *Third Pennsylvania*, 546–47.

14. This movement, which was commanded by Colonel Taylor of the 1st Pennsylvania Cavalry and included most of Gregg's division, was a scouting mission to reconnoiter the lower Shenandoah Valley. The expedition advanced as far as Front Royal on their first day out, but the weather deteriorated and the men found the Shenandoah River impassable. The Northern troopers returned to the vicinity of Warrenton the next day. "It was a hard, cold time," wrote a diarist in the 1st Maine Cavalry, "and what it amounts to no one knows." Tobie, *First Maine Cavalry*, 229–31.

15. The Rebels who carried out this surprise attack were under the command of Lt. Thomas A. Turner, a member of Mosby's Rangers. The party, thirty-two strong, had departed Salem at sundown of January 6 and arrived near Warrenton at 9:00 PM. They soon captured a Federal sentry, and in the early morning hours of January 7, their prisoner led them to the rear of the picket reserve of the 3rd, which they charged, wounding eight of the Pennsylvanians (two of whom later died) and capturing eighteen men and over forty horses. In a similar raid near Harpers Ferry four days later, Lieutenant Turner was mortally wounded. Regimental History Committee, *Third Pennsylvania*, 393–97; Williamson, *Mosby's Rangers*, 121–25.

16. The actual number of veterans of the 3rd who signed on for an additional three-year term varies between sixty-five and seventy-five, depending on the source. Regardless, the number recruited was far lower than was desired, and the decision whether or not to reenlist was undoubtedly influenced by the exhausting nature of the service the regiment was engaged in at this time. "The depressing circumstances attending the kinds of work the men of the regiment were without interruption called upon to perform . . . militated against the success which had been hoped for, and the majority of them declined the tempting bait offered by the Government." Cpl. Andrew Speese of Company H recalled that in spite of the sizeable bounty and monthlong furlough being offered, "the vast amount of duty exacted of them at this time . . . had such a discouraging effect, that less than one hundred men were induced to re-enter the service." He concluded, "The boys wouldn't bite well under these circumstances." Similar sentiments were expressed in the 1st Massachusetts Cavalry, which reenlisted a single company. "Those with the colors were having an unusually tedious and severe winter, with ceaseless picket duty and scouting, and for various reasons were discouraged." Regimental History Committee, *Third Pennsylvania*, 390; Speese, *Story of Companies H, A, and C*, 54;

Crowninshield, *First Regiment of Massachusetts Cavalry,* 198–99. A contrasting opinion by a member of the 1st New Jersey Cavalry is in Pyne, *First New Jersey Cavalry,* 212.

17. Hussars were distinctively attired light cavalry units originating in Hungary during the fifteenth century. They gained prominence during the American Revolution and Napoleonic Wars.

18. This was the Battle of Morton's Ford, which took place on February 6. Intended as a diversion to distract Confederate attention from an attack planned against Richmond by troops from the Army of the James under Maj. Gen. Benjamin Butler, the action occurred when the II Corps division of Brig. Gen. Alexander Hays crossed the Rapidan River at Morton's Ford, four miles south of Stevensburg, expecting to surprise the Rebels on the south bank. Though it was hoped that Hays would keep the Southerners occupied for several days, he was driven back across the river at nightfall, having suffered over 250 casualties with nothing to show for them. *OR* 33:113–43.

19. Edwin Booth (1833–93), one of the most well-known actors of his time, was the older brother of John Wilkes Booth. The Kirkwood House Hotel was located at Pennsylvania Avenue and Twelfth Street. A Pennsylvania officer who boarded there during the war called it a "one horse hotel, awful for accommodations." Upon Lincoln's death in April 1865, Vice Pres. Andrew Johnson was sworn in as president at the Kirkwood. Acken, *Service with the Signal Corps,* 340.

20. WBR has allowed the understandable pride he felt for the 3rd Pennsylvania to cloud his judgement. While the 3rd was one of the first volunteer cavalry regiments raised in the North (and the first to take the field) and had seen hard service since mid-1861, it is unlikely that it had experienced higher casualty levels than any other cavalry regiment serving with the Army of the Potomac. Units such as the 6th Pennsylvania, 1st Maine, 1st Michigan, 2nd New York, and 1st Vermont had all seen hard service since early in the war and, unlike the 3rd Pennsylvania, had experienced individual battles in which large numbers of their men were killed or mortally wounded. Furthermore, as WBR mentioned in his October 1863 letter describing the incident, his friend Ellwood Davis was the first officer killed in the 3rd Pennsylvania—this after over two years of active service.

21. Capt. John Redman Coxe of Philadelphia was serving as the acting commissary of subsistence on Meade's staff. George Gordon Meade Jr. (1843–97) had garnered enough demerits while attending West Point to be dismissed from the academy after his second year. Although offered a commission in the 3rd Pennsylvania (which Meade Sr. regretted his not accepting), he joined the 6th Pennsylvania Cavalry as a lieutenant in November 1862. In May 1863 he became an aide to his father, who then commanded the V Corps, and remained on his staff for the rest of the war. Capt. Arthur McClellan (1839–1904) was the younger brother of the former commander of the Army of the Potomac. He had graduated from the University of Pennsylvania in 1858 and was serving at this time as an aide to Maj. Gen. John Sedgwick, commander of the VI Corps, and was not a member of Meade's staff. Maj. James C. Biddle (1835–98), yet another Philadelphia blueblood, was also an aide on the headquarters staff. The official designation of Collis's Zouaves, named for their colonel, Philadelphia native Charles H. T. Collis, was the 114th Pennsylvania Infantry. Lowe, *Meade's Army,* 154, 218, 402; *OR* 37(2):487; Cleaves, *Meade of Gettysburg,* 60–61, 83; Sedgwick, *Correspondence of John Sedgwick,* 174; Gracey, *Annals of the Sixth Pennsylvania Cavalry,* 214.

22. Rev. Benjamin Dorr (1796–1869) served as rector of Philadelphia's Christ Church from 1837 to 1869. WBR had attended school with his son, Will, who was serving as a captain in the 121st Pennsylvania Infantry. Gough, *Christ Church Philadelphia,* 225–27, 244–46.

23. Fifteen hundred cavalrymen under Brigadier General Custer embarked on a raid against the Virginia Central Railroad near Charlottesville on February 28. Custer reported

capturing 100 slaves, 50 prisoners, and 500 horses without any Federal loss. The VI Corps was sent to Madison Court House to support this movement. *OR* 33:162–63.

24. On February 28 Brigadier General Kilpatrick, with 3,000 men, and Col. Ulric Dahlgren, son of a navy admiral, with 500 troopers, had embarked on a two-pronged cavalry raid against Richmond to attempt to free the 15,000 Union prisoners being held in the Rebel capital. The larger force under Kilpatrick was to move against its northern defenses and draw attention away from Dahlgren's charge into the city from the south. Abysmal weather, Kilpatrick's temerity, and determined resistance by Confederate defenders stopped the raiders on the outskirts of Richmond. Dahlgren was killed, and 340 men and approximately 1,000 horses were lost. WBR shared the opinion of many regarding Kilpatrick. Cavalry historian Steven Starr wrote of him: "His chief talents were a reckless bravery and a gift for leadership in combat, unmatched by sound judgment or the intellect needed for high command." Starr, *Union Cavalry,* 2:9, 417.

25. Ulysses S. Grant had been promoted to lieutenant general effective March 9, assuming command of all Union armies. "In a drenching rain, on March 10, the headquarters guard . . . turned out under Lieutenant Rawle Brooke, as Brigade Officer of the Day, to receive Lieutenant General Grant on the occasion of his first visit to the Army of the Potomac, for the purpose of a conference with General Meade as to the future movements of the army." Regimental History Committee, *Third Pennsylvania,* 411.

26. Not to be confused with his sister Charlotte, who was nicknamed Lottie, this was WBR's cousin Lottie Lloyd. Her father, Clinton Lloyd (1828–1901), had recently been appointed chief clerk of the US House of Representatives, a position he would hold until 1875.

27. Brig. Gen. Rufus Ingalls (1818–93) of Maine, an 1843 West Point graduate, was at this time the chief quartermaster of the Army of the Potomac and would later hold supply and logistics responsibilities for all of the armies operating against Richmond and Petersburg. Brig. Gen. Seth Williams (1822–66), also from Maine, was an 1842 graduate of the US Military Academy. He had served as assistant adjutant general (essentially the chief administrative officer) of the Army of the Potomac since its inception and had recently been appointed inspector general on the staff of General Grant. Both men were exceptionally efficient officers. WBR recounted his meeting with Ingalls in his diary: "I found him anxious to have me as his A.D.C. I told him that though I preferred being with my regiment, so as not to lose my chances of promotion, yet I would accept his kind offer. The position is a nice one, especially since our Regiment is on duty here." WBR Diary, Apr. 7, 1864, transcript.

28. It was not uncommon for Meade's soldiers to express misgivings about Grant's chances for success against Lee and the Army of Northern Virginia, who, they felt, were superior to the Southern generals and armies Grant had opposed in the West. Writing in December 1863, three months before Grant was appointed general in chief, General Meade informed his wife that he did not begrudge Grant his success but that the Confederates "have never had in any of their Western armies either the generals or the troops they have had in Virginia." A Massachusetts soldier reckoned that "Grant has a far different enemy to cope with than he overcame in his past victories," ominously declaring that "Gen. Lee's is not a power to be considered lightly." Meade, *Life and Letters,* 2:162–63; Hennessy, *Fighting with the Eighteenth Massachusetts,* 225. For other examples of this thinking in the weeks preceding the Overland Campaign, see Osceola, *History of the One Hundred and Thirty Eighth Regiment, Pennsylvania Volunteer Infantry,* 77; Blight, *When This Cruel War Is Over,* 280; Allen, *Down in Dixie,* 180–81; and Goss, *Recollections of a Private,* 262–64.

29. *Holmby House: A Tale of Northamptonshire* is a novel by one of WBR's favorite authors, George Whyte-Melville, first published in 1860.

30. An educated, erudite volunteer aide on Meade's staff who also attended this service, Lt. Col. Theodore Lyman, wrote of the proceedings: "Dr. Kirk, with a strong Boston deputation

of the Chr. Commission, turned up and he preached for us a severe but good sermon. He is a man of ability but rather oratorical." A Boston blueblood with a keen sense of observation, Lyman left a fascinating, gossipy, intimately detailed account of his time serving under Meade. His recollections, long a cornerstone in any study of the Army of the Potomac, were originally published in an abridged format in 1922 but were reissued in 2007, deftly edited by David W. Lowe and expanded to include additional material that was left out of the original publication. The new edition is one of the best primary sources on the Army of the Potomac ever published. I have relied on this later version to verify (and augment) many of the future events and experiences WBR describes. Lowe, *Meade's Army*, 120.

31. Capt. Joseph Penrose Ash of Philadelphia (1839–64) commanded Company A of the 5th US Cavalry. He had been commissioned a second lieutenant in the regiment from civil life by President Lincoln in April 1861. Ash had suffered multiple wounds during a cavalry skirmish near Warrenton in November 1862 and had distinguished himself in a diversionary movement against Charlottesville attendant to the Kilpatrick-Dahlgren Raid in February 1864. He was killed on May 8 near Todd's Tavern, Virginia, and was posthumously promoted to the rank of lieutenant colonel.

32. While on leave in Philadelphia, Rawle had purchased this piccolo "for my amusement in camp. ($6)." WBR Diary, Apr. 4, 1864, transcript.

33. WBR was carrying letters, money, and a bundle on behalf of Alfred Horner of Philadelphia to his brother, Joseph Horner, in Warrenton, Virginia. It seems likely that Horner of Warrenton was a relative—and possibly the father—of Mary Horner, mentioned above in note 7.

34. Before his appointment as commissary of subsistence in the Cavalry Corps, Capt. J. Nelson Potter (b. 1841) had been an aide-de-camp to II Corps commander Maj. Gen. Darius Couch, serving under him at Fredericksburg, Chancellorsville, and during the Gettysburg Campaign, when Couch commanded the Department of the Susquehanna. Potter was, as WBR states, the son of the Episcopalian bishop of Philadelphia, Alonzo Potter (1800–1865), and also the half brother of Brig. Gen. Robert B. Potter (see chapter 7, note 18). Originally the commissary sergeant of Company H of the 3rd, Samuel C. Wagner of Cumberland County, Pennsylvania, was promoted to second lieutenant of Company I in November 1862 and to first lieutenant and regimental commissary on May 1, 1863. Less than two months later, he joined the staff of the 1st Brigade, 2nd Division, Cavalry Corps, and was later advanced to the position of divisional commissary. He mustered out in August 1864. *OR* 21:224, 25(1):308, 27(3):635, 651; Regimental History Committee, *Third Pennsylvania*, 566–67, 572–73.

35. The Invalid Corps had been established in April 1863 to allow Federal soldiers who had become unfit for active duty due to wounds or illness to continue to serve. Many men performed light guard and garrison duty, while those more severely disabled filled administrative and nursing roles in hospitals and government-run institutions. WBR's designation of them as "Condemned Yankees" stemmed from a nickname that the corps had been saddled with by able-bodied soldiers. Boxes of rations that were determined by quartermasters to be spoiled or otherwise unsafe for consumption were stamped with the initials "I C," which stood for "inspected, condemned." Northern soldiers began to refer to their comrades in the Invalid Corps as "inspected, condemned" because the initials were the same. In March 1864, partly because of the negative connotation associated with the abbreviation, the organization was renamed the Veteran Reserve Corps.

36. "I subsequently learned," WBR added in a postwar notation, "that Major Robinson went to Hd. Qrs., without informing me, and stated that I could not be spared from the Regiment, and prevented the detail. He then tried to obtain some similar staff position for himself, and failing in this, obtained his detail to go home on recruiting service." His own attempt to obtain a staff position "was all knocked on the head by the contemptible underhand

conduct of Maj. Robinson," WBR confided to his diary, "a man who will let no officer of the Regiment get a soft thing, but who is almost always away from his Regiment himself." WBR Diary, Apr. 7, 1864, transcript.

5. THE OVERLAND CAMPAIGN AND THE EARLY ACTIONS NEAR PETERSBURG

1. Grant, *Personal Memoirs*, 2:129–32. Sigel's orders involved two movements—his own up the Shenandoah Valley (in which he failed), and a slightly more successful venture by Maj. Gen. George Crook in West Virginia, which resulted in the destruction of a large cache of supplies and a portion of the Virginia & Tennessee Railroad.

2. Of his decision to campaign with Meade and the Army of the Potomac, Grant writes, "No one else could, probably, resist the pressure that would be brought to bear upon him to desist from his own plans and pursue others." Grant, *Personal Memoirs*, 2:116.

3. Grant, *Personal Memoirs*, 2:135.

4. Anderson, *Fifty-Seventh Regiment of Massachusetts Volunteers*, 23.

5. Provost Marshal General Patrick's Headquarters Brigade was commanded by Colonel Collis of the 114th Pennsylvania and consisted of the 114th, the 3rd Pennsylvania Cavalry, the 68th Pennsylvania Infantry, and the 20th New York State Militia (known also as the 80th New York Infantry).

6. Col. Theodore B. Gates commanded the 20th New York State Militia. *OR* 36(1):198.

7. Captain Ash was killed on May 8 at Todd's Tavern while trying to rally an infantry regiment that had mistakenly fired into a line of Union cavalry posted to their front. Lt. Robert P. Wilson of the 5th US Cavalry had been appointed from the army as first lieutenant and adjutant of the 3rd Pennsylvania in January 1862 and was honorably discharged after serving with the regiment for eight months. After a brief stint as an enlisted man in the regular infantry, Wilson was commissioned second lieutenant in the 5th Cavalry in June 1863 and promoted to first lieutenant on May 8, 1864, only to be captured two days later. He remained in the army after the war, attaining the rank of captain, and resigned in 1876. Maj. James Starr, commanding the 6th Pennsylvania Cavalry, and WBR's friend Lieutenant Coxe were both wounded on May 7; Coxe was disabled by a shoulder wound, while Starr was shot in the face. Lt. William Kirk, the acting adjutant of the 6th, was wounded by a shot that shattered his thigh, which led to his death on June 24. *OR* 36(1): 812; Regimental History Committee, *Third Pennsylvania*, 564; Wittenberg, *Rush's Lancers*, 173; Gracey, *Annals of the Sixth Pennsylvania Cavalry*, 235.

8. Lt. Gen. James Longstreet, commander of the Army of Northern Virginia's First Corps, had been seriously wounded by friendly fire on May 6. Although Maj. Gen. George Pickett led a division in Longstreet's Corps, he and his troops were serving on detached duty near Richmond, thus the rumor that the general had been killed was untrue. "Uncle John" Sedgwick, the popular commander of the VI Corps, was killed by a sniper on May 9 only moments after chiding a nearby soldier for dodging the bullets of Confederate marksmen.

9. The predawn May 12 assault by the Union II Corps against the Mule Shoe salient resulted in the capture of thousands of prisoners, among them a majority of the famed Stonewall Brigade. Of the five infantry regiments that composed it—the 2nd, 4th, 5th, 27th, and 33rd Virginia—only the 2nd Virginia (contrary to WBR's belief) escaped wholesale capture. WBR's cousin, Mordecai Lewis, was serving in Company C of the 2nd Virginia. He had enlisted as a private at age eighteen in April 1861, was promoted to sergeant in November 1862, and survived wounds and several stretches in hospitals before surrendering at Appomattox. Matter, *If It Takes All Summer*, 199–200; Compiled Service Record of Mordecai Lewis, US National Archives, at Fold3.com, https://www.fold3.com/search/#s_given_name=Mordecai&s_surnam e=Lewis&ocr=1&offset=1&preview=1&t=42,872,19 (accessed Feb. 17, 2018).

10. Twenty-six-year-old William White Dorr, "a man of unflinching character and integrity," had commanded Company K of the 121st Pennsylvania Infantry. He was killed at Laurel Hill on May 10, 1864, while in temporary command of the regiment. Dorr had joined the 121st as first lieutenant on September 4, 1862, and was promoted to captain on October 5, 1863. His regimental commander had mentioned him for gallantry at Gettysburg. Dorr was the son of the Rev. Benjamin Dorr, rector of Philadelphia's Christ Church, who WBR mentions in his letter of February 28, 1864. Bates, *History of Pennsylvania Volunteers*, 3:51; Survivor's Association, *History of the 121st Pennsylvania*, 17, 81, 146–47.

11. The 2nd Ohio was actually a veteran cavalry regiment, having served in Kentucky and Tennessee prior to its assignment to the Army of the Potomac just before the Overland Campaign. Venturing into the Wilderness with the IX Corps on May 5, one of the Buckeyes wrote that they felt "like strangers in a strange land. . . . There were many young staff officers that appeared to want to do something, but they did not appear to know what to do but to make some fuss." Gause, *Four Years with Five Armies*, 223.

12. Brig. Gen. James B. Ricketts (1817–87), an 1839 West Point graduate, commanded the 3rd Division of the VI Corps. Brig. Gen. William H. Morris of New York (1827–1900), an 1851 West Point graduate, commanded the 1st Brigade of Ricketts's division; he would receive a wound four days later, on May 9, that would preclude his return to active service.

13. Maj. Gen. Winfield Scott Hancock's II Corps, supported by a VI Corps division to its north, had initiated the fighting on May 6 by attacking west along the Orange Plank Road at 5:00 A.M.; only the timely arrival of Longstreet's First Corps staved off disaster for the Confederates. Longstreet then mounted a full counterattack at 11:00 A.M. against the left of the II Corps, now positioned south of the Plank Road, and in Hancock's words "rolled it up like a wet blanket." The Rebels nearly succeeded in reaching the Brock Road, a key north–south avenue running behind Union lines, before being stopped. To the south of the II Corps, Maj. Gen. Ambrose Burnside had dispatched two divisions of his IX Corps in a listless attack bereft of results between 1:00 P.M. and 3:00 P.M. Brig. Gen. John B. Gordon's brigade of Georgians attacked the exposed right flank of the VI Corps in the early evening of May 6 and sent the brigades of Brig. Gens. Alexander Shaler and Truman Seymour reeling in disarray. Sedgwick, commanding the VI Corps, soon sent reinforcements from the left of his line, which eventually blunted the force of the Rebel attack. Brig. Gen. Thomas G. Stevenson's 1st Division of the IX Corps had supported the attack of Hancock's corps along the Plank Road that morning. Scott, *Into the Wilderness*, 109–28, 147–63, 171–78.

14. The fighting on May 5–6 produced over 17,000 casualties for the Northerners and over 11,000 for the Confederates. During the two days, 209 Federal officers were killed or mortally wounded, including Brig. Gen. James Wadsworth, commanding a division of the V Corps, and Brigadier General Hays, commanding a II Corps brigade. Rhea, *Battle of the Wilderness*, 435–36, 440.

15. An engineer officer serving on Grant's staff, Cyrus Comstock, discovered that the high-ranking party and their escorts, while moving south along the Brock Road, had gone off track in the darkness and were headed dangerously close to Confederate lines. The group decided to return to the Brock Road, but Grant was loath to backtrack, which, another officer present observed, was proof of "his marked aversion to turning back, which amounted almost to a superstition." Trudeau, *Bloody Roads South*, 127–28. "Our Regiment went ahead of the column following Gens. Grant, Meade and Patrick," WBR noted, "who rode very fast and we had a hard time keeping up, getting off the road in the woods several times." WBR Diary, May 7, 1864, transcript.

16. The fighting on May 7, as the Army of the Potomac prepared to move south to Spotsylvania Court House, essentially amounted to heavy skirmishing and did not come close to approaching the ferocity of the two previous days.

17. After sparring with Meade about the cavalry's inability to clear the road to Spotsylvania on May 8, Maj. Gen. Phil Sheridan, commander of the Cavalry Corps, had left the main body of the army on May 9 with his three divisions, intending to "whip Jeb Stuart." This movement, which became known as Sheridan's Richmond Raid, would last over two weeks, take the Union horsemen to the outskirts of the Rebel capital, and, though Sheridan failed to gain decisive victories over his Southern foes, succeeded in killing the daring General Stuart, commander of the Army of Northern Virginia's cavalry.

18. "More like 20,000, I guess." WBR Diary, May 9, 1864, transcript.

19. As it related to Butler's Army of the James, this was an optimistic assessment. Butler had landed fifteen miles south of Richmond, at Bermuda Hundred, on May 5 and commenced what ultimately proved to be a failed offensive against Confederate forces under Gen. P. G. T. Beauregard. Sherman had embarked on the Atlanta Campaign during the first week of May; by May 10, when WBR wrote this, he had advanced from southern Tennessee into northern Georgia and was attempting to outflank forces under Confederate general Joseph E. Johnston (not Johnson) near Resaca. Late in the afternoon of the tenth, Col. Emory Upton of the 121st New York, commander of a VI Corps brigade, personally led an assault of twelve regiments from his corps against a fortified Rebel position near Spotsylvania. Upton's men succeeded in punching through the enemy line, but promised reinforcements from the II Corps never arrived, and they were forced to retreat, with a loss of approximately 1,000 men. Confederate losses are harder to pinpoint, though the Northerners recorded the capture of over 1,000 prisoners.

20. Impressed by the initial success that had attended Upton's audacious charge on May 10, Grant decided to duplicate the effort on a larger scale. On the evening of May 11–12, the entire II Corps (over 19,000 men), supported by parts of the VI Corps, assembled quietly opposite a bulge in the Confederate entrenchments known as the Mule Shoe salient. As dawn broke on the twelfth, the Federal assault succeeded in overrunning the Rebel defenders, in the process capturing 4,000 prisoners, including Brig. Gen. George Steuart and Maj. Gen. Edward Johnson. Skillful resistance by the surprised Rebels limited the Union breakthrough to the area within the salient, while weak supporting attacks by Burnside's IX and Warren's V Corps allowed Lee to continue to dispatch reinforcements to shore up his breached lines. After over twenty-two hours of what may have been the most intense, sustained close-quarter combat of the Civil War, the armies disengaged. More than 6,800 Federals were lost, while Lee's army counted approximately 8,000 casualties. A detailed recounting of the attack and the events that preceded it is in Rhea, *Battles for Spotsylvania Court House*, 214–312.

21. While reconnoitering along the VI Corps front with corps commander Maj. Gen. Horatio Wright on May 14, Meade was surprised and almost captured by a sudden rush of Confederate cavalry. The Rebel major mentioned by WBR nearly overtook the Union commander, and in fact was able to grab the general's bridle, before he was overcome and captured. Meade was fortunate to have been accompanied by a topographical-engineer officer who knew of a nearby ford on the Ni River, which allowed him to escape. Huntington, *Searching for George Gordon Meade*, 280; James C. Biddle to Wife, May 16, 1864, Biddle Papers, HSP.

22. J. Harrison Lambdin (1840–70) of Philadelphia began his war service as a second lieutenant in the 121st Pennsylvania Infantry. Transferred to staff duty, he served as aide-de-camp at headquarters of the I Corps at Gettysburg and later held staff roles at the divisional level in the V Corps. He received the brevet ranks of major and lieutenant colonel for gallantry near the close of the war. Heitman, *Historical Register and Dictionary of the United States Army*, 1:612.

23. Believing Lee had weakened his northernmost positions at Spotsylvania, Grant had shifted the VI Corps from the left (southern) end of his line on the evening of May 17 to the far right of his line. In the early dawn of the eighteenth, Thomas Neill's division of the VI

Corps and most of Hancock's II Corps attacked south against works manned by Confederate general Ewell's Second Corps. But before reaching the Southern positions, the assault was broken up by accurate, concentrated artillery fire from twenty-nine Confederate guns. For an account of the failed attack, see Rhea, *To the North Anna River,* 126–53.

24. Grant had begun to disengage from positions near Spotsylvania Court House. In an effort to discern the next Federal movement, Lee sent Ewell's corps on a reconnaissance around the Union right flank near Harris Farm on May 19. The Rebels approached the Fredericksburg Road, which was the primary supply line for the Northern army, but were soon engaged, primarily by newly arrived regiments of heavy artillery (now serving as infantry) sent from the defenses of Washington as reinforcements. Ewell, having verified that the Federals were preparing to move, withdrew, suffering a loss of 900 men. Union losses were just over 1,500.

25. While home on leave in March, WBR had received a letter from Lt. Miles Carter informing him, erroneously, that he had been appointed to the staff of Brig. Gen. Henry J. Hunt, who commanded the artillery of the Army of the Potomac.

26. "Dabner's Ford" was properly known as Dabney's Ferry. Cavalry under General Custer had forced a crossing at this site early on the morning of May 27, after which a pontoon bridge was strung across to facilitate crossing the infantry.

27. Downer's Bridge was located on the Mattaponi River about midway between the Richmond, Fredericksburg, & Potomac Railroad stops of Guinea Station and Milford Station. "The inhabitants were old Mrs. Tyler and her daughter-in-law," wrote Lieutenant Colonel Lyman, "both strong rebels, and the younger cried, at first, from fear & anger, but recovered and talked quite reasonably. The older was a simple and narrow person; she had lost a son at 'Sharpsburg' (Antietam)." *OR Atlas,* plate 74, map 1; Lowe, *Meade's Army,* 169–70.

28. Carmel Church (properly known as Mt. Carmel Church) was located in an angle of the crossroads formed by the intersection of the Telegraph Road (which ran north–south) and an east–west road that ran to Milford Station on the Richmond, Fredericksburg, & Potomac Railroad. The V and VI Corps, moving in one column, and the II and IX Corps, moving in another, were to converge at the church on May 23. Jericho Bridge, as WBR relates shortly, did not exist. Union engineers, however, constructed a pontoon bridge at Jericho Mills on the North Anna; Warren's V Corps utilized that crossing on May 23. Hanover Junction was seated at the juncture of the Virginia Central Railroad, a key supply artery that carried goods from the Shenandoah Valley, and the Richmond, Fredericksburg, & Potomac Railroad, another important supply line. Rhea, *To the North Anna,* 280–82.

29. "I . . . got some of the natural leaf tobacco, took it to camp, stemmed it, dried it, and crumpled it up. It is the best natural, pure tobacco I ever smoked, though very strong." WBR Diary, May 25, 1864, transcript.

30. Chesterfield Station, on the Richmond, Fredericksburg, & Potomac Railroad, was located approximately two miles northeast of Jericho Mills. Mangohick Church, "built of old bricks brought from England, and laid 'header and stretcher' fashion," lay several miles northeast of the Pamunkey River. *OR Atlas,* plate 74, map 1; Lowe, *Meade's Army,* 178.

31. This was the Battle of Haw's Shop, which resulted when Lee dispatched his cavalry under Hampton to determine whether the Federals had a presence south of the Pamunkey River. The Southern cavalrymen collided with Sheridan's troopers near Haw's Shop, approximately fourteen miles north-northeast of Richmond, on May 28 and fought a seven-hour battle to a draw. Brig. Gen. Henry E. Davies's 1st Brigade of Gregg's 2nd Division lost 23 officers and 151 enlisted men during the fight. Trudeau, *Bloody Roads South,* 248–50; *OR* 36(1):858.

32. Only a portion of the regiment was idle. James Walsh, now a major, and 100 men of the 3rd Pennsylvania were sent by General Patrick back to Mangohick Church on May 29 to drive up stragglers. White House was located on the Pamunkey River, a tributary of the York River. Sparks, *Inside Lincoln's Army,* 378.

33. While none of the four regiments that composed Colonel McIntosh's 1st Brigade of the 3rd Division of the Cavalry Corps had been in service for as long as the 3rd Pennsylvania, only one, the 1st Connecticut Cavalry, could be characterized as inexperienced. The Connecticut men were originally organized as a battalion before they expanded into a fully staffed regiment. They joined the Cavalry Corps soon after completing the formation of their enlarged organization in March 1864.

34. Writing to his father on the same day that WBR penned his observation, the commander of another squadron of horsemen attached to headquarters, Charles Francis Adams of the 1st Massachusetts Cavalry, mirrored his comment respecting the esprit de corps of the Army of the Potomac: "Hammered and pounded as this Army has been; worked, marched, fought and reduced as it is, it is in better spirits and better fighting trim today than it was in the first day's fight in the Wilderness. I believe, yet the fact, that this Army is now just on its second wind, and is more formidable than it ever was before." Ford, *Cycle of Adams Letters* 2:131.

35. Hyde, *Following the Greek Cross*, 211; Grant, *Memoirs* 2:276.

36. WBR is referring to the area around Haw's Shop, where the cavalry fighting on May 28 (mentioned above in note 27) took place. Salem Church was part of the Haw's Shop community.

37. The XVIII Corps, under the command of Maj. Gen. William F. "Baldy" Smith, had been detached from the Army of the James, then operating below Richmond, and reinforced the Army of the Potomac on June 1. The fighting on this day involved principally the VI and XVIII Corps and resulted in Federal losses of over 2,500 men. Trudeau, *Bloody Roads South*, 267.

38. On June 2 the Federals repositioned their corps in preparation for an attack, but the troops' fatigue compelled a postponement until the third. Lee spent the day repositioning his men to receive the Northerners and in strengthening his fieldworks. The Confederate chief also ordered minor assaults against both flanks of the Army of the Potomac, but these actions did not result in "hard fighting."

39. Although the initial attacks by the three southernmost Union corps against the Confederate right in the early morning hours of June 3 met with initial success, especially on the II Corps front, any gains they experienced were soon erased, and the Federals were forcefully repulsed. Northern losses amounted to over 7,000 men, while the Rebels lost fewer than 1,500. "We charged the enemy in the earthworks, and our men fell in heaps," reported a regimental commander in the II Corps. The historians of the 3rd Pennsylvania wrote that June 3 near Cold Harbor "was probably one of the worst days of our whole experience. The piles of dead, the immense numbers of wounded, the ghastly spectacle of blood and suffering, can never be effaced from our minds." OR 36(1):390; Regimental History Committee, *Third Pennsylvania*, 433.

40. Due to an inherent antipathy toward the press, Meade had never been a favorite with the reporters who covered the Army of the Potomac. But by early June 1864, members of his inner circle had grown increasingly sensitive to reporting favorable to Grant that neglected to mention Meade. "It sickens me the way Gen. Meade has been ignored," Major Biddle of the general's staff had written in a mid-May letter to his wife. "I do not want you to be deceived by the newspapers, they are made up of untruths, the reporters who make up public opinion are the scum of the earth." Meade also took notice. "The papers are giving Grant all the credit of what they call successes," he wrote to his wife on June 4. "I hope they will remember this if anything goes wrong." Later in the month, he took issue with official dispatches issued by Secretary of War Edwin M. Stanton, bemoaning the fact that his name was left out in favor of Grant's. "I cannot imagine," he complained, "why I am thus ignored." Meade would later compound the problem when he ordered Edward Crapsey, correspondent for the *Philadelphia Inquirer*, banished from the army and publicly humiliated for writing an account that accused him of wanting to turn back after the fighting in the Wilderness. James C. Biddle to wife, May 16, 1864, Biddle Papers, HSP; Meade, *Life and Letters* 2:200; Cleaves, *Meade of Gettysburg*, 253–55.

41. The Sanitary Fair held in Philadelphia, also known as the Great Central Fair, was one of several such events staged in Northern cities by the US Sanitary Commission, a civilian-led benevolent organization that helped care for wounded and sick soldiers and their families. Proceeds from these fairs went to support the work of the commission. The Philadelphia event, which took place June 7–28, raised over $1 million, a spectacular sum for that time. WBR's mother composed and published a fifty-four-page poem entitled *The Days of Sixty-Three!* for the benefit of the Sanitary Fair. Gallman, *Mastering Wartime*, 146.

42. Lt. Col. John M. Wetherill (1829–95) of the 82nd Pennsylvania Infantry, which formed a part of General Russell's division of the VI Corps, was the brother of WBR's close friend Captain Wetherill. During the assaults at Cold Harbor, the colonel of the 82nd was wounded, and command devolved on Wetherill. He led the regiment thereafter until he mustered out at the expiration of its term of service in September 1864. Bates, *History of Pennsylvania Volunteers*, 2:1207–9.

43. In a movement known as Sheridan's Second Raid, the general and his horsemen, on Grant's orders, ventured north from Cold Harbor on June 7 to destroy the Virginia Central Railroad between Charlottesville and Richmond. As they followed the railway west, they would attempt to link up with forces under Maj. Gen. David Hunter, who were then moving east from the Shenandoah Valley; once united, the combined force was to join the Army of the Potomac. In addition to the benefit gained by disrupting the rail line, the movement was intended to occupy the attention of Rebel horsemen who might otherwise learn of Grant's planned repositioning from Cold Harbor to the James River. Fighting began on June 11 near Trevilian Station, sixty miles northwest of Richmond, when Confederate cavalry under General Hampton intercepted the Federal column. After two days of combat, Sheridan was defeated, and both sides broke off the engagement and moved back to their lines. Of the approximately 16,000 troopers engaged between both sides, almost 2,000 became casualties. Longacre, *Lincoln's Cavalrymen*, 275–81. An excellent book-length study of the raid is Eric J. Wittenberg, *Glory Enough for All: Sheridan's Second Raid and the Battle of Trevilian Station* (Washington, DC: Brassey's, 2001).

44. Even though WBR acknowledges Union losses of 5,000–6,000 men (though closer to 7,000 were lost), he seems unaware of the magnitude of the defeat at Cold Harbor. The action on the evening of June 5 was an attack against elements of Brig. Gen. Francis Barlow's 1st Division of the II Corps, which lasted less than thirty minutes. Brig. Gen. John Gibbon commanded the 2nd Division of the II (not VI) Corps. *OR* 36(1):452.

45. New Castle was located along the south bank of the Pamunkey River, four miles below Hanover Town. Much of the Federal cavalry would cross the river here on June 8 during Sheridan's Second Raid.

46. Parsley's Mill was located along Matadequin Creek, five miles west of the Pamunkey River and approximately three miles due south of New Castle. *OR Atlas*, plate 17, map 1.

47. *OR* 36(3):598.

48. Hess, *Trenches at Petersburg*, 18. The Federals moving to assault the city numbered approximately 14,000 men.

49. De Trobriand, *Four Years with the Army of the Potomac*, 591.

50. "The Third Pennsylvania Cavalry has been on several occasions called upon to act upon the flanks of the army, and in the advance, besides detachments of it being frequently sent out as scouting parties," wrote Provost Marshal General Patrick in one of his reports of the Overland Campaign, "on all of which occasions it has behaved with great coolness and judgment." *OR* 40(1):272.

51. Heading east from Richmond on the Richmond & York River Railroad, Dispatch Station was the first station stop after crossing the Chickahominy River. Moody's Cross Roads lay south of the rail bed a mile northeast of Dispatch Station. *OR Atlas*, plate 17, map 1.

52. WBR misspells the name of the church; it was Emmaus (not Emman's) Church, completed in 1852, which still stands (as of this writing) in New Kent County, Virginia. He also seems to have been confused regarding when he passed near the residence of former president John Tyler. WBR records that he observed Tyler's residence, known as Sherwood Forest, before crossing the Chickahominy over Long Bridge, when actually it was twelve miles below Emmaus Church and well south of the Chickahominy. IX Corps troops had visited the plantation, with the result, wrote a staff officer, that "the place was a wreck, furniture smashed and bureaus turned upside down, bed's ripped open, Library upside down, and papers mutilated." Theodore Lyman judged, "it was but a moderately good house," apparently overlooking the destruction, "with rather a good, ornamented chimney." *OR Atlas*, plate 17, map 1; Daniel Reed Larned to Sister, June 15, 1864, quoted in Rhea, *On to Petersburg*, 229; Lowe, *Meade's Army*, 202.

53. This pontoon bridge, which spanned the James River between Weyanoke Point on the north bank and Fort Powhatan on the south bank, was actually three times as long (2,100 feet) as WBR estimated, though it is possible he may have meant to record the distance in yards instead of feet when referring to its length.

54. Though it may appear at first blush that WBR is repeating a rumor regarding depredations attributable to the IX Corps during its march from the James River to Petersburg—I have found almost no other accounts corroborating his statement—his accusation is backed up by none other than Provost Marshal General Patrick: "We crossed the [James] River," the general wrote in his diary on June 16, "following Meade & *kept* following, over a terrible dusty road, full of trains & troops with houses burning, on either side, attesting to the march of the 9th Corps." With regard to WBR's assertion that the IX was the "worst corps in the army," my belief is that his opinion was formed partly as a result of his unfamiliarity with the command. The IX Corps was certainly something of an outlier in the Army of the Potomac at this time, in some measure because it had experienced a nomadic existence since its inception, campaigning along the Atlantic coast in North and South Carolina, in Virginia and Maryland as part of the Army of the Potomac (it had fought at Second Manassas, Antietam, and Fredericksburg), and subsequently in Kentucky, Mississippi, and Tennessee. It had only recently been sent back to fight with the Army of the Potomac after a fourteen month absence; because Burnside outranked Meade by seniority, he initially reported directly to Grant, which only reinforced the impression of the IX's outsider status. Assigned as it was to five different armies or departments throughout its service, only those soldiers who had served in the Army of the Potomac during August 1862–February 1863, when it was attached to that army, would have been familiar with the fighting qualities of its men. During the movements prior to the North Anna, Patrick had also expressed his disgust with Burnside's troops: "There is any quantity of straggling on these marches, from 9th Corps—which is in very bad discipline & its Staff Departments worthless." Lyman had commented on May 24 that "the inferiority of the 9th Corps begins now to show a good deal, in the straggling and the general comparative want of tone and discipline." The animus was not lost on Burnside's soldiers: "the 9th Corps has been considered not an integral part of the old Army of the Potomac," wrote one of its division commanders a week after the disaster that befell the corps at the Battle of the Crater on July 30, "& there are not wanting those in the other corps that are glad to get a kick at the brave old dog now he is down." Later that summer a IX Corps captain complained, "We do about as much fighting as any of the Corps, and *do it well*, but get no credit." A IX Corps staff officer also weighed in: "We have been bullyragged round so—& the Corps is spoken of as a superfluity—and no end to the insults & taunts we have received." Sparks, *Inside Lincoln's Army*, 376, 384; Lowe, *Meade's Army*, 173; Scott, *Forgotten Valor*, 562; Coco, *Through Blood and Fire*, 147, 159–60; Sears, *Lincoln's Lieutenants*, 685.

55. The reasons behind the failure of elements of the Army of the Potomac and the Army of the James to capture Petersburg at this time have been the subject of much debate and

discussion. Baldy Smith's XVIII Corps had arrived in front of Petersburg from Cold Harbor early on the morning of June 15 and conducted dilatory attacks, with limited success, against the outer defenses of Petersburg, called the Dimmock Line. In the early evening a renewed assault overran the thinly manned Confederate works east of the city, forcing the Rebels to retreat to a secondary position—called the Hagood Line—along Harrison's Creek. Mention has been made of the over three-to-one advantage the attackers enjoyed on June 15, and Federal reticence to press their assaults before the Southerners could be reinforced—coupled with agile resistance by General Beauregard and the city's outnumbered defenders—cost them control of the town and its railroad connections until the following spring. The most recent and complete evaluation of the events surrounding the Federal effort to capture the city is in Greene, *Campaign of Giants,* 65–219. See also Trudeau, *Last Citadel,* 29–55; Longacre, *Army of Amateurs,* 143–62; and Hess, *Trenches at Petersburg,* 14–37.

56. Pvt. John Burns of Company L had joined the 3rd on October 23, 1863. Regimental History Committee, *Third Pennsylvania,* 606.

57. "The General has again taken all my cavalry," complained Patrick in his diary on June 17, "and placed it at Warren's disposal, who, for some reason, failed to attack." Sparks, *Inside Lincoln's Army,* 385.

58. As noted earlier, Baldy Smith's XVIII Corps had been attacking the Petersburg defenses with limited success since June 15. Attacks on the sixteenth and seventeenth by the newly arrived II and IX Corps also met with minor success but failed to pierce the main defensive line. On June 18, his patience nearly exhausted at this inability to overrun the outnumbered Confederate defenders, Meade ordered a general assault by the II, IX, V, and part of the XVIII Corps. An early morning advance revealed that the Rebels had retreated to an inner line of defenses (called the Harris Line), and attacks against it later in the day, in addition to being disjointed and lacking in vigor, came up against Lee's veterans, who had just arrived from Cold Harbor. On Warren's V Corps line, uneven terrain and the distance the men had to travel to initiate their attack diluted the power of their assault. Powell, *Fifth Army Corps,* 700–702. A photograph of Warren and his staff at the Avery Farm, taken several days after the failed attacks, is in William Frassanito, *Grant and Lee: The Virginia Campaigns, 1864–1865* (New York: Charles Scribner's Sons, 1983), 250.

59. Lee was confused about Grant's intentions after the Federals left Cold Harbor, believing that his opponent might advance up the north side of the James to operate against Richmond instead of crossing the river and moving against Petersburg. General Beauregard, who commanded the troops manning the Petersburg defenses, pleaded for reinforcements at this time, and as late as the second day of Federal attacks, Lee still hesitated to commit additional men to support him. "I do not know the position of Grant's troops," he wrote on June 16, then told Beauregard the next day, "Until I get more definite information of Grant's movements, I do not think it prudent to draw more troops to this side of the river." Lee finally grasped Grant's objective and began dispatching his infantry to the beleaguered city on the afternoon of the seventeenth. Alexander, *Military Memoirs,* 551.

60. This was the beginning of Grant's Second Offensive, the first attempt to cut the Southern supply lines leading into Petersburg west of the Jerusalem Plank Road. Moving against the Weldon Railroad on June 22, a gap developed between the II and VI Corps. Confederate brigadier general William Mahone led his division into the void and crushed the exposed flank of the II Corps. Fighting continued on June 23 as the VI Corps was driven away. In the end, almost 3,000 Federals became casualties, including 1,700 prisoners taken from the II Corps. A number of new regiments that had joined the II Corps—notably its heavy artillery units recently cleaved from the capital defenses—behaved badly, and some of the most experienced regiments of the corps, like the 15th and 19th Massachusetts, reduced by the recent fighting, were captured nearly whole. The reverse of June 22 prompted II Corps commander Hancock,

who had been on leave during the battle, to issue an order promising that "hereafter those skulkers who abandon the field on the plea of carrying off the wounded . . . and those who run away while their comrades are fighting, will be shot down by the Provost Guard." Hess, *Trenches at Petersburg,* 38–39; Stevens, *Berdan's United States Sharpshooters,* 471.

61. The heat near Petersburg during late June was oppressive, especially so for men clothed in flannel and woolen uniforms. The day before WBR wrote this letter, a New York surgeon jotted in his diary: "I do not know how this army is to live and do duty these intensely hot days. I have never suffered so from heat as to-day. We are encamped on ground which has been burned over, and completely covered with underbrush. . . . A coal pit is a more comfortable place." Explained a VI Corps chaplain: "The weather is intensely, awfully, roastingly hot. You see nothing but dust—you smell dust, you eat dust, you drink dust. Your clothes, blanket, tent, food, drink are all permeated with dust." An artillery officer in the V Corps reported a temperature reading of 101 degrees in the shade on June 26. Greiner, Coryell, and Smither, *Surgeon's Civil War,* 210; Stewart, *Camp, March, and Battlefield,* 398–99; Nevins, *Diary of Battle,* 429. For more on the soldiers' battle with the heat and dust near Petersburg, see Lord, *History of the Ninth Regiment New Hampshire Volunteers,* 454–55; Kent, *Three Years with Company K,* 291–92; and J. Perry, *Letters from a Surgeon,* 208, 213.

62. WBR phonetically spelled the name of his campsite; it was actually near Cocke's Mills (also referred to Cocke's Burnt Mills), located at the headwaters of Powell's Creek, approximately fourteen miles west of central Petersburg in King George County. *OR Atlas,* plate 100, map 2.

63. The action described by WBR was the Battle of St. Mary's Church, or Nance's Shop, which took place on June 24. As Sheridan returned from his raid against the Virginia Central Railroad, he incorporated 900 wagons from the abandoned Union supply base at White House Landing into his supply train and moved toward the James River to reunite with the Army of the Potomac. Confederate cavalry under Hampton attacked the column, which was guarded principally by Gregg's 2nd Division. Despite being outnumbered by a nearly two-to-one margin, Gregg's men were able to repulse repeated Southern assaults. Lt. Col. George H. Covode (1835–64) of the 4th Pennsylvania Cavalry was mortally wounded during the fighting; Capt. Walstein Phillips (1837–64) of the 1st Maine Cavalry, Gregg's commissary of musters and "a true gentleman and excellent soldier," was struck by a shell and killed. Longacre, *Lincoln's Cavalrymen,* 282–85; *OR* 36(1):856; Tobie, *First Maine Cavalry,* 294.

64. Brig. Gen. James H. Wilson (1837–1925), an 1860 graduate of West Point, now commanded the 3rd Division of the Army of the Potomac's Cavalry Corps. In an effort to interdict Confederate supply lines, Wilson's division and the cavalry division of Brig. Gen. Augustus Kautz from the Army of the James had left Union lines on June 22 to destroy sections of the Southside, Richmond & Danville, and Weldon Railroads to the west and southwest of Petersburg. Though they wrecked approximately sixty miles of track during the course of their movement, known as the Wilson-Kautz Raid, the cavalrymen were surrounded and forced to abandon their artillery and supply wagons as they fought their way back east to the safety of Federal positions near Petersburg. Wilson lost approximately 1,000 men in the effort, and the Southerners quickly repaired the torn-up track. Longacre, *Lincoln's Cavalrymen,* 287–93.

65. "During the morning, two Rebs, dismounted, of 10th Va. Cavy., disrespecting his papers, took Murphy of 'C' Co., safeguard at a house of Mr. Livesey." WBR Diary, July 3, 1864, transcript. Pvt. John Murphy, an original member of Philadelphia-raised Company C, would be returned to the regiment after Meade requested his release from Lee. He mustered out of the 3rd in February 1865. Regimental History Committee, *Third Pennsylvania,* 443, 588.

66. A sergeant in the 6th Pennsylvania Cavalry reported that cumulative losses in the regiment since crossing the Rapidan in early May were ten officers and 166 enlisted men. Eric Wittenberg, in his modern history of the regiment, puts losses for the Lancers during

the Wilson-Kautz Raid at between 67 and 79. Captain Leiper had been wounded on May 30, prior to the raid on the Virginia Central Railroad, while commanding the regiment. Wittenberg, *We Have It Damn Hard Out Here*, 126; Wittenberg, *Rush's Lancers*, 182, 187–88.

67. "I have also sent out an order," Provost Marshal General Patrick complained in his diary two days later, "restoring Safe Guards to families within the lines—they having been called in by an Order of Genl. Meade, three days ago, though now he disowns the *intention* to give any such order." Sparks, *Inside Lincoln's Army*, 396.

68. Contrary to WBR's statement, the USS *Kearsarge* had not been sunk. On June 19, off the coast of France, the *Kearsarge* instead had sunk the CSS *Alabama*. In response to Lt. Gen. Jubal Early's threatening movements in the Shenandoah Valley, Pennsylvania governor Curtin had issued a call on July 6 for 12,000 men to serve for one hundred days. Just over 7,500 Pennsylvanians answered his request. "If some were not tempted by a shoulder strap and brass buttons in profusion to recruit a company and regiment," scoffed a Pennsylvanian in the V Corps, "not a thousand of the twelve asked for would respond." Egle, *Life and Times of Andrew Gregg Curtin*, 254; Henry T. Peck to Mother, July 10, 1864, Henry T. Peck Letters, National Guard of Pennsylvania Library, Philadelphia.

69. Fire-eating slaveowner Edmund Ruffin (1794–1865) was a successful farmer and agriculturalist in antebellum Virginia who had campaigned widely in support of secession and the preservation of slavery in the years leading up to the war. He had participated in the April 1861 bombardment of Fort Sumter, where it was widely believed he had fired the first shot directed at the Federal garrison in Charleston Harbor, earning him acclaim throughout the South. Ruffin had inherited this property, called Beechwood, from his grandfather in the 1840s; during the war, it was owned by his son, Edmund Jr. The estate had been thoroughly sacked and vandalized by Union troops during the Peninsula Campaign in 1862. Craven, *Edmund Ruffin*, 238–41; Marten, *Civil War America*, 3–10.

70. The continuing excavation of a tunnel—to be filled with 8,000 pounds of explosives and detonated—reaching beneath Confederate works at Elliott's Salient by soldiers of the IX Corps was a poorly kept secret. For examples of comments by soldiers who, like WBR, made note of its construction in the weeks leading up to its completion, see Robertson, *Civil War Letters of General Robert McAllister*, 457; Campbell, *Grand Terrible Dramma*, 238; Nevins, *Diary of Battle*, 439, Weld, *War Diary*, 333; and Coco, *Through Blood and Fire*, 124.

71. Cpl. Charles Bickley of Company L had joined the 3rd in August 1861 and was absent when his term of enlistment expired in August 1864, as was Pvt. James York of the same company. Pvt. Charles A. Smith of Company C had joined the 3rd less than two months prior to his capture. He was paroled in December 1864 and returned to the regiment. Regimental History Committee, *Third Pennsylvania*, 588, 606, 608.

72. The men from the 72nd New York were eighteen-year-old Pvt. Daniel Geary of Company G and Pvt. Ransom S. Gordon, twenty-three, of Company E. Both had been found guilty of raping Mary Stiles at her home in Prince George County. The pair served as teamsters in their regiment and had been mustered out at the expiration of their term of service just before committing this crime. Chaplain Rammel of the 3rd Pennsylvania ministered to the convicted soldiers, relating afterward that they both acknowledged the justice of their sentence immediately before their execution. Provost Marshal General Patrick was determined to use their punishment as a deterrent to crime. While their lifeless bodies still swung from the ropes, he mounted the scaffold and addressed the assembled troops, imparting, he wrote, "such words of warning, of reproof & of correction as seemed proper in the presence of such a mass of life as stood before & around me.... My words will not soon be forgotten." Sparks, *Inside Lincoln's Army*, 388–89, 397–99; de Trobriand, *Four Years with the Army of the Potomac*, 604–5.

73. Following their repulse at the Battle of Fort Stevens outside of Washington, DC, on July 11–12, Early's Confederates had crossed the Potomac back into Virginia on the evening of the thirteenth.

74. Second Lt. Vidal L. Thom from the 1st New Hampshire Cavalry's Company A was killed on July 18 by guerillas in the vicinity of Cocke's Mills. *Official Army Register of the Volunteer Forces of the United States Army for the Years 1861, 1862, 1863, 1864, 1865. Part 1, New England States* (Washington: n.p., 1865), 64; Tenney, *War Diary,* 124.

75. "Rain! Actually rain!! The first for 47 days," wrote staff officer Lieutenant Colonel Lyman on July 19. "It rained nearly all day and soaked the dust to the hard pan." Lowe, *Meade's Army,* 235.

76. *Bleak House,* by Charles Dickens, was published in 1852–53.

77. This was Sgt. Thomas Gregg of Company A (not I). Despite WBR's misgivings about his fitness to hold a commission, Gregg was undoubtedly brave. During the hand-to-hand fighting on July 3 at Gettysburg, a trooper of the 3rd was taken prisoner by a Confederate cavalryman. Gregg came upon the pair and, according to another member of the 3rd who witnessed the scene, "cut the Confederate to the ground." At that moment another Rebel rode up and, with a swing of his saber, "scalped Gregg as clear as a Sioux Indian could have done it." Gregg eventually rose to be captain of Company E in the 3rd. When he had occasion to remove his hat in the months following his wounding, he could, recalled the same veteran several decades after the war, "show as hairless a pate as many of us can now do with thirty years of cultivation." Gilmore, "With General Gregg at Gettysburg," 111; Regimental History Committee, *Third Pennsylvania,* 568–71.

78. The surfeit of seemingly trivial expenses incurred by cavalry officers led several sergeants in the 1st Massachusetts Cavalry to decline commissions since their promotions would have resulted in "excessive responsibility and totally inadequate pay—in some cases, indebtedness instead of pay." Crowninshield, *First Regiment of Massachusetts Cavalry,* 233.

79. John J. Brandon entered the service as sergeant of Philadelphia-raised Company C in August 1861. He was promoted to first sergeant on June 1, 1863, and mustered out with the original complement of the 3rd in August 1864. Regimental History Committee, *Third Pennsylvania,* 586.

6. OPERATIONS NEAR PETERSBURG

1. Grant, *Memoirs,* 2:307–10; Hess, *Trenches at Petersburg,* 78–85.

2. Coco, *Through Blood and Fire,* 118. The same officer, however, further noted that Grant had overcome significant difficulties earlier in the war and that, despite the seeming lack of progress, he still had confidence in the general in chief.

3. Colonel McIntosh had commanded brigades within the Cavalry Corps since March 1863. His overdue promotion to brigadier general of volunteers was effective to date from July 21, 1864.

4. African American troops from Brig. Gen. Edward Ferrero's 4th Division of the IX Corps were initially slated to lead the assault that would follow the explosion of the mine. The day before the attack, however, General Meade, concerned about public opinion should the black soldiers fail, directed that the other three divisions of the IX Corps, composed of white soldiers, would initiate the attack and that Ferrero's men would act as supports. Although the detonation created the opening in the Southern works as intended, many of the onrushing Federals, instead of moving around the crater the blast had created and widening the breach, rushed headlong into the crater itself and were slaughtered by the Confeder-

ates, who recovered quickly from the surprise of the explosion. Many, like WBR, mistakenly blamed the black soldiers of the 4th Division for the disaster, but in point of fact the attack was poorly led, uncoordinated, and unsupported. Federal losses totaled nearly 3,800 men, while the Confederates lost approximately 1,500.

5. As jarring as this passage is to read, WBR's opinions regarding the combat effectiveness of the African American troops then serving in Virginia were shared by many of his fellow soldiers. "The prejudices entertained by the veterans of the Army of the Potomac at this time," wrote a Massachusetts infantryman with some understatement, "were very decidedly against the negro race as soldiers." It should be noted, however, that in a number of cases the preconceptions white soldiers held regarding the usefulness of African American troops were changed after they had fought with them or witnessed them in battle. "This army is fast coming to a knowledge that its colored troops are an honor to it," wrote a Regular Army infantryman in late June 1864. Hennessy, *Fighting with the Eighteenth Massachusetts,* 231; Cassedy, *Dear Friends at Home,* 509. For more comments by Army of the Potomac soldiers regarding African American troops, see Bennett, *Musket and Sword,* 318–20; Scott, *Fallen Leaves,* 198–99; Coco, *Through Blood and Fire,* 139, 142; and Herdegen and Murphy, *Four Years with the Iron Brigade,* 299.

6. The Cavalry Corps and the II Corps had been participating in the aforementioned Third Offensive operation north of the James River at Deep Bottom.

7. Eugene M. Smyser (1842–1916), a native of Gettysburg, Pennsylvania, had joined the 48th Pennsylvania Infantry of the IX Corps as an assistant surgeon in April 1864, serving until his discharge in July 1865. Bosbyshell, *Campaigns of the 48th Regiment,* 194.

8. Those veterans slated to be mustered out were hurriedly refitted and sent from their encampment near Washington, DC, to western Maryland on July 30 to help counter the Southern incursion into Pennsylvania. Reaching Harpers Ferry, the men of the 3rd were sent on to Charlestown, Virginia, where they briefly skirmished with retreating Confederates. "The men were now getting careless," remembered one of them, "their time having expired they preferred marching the other way." According to this same trooper, some of the men got drunk and fired at the unnamed general who commanded them there. "He made a speech to the men, but was so much disgusted with them that he ordered the Regiment back to Harpers Ferry, where all public property was taken in, and cars taken to Philadelphia." Speese, *Story of Companies H, A, and C,* 56–57.

9. The court of inquiry, composed entirely of army officers, formed to investigate the reasons behind the Union failure at the Battle of the Crater faulted IX Corps commander General Burnside; Brig. Gen. James Ledlie, who commanded the division which led the assault of the corps; and the commander of the all-black 4th Division of the corps, General Ferrero. Ledlie and Ferrero, instead of leading or even supervising the attack, were reported to have remained sheltered behind the lines drinking while the action took place. Ledlie had exhibited similar behavior during the May battles along the North Anna and in the initial assaults on Petersburg in mid-June, leading a Massachusetts officer to observe that the general "was a good soul, but a very weak man, and no more fit to command a division than half of the privates under him." Burnside would be shelved, Ledlie would resign before he could be run out of the army, and, startlingly, Ferrero found himself promoted to the brevet rank of major general but also transferred out of the Army of the Potomac. Congress, via the Joint Committee on the Conduct of the War, later initiated their own investigation and in addition to blaming Burnside also censured Meade for abandoning the original plan of attack. Hess, *Trenches at Petersburg,* 105; Anderson, *Fifty-Seventh Regiment of Massachusetts Volunteers,* 140; J. Perry, *Letters from a Surgeon,* 220.

10. Early had led his corps of the Army of Northern Virginia into the Shenandoah Valley in mid-June, driven away Hunter's Army of West Virginia, secured nearly a quarter of a million dollars in ransom from several Maryland cities, and marched east to threaten Washington,

DC, before retreating south across the Potomac on July 13. Later that month he sent two brigades of cavalry on a raid into southern Pennsylvania and burned most of the business district of Chambersburg, Pennsylvania, after its citizens refused to pay a ransom. In response to these developments, Grant in the early days of August appointed Sheridan to command the newly created Middle Military Department. Little Phil's orders were to clear the Valley of Confederate troops and to lay waste to the foodstuffs and forage there that supplied both the local Rebel forces and Lee's troops near Richmond and Petersburg. In addition to Hunter's former troops, Sheridan's command included two divisions of the XIX Corps, newly arrived from the Deep South; Wright's VI Corps, which had been sent north to help defend the capital in early July; and two of the three cavalry divisions attached to the Army of the Potomac. The Army of the Shenandoah, as the combined forces were to be known, totaled some 50,000 men, initially faced by about one-third as many Southerners. Wert, *Custer,* 168–71.

11. Confederates had dug a mine in the vicinity of what would become Fort Stedman, on the XVIII Corps front, and exploded it on August 5. A miscalculation in the distance the underground tunnel would need to extend led to the detonation of the powder charges forty yards short of the Federal entrenchments. Although there was only skirmishing and an exchange of artillery fire following the explosion, a number of memoirists believed that an all-out Confederate assault had taken place. OR 42(2):51; Hess, *Trenches at Petersburg,* 118–19; Boston, *Civil War Diary,* 57.

12. *Doctor Antonio,* a novel by Giovanni Ruffini, was published in 1855.

13. WBR notes the sailor was Lt. John Weidman, executive officer of the USS *Osceola,* and that he was accompanied by a Lieutenant Churchman of the 5th US Cavalry, who I have not been unable to identify fully.

14. August 12 marked the commencement of Grant's Fourth Offensive, which accounted for the combat WBR was then hearing and the activity he observed. He discusses the movement further in a later diary entry.

15. See chapter 1, note 6.

16. Good descriptions of life in the works before Petersburg as experienced by the Federals who occupied them are in Lord, *History of the Ninth Regiment New Hampshire Volunteers,* 457–61; Cowtan, *Services of the Tenth New York Volunteers,* 318–21; Parker, *Story of the Thirty-Second Regiment Massachusetts Infantry,* 224–26; Anderson, *Fifty-Seventh Regiment of Massachusetts Volunteers,* 150–52, 154–55; and Ward, *History of the Second Pennsylvania Veteran Heavy Artillery,* 76–78.

17. "The mortar shells look very fine at night," wrote an officer serving in a Wisconsin regiment, "as they describe an arc with the sparks from their burning fuses. At times it would seem as the mortars were loaded with a dozen shells in each. There would be as many as thirty or forty in the air at once, with their comet-like tails, and apparently, from the sound of Whit you! Whit you!, they were kissing each other as they passed. Our guns fire about six shots to the Johnnies one." A New York artilleryman who watched an exchange of fire between the opposing lines wrote: "It was a grand Fourth of July display, once seen never forgotten. As soon as the mortars began the pickets, (who were but twenty feet apart at this point) stopped firing and began to exchange compliments. As our shells would pass over the Yank would hallo 'There is a pass for Richmond, Johnnie!' As their shells would come, the rebs would yell 'There is a thirty day furlough Yank!'" Aubrey, *Thirty Sixth Wisconsin Infantry,* 163; Kirk, *Heavy Guns and Light,* 320.

18. The August 9 disaster at City Point was precipitated by Confederate agents who detonated an ammunition barge moored nearby, triggering a series of explosions from the stockpiles of ordnance and ammunition stored there. Forty-three people were killed and 126 wounded, many of whom were African American laborers working on the docks. A thorough explanation of the event is in Trudeau, *Last Citadel,* 131–41.

19. A jackanapes is "one who is impudent or self-important."

20. This movement by the II Corps, which WBR mentions in his letter of August 12, was joined in by Gregg's cavalry division and two divisions from the X Corps of the Army of the James. It represented the first of three aspects of Grant's Fourth Offensive and resulted in the Second Battle of Deep Bottom. Grant believed that Lee had weakened his lines to the point of vulnerability by siphoning off troops to the Shenandoah Valley and dispatched Hancock to lead this patchwork force in an attack on Richmond. Fighting took place between August 14 and 18 in the same area as First Deep Bottom in late July. But finding the Confederate defenses there too strong, Hancock withdrew on the night of August 20. Hess, *Trenches at Petersburg*, 124–29.

21. The rains of August 14–15 were heavy enough to collapse sections of the entrenchments and wash away breastworks on the IX Corps front. See Cuffel, *History of Durell's Battery*, 203.

22. John Rufus Edie of Pennsylvania was actually a captain at this time. Morris Schaff of Ohio would write one of the first book-length accounts of the Battle of the Wilderness (published in 1910). Edward Jenner Strang was an officer from New York. Heitman, *Historical Register and Dictionary of the United States Army*, 1:397, 863, 931.

23. Lt. Col. Hugh Janeway (1842–65) of the 1st New Jersey Cavalry had a finger shot away in the early stages of the Second Battle of Deep Bottom. Miers, *Ride to War*, 238.

24. Grant's views were in concert with those expressed by WBR. The general believed that Lee had removed an entire corps from his lines north of the James River to send to the support of Early in the Shenandoah. Lee had, in fact, sent only a division each of infantry and cavalry. The movement by Hancock to the right that WBR notes resulted in the aforementioned Second Battle of Deep Bottom. The movement on the left by Warren's V Corps was also a part of the Fourth Offensive: an attempt to capture the Weldon Railroad, which was the main logistical route supplying Petersburg and Richmond. Moving west from established Union lines early on August 18, Warren cut the railroad at Globe Tavern, then held it stubbornly, with support from the IX Corps, against successive Southern attempts to dislodge him over the next three days. Over 4,000 Federals became casualties, compared with 2,300 Confederates, but Grant had succeeded in slowing the flow of supplies reaching the Rebels in Petersburg. Hess, *Trenches at Petersburg*, 129–35; Powell, *Fifth Army Corps*, 710–27.

25. Theodore Winthrop, a writer and lawyer, was one of the first Northern officers to die in combat when he was killed at the Battle of Big Bethel, Virginia, on June 10, 1861. *Cecil Dreeme*, a novel, was published posthumously in late 1861.

26. Although Averell may have been notified that his promotion to brevet major general was in the offing (he received it for his services at the Battle of Moorfield on August 7, 1864), his elevation to that grade was not effective until March 13, 1865. Even so, it provided an occasion for men of the 3rd to celebrate: "Hearing that 'Little Billy' Averill had got another star the officers thought it incumbent upon them to get on a spree, and they were in a jolly humor accordingly." WBR Diary, Aug. 24, 1864, transcript. WBR's comment about the three stars for the 3rd Pennsylvania are in reference to the two stars represented in Averell's promotion to major general and McIntosh's recent advancement to brigadier general. Powell, *Officers of the Army and Navy*, 136.

27. Henry Boyden Blood of Massachusetts had been appointed a captain in the Quartermaster Department on October 15, 1862. Heitman, *Historical Register and Dictionary of the United States Army*, 1:225.

28. WBR is describing the Battle of Reams Station (August 25), which was the third and final component of Grant's Fourth Offensive. Hancock's II Corps, supported by cavalry, had been destroying the tracks of the Weldon Railroad near Reams Station, seven miles south of Petersburg, when they were attacked by Confederates under the command of Lt. Gen. A. P. Hill. Though the Federals were able to fight off the first two assaults, a third effort broke

through their lines, which soon disintegrated. Hancock was distraught that his formerly formidable corps, worn down by over one hundred days of near-continuous combat and movement while rendered less potent by an influx of inexperienced troops, had been routed. "Come on, we can beat them!" he pleaded with his retreating men as he rode among them. "Don't leave me for God's sake!" Hancock lost over 2,500 men and nine pieces of artillery, including all four guns from Capt. J. Henry Sleeper's 10th Massachusetts Light Artillery Battery, as a result. Sleeper took a bullet in the arm during the action. Billings, *History of the Tenth Massachusetts Battery*, 322, 324; *OR* 42(1):408–9.

29. August 29, 1864, was WBR's twenty-first birthday.

30. Silas W. Pettit (1844–1908) was the first lieutenant of Company F of the 196th Pennsylvania. He had served briefly in two Regular Army regiments earlier in the war. Following the expiration of his term in the 196th, he was commissioned as the captain of Company C of the 213th Pennsylvania Infantry in March 1865. Heitman, *Historical Register and Dictionary of the United States Army*, 1:787; Bates, *History of Pennsylvania Volunteers*, 5:443, 806.

31. "Most probably," WBR wrote of the recruits in his diary on August 28, "they will be organized into a new company, which may give some of us a hoist." While he was generally pleased with the quality of the men the regiment received, the Army of the Potomac's veterans held a range of opinions on the effectiveness of their newest soldiers. The commander of the 1st Massachusetts Cavalry, which was serving with the 3rd Pennsylvania at army headquarters, decried the mediocrity he witnessed in the recruits he received at this time: "We want men, not a lot of sickly Boys and cripples, where is all of the boasted patriotism of Massachusetts, gone too, to have her send agents to collect such scum and trash, that has been sent of late. They are a source of weakness, instead of strength to the cause." Likewise, many of the veterans of the 2nd New Hampshire Infantry, which had served through most of its existence with the Army of the Potomac, decided not to extend their enlistments because of the caliber of the men the regiment had received: "Their refusal to reenlist in the Second was in a great measure influenced by their dislike of the uncongenial mass of mercenaries in which their state had submerged them." B. Perry, *Life and Letters of Henry Lee Higginson*, 230; Haynes, *History of the Second Regiment New Hampshire Volunteer Infantry*, 243.

32. This was the City Point & Army (or US Military) Railroad, which utilized part of the existing railroad connecting Petersburg with City Point, nine miles east on the James River. The prewar tracks ran from the supply wharves at City Point to Pitkin Station, six miles away, where a newly constructed spur branched off to the south and west, roughly paralleling the Union lines, which nearly formed a semicircle below Petersburg; crossed the Norfolk & Petersburg Railroad; linked up with the Weldon Railroad; and eventually ended at Humphreys Station, near Hatcher's Run. Stations along the twenty-one-mile route were named for prominent Union officers, including Meade, Gregg, Warren, Hancock, and Patrick. "It was a novelty in railroad construction," recalled a Pennsylvanian in the IX Corps. "There was no grading of any account; the ties were laid on the surface of the ground without ballast; the tracks ran up and down over hill and dale. Heavy trains of ammunition and supplies passed over the road, and when at the top of a grade or hill, a full head of steam was put on to give the train sufficient momentum to carry it up the next grade. If it did not succeed, the train was backed down across the hollow and a fresh start was taken. Sometimes, with the aid of troops pushing, it was carried over the ascent." The engineers and firemen who operated the trains were civilians who, approvingly noted another soldier, "faced danger with remarkable courage and fidelity." *Map of the City Point and Army Line with Its Branches and Connections*, Record Group 77, US National Archives, Washington, DC, viewed online at www.loc.gov; Cuffel, *History of Durell's Battery*, 208–9; Bennett, *Musket and Sword*, 292.

33. Almayne H. G. Richardson had served in the 19th Pennsylvania Infantry, a three-month regiment, early in the war and was commissioned as a second lieutenant in the 114th

Pennsylvania in August 1862. He had been promoted to first lieutenant on July 1, 1863, and was singled out for bravery by his regimental commander for his actions at Gettysburg on July 2. Advanced to captain in February 1864, he mustered out with his company on May 29, 1865. Bates, *History of Pennsylvania Volunteers,* 3:1205; *Annual Report of the Adjutant General of Pennsylvania,* 472; *OR* 27(1):504.

34. Sherman had occupied Atlanta on September 2.

35. An 1861 West Point graduate, Joseph Pearson Farley (1839–1912) had originally been commissioned in the artillery but shortly after transferred to the Ordnance Department and spent his career there, eventually rising to the rank of colonel of ordnance and later brigadier general before his retirement in 1903. He had married Fannie Elizabeth Brinley of Philadelphia in April 1864. *Forty Second Annual Reunion of the Association of the Graduates of the United States Military Academy,* 142–47.

36. "The Rebs amuse themselves by firing at the trains on the new R.R.," WBR notes in his diary on September 10, "which is plainly visible from their position. . . . Today they hit the train, and on Wednesday they sent a Whitworth bolt clear over our camp." Federal engineers eventually solved the problem caused by the exposure of the train to enemy artillery. "They have at last stopped the Whitworth bolts," explained Meade's aide Theodore Lyman on September 29, "by putting the railroad, between Meade's and Hancock's stations, in a *covered* way." Lowe, *Meade's Army,* 272.

37. An 1863 West Point graduate, Jacob H. Counselman (1840–75) of Maryland took the field immediately upon his graduation from the academy, assuming command of Battery K of the 1st US Artillery, part of the Horse Artillery Brigade of the Army of the Potomac's Cavalry Corps. It was likely during his service with the corps that WBR made his acquaintance. Counselman was appointed lieutenant colonel of the 1st Maryland Cavalry, which was attached to the Army of the James, in June 1864. The 1st Maryland had been serving dismounted as infantry with the X Corps for some time. Unsurprisingly, this left the men "much discouraged," as Brigadier General Kautz, commander of that army's cavalry, complained. Three weeks after WBR wrote this letter, however, the Marylanders' assignment as foot soldiers ended when they received horses and equipment and transferred to Kautz's command. Starr, *Union Cavalry,* 2:396–97.

38. "I have commenced a registration of all Citizens within our lines," remarked Provost Marshal General Patrick in his diary on September 14, "through the Officers of the 3d Penn. Cavy. with reference to sending them out of the lines unless they take the Oath." Sparks, *Inside Lincoln's Army,* 421.

39. While rumors regarding Lieutenant Colonel Jones's attempts to raise a new regiment may have had some basis in fact, he was not successful. Eugene L. Cauffman was originally the second lieutenant of Philadelphia-raised Company F, joining the 3rd in July 1861. Promoted to first lieutenant of Company H in December 1862, he mustered out of the service in August 1864. Regimental History Committee, *Third Pennsylvania,* 570, 572.

40. This incident, known as the Beefsteak Raid, resulted when Confederate cavalry leader Wade Hampton learned that a large herd of lightly guarded livestock was grazing near Coggins Point on the James River. Leaving his lines near Petersburg on September 14, Hampton rode in a wide counterclockwise arc around the Federal lines. Surprising the troopers charged with protecting the 2,500 animals, the Rebels captured the beeves on September 16 and led them back to Petersburg. The commissary officer charged with management of the herd, pointed out one of Meade's staff, "had often been notified of their insecurity. . . . My only surprise has been that they have not done it before. What good is there in our occupying railroads of the enemy if we are to supply them in this way?" With their beef rations temporarily disrupted, Union quartermasters substituted salted codfish, which, recalled a Maine soldier, "after being carried in a dirty haversack and wet a few times . . . is not a specially

inviting diet." James C. Biddle to wife, Sept. 18, 1864, Biddle Papers, HSP; Smith, *History of the Nineteenth Regiment of Maine Volunteer Infantry,* 244.

41. Sgts. Guy C. Humphreys (also spelled Humphries) of Company A, Thomas Ewing of Company B, Alexander B. Frazer of Company M, and Horace W. Hayden of Company C were commissioned as second lieutenants in Companies F, M, B, and C respectively in early October. Humphreys, who had joined the 3rd in August 1861, was formerly sergeant major of the regiment; he resigned his commission in January 1865 under duress (as WBR will explain). Ewing (who had joined the regiment in March 1864) would rise to first lieutenant and captain of Company I. Frazer, who also was one of the original cadre of men who enlisted in August 1861, would be promoted to first lieutenant and captain of Company D. Hayden, who joined the 3rd as a private in November 1862, would rise to first lieutenant of Company C. Regimental History Committee, *Third Pennsylvania,* 458, 568–71, 574–76, 587, 591.

42. The Chicago platform refers to the positions adopted by the Democrats and their 1864 presidential candidate, George B. McClellan, which included a call for an end to the war and the preservation of the Union while leaving slavery intact. Many in the Army of the Potomac were incensed that their former commander, after three years of protracted conflict that had claimed tens of thousands of lives, would align himself with a policy that promoted peace at any cost.

43. Sheridan's Army of the Shenandoah had emerged victorious at the Third Battle of Winchester (also known as Opequon) on September 19, 1864, overwhelming Early's Army of the Valley and driving the Confederates from the battlefield. McIntosh, who was commanding a brigade in Wilson's cavalry division, suffered a wound that resulted in the amputation of one of his legs below the knee. Longacre, *Lincoln's Cavalrymen,* 304–6.

44. Federal tax rates on annual incomes between $600 and $5,000 had risen from 3 percent to 5 percent effective in June, when Lincoln signed the Revenue Act of 1864. The levies were not, as WBR feared, applied retroactively.

45. The actions WBR recounts have been categorized by Earl Hess as Grant's Fifth Offensive. Butler's troops north of the James were to strike against Richmond while Meade's V and IX Corps, supported by cavalry, were to target the South Side Railroad, which ran parallel to the Appomattox River as it entered Petersburg from the west. Fighting by the Army of the James during September 29–30, known as the Battle of Chaffin's Bluff, secured Fort Harrison, a key fortification in the Southern defense line, but the Northerners failed to seriously threaten Richmond, though they could see the city from their newly secured positions. On the left the Federals moved west of the Weldon Railroad on September 30, in an action known as the Battle of Peebles' Farm, but only got within six miles of the South Side. Fighting took place between September 30 and October 2; on the first Davies's brigade of Gregg's division repulsed several brigades under Hampton attempting to outflank the Federals from their newly won positions. The 2nd Division reported casualties of 174 over the four days of combat. Trudeau, *Last Citadel,* 207–15; Longacre, *Lincoln's Cavalrymen,* 321; OR 42(1):619–20.

46. The Gurley House was located just south of the US Military Railroad several miles due east of its junction with the Weldon Railroad and not far from Globe Tavern. Fort Davison was constructed immediately behind the house and outbuildings.

47. There are several pieces of contradictory information concerning the military career of Thomas Woods. A twenty-three-year-old Irish-born Philadelphian, Woods had been commissioned as the second lieutenant of Company E of the predominately Irish 69th Pennsylvania Infantry in the fall of 1861. He was wounded at Antietam in September 1862, promoted to first lieutenant in April or May 1863, and that same year advanced to captain (with dates of promotion reported variously in May, October, and November). Woods would be wounded again at Gettysburg. He is also listed in the *Official Records* as the commander of the 69th Pennsylvania on January 1, 1864. Woods was discharged from the 69th in August 1864 and,

as WBR notes, joined the 3rd Pennsylvania. There is no mention, however, in the published roster of the 3rd of Woods ever having been a member of the regiment. Bates, *History of Pennsylvania Volunteers*, 2:722; *OR* 33:465; *Annual Report of the Adjutant General of Pennsylvania*, 286; "Paul Conley Kline Family Home Page: Information about Thomas Woods," Genealogy.com, https://www.genealogy.com/ftm/k/l/i/Paul-C-Kline/WEBSITE-0001/UHP-0409.html (accessed Dec. 15, 2017); Roster, Company E, 69th Pennsylvania Infantry, p. 15, https://www.69thpa.co.uk/coe.pdf (accessed Jan. 5, 2018; website discontinued, printout in editor's possession).

48. Parke's Station, named for IX Corps commander Maj. Gen. John Grubb Parke, was a stop on the US Military Railroad immediately east of the Gurley House.

49. Prior to the 1864 elections, only Pennsylvania soldiers present in the state on Election Day could vote; that law was changed in August 1864 to allow soldiers in the field to cast ballots as well. Pennsylvania, one of nineteen states to allow this practice, held two elections: one for state, county, and local offices in October, and the other for national offices in November. Benton, *Voting in the Field*, 196–203.

50. Kautz, who at this time commanded the cavalry of the Army of the James, had written *The Company Clerk*, which was first published in 1863 and went through numerous reprintings in subsequent years. T. B. Peterson and Brothers Publishers and Booksellers was located at 306 Chestnut Street in Philadelphia. *McElroy's Philadelphia City Directory 1860*, 780.

51. Admired for their obedience, coolness and devotion to duty, no higher compliment could be paid to a volunteer regiment in the North during the Civil War than to have themselves compared to the soldiers, artillerists, or cavalrymen of the Regular Army. Many officers and men aspired to attain the level of discipline that would lead to such recognition for their units. A number of volunteer organizations, including the 121st New York Infantry, 5th New York Infantry, 20th Massachusetts Infantry, 6th Pennsylvania Cavalry, and the Iron Brigade of the I Corps, to name but a few, proudly likened themselves to units of the Regular Army.

52. "Dum vivimus" appears to be an abbreviation of *Dum vivimus vivamus*, Latin for "while we live, let us live."

53. Grant had anticipated that the troops serving in the Shenandoah Valley, including the VI Corps, would return to Petersburg and enable him to continue his envelopment of the city. Early's attack on October 19, which precipitated the Battle of Cedar Creek, delayed their redeployment to the Army of the Potomac. Hess, *Trenches at Petersburg*, 189–90.

54. Secretary of War Stanton, who Lieutenant Colonel Lyman aptly described as "short, very stout, with a big head and beard; a face expressive of large intelligence, but coarse," had visited the army, accompanied by a retinue of elected and government officials, on October 17. Lowe, *Meade's Army*, 281.

55. First Lt. Harvey Fisher, twenty, was serving in Col. Langhorne Wister's 150th Pennsylvania Infantry. He left the University of Pennsylvania and joined the regiment as second lieutenant of Company A in August 1862. He was promoted to captain of his company, but not mustered in at that rank, in March 1864. His predecessor had been captured at Gettysburg, and, "from the autumn of 1863 until the close of hostilities," recalled the regiment's historian, Fisher "commanded his company with marked ability." He left the army upon the expiration of the regiment's term of service in June 1865. Bates, *History of Pennsylvania Volunteers*, 4:659; Chamberlin, *History of the One Hundred and Fiftieth Regiment Pennsylvania Volunteers*, 302.

56. Hess, *Trenches at Petersburg*, 191–92; Trudeau, *Last Citadel*, 223–24; Regimental History Committee, *Third Pennsylvania*, 460–61.

57. Poplar Grove Church had been constructed by Federal engineers near the site of the former Poplar Springs Church, which had been destroyed during the Fifth Offensive in early October. The church was just under a mile due west of Globe Tavern and the Weldon Railroad. *OR Atlas*, plate 76, map 2.

58. Much of the geography mentioned by WBR in his account of the Boydton Plank Road fighting is shown on *OR Atlas,* plate 74, map 2.

59. "In the early part of the skirmish at the mill," wrote Lieutenant Colonel Walsh of the 3rd in his official report, "my command became separated by the enemy advancing up a ravine on my left. Two companies, commanded by Capt. Stille and Lieutenant Brooke [Rawle] were thus separated. . . . These two companies . . . according to my previous instructions fell back on the Vaughan Road in rear of [Brig.] General [Thomas] Egan's command." *OR* 42(1):215.

60. Yellow House, also known as Yellow Tavern or Globe Tavern, stood on the Weldon Railroad between Fort Dushane and Fort Wadsworth. The US Military Railroad intersected the Weldon near the structure, which served as V Corps headquarters during the operations near Petersburg.

61. Hancock and the II Corps, supported by Gregg's cavalry, had made good progress on the rain-soaked day of October 27, driving Confederates away from the Boydton Plank Road, but reinforcements from the V Corps could not get up in time to assist and the IX Corps failed to penetrate the Southern lines farther north on the road, above Hatcher's Run. Hancock, assisted by Gregg's horsemen, beat back several Rebel assaults, capturing 900 men. But the Northerners indeed fell back on October 28, relinquishing control of the section of the Boydton Plank Road they had secured. Total Union casualties were 1,758; the Confederates lost another 400 men in addition to those taken prisoner. On Butler's front, where a diversionary attack was carried out, effective resistance by Longstreet along the Darbytown Road stymied the Army of the James, resulting in the loss of 1,600 Federals. Longstreet lost 64. Cleaves, *Meade of Gettysburg,* 295–96; Hess, *Trenches at Petersburg,* 192–96.

62. The new 3rd Brigade had been formed in October and was commanded by Col. Charles H. Smith of the 1st Maine Cavalry. It consisted of two veteran cavalry regiments, the 1st Maine and 6th Ohio, and the 21st Pennsylvania Cavalry. The 21st had been recruited in late 1863 and had fought dismounted as infantry with the V Corps between June 1 and October 5, 1864, when it received horses and joined Gregg's 2nd Division. The 3rd Brigade lost 171 men in the fighting along the Boydton Plank Road, nearly twice as many as the 1st and 2nd Brigades combined. Bates, *History of Pennsylvania Volunteers,* 5:77–79; *OR* 42(1):160. For Colonel Smith's report, see *OR* 42(1):647–48. For the report by the chief surgeon of the 2nd Division, Dr. Elias Marsh, which is surprisingly far more detailed than the one written by Brigadier General Gregg, see *OR* 42(1):620–22.

63. The books mentioned here are *Maurice Tiernay: The Soldier of Fortune* (1852), by Irish author Charles Lever; *Barren Honour* (1862), by British novelist George Alfred Lawrence; and William Thackeray's *The Irish Sketchbook* (1843).

64. WBR is again referring to George Whyte-Melville's *The Interpreter,* referenced in chapter 1, note 6.

65. There are innumerable examples in regiments on both sides of the conflict where soldiers commissioned from the ranks performed superbly as officers. It is worth mentioning that another Philadelphia-raised cavalry regiment, the 6th Pennsylvania, experienced the same issues as WBR describes with men promoted from sergeant to commissioned officer to such an extent that its colonel wrote to Governor Curtin in March 1865 requesting that only men from civil life be commissioned in his regiment: "The sergeants who were promoted were first class men as sergeants, but after their promotion they have invariably . . . become inefficient and have to be driven to do anything, except fight." Many of them, he continued, had "no idea of discipline and of the simplest duty of an officer." Wittenberg, *Rush's Lancers,* 215.

7. WINTER AT PETERSBURG

1. "Billy duxes" is slang for *billet doux,* a love letter.

2. For an account of the search by WBR, see *New York World,* Nov. 11, 1864.

3. "Flocks of election commissioners, scurvy looking fellows, are coming down here to look after the presidential vote," wrote Lyman on November 3. Lowe, *Meade's Army,* 292.

4. *Maurice Dering* is a novel by George Alfred Lawrence published in 1864.

5. Jeremiah McKibbin (1820–81) was a Philadelphia hotelier. His father, Chambers, was active in Democrat politics throughout his life. Four of his brothers were serving in the Union army, including David, who was promoted to brevet brigadier general at war's end, and Joseph, a prewar congressman from California. Word of irregularities stemming from McKibbin's activities reached Washington, prompting Secretary of War Stanton to order the Philadelphian arrested and sent to the capital two days after the election. Sparks, *Inside Lincoln's Army,* 436, 440–41; Nevin, *Centennial Biography,* 443–45. "Many commissioners and party agents were about the camps, and as the spiritual exhilaration of camp influences was too strong for some of them, especially those of the Democratic party, many of their ballots and other papers mysteriously disappeared, as well as they themselves, temporarily." Regimental History Committee, *Third Pennsylvania,* 465.

6. A soldier in the 4th Pennsylvania Cavalry recorded a similar phenomenon regarding the voting proclivities of his command's newest soldiers. When state and local elections were held in October, three-fourths of the regiment voted Republican. Recruits and draftees were absorbed into the unit later in October, and in the presidential election held in November, only two-thirds of the regiment voted for Lincoln, with the balance favoring McClellan. The change, he believed, "showed that by the addition of new recruits from the Northern States, and gradual fluctuations in public sentiment, the Democratic feeling had grown slightly in the regiment." Another Pennsylvanian remarked: "Almost all of the new regiments are giving a large majority for McClellan; but you will find that most of the men (I will not say all) who are voting the Democratic ticket have either lately come out for the large *bounties* and not for the sake of the country, or have forever 'bummed' in the hospital and never fired a gun. You will find no soldier who is simply fighting for the good of the country that will cast a vote for McClellan or Pendleton." In contrast, a long-serving artillery officer in the V Corps who supported McClellan believed that the newest recruits (who he called "thousand-dollar patriots" because of the bounties many received for enlisting) "all vote for Lincoln, while a majority of the old soldiers go the other way." But he accurately predicted, "The army vote . . . will be decidedly Republican." The Army of the Potomac indeed voted overwhelmingly for Lincoln; various accounts credit him with receiving between three and up to seven times as many votes as McClellan. Lincoln carried the popular vote by over 400,000. In a notable incident a regiment of the Iron Brigade (which went for Lincoln by a vote of 543 to 116) took in a Confederate on Election Day who told his captors that he deserted because he wanted to cast a vote for Lincoln. Hyndman, *History of a Cavalry Company,* 236, 250–52; Chamberlin, *150th Pennsylvania,* 290; Nevins, *Diary of Battle,* 476; de Trobriand, *Four Years with the Army of the Potomac,* 683; Lewis, *History of Battery E,* 389; Curtis, *History of the Twenty-Fourth Michigan,* 280. An excellent discussion—though not limited to the Army of the Potomac— on Lincoln and the soldier vote in 1864 is Davis, *Lincoln's Men,* 192–227. Though resigned to its implications, soldiers in the Army of Northern Virginia were understandably despondent at the outcome of the election. For a sampling of their reactions, see Power, *Lee's Miserables,* 217–19; and Pierce, *Battlefields and Camp Fires,* 69–70.

7. Many of the veteran regiments of the Army of the Potomac were disdainful regarding the recruits they received at this time. Despite WBR's comments, the new men received by the 3rd Pennsylvania became good soldiers. They "all had a taste, soon after joining, of

what was expected of them, and they behaved splendidly. Many of them had served in other regiments earlier in the war, and had re-enlisted after their first discharge and a short rest at home. They were forcibly impressed with the fact that the standard of discipline and efficiency for which the Third had always been remarkable must and would be maintained, and they strove hard and successfully to attain that standard." Regimental History Committee, *Third Pennsylvania,* 464.

8. Grant did not, in fact, spend the winter in Washington but remained in command of all Union forces from his headquarters at City Point, Virginia. Major General Hancock would be relieved of command of the II Corps in late November in order to organize a corps of veterans "of not less than 20,000 infantrymen, to be composed of able-bodied men who had served honorably for at least two years and to be led by officers who also had at least two years' service." Meade's chief of staff, Maj. Gen. Andrew Atkinson Humphreys, replaced Hancock at the head of the II Corps. *OR* 52(3):337.

9. WBR saved the order and pasted it to the back of this letter. Dated August 15, 1864, and signed by Gen. Samuel Cooper, the adjutant and inspector general of the Confederate armies, it enjoined Federal soldiers—foreigners in particular—to desert "the military and naval service of the United States," going on to direct Southerners "that all such persons coming within the lines of the Confederate armies shall be received, protected and supplied with means of subsistence until such of them as desire it can be forwarded to the most convenient points on the border, where all facilities will be afforded them to return to their homes."

10. Camp Distribution was located at Alexandria, Virginia, and held, at various times, between 2,000 and 10,000 recruits, conscripts, convalescents, and deserters. A member of the 9th New Hampshire who was sent there after recovering from an illness in a Washington, DC, hospital called it "one of the most dismal holes that I ever got into. It is where they keep all of the deserters and we are guarded as close as though we were prisoners." *OR* ser. 3, 5:563; Edson Justus Cheever to "Dear Uncle," May 25, 1863, J. Gregory Acken personal collection.

11. After a highly successful two-year career as a commerce raider, the CSS *Florida* had been seized during what was later determined to be an illegal attack by US Navy forces at Bahia, Brazil, on October 7, 1864. Brought back to Newport News, Virginia, where WBR saw it, the ship sank after what may have been an intentional collision with a Federal troop transport (to prevent it being returned to Confederate service) on November 28.

12. Supplies from points south in the Confederacy were still able to reach as far as north as Stony Creek Station on the Petersburg & Weldon Railroad, eighteen miles south of Petersburg. From that point they were loaded into wagons and entered the city from the west via the Boydton Plank Road. Gregg's 2nd Cavalry Division went on a raid to the station on December 1. His troopers burned the supply depot and other public buildings and captured 190 Rebels, two artillery pieces, and thirty wagons along with food, clothing, and ammunition. *OR* 52(1):610–11.

13. *Guy Livingstone* (1857) is a novel by the English writer George Alfred Lawrence.

14. Trudeau, *Last Citadel,* 263–75.

15. A native of Ireland, Michael Kerwin (1837–1912) had joined the 13th Pennsylvania Cavalry as the captain of Company B in April 1862 and was promoted to major six months later. He commanded the regiment from the late summer of 1863 until July 1864, when he was promoted to colonel. Bates, *History of Pennsylvania Volunteers,* 3:1268, 1272.

16. "The rebels opened on the 13[th Pennsylvania Cavalry] which was in advance," wrote a soldier of the 3rd Pennsylvania the day after this action. "We formed on but the 13 had them on the skedaddle. We then went on about a mile to the creek and formed in line when the 13 advanced about 200 yards to the creek where they were met by the Rebs with a yell, but they were not so easily scared and a general engagement took place, our Cavalry being on one side and the Rebel Infantry on the other. After about ½ an hours fight our men finding they could

not cross the order was given Retreat which was done in good order." Charles Woolston to Benjamin A. Woolston, Dec. 9, 1864, Charles Woolston Correspondence, Gilder Lehrman Institute of American History.

17. On the heels of Captain Ward's wounding, Pvt. Edward Coyle of Company M crawled forward to try to pick off the Rebels who had shot the officer. After firing a few rounds in their direction, he carelessly exposed himself and took a bullet through his chest, which coursed lengthwise through his body, mortally wounding him. When the fighting ended, his comrades retrieved him. As he was carried from the field, he locked eyes with Maj. Frank Hess. "Major," said the dying man, "it's the last of poor Coyle." Regimental History Committee, *Third Pennsylvania*, 467.

18. Brig. Gen. Robert B. Potter (1829–87) commanded the 2nd Division of the IX Corps. His father was the bishop of the Protestant Episcopal Church of Pennsylvania, while his half-brother served as an officer in the Cavalry Corps. See chapter 4, note 34.

19. The V Corps did destroy fifteen miles of the Weldon Railroad during the raid. It took three months for the Confederates to restore the track. Hess, *Trenches at Petersburg*, 214.

20. The countryside south of Petersburg through which the Hicksford Raid took place had been relatively unscathed up to this point in the war, though a Michigan soldier thought it had been "pretty badly used by the enemy themselves." There is little doubt that the discovery of hidden stores of alcohol in houses along its route contributed to the depredations that WBR mentions. "No mention is made in the official report," allowed a Massachusetts soldier, "of the quantity of apple jack, which the curiously inclined Yankees sought and found, and to their own harm, imbibed. . . . [B]etter stored farm houses were found than the men had been seeing of late and, notwithstanding the rigors of the campaign, possibly on account of them, they made merry with the seductive liquids made from innocent cider." A Pennsylvania infantrymen recalled: "The dead bodies of soldiers were found along the roadside; in one case, it was said, with the throat cut, and other instances were reported of still more revolting barbarities. The stories of these cruelties aroused a spirit of vengeance, and in retaliation the torch was applied to almost every house along the route. The efforts of the officers to stop this incendiarism were but partially successful." A cavalry officer commanding a regiment in Gregg's division recorded other scenes: "On this homeward march . . . I witnessed the sickening site of some of our men lying dead with their hearts and private parts cut out and thrust in their mouths. These atrocities were supposed to have been committed by citizens of the neighborhood out 'bush-whacking.' The poor fellows who met with such horrible treatment had become intoxicated from the large quantity of apple-jack found in that section of the country and were murdered in cold blood." Evidence exists, however, that some of the Federals may have brought the punishment on themselves. A Maine soldier wrote that, on the night of December 10, he saw a drunken Pennsylvania colonel and his adjutant "perpetuating one of the foulest outrages on two defenseless women whose house was within our lines. These women were compelled to submit to their infamous proposals or have their house burned down and themselves turned out into the bleak December. Had this been the work of privates, said privates would have suffered death." Artilleryman Charles Wainwright was appalled by the destruction: "So pitiable a sight as the women and children turned adrift at nightfall, and a most severe winter night too, I never saw before and never want to see again. If this is a raid, deliver me from going on another." Curtis, *History of the Twenty-Fourth Michigan*, 283; Roe, *Thirty-Ninth Regiment Massachusetts Volunteers*, 266; Survivor's Association, *History of the Corn Exchange Regiment*, 540; Thomas, "Some Personal Reminiscences," 22; Silliker, *Rebel Yell and the Yankee Hurrah*, 226–27; Nevins, *Diary of Battle*, 490. For more soldiers' comments on their experiences during this movement, see Carter, *Four Brothers in Blue*, 496; Regimental Association, *Under the Maltese Cross*, 328–30; Spear et al., *Civil War Recollections of General Ellis Spear*, 158–64; and Greenleaf, *Letters to Eliza*, 142–47.

21. Sherman had captured Fort McAllister, a key defensive position guarding Savannah on December 13. Maj. Gen. George Thomas had soundly defeated Gen. John Bell Hood's Army of Tennessee at the Battle of Nashville on December 15–16, effectively wiping it out as a cohesive fighting force.

22. Sherman's March to the Sea had culminated in the capture of Savannah on December 21, 1864, the general offering the city to President Lincoln as a "Christmas gift." Confederate lieutenant general William Hardee, overseeing the defense of the city, had evacuated most of his 10,000 troops before Sherman could attack, so only around 800 Rebels were captured. Union attacks against Fort Fisher, guardian of the Cape Fear River and the vital port city of Wilmington, had begun under the supervision of General Butler the day that WBR penned this letter, December 24, and lasted until December 27, when Butler withdrew the infantry he had landed to assault the fort. A second, ultimately successful attempt to capture the fort was led by Maj. Gen Alfred Terry, who bombarded the bastion for over two days, beginning on January 12, 1865, before overrunning it on January 15 with a combined force of infantry and sailors pressed into duty as foot soldiers. The rumor that Jefferson Davis was dead was unfounded, though he had been prostrated by an attack of neuralgia in December. Cooper, *Jefferson Davis*, 558.

23. Dr. George Emlen Hare was the headmaster of Philadelphia's Episcopal Academy, founded in 1785 (and still in operation). Students between the ages of nine and fourteen attended the school, which since 1846 had attracted pupils from the upper caste of Philadelphia society. Hare was such an influential educator that, during the time he led it, the institution was referred to as "Hare's Academy." Harrison, *Harrison, Waples, and Allied Families*, 41; George, *Life of Henry George*, 8.

24. Francis C. Grugan had formerly served as adjutant of the 114th Pennsylvania and as the post adjutant at the headquarters of the Army of the Potomac. Described as "a charming gentleman and ideal staff officer," he joined the 3rd as first lieutenant and adjutant on December 19, 1864. He entered the Regular Army after the war, serving in the cavalry and artillery, and retired as a major in 1899. Regimental History Committee, *Third Pennsylvania*, 471, 474, 561, 570–71.

25. "Yesterday morning about 4 o'clock the Rebs made an attack right here in front of us but they were well paid for it. They drove in our pickets and mad[e] an awfle yell but were drove off when they came to our works. They got within ¼ of a mile of us. We were called out of bed some without shoes on and every fashion. We were formed out on the front of camp in line of battle but the 1 division 6 corpse [*sic*] gave them enough." Charles Woolston to Maria Woolston, Jan. 1, 1865, Woolston Correspondence, Gilder Lehrman Institute.

26. General Butler had begun expanding a small canal, known as Dutch Gap, at a bend of the James River in August 1864 to bypass a group of strong Southern batteries that controlled the waterway north of Petersburg. After five months of digging, almost wholly by African American troops, the remaining obstruction was blown up on January 1, 1865, but instead of creating the anticipated shortcut, much of the loosened earth fell back into the excavation from which it had been removed. "Butler's Dutch Gap blew up yesterday and made a perfect fizzle!" wrote a general in the Army of the Potomac. Longacre, *Army of Amateurs*, 259; Sparks, *Lincoln's Army*, 455.

27. Lt. Col. Edward B. Dalton (1834–72) of New York had entered the service in 1861 as surgeon of the 36th New York Infantry; by late June 1864, he had risen to become the chief medical officer in charge of the Depot Field Hospital of the Army of the Potomac at City Point. On March 25, 1865, he was appointed medical director of the IX Corps. Philadelphia native Felix Octavius Carr Darley (1822–88) was one of the most popular American artists of the period. His works graced many periodicals and books of the mid- to late nineteenth century. Heitman, *Historical Register and Dictionary of the United States Army*, 1:351; *OR* 46(1): 615; Dalton, *Memorial of Edward B. Dalton*; Marter, *Grove Encyclopedia of American Art*, 1:21–22.

28. WBR noted in a typed addition to his diary transcript that Humphries resigned before being court-martialed, and that his resignation was accepted. WBR Diary, Jan. 10, 1865, transcript.

29. "I have never seen a deeper depression of spirit among the rebels than there seems to be at present," wrote a IX Corps soldier on January 17, "nor a more jubilant and confident spirit among our men." A number of factors, including the quality and the paucity of their rations, along with a sense of the inevitability of their defeat, led increasing numbers of soldiers to desert from the Army of Northern Virginia throughout the winter and spring of 1864–65. Pierce, *Battlefields and Campfires,* 84. Comments by Federals who interacted with Rebel deserters at this time are legion. Thorough explorations of the mindset of Confederates in the trenches are in Powers, *Lee's Miserables,* 6–9, 236–38, 255–57; and Greene, *Final Battles of the Petersburg Campaign,* 83–93.

30. A prewar attorney, George H. Sharpe (1828–1900) of New York had raised the 120th New York and served as its colonel before his assignment in February 1863 as the chief intelligence officer of the Army of the Potomac. He built and oversaw an intelligence-gathering operation, initially referred to as the Secret Service Department but later renamed the Bureau of Military Information, that provided important information on enemy strength, organization, and movements to every subsequent commander of the army—and ultimately to General Grant during the 1864–65 campaigns. The secret duty referred to here, as WBR divulged in a postwar notation to his diary, "was running the mail to & recovering it from Richmond per Underground Rail Road. I got files of the Richmond Papers of the same day." Fishel, *Secret War for the Union,* 287–91, 546–48.

31. Upon reaching Harrison's Landing on the north bank of the James, WBR wrote that he and his party rode to Long Bridge on the Chickahominy, where he secured mail, newspapers, and an almanac. "Saw a few Rebel scouts and got on the track of some guerillas but could not find them. Just at dark we saw some figures some distance off and gave chase, but found them to be three pretty girls. . . . We brought in to Gen. Grant cypher despatches from Richmond of the gunboat attack on the following Monday." WBR Diary, Jan. 17, 1865, transcript. The information he secured was brought to him by a Union sympathizer from Richmond, who provided him a small, foil-covered pellet that contained the coded dispatches. The informant instructed WBR to deliver the pellet to Colonel Sharpe of the Bureau of Military Information; if he encountered a situation in which his capture was imminent, WBR was to destroy or swallow it. Regimental History Committee, *Third Pennsylvania,* 478.

32. Septima Levy Collis was a native of Charleston, South Carolina, and spent a considerable amount of time during the war in camp with her husband, Col. Charles H. T. Collis (later breveted brigadier general), whom she had wed in December 1861. "Being a crisp, dry winter," Mrs. Collis wrote of her time spent at City Point, "I was constantly in the saddle, galloping to the different headquarters." Hagerty, *Collis Zouaves,* 14, 29; Collis, *Woman's War Record,* 37–38.

33. Stephen H. Brooke (d. 1886), WBR's uncle, was his father's brother. He was an attorney and merchant in Philadelphia. For unknown reasons, his grave in Philadelphia's Laurel Hill Cemetery lies between those of WBR and his wife, Elizabeth.

34. WBR recorded in his diary that the ship sunk was the CSS *Drewry.* A 106-ton wooden gunboat, it was destroyed by gunners of the 1st Connecticut Heavy Artillery firing from Fort McPherson during the early morning hours of January 24. Gaines, *Encyclopedia of Civil War Shipwrecks,* 179.

35. Pvt. Newell Root of the 1st Connecticut Heavy Artillery, convicted of desertion, was the soldier executed on January 27, 1865.

36. Hess, *Trenches at Petersburg,* 229–32.

37. Andrew J. Pemberton (1831–1900) was the younger brother of Confederate lieutenant general John C. Pemberton, best known for his surrender of Vicksburg to Grant in July 1863. Pemberton had served in a three-month militia unit in the early months of the war and later as a captain in the 3rd Maryland Cavalry. He had been commissioned as first lieutenant of Company D of the 3rd Pennsylvania to date from January 14, 1865. Pemberton mustered out in August 1865. Regimental History Committee, *Third Pennsylvania*, 479, 505, 571.

38. "Had to pay $7.50 fare to the front. Great injustice." WBR Diary, Feb. 19, 1865, transcript.

39. Brig. Gen. Adam R. "Stovepipe" Johnson (1834–1922) was permanently blinded when he was accidentally shot by one of his own men during a skirmish in Kentucky in August 1864. Captured by Federals shortly thereafter, he was sent to prison at Fort Warren near Boston. Col. Richard Curd Morgan (1836–1918), brother of famed Confederate raider Brig. Gen. John Hunt Morgan, had been captured by the Federals on July 19, 1863, following a fight at Buffington Island, near Portsmouth, Ohio, while participating in his brother's raid of that state.

40. Capt. Julius W. Mason (1835–82) had charge of a three-company detachment of the 5th US Cavalry that served as escort at General Grant's headquarters. Mason received brevet promotions for gallant and meritorious service at the Battles of Beverly Ford and Brandy Station and had commanded his regiment at Gettysburg. Heitman, *Historical Register and Dictionary of the United States Army*, 1:695.

41. James Kennedy Moorhead (1806–84) was a Republican congressman from western Pennsylvania. He had served as adjutant general of Pennsylvania in the 1830s before representing his district in Congress from 1859 to 1869.

42. Lt. Col. Horace Porter (1837–1921), an 1859 West Point graduate, was at this time serving on Grant's staff as an aide-de-camp, a position he had held since just before the start of the Overland Campaign. He would end the war as a brevet brigadier general, pen an excellent memoir of his experiences under Grant, and later in life receive the Medal of Honor for his actions during the Battle of Chickamauga. As WBR subsequently discloses, he and Porter were related.

43. Most of Early's troops had been withdrawn from the Valley and sent to reinforce Lee at Petersburg. The remnants, numbering 1,600 men, were drawn up on the western outskirts of Waynesboro, Virginia, on the afternoon of March 2. The Federal cavalry divisions of Custer and Brig. Gen. Thomas Devin, advancing east from Staunton with 2,500 troopers, made contact with the Southerners, and Custer exploited an unprotected flank to roll up and rout the Rebels, capturing 1200 men and clearing the Valley permanently of the presence of organized bodies of Confederate troops.

44. The condemned man was Pvt. William T. Griffin (alias George Bolter) of Company C of the 8th Delaware Volunteers. He was shot for desertion. *Index to General Orders, Army of the Potomac*, unpaginated.

45. Constructed on ground fought over near Peeble's Farm during Grant's Fifth Offensive, Fort Welch, located between Duncan Road and Church Road near Arthur's Swamp, was the westernmost fort in the Federal lines around Petersburg. The VI Corps attacks that broke through the Confederate lines on April 2, 1865, originated from the area immediately northwest of Welch.

46. Patrick Station, named for Provost Marshal General Patrick, was the western terminus of the US Military Railroad.

47. Maj. Gen. Edward O. C. Ord (1818–83), an 1839 West Point graduate, commanded the XVIII Corps of the Army of the James; within weeks he would rise to command of that army, replacing Butler.

8. THE FALL OF PETERSBURG AND THE APPOMATTOX CAMPAIGN

1. Norton, *Army Letters,* 254; Billings, *History of the Tenth Massachusetts Battery,* 396.

2. There are many mentions at this time by Federal soldiers on the inevitability of Confederate defeat. For examples, see Rosenblatt and Rosenblatt, *Anti-Rebel,* 318–19; Silliker, *Rebel Yell,* 247; Styple, *Writing and Fighting the Civil War,* 341; Nevins, *Diary of Battle,* 492–93; and Gerrish, *Army Life,* 225.

3. "One of the most anxious periods of my experience during the rebellion was the last few weeks before Petersburg. I felt that the situation of the Confederate army was such that they would try to make an escape at the earliest practicable moment, and I was afraid, every morning, that I would awake from my sleep to hear that Lee had gone, and that nothing was left but a picket line." Grant, *Memoirs,* 2:424.

4. Grant, *Memoirs,* 2:434.

5. This was the sidewheel steamer *Thomas Collyer.*

6. Brevet Brigadier General Collis was given charge of an independent command at City Point, known alternately as the Provisional or Independent Brigade, consisting of his own 114th Pennsylvania, the 68th Pennsylvania, the 20th New York, the 61st Massachusetts, and the 1st Massachusetts Cavalry. Sparks, *Inside Lincoln's Army,* 480; *OR* 46(1):590.

7. Bvt. Brig. Gen. George N. Macy (1837–75) had relieved Patrick as provost marshal on March 16. Macy had lost a hand at Gettysburg while commanding the 20th Massachusetts Infantry and was injured again when his horse was shot and fell on him while leading a II Corps brigade during the fighting near Deep Bottom in August 1864. The 3rd US Infantry were the headquarters guard for the Army of the Potomac; the 1st Battalion of the 11th US Infantry was serving with WBR as part of the provost guard. *OR* 46(1):581.

8. Calvin D. Ludwig had joined Philadelphia-raised Company A of the 3rd as a corporal in September 1862 and was promoted to sergeant on August 1, 1864. He was commissioned in Company B in December 1864. Regimental History Committee, *Third Pennsylvania,* 568, 578.

9. These were no ordinary early spring winds. "Yesterday afternoon it blew a perfect hurricane," recorded a clerk in the V Corps on March 24, "and you would have laughed to see the results of it in our camps; scarcely a house withstood its fury. Canvas roofs were flying around in a marvelous manner; tents strained on their ropes, till, finally breaking loose, they fell enveloping their occupants; here a foot was seen sticking out; there a head appeared; its owner desperately endeavoring to work out from under the ruins; clouds of dust so thick, they filled the air as sensibly to diminish the sun's light." Lieutenant Colonel Lyman, who accompanied this group of guests on the twenty-third, declared, "The wind rose to a furious gale, and in this flat region without turf, and shorn of its wood, swept such clouds of sand and dust as never yet saw in all my army experience." The gusts eventually grew so strong that several of the few trees left near the V Corps camps were blown over. Tilney, *Life in the Army,* 191–92; Lowe, *Meade's Army,* 348–49.

10. These individuals were part of a large group of civilians and former officers who visited the army at this time. Those singled out by WBR were General Meade's wife, Margaretta Sergeant Meade (1814–86), and their daughter, Maggie (Margaret) (1845–1905); William Wharton Jr. (1830–1907), a Philadelphia businessman; Meade's staff officer James C. Biddle and his wife, Gertrude; Fannie and Annie Cadwalader, sisters of Meade's staff officer Captain Cadwalader; and Morton Pearson Henry (1826–1901), a Philadelphia attorney. Hardman Norris is unidentified. Others in the party included Meade's chief of staff, Maj. Gen. Alexander Webb, and his wife and Bvt. Brig. Gen. James Hardie, inspector general of the army. Lowe, *Meade's Army,* 348.

11. WBR mentions later that this camp was located near Parke's Station on the US Military Railroad.

12. Although it initially met with success, surprising and overwhelming the IX Corps picket line and capturing Fort Stedman, the Southern assault on March 25 was soon contained and the fort retaken after heavy fighting. Recognizing that this concentration of force would have produced weak spots elsewhere in the Rebel defenses, Humphreys's II Corps and Wright's VI Corps initiated attacks later in the day that secured four miles of the Confederate picket line in their front. Wright reported the capture of 547 prisoners; Humphreys captured 358. "Wish they would try it every day," commented Meade to one of his officers after the Rebels retreated. President Lincoln, accompanied by his wife, had arrived at City Point on March 25 for conferences with Grant, and the fighting he witnessed (from the safety of Fort Wadsworth, along the Weldon Railroad) occurred on the VI Corps front. Mrs. Lincoln; Grant and his wife, Julia; and Meade were also present. The president had reviewed Brig. Gen. Samuel Crawford's V Corps division before watching the fighting. Greene, *Final Battles of the Petersburg Campaign*, 116, 133, 135; *OR* 46(3):182; Nevins, *Diary of Battle*, 504; Walker, *Second Corps*, 651; Lowe, *Meade's Army*, 350.

13. Properly known as Fort Sedgwick, "Fort Hell," which sat astride the Jerusalem Plank Road, earned its cognomen due to the severity of the picket fire and shelling its occupants experienced. Located only several hundred yards away from Rebel Fort Mahone (nicknamed Fort Damnation), it had been constructed by V Corps troops and engineers in July 1864. Sheridan and his two divisions of cavalry, numbering approximately 10,000 men, reached the Army of the Potomac on March 26. Hess, *Trenches at Petersburg*, 57; Grant, *Memoirs* 2:428.

14. Two divisions of the XXIV Corps and one division of the XXV Corps, accompanied by the cavalry division of the Army of the James under Brig. Gen. Ranald Mackenzie, were transferred to man the lines being vacated by the Army of the Potomac prior to their movement against the Confederate left. Mackenzie's horsemen would later join Sheridan's cavalry command. Grant, *Memoirs* 2:434.

15. Greene, *Final Battles of the Petersburg Campaign*, 152.

16. WBR was unaware that the X Corps had been broken up in December 1864. Its black brigades were absorbed by the XXV Corps, while its white troops were used to form the XXIV Corps, both of which belonged to the Army of the James. None of these troops were involved in the movements described by WBR, although, as noted earlier, elements of both corps backfilled the trenches vacated by the II Corps when it moved west.

17. On March 29 Sheridan and his cavalry divisions (which were led by Brigadier Generals Devin and Custer—both under the command of Major General Merritt—and Major General Crook, who had taken command of Gregg's 2nd Division in late March after Gregg's resignation in February) marched south to Reams Station on the Weldon Railroad and then headed west to Dinwiddie Court House, along the Boydton Plank Road. This movement put Sheridan on the far right flank of the Army of Northern Virginia, five miles from a strategic crossroads known as Five Forks, itself only three miles due south of the vital South Side Railroad. The cavalry division of the Army of the James, which had been under the command of Kautz but was now led by Mackenzie, would join Sheridan's command on the morning of April 1. Longacre, *Lincoln's Cavalrymen*, 324; Longacre, *Army of Amateurs*, 292.

18. Sheridan was riding to meet with Grant at his headquarters on March 30. An aide who was with him recalled that the group was made up of Sheridan, several staff officers, and a dozen escorts and noted the disturbance they created: "This little party raised an immense commotion on the picket line of the army, and only after such persevering dumb-show as the friendly Friday made to Robinson Crusoe was it permitted to approach." Grant had received word from his commanders fronting Petersburg a day earlier that the Rebel lines they faced looked vulnerable. Sheridan informed him at this meeting that, with infantry support, he believed he was in a position to roll up Lee's right flank. Grant placed Warren's V Corps under Sheridan and ordered his troops fronting Petersburg to prepare to attack. Wittenberg, *With Sheridan in the Final Campaign*, 31; Catton, *Grant Takes Command*, 441.

19. Sherman had actually arrived to meet with Grant on March 27. The following day the pair, with Sheridan present, conferenced with Lincoln aboard the *River Queen,* the steamer that had ferried him from the capital. The president was uneasy at the possibility of Lee linking up with Johnston but was mollified by reassurances from his generals. The group also discussed the future movements of the armies and the terms of surrender to be offered in the event of victory. Catton, *Grant Takes Command,* 435–39.

20. Lee had reacted to the late March movements of the Federals by sending five infantry brigades (later joined by a sixth from Petersburg), under Maj. Gen. George Pickett, from the Bermuda Hundred front near Richmond to secure the area around the crossroads at Five Forks—safeguarding the South Side Railroad in the process—and to bolster the cavalry that had been disputing Sheridan's advance. These troops were soon reinforced by cavalry under the Confederate commander's son Maj. Gen. W. H. F. "Rooney" Lee, his nephew Maj. Gen. Fitzhugh Lee, and additional infantry under Maj. Gen. Thomas L. Rosser. On March 31 Sheridan had moved north from Dinwiddie Court House toward Five Forks but was hit on his western flank by Southern cavalry and in front by Pickett's infantry, which forced him back. In conjunction with Sheridan's advance, Warren's V Corps had been ordered to move against the Southern positions at Five Forks in hopes of breaking through and cutting off the Rebels to the west. As he approached the White Oak Road, Warren was preemptively attacked by four Southern infantry brigades and sent back in disarray, though he recovered and stabilized his line.

21. Dabney's Mill was located on the western (southern) side of Hatcher's Run, one-half mile southwest of Armstrong's Mill, three-fourths of a mile northwest of the Vaughan Road. *OR Atlas,* plate 74, map 2.

22. The hamlet of Jetersville, located seven and a half miles southwest of Amelia Court House, was situated near the Richmond & Danville Railroad. WBR mistakenly refers to it as Jetersville Station.

23. Following the fighting on March 31, Warren and his V Corps had been ordered to move west to join with Sheridan. Sheridan had hoped the infantry would arrive in time to hit Pickett in the open on his left flank, but the Virginian, alive to the danger the V Corps posed, returned to his lines on the White Oak Road near Five Forks before Warren's men could attack. Although they were protected by hastily reinforced fieldworks, the Rebels at Five Forks were isolated three miles outside of their lines. Sheridan devised a plan for April 1 that called for the V Corps to hit the Southern works through the gap on their left while his cavalry would move against the Rebels' right and center. Fighting began that afternoon and turned into a Confederate rout when the V Corps collapsed the Pickett's left flank and penetrated through to the rear of his defenses. Despite this overwhelming success—over 4,000 prisoners were taken, 600 Rebels were killed, and the South Side Railroad was all but under Northern control—Sheridan was displeased with Warren, believing him too slow in forming for the attack, and relieved the general of corps command, replacing him with 1st Division commander Maj. Gen. Charles Griffin. Longacre, *Lincoln's Cavalrymen,* 326–27; Hess, *Trenches at Petersburg,* 262–63.

24. As a result of the success of his Eighth Offensive, Grant launched his Ninth (and final) Offensive beginning on April 2. "I have ordered an immediate assault all along the lines," he told his staff officers on the night of April 1. Following a three-hour bombardment, assaults began in the early dawn hours by Parke's IX Corps east of Petersburg and Wright's VI Corps to the city's southwest. The VI Corps attack broke through the Rebel fieldworks, and, supported by troops of the XXIV and XXV Corps from Ord's Army of the James, Wright's troops turned to the east and swept toward Petersburg. Humphreys's II Corps, positioned to the left of the XXIV Corps, also attacked on April 2 and, after several assaults were repulsed, secured Sutherland's Station on the South Side Railroad. Porter, *Campaigning With Grant,* 443; Hess, *Trenches at Petersburg,* 277–78.

25. *OR* 46(3):1379.

26. Trudeau, *Out of the Storm*, 89; Calkins, *Appomattox Campaign*, 58.

27. Custer's cavalry division, leading the pursuit of Lee's army, encountered rearguard Confederate cavalry and infantry blocking its advance on the western side of Namozine Creek on the morning of April 3. The general sent a regiment across the creek to flank the troops opposing him, forcing the Southerners, under the command of Brig. Gen. William P. Roberts, to retreat. Later that day, three of Custer's regiments again defeated a blocking force of cavalry posted at Namozine Church, capturing 350 Southerners. Calkins, *Appomattox Campaign*, 70–71.

28. "A funny incident occurred when Paddy Walsh, Lt. Col. of the Third Penn. Cav. passed with his regiment," Meade's sharp-eyed aide Lyman wrote on April 4. "The troops mistook him for Grant and cheered him; all of which he took with great dignity!" Dennisville, a small hamlet in southern Amelia County, lay along the Namozine Road approximately six miles northwest of Burkeville Junction on the South Side Railroad (here also known as the Lynchburg & Petersburg). Lowe, *Meade's Army*, 360.

29. The rations that Lee had anticipated would be waiting for his army at Amelia Court House had not materialized when he arrived on the morning of April 4 (though there were ample supplies of ammunition). With his troops converging on the town throughout the day, the general appealed to the local citizens for provisions. By midday on April 5, however, it was apparent that little would be gleaned from the neighboring countryside, and Lee ordered his men to continue southwest along the general line of the Richmond & Danville Railroad. The charge mentioned by WBR was made on April 5 by Davies's 1st Brigade of Crook's 2nd Division. Davies had learned that a large supply train was moving four miles from his position at Painesville and attacked it, capturing a battery and scattering the guards protecting the wagons. He then seized the men and horses and burned the wagons: "in a short time I was on my return to Jetersville with 5 guns, 11 flags, 320 white prisoners, and equal number of colored teamsters and over 400 animals captured from the enemy, leaving behind me 200 blazing ammunition and headquarters wagons, caissons and ambulances." The commander of the 1st Pennsylvania Cavalry wrote that his regiment secured, among other prizes, "a bright new, spick-and-span battery of Armstrong field guns, which shortly before had been presented by the ladies of Liverpool to the corporation of the city of Richmond." Calkins, *Appomattox Campaign*, 75–76, 85; *OR* 46(1):1145; Thomas, "Some Personal Reminiscences," 24.

30. As the Army of Northern Virginia moved out of Amelia Court House on April 5, they found their route to the southwest blocked at Jetersville by Sheridan's cavalry and Griffin's V Corps. Instead of attacking, Lee directed a move around the Federal left and a march west to Farmville, located on the South Side Railroad twenty-three miles away. Once there, his army would resupply, move due south to link with the Richmond & Danville Railroad again, and head southwest toward Danville. On April 6, Federal cavalry pursuing the Rebels on a parallel line to their south initiated attacks against Lee's supply trains wending westward. Gaps developed in the Southern column as a result, and during several separate pitched battles near Sailor's Creek, assaults by Federal cavalry, the VI Corps, and the II Corps resulted in the capture of over 7,000 of Lee's veterans and eight general officers, including Lieutenant General Ewell, Maj. Gen. Joseph Kershaw, and Maj. Gen. G. W. "Custis" Lee, eldest son of the Confederate commander. Calkins, *Appomattox Campaign*, 90–92, 99–100, 105–15.

31. Fourteen hundred wagons were used by the Army of Northern Virginia in the evacuation of Richmond and Petersburg; of that number up to three hundred were designated to carry paperwork belonging to organizations and units ranging in size from corps to regiment. A portion of Ewell's trains were attacked, ransacked, and burned on the morning of April 5 near Painesville. For an overview of this aspect of Lee's retreat and the Federal response to it, see Bohannon, "Many Valuable Records and Documents Were Lost to History," 170–91.

32. Following the setbacks at Sailor's Creek, Lee continued to move to Farmville, reaching the small railroad town on the morning of April 7, the Federals following close behind. The first government rations the Southern soldiers had seen since leaving the environs of Petersburg and Richmond were waiting there, and after issuing them to his exhausted men, Lee ordered his army to cross to the north side of the Appomattox River. He had given up hope of reaching Danville to the southwest; instead he determined to march due west to Lynchburg, destroying the river crossings behind him to slow his pursuers. Lee had directed that a key crossing of the Appomattox, a 2,400-foot structure known as High Bridge, four miles east of Farmville, be burned after a portion of his army crossed it. But troops of the Union II Corps secured the crossing before it was consumed, enabling them to continue a close pursuit of the Army of Northern Virginia north of the river. Calkins, *Appomattox Campaign*, 116.

33. After crossing the Appomattox River at High Bridge, Humphreys's II Corps, followed by the VI Corps, which had also moved to the north side of the river, pursued Lee, catching up with his rear guard late in afternoon of April 8. WBR, attached to Meade's headquarters, accompanied this column. South of the river, Sheridan and the cavalry, along with the infantry from Ord's Army of the James and Griffin's V Corps, followed on a roughly parallel route. Sheridan had learned that Lee was headed for Appomattox Station to secure supplies, and by dint of hard riding by his troopers (and willful marching by the infantry, some of whom covered nearly forty miles this day), he had his cavalry blocking the Rebels' path on the Lynchburg Road at Appomattox, the Union infantry within supporting distance. Longacre, *Army of Amateurs*, 307.

34. New Stores, which is shown on period maps as New Store, was located on the Lynchburg Road west of Curdsville and approximately fifteen miles east of Appomattox Court House on a direct line. *OR Atlas*, plate 5, map 76.

35. Lee attacked the Federal cavalry cordon preventing his move to the west on April 9, but troops from the Army of the James arrived in time to reinforce the cavalrymen and block any breakthrough. This reverse, combined with the II and VI Corps advancing on his rear, convinced the Confederate commander that he had no alternative but to surrender. Lee was hemmed in in nearly every direction except to his northwest, which, as WBR has alluded to, was without a road network that could support his troops and trains. During the surrender proceedings over the next several days, 23,500 infantry, 2,500 artillerymen, and just over 1,550 cavalrymen gave up their arms. Calkins, *Appomattox Campaign*, 165, 187–88, 192.

36. Coleman Hall Watts (1845–96) was formerly a member of the 7th Pennsylvania Cavalry. He had joined the 7th, which campaigned exclusively in the western theater, in March 1864, serving as a sergeant of Company M and as sergeant major of the regiment. Although Watts had been commissioned as first lieutenant in WBR's Company B to date from January 17, 1865, he did not join the 3rd until April 3. Regimental History Committee, *Third Pennsylvania*, 568–69, 489; Bates, *History of Pennsylvania Volunteers*, 2:1122, 1162; Sipes, *Seventh Pennsylvania Veteran Volunteer Cavalry*, 136.

37. New Orleans native Francis Rawle (1835–1913) had been commissioned as the captain of Company C of the 1st Louisiana Infantry in April 1861 and became the regimental quartermaster of the 10th Louisiana in June 1862. Promoted to major and quartermaster in October 1862, he served in several brigade-level assignments (including quartermaster of the Louisiana Brigade) during the balance of the war. Rawle was among the remaining members of the Army of Northern Virginia surrendered at Appomattox. Krick, *Staff Officers in Gray*, 250; *OR* 36(3):879.

38. The inference here being that most of the 2nd Virginia Infantry, of which WBR's cousin Sergeant Lewis was a member (and mentioned in WBR's letters of January 31, May 16, and May 19, 1864), was captured and being held at the Federal prison at Point Lookout,

Maryland. The statement was not entirely untruthful. When the 2nd Virginia surrendered at Appomattox, it counted only seventy-one men in its ranks, including Lewis.

39. Regimental History Committee, *Third Pennsylvania,* 548–49.

40. An error. Lincoln was not interred until May 4.

41. Johnston and Sherman had agreed to and signed the terms of surrender for Johnston's troops on April 18, but authorities in Washington, believing them to be too far reaching and lenient, ordered them withdrawn. New terms were agreed to and ratified by both sides on April 26. Catton, *This Hallowed Ground,* 392–93.

42. "The country through which the army was moving had seen nothing of the war," wrote a member of the V Corps regarding their march through Prince Edward County. "It was a fertile, productive region, and the well-stocked larders of what were yet thrifty plantations paid handsome tribute to the exorbitant exactions of the hungry soldiers." A soldier of the 20th Maine remembered: "Foraging was good. . . . Tobacco, molasses, bacon, cattle, sheep, pigs and poultry were occasionally found, and were quickly appropriated to our use. . . . Thus the whole route from Five Forks to Appomattox was filled with incidents never to be forgotten." Survivor's Association, *History of the Corn Exchange Regiment,* 587; Gerrish, *Army Life,* 252.

43. A. D. Dickinson, a member of the Virginia House of Delegates (1859–60), is otherwise unidentifiable.

44. Capt. William H. Atwell had joined 7th Tennessee Infantry as a private in May 1861. Present at Lee's surrender at Appomattox, he had been the acting commissary of subsistence on the staff of Major General Heth. Originally a division commander in the Third Corps, Heth had assumed command of the corps following Lieutenant General Hill's death near Petersburg on April 2. Krick, *Staff Officers in Gray,* 64.

45. The Shockoe Bottom section of Richmond lies to the southeast of the downtown area, fronting the James River. Much of it was burned when retreating Confederate soldiers set fire to tobacco-filled warehouses during the evacuation of the capital on the night of April 2–3. Church Hill, comprising the earliest settled area of Richmond, is a thirty-two-block area in the center of the city.

46. Two unrelated individuals with the surname Turner played a prominent role in the lives of Union soldiers held at Libby Prison. Maj. Thomas P. Turner was the commandant of Libby. Richard R. "Dick" Turner was the jailer and was responsible for enforcing discipline within the prison, which he meted out, sometimes severely, with regularity. Turner the jailer was captured soon after Lee's surrender and incarcerated in Libby, so he is likely the man WBR mentions. Parker, *Richmond's Civil War Prisons,* 11, 67–68.

47. Early was not near Richmond when the fires that devoured a large section of the city were started, but Ewell was, as he commanded the military forces defending the Confederate capital. Directed to prevent tobacco, cotton, and other supplies from falling into enemy hands in the event of the city's evacuation, Ewell had ordered the consolidation of the tobacco into several warehouses near the James River, where it was thought it could be burned without danger to neighboring structures. Firemen were assigned to monitor the blazes but unaccountably found their hoses cut and were thus unable to contain the flames. Furgurson, *Ashes of Glory,* 328, 333–36.

48. Winder Hospital, located on the western outskirts of Richmond, was the largest hospital in the Confederacy. The facility comprised ninety-eight buildings and could accommodate 4,300 patients. Waitt, *Confederate Military Hospitals in Richmond,* 21–22.

49. An intimate of the unapologetic secessionist Edmund Ruffin, William Boulware (1811–70) served as US minister to Naples from 1841 until 1845. Accounts differ as to whether Pres. William Henry Harrison, who died in April 1841 after a month in office, or John Tyler, who succeeded him, was responsible for Boulware's appointment, but it was not Franklin Pierce (as

WBR believed). As of this writing, the house in Newton, Virginia, where WBR arrested Boulware survives as a sportsman's club.

50. Robert Mercer Taliaferro Hunter (1809–87) had served as Speaker of the House of Representatives from 1839 to 1841 and was elected to represent Virginia in the Senate in 1847, serving until just before the outbreak of war, which he had labored to prevent by compromise. Following a brief stint in the Confederate Congress, Hunter was appointed secretary of state, serving until February 1862, when he was elected to the Confederate Senate. He served as a senator until the collapse of the Confederacy. After his imprisonment and release, Hunter resisted Reconstruction efforts in his state.

EPILOGUE

1. WBR to Mother, June 5, 1865.

2. WBR to Mother, May 19, 1865

3. War Department General Orders no. 83, May 8, 1865, quoted in Regimental History Committee, *Third Pennsylvania*, 498.

4. The soldiers who deserted were Sgt. John Deans and a Private Pettinger, who I have been unable to more completely identify. Deans was an original member of Philadelphia-raised Company C. He had deserted earlier in the war at an unspecified date (as had Pettinger, according to WBR) but had returned and was transferred to the veteran battalion in July 1864. He was then promoted to corporal, sergeant, and first sergeant. Regimental History Committee, *Third Pennsylvania*, 587.

5. WBR to Mother, May 29, 1865.

6. McCulloh (1818–94) would be captured in Florida at the end of May and imprisoned at Washington, DC, and later Richmond until his release in March 1866. Several months later, at the invitation of Robert E. Lee, he joined the faculty of Washington College, where the former general was serving as president. Thomas, "Professor McCulloh," 17–29.

7. Information regarding the 5th Pennsylvania was assembled from the short historical sketch of the regiment in Bates, *History of Pennsylvania Volunteers*, 2:568–77; Sauers, *Advance the Colors!*, 1:182–83; and Longacre, "Most Inept Regiment," 4–7.

8. WBR to Mother, June 5, 1865.

9. The 3rd's four companies were designated I, K, L (commanded by WBR), and M in the 5th Pennsylvania. Six officers of the 3rd were discharged as a result of the consolidation. Regimental History Committee, *Third Pennsylvania*, 500.

10. "During the *skedaddle* from Richmond, this box was thrown into a car and let go to the 'Old Harry.'" WBR to Mother, June 22, 1865.

11. WBR to Mother, June 25, 1865.

12. Capt. Clarence Morfit was an assistant quartermaster in Richmond and had reported to his superiors in late April that "the chest of valuables, containing also the books and papers relating to the prisoners' funds," had been left in Danville and, he believed, had been turned over to civil authorities. Morfit had been in charge of collecting and providing receipts for all of the US currency confiscated from Federal prisoners in Richmond but was arrested in the aftermath of the war on suspicion mishandling these funds. The board assembled to investigate the alleged improprieties exonerated Morfit of any wrongdoing. *OR* ser. 2, 8:457, 512, 706–7.

13. WBR to Mother, June 25, 1865. As a former Confederate officer remarked to WBR during his stay there, "It was Confederate fare, at Confederate prices, paid in Federal money." WBR Diary, June 20, 1865, transcript.

14. WBR explained that the money he received had been entrusted to the Reverend Dame by "Maj. Carrington, late C.S. Provost Marshal of Richmond." Reverend Dame would be warmly recalled by many of the prisoners who were held in Danville: "Though Northern born, his early going to the South, his education at Hampden-Sidney, his marriage and long residence in Virginia, all combined to make his prejudices in favor of secession; but he was more than rebel or federal, he was a Christian man. . . . His talks to the men were always most respectfully received, and when in the following April, the Sixth corps entered Danville, no one received more considerate attention than the Rev George W. Dame." Roe, "In a Rebel Prison."

15. WBR to Mother, July 3, 1865.

16. WBR complained that the 5th Pennsylvania was also better equipped than the 3rd had been: "Somehow the Army of the James could get a great many more things than we of the Potomac, and as the 5th was with the A. of J., they have all they want. While we had 3 wagons the 5th had 14." WBR Diary, June 26, 1865, transcript.

17. WBR to Mother, June 11, 1865.

18. WBR to Mother, May 19, 29, 1865.

19. WBR to Mother, July 13, 1865.

20. WBR to Mother, July 21, 1865. WBR wrote in his diary that rather than pleading with the men, "a regiment of infantry, and short range," would have been far more persuasive but noted that General Terry had ordered that no bloodshed take place. "Dissatisfaction with the consolidation is at the bottom of the whole thing," he observed.

21. WBR Diary, July 18, 1865, transcript. Thirty-three men were identified as organizers of the mutiny and remained in prison. They were tried by court-martial and sentenced to be dishonorably discharged, forfeit their pay, and perform hard labor for up to eighteen months in the Dry Tortugas. Their sentences were never carried out. Regimental History Committee, *Third Pennsylvania,* 511.

22. WBR to Mother, July 27, 1865.

23. WBR Diary, Aug. 11, 1865, typescript; Elizabeth T. Rawle to Mama, Aug. 14, 1865, WBR Letters, Foundations of the Union League of Philadelphia.

24. WBR Diary, Aug. 12, 1865, transcript.

25. WBR to Mother June 11, 1865.

26. General Orders no. 84 (Washington, DC: War Department, Oct. 14, 1868), 10, 16.

BIBLIOGRAPHY

MANUSCRIPT SOURCES

J. GREGORY ACKEN PERSONAL COLLECTION
Edson Justus Cheever letters (typescript copies)

THE FOUNDATIONS OF THE UNION LEAGUE OF PHILADELPHIA
William Brooke Rawle Letters
William Brooke Rawle Diary (typescript copy)

GILDER LEHRMAN INSTITUTE OF AMERICAN HISTORY, NEW YORK
Charles Woolston Correspondence

HISTORICAL SOCIETY OF PENNSYLVANIA, PHILADELPHIA
William Brooke Rawle Papers
Walter S. Newhall, Correspondence and Diary, Newhall Family Papers
James C. Biddle Papers

NATIONAL GUARD OF PENNSYLVANIA LIBRARY, PHILADELPHIA
Henry T. Peck Letters

NEW YORK PUBLIC LIBRARY
Joseph D. Galloway Diaries

US ARMY HERITAGE AND EDUCATION CENTER, CARLISLE, PA
Robert L. Brake Collection
Francis Dring Wetherill memoir

NEWSPAPERS

Philadelphia Inquirer
New York World
New York American

BOOKS AND ARTICLES

Acken, J. Gregory, ed. *Inside the Army of the Potomac: The Civil War Experience of Captain Francis Adams Donaldson*. Mechanicsburg, PA: Stackpole Books, 1998.

——, ed. *Service with the Signal Corps: The Civil War Memoir of Captain Louis R. Fortescue*. Knoxville: Univ. of Tennessee Press, 2015.

Adams, Charles Francis. *Charles Francis Adams, 1835–1915: An Autobiography*. Boston: Houghton Mifflin, 1916.

Aggasiz, George R., ed. *Meade's Headquarters, 1863–1865: Letters of Colonel Theodore Lyman from the Wilderness to Appomattox*. Boston: Atlantic Monthly Press, 1922.

Alexander, Edward Porter. *Military Memoirs of a Confederate: A Critical Narrative*. New York: Charles Scribner's Sons, 1907.

Allen, Stanton P. *Down in Dixie: Life in a Cavalry Regiment in the War Days, from the Wilderness to Appomattox*. Boston: D. Lothrop, 1893.

Anderson, John A. *The Fifty-Seventh Regiment of Massachusetts Volunteers in the War of the Rebellion, Army of the Potomac*. Boston: E. B. Stillings, 1896.

The Annals of the War, Written by Leading Participants North and South. Philadelphia: Times Publishing, 1879.

Annual Report of the Adjutant General of Pennsylvania. . . . for the Year 1863. Harrisburg: Singerly and Myers, 1864.

Aubrey, James M. *The Thirty-Sixth Wisconsin Infantry, 1st Brigade, 2nd Division, 2nd Army Corps, Army of the Potomac*. Milwaukee: Evening Wisconsin, 1900.

Basler, Roy P., ed. *The Collected Works of Abraham Lincoln*. 10 vols. and index. New Brunswick, NJ: Rutgers University Press, 1953.

Bates, Samuel P. *History of Pennsylvania Volunteers, 1861–5; Prepared in Compliance with Acts of the Legislature*. 5 vols. Harrisburg: PA: State Printer, 1869–71.

Bennett, Edwin C. *Musket and Sword*. Boston: Coburn, 1900.

Benton, Josiah. *Voting in the Field: A Forgotten Chapter of the Civil War*. Boston: privately printed, 1915.

Bigelow, John C. *The Campaign of Chancellorsville*. New Haven, CT: Yale Univ. Press, 1910.

Billings, John D. *The History of the Tenth Massachusetts Battery of Light Artillery in the War of the Rebellion, 1862–1865*. Boston: Arakelyan, 1909.

Bledsoe, Andrew S. *Citizen Officers: The Union and Confederate Volunteer Junior Officer Corps in the American Civil War*. Baton Rouge: Louisiana State Univ. Press, 2015.

Blight, David W., ed. *When This Cruel War Is Over: The Civil War Letters of Charles Harvey Brewster*. Amherst: University of Massachusetts Press, 1992.

Bohannon, Keith. "Many Valuable Records and Documents Were Lost to History: The Destruction of Confederate Military Records during the Appomattox Campaign." In Janney, *Petersburg to Appomattox*, 170–91.

Bosbyshell, Oliver. *Campaigns of the 48th Regiment, Infantry, Pennsylvania Veteran Volunteers, during the War of the Rebellion*. Philadelphia: Avil Printing, 1895.

Boston, William. *The Civil War Diary of William Boston, a Union Soldier of Company H, Twentieth Michigan Volunteer Infantry, Ninth Corps*. Ann Arbor, 1937.

Buckingham, Peter, ed. *All's for the Best: The Civil War Reminiscences and Letters of Daniel W. Sawtelle, Eighth Maine Volunteer Infantry*. Knoxville: Univ. of Tennessee Press, 2001.

Burnett, William G. *Better a Patriot Soldier's Grave: The History of the Sixth Ohio Volunteer Cavalry*. N.p.,1982.

Burns, Vincent L. *The Fifth New York Cavalry in the Civil War*. Jefferson, NC: McFarland, 2014.

Burt, Nathaniel. *The Perennial Philadelphians: The Anatomy of an American Aristocracy*. Philadelphia: Univ. of Pennsylvania Press, 1963.

Calkins, Chris. *The Appomattox Campaign, March 29–April 9, 1865*. Conshohocken, PA: Combined Books, 1997.

Campbell, Eric A., ed. *A Grand Terrible Dramma. From Gettysburg to Petersburg: The Civil War Letters of Charles Wellington Reed*. NY: Fordham Univ. Press, 2000.

Carhart, Tom. *Lost Triumph: Lee's Real Plan at Gettysburg and Why It Failed*. New York: G. P. Putnam's Sons, 2005.

Carpenter, J. Edward. "Gregg's Cavalry at Gettysburg." In *Annals of the War*, 527–35.

Carter, Robert Goldthwaite. *Four Brothers in Blue; or, Sunshine and Shadows of the War of the Rebellion: A Story of the Great Civil War from Bull Run to Appomattox*. 1913. Reprint, Austin: Univ. of Texas Press, 1979.

———. *Tragedies of Canon Blanco: A Story of the Texas Panhandle*. Washington, DC: Gibson Brothers, 1919.

Cassedy, Edward K., ed. *Dear Friends at Home: The Civil War Letters and Diaries of Sergeant Charles T. Bowen, Twelfth United States Infantry, 1861–1864*. Baltimore: Butternut and Blue, 1991.

Catton, Bruce. *Grant Takes Command*. Boston: Little, Brown, 1968.

———. *This Hallowed Ground: The Story of the Union Side of the Civil War*. Garden City, NY: Doubleday, 1956.

Chamberlin, Thomas. *History of the One Hundred and Fiftieth Regiment Pennsylvania Volunteers, Second Regiment, Bucktail Brigade*. Philadelphia: F. McManus Jr., 1905.

Charles, Henry Fitzgerald. *Civil War Record, 1862–1865*. Compiled by Edwin Fitzgerald Charles and John Elwood Charles. N.p., 1969.

Cheney, Newell. *History of the Ninth Regiment New York Volunteer Cavalry, War of 1861 to 1865*. Jamestown, NY: Martin Merz and Son, 1901.

Cleaves, Freeman. *Meade of Gettysburg*. Norman: Univ. of Oklahoma Press, 1960.

Coco, Gregory A., ed. *Through Blood and Fire: The Civil War Letters of Major Charles J. Mills, 1862–1865*. Gettysburg, PA, 1982.

Collis, Septima Levy. *A Woman's War Record, 1861–1865*. New York: G. P. Putnam's Sons, 1889.

Constitution and By-laws of Company H, Third Pennsylvania Cavalry, with a Brief History and Muster Roll. Shippensburg, PA: D. K. and J. C. Wagner, Printers, 1878.

Cooper, William J. *Jefferson Davis: American*. New York: Alfred A. Knopf, 2000.

Cowtan, Charles H. *Services of the Tenth New York Volunteers (National Zouaves) in the War of the Rebellion*. New York: Charles H. Ludwig, 1882.

Craven, Avery. *Edmund Ruffin, Southerner*. New York: D. Appleton, 1932.

Crowninshield, Benjamin W. *A History of the First Regiment of Massachusetts Cavalry Volunteers*. Boston: Houghton Mifflin, 1891.

Cuffel, Charles A. *History of Durell's Battery in the Civil War (Independent Battery D, Pennsylvania Volunteer Artillery): A Narrative of the Campaigns and Battles of the Berks and Bucks Counties' Artillerists in the War of the Rebellion from the Battery's Organization, September 24, 1861, to Its Muster Out of Service, June 13, 1865*. Philadelphia: Craig, Finley, 1903.

Curtis, Orson B. *History of the Twenty-Fourth Michigan of the Iron Brigade, Known as the Detroit and Wayne County Regiment*. Detroit: Winn and Hammond, 1891.

Dalton, John C. *Memorial of Edward B. Dalton, M.D.* New York, 1872.

Davis, William C. *Lincoln's Men: How President Lincoln Became Father to an Army and a Nation*. New York: Free Press, 1999.

Denison, Rev. Frederic. *Sabres and Spurs: The First Regiment Rhode Island Cavalry in the Civil War, 1861–1865*. Central Falls, RI: E. L. Freeman, 1876.

De Trobriand, Regis. *Four Years with the Army of the Potomac*. Boston: Ticknor, 1889.

Eckert, Edward K., and Nicholas J. Amato, eds. *Ten Years in the Saddle: The Memoir of William Woods Averell, 1851–1862*. San Rafael, CA: Presidio, 1978.

Eden, Robert C. *Sword and Gun: A History of the 37th Wis. Volunteer Infantry, from Its Organization to Its Final Muster Out.* Madison, WI: Atwood and Rublee, 1865.

Edmonds, Howard Owen. *Owen Edmonds, Incidents of the American Civil War, 1861–1865, Prepared from Family Records by Howard Owen Edmonds.* Chicago: Lakeside, 1928.

Egle, William H. *Life and Times of Andrew Gregg Curtin.* Philadelphia: Thompson, 1896.

Fishel, Edwin C. *The Secret War for the Union: The Untold Story of Military Intelligence in the Civil War.* Boston: Houghton Mifflin, 1996.

Foote, Lorien. *The Gentlemen and the Roughs: Violence, Honor, and Manhood in the Union Army.* New York: New York Univ. Press, 2010.

Ford, Worthington C., ed. *A Cycle of Adams Letters, 1861–1865.* 2 vols. Boston: Houghton Mifflin, 1920.

Forty Second Annual Reunion of the Association of the Graduates of the United States Military Academy at West Point, New York, June 12th, 1911. Saginaw, MI: Seeman and Peters, 1911.

Fox, William F. *New York at Gettysburg.* 3 vols. Albany, NY: J. B. Lyon, 1900.

Gaines, W. Craig. *Encyclopedia of Civil War Shipwrecks.* Baton Rouge: Louisiana State Univ. Press, 2008.

Gallagher, Gary W., ed. *Chancellorsville: The Battle and Its Aftermath.* Chapel Hill: Univ. of North Carolina Press, 1996.

———, ed. *The Spotsylvania Campaign.* Chapel Hill: Univ. of North Carolina Press, 1997.

———. *The Union War.* Cambridge, MA: Harvard Univ. Press, 2011.

———, ed. *The Wilderness Campaign.* Chapel Hill: Univ. of North Carolina Press, 1998.

Gallagher, Gary W., and Caroline E. Janney, eds. *Cold Harbor to the Crater: The End of the Overland Campaign.* Chapel Hill: Univ. of North Carolina Press, 2015.

Gallman, J. Matthew. *Mastering Wartime: A Social History of Philadelphia during the Civil War.* Philadelphia: Univ. of Pennsylvania Press, 2000.

Gause, Isaac. *Four Years with Five Armies: Army of the Frontier, Army of the Potomac, Army of the Missouri, Army of the Ohio, Army of the Shenandoah.* New York: Neale, 1908.

George, Henry, Jr. *The Life of Henry George, by His Son, Henry George, Jr.* London: William Reeves, 1900.

Gerrish, Theodore. *Army Life: A Private's Reminiscences of the Civil War.* Portland, ME: Hoyt, Fogg, and Dunham, 1882.

Gienapp, William E., and Erica L. Gienapp, eds. *The Civil War Diary of Gideon Welles, Lincoln's Secretary of the Navy: The Original Manuscript Edition.* Urbana: Univ. of Illinois Press, 2014.

Gilmore, David M. "Cavalry: Its Use and Value as Illustrated by Reference to the Engagements of Kelly's Ford and Gettysburg." *Military Order of the Loyal Legion of the United States, Minnesota Commandery, Glimpses of the Nation's Struggles,* 2nd ser., 2:38–51. St. Paul, MN: St. Paul Book and Stationery, 1890.

———. "With General Gregg at Gettysburg." *Military Order of the Loyal Legion of the United States, Minnesota Commandery, Glimpses of the Nation's Struggles.* 2nd ser., 4:92–111. St. Paul, MN: St. Paul Book and Stationery, 1893.

Goss, Warren Lee. *Recollections of a Private: A Story of the Army of the Potomac.* New York: Thomas Y. Crowell, 1890.

Gough, Deborah Mathias. *Christ Church Philadelphia: The Nation's Church in a Changing City.* Philadelphia: Univ. of Pennsylvania Press, 1995.

Gracey, Samuel L. *Annals of the Sixth Pennsylvania Cavalry.* Philadelphia: H. E. Butler, 1868.

Grant, Ulysses S. *Personal Memoirs of U. S. Grant.* 2 vols. New York: Charles L. Webster, 1886.

Gray, John Chipman, and John Codman Ropes. *War Letters, 1862–1865.* Boston: Houghton Mifflin, 1927.

Greene, A. Wilson. *A Campaign of Giants: The Battle for Petersburg.* Chapel Hill: Univ. of North Carolina Press, 2018.

————. *Civil War Petersburg: Confederate City in the Crucible of War.* Charlottesville: Univ. of Virginia Press, 2006.

————. *The Final Battles of the Petersburg Campaign: Breaking the Backbone of the Rebellion.* Knoxville: Univ. of Tennessee Press, 2012.

Greenleaf, Margery, ed. *Letters to Eliza from a Union Soldier, 1862–1865.* Chicago: Follett, 1970.

Gregg, David McMurtrie. *The Second Cavalry Division of the Army of the Potomac in the Gettysburg Campaign.* Philadelphia, 1907.

————. "The Union Cavalry at Gettysburg." In *Annals of the War,* 372–79.

Greiner, James M., Janet L. Coryell, and James R. Smither, eds. *A Surgeon's Civil War: The Letters & Diary of Daniel M. Holt, M.D.* Kent, OH: Kent State Univ. Press, 1994.

Griffin, Richard N., ed. *Three Years a Soldier: The Diary and Newspaper Correspondence of Private George Perkins, Sixth New York Independent Battery, 1861–1864.* Knoxville: Univ. of Tennessee Press, 2006.

Guelzo, Allen C. *Gettysburg: The Last Invasion.* New York: Alfred A. Knopf, 2013.

Hagerty, Edward J. *Collis' Zouaves: The 114th Pennsylvania Volunteers in the Civil War.* Baton Rouge: Louisiana State Univ. Press, 1997.

Halsey, Milton Thomas. "Professor McCulloh of Princeton, Columbia, and Points South." *Princeton University Library Chronicle* 9, no. 1 (Nov. 1947): 17–29.

Hand, Harold, Jr., *One Good Regiment: The 13th Pennsylvania Cavalry in the Civil War, 1861–1865.* Victoria, BC: Trafford, 2000.

Harrison, William Welsh. *Harrison, Waples, and Allied Families: Being the Ancestry of George Leib Harrison of Philadelphia, and of His Wife Sarah Ann Waples.* Philadelphia: privately printed, 1910.

Haynes, Martin A. *A History of the Second Regiment New Hampshire Volunteer Infantry in the War of the Rebellion.* Lakeport, NH, 1896.

Hays, Gilbert Adams. *Under the Red Patch: Story of the Sixty-Third Regiment Pennsylvania Volunteers, 1861–1864.* Pittsburgh: Sixty-Third Pennsylvania Volunteers Regimental Association, 1908.

Heitman, Francis B. *Historical Register and Dictionary of the United States Army, from Its Organization, September 29, 1789, to March 2, 1903.* 2 vols. Washington, DC: Government Printing Office, 1903.

Henderson, William D. *The Road to Bristoe Station: Campaigning with Lee and Meade, August 1–October 20, 1863.* Lynchburg, VA: H. E. Howard, 1987.

Hennessy, John J., ed. *Fighting with the Eighteenth Massachusetts: The Civil War Memoir of Thomas H. Mann.* Baton Rouge: Louisiana State Univ. Press, 2000.

————. "The Scourge of the Confederacy: The Story of John Minor Botts, Virginia's Most Outspoken Unionist." *Civil War Monitor* 7, no. 1 (Spring 2017): 32–41, 75–77.

————. "We Shall Make Richmond Howl: The Army of the Potomac on the Eve of Chancellorsville." In Gallagher, *Chancellorsville,* 1–35.

Herdegen, Lance, and Sherry Murphy, eds. *Four Years with the Iron Brigade: The Civil War Journal of William Ray.* New York: Da Capo, 1992.

Hess, Earl J. *In the Trenches at Petersburg: Field Fortifications and Confederate Defeat.* Chapel Hill: Univ. of North Carolina Press, 2009.

————. *Trench Warfare under Grant and Lee: Field Fortifications in the Overland Campaign.* Chapel Hill: Univ. of North Carolina Press, 1997.

————. *The Union Soldier in Battle: Enduring the Ordeal of Combat.* Lawrence: Univ. Press of Kansas, 1997.

Hess, Frank W. "The First Cavalry Battle at Kelly's Ford, Va." *First Maine Bugle, Campaign III, Call 3* (July 1893): 3–16.

Hesseltine, William B. *Lincoln and the War Governors.* New York: Alfred A. Knopf, 1948.

Houghton, Edwin B. *Campaigns of the Seventeenth Maine.* Portland, ME: Short and Loring, 1866.

Humphreys, Andrew A. *From Gettysburg to the Rapidan: The Army of the Potomac, July 1863 to April 1864.* New York: Charles Scribner's Sons, 1883.

———. *The Virginia Campaign of '64 and '65: The Army of the Potomac and the Army of the James.* New York: Charles Scribner's Sons, 1883.

Huntington, Tom. *Searching for George Gordon Meade: The Forgotten Victor of Gettysburg.* Mechanicsburg, PA: Stackpole Books, 2013.

Hyde, Thomas W. *Following the Greek Cross; or, Memories of the Sixth Army Corps.* Boston: Houghton Mifflin, 1894.

Hyndman, William. *History of a Cavalry Company: A Complete Record of Company A, Fourth Pennsylvania Cavalry.* Philadelphia: J. B. Rodgers, 1870.

Index to General Orders, the Army of the Potomac, 1865. Philadelphia: Printing Department, Military Division of the Atlantic, 1865.

James, Henry B. *Memories of the Civil War.* New Bedford, MA: Franklin E. James, 1898.

Janney, Caroline E., ed., *Petersburg to Appomattox: The End of the War in Virginia.* Chapel Hill: Univ. of North Carolina Press, 2018.

Jenkins, Howard M. *The Family of William Penn, Founder of Pennsylvania, Ancestry of Descendants.* Philadelphia: By the author, 1899.

Johnson, Robert Underwood, and Clarence Clough Buel, eds. *Battles and Leaders of the Civil War.* 4 vols. New York: Century, 1887.

Jordan, John W., LLD, ed. *Colonial and Revolutionary Families of Philadelphia, Genealogical and Personal Memoirs.* 3 vols. New York, 1911. Reprint, Clearfield, 2004.

Kenner, Charles L. *Buffalo Soldiers and Officers of the Ninth Cavalry, 1867–1898: Black & White Together.* Norman: Univ. of Oklahoma Press, 1999.

Kent, Arthur A., ed. *Three Years with Company K: Sergt. Austin C. Stearns.* Rutherford, NJ: Fairleigh Dickinson Univ. Press, 1976.

Kester, Donald E. *Cavalryman in Blue: Colonel John Wood Kester of the First New Jersey Cavalry in the Civil War.* Hightstown, NJ: Longstreet House, 1997.

Kirk, Hyland C. *Heavy Guns and Light: A History of the Fourth New York Heavy Artillery.* New York: C. T. Dillingham, 1890.

Krick, Robert K. *Staff Officers in Gray: A Biographical Register of Staff Officers in the Army of Northern Virginia.* Chapel Hill: Univ. of North Carolina Press, 2003.

Lewis, George. *The History of Battery E, First Regiment Rhode Island Light Artillery, in the War of 1861 and 1865, to Preserve the Union.* Providence, RI: Snow and Farnham, 1892.

Lewis, John Frederick. "Presentation of Portrait of Colonel William Brooke Rawle, and an Address on His Military Record." *Pennsylvania Magazine of History and Biography* 41 (1917): 126–42.

Lloyd, William P. *History of the First Reg't Pennsylvania Reserve Cavalry, from Its Organization, August, 1861, to September, 1864.* Philadelphia: King and Baird, 1864.

Locke, William Henry. *The Story of the Regiment.* Philadelphia: J. B. Lippincott, 1868.

Longacre, Edward G. *Army of Amateurs: General Benjamin F. Butler and the Army of the James, 1863–65.* Mechanicsburg, PA: Stackpole Books, 1997.

———. *The Cavalry at Gettysburg: A Tactical Study of Mounted Operations during the Civil War's Pivotal Campaign, 9 June–14 July 1863.* Rutherford, NJ: Associated University Presses, 1986.

———. *Lincoln's Cavalrymen: A History of the Mounted Forces of the Army of the Potomac.* Mechanicsburg, PA: Stackpole Books, 2000.

———. "The Most Inept Regiment of the Civil War." *Civil War Times Illustrated* 8 (Nov. 1969): 4–7.

———. *To Gettysburg and Beyond: The Twelfth New Jersey Volunteer Infantry, II Corps, Army of the Potomac, 1861–1865*. Hightstown, NJ: Longstreet House, 1988.

Lord, Edward O., ed. *History of the Ninth Regiment New Hampshire Volunteers in the War of the Rebellion*. Concord, NH: Republican Press Association, 1895.

Lowe, David W., ed. *Meade's Army: The Private Notebooks of Lt. Col. Theodore Lyman*. Kent, OH: Kent State Univ. Press, 2007.

Macnamara, Daniel George. *The History of the Ninth Regiment Massachusetts Volunteer Infantry . . . June, 1861–June, 1864*. Boston: E. B. Stillings, 1899.

Marbaker, Thomas D. *History of the Eleventh New Jersey Volunteers, from Its Organization to Appomattox*. Trenton, NJ: MacQuellish and Quigley, 1898.

Marten, James Alan. *Civil War America: Voices from the Home Front*. New York: Fordham Univ. Press, 2007.

Marter, Joan, ed. *The Grove Encyclopedia of American Art*. 5 vols. New York: Oxford Univ. Press, 2013.

Matter, William D. *If It Takes All Summer: The Battle of Spotsylvania*. Chapel Hill: Univ. of North Carolina Press, 1988.

Maxwell, W. J. *General Alumni Catalog of the University of Pennsylvania, 1922*. Philadelphia: Alumni Association, 1922.

McClellan, H. B. *The Life and Campaigns of Major General J. E. B. Stuart*. Boston: Houghton Mifflin, 1885.

Meade, George Gordon, Jr., ed. *The Life and Letters of George Gordon Meade*. 2 vols. New York: Charles Scribner's Sons, 1913.

Miers, Earl Schenck, ed. *Ride to War: The History of the First New Jersey Cavalry, by Henry R. Pyne*. New Brunswick, NJ: Rutgers Univ. Press, 1961.

Miller, William E. "The Cavalry Battle near Gettysburg." In Johnson and Buel, *Battles and Leaders*, 3:397–406.

Mohr, James C., ed. *The Cormany Diaries: A Northern Family in the Civil War*. Pittsburgh: Univ. of Pittsburgh Press, 1982.

Nevin, Alfred. *Centennial Biography: Men of Mark of Cumberland Valley, PA, 1776–1876*. Philadelphia: Fulton, 1876.

Nevins, Allan, ed. *A Diary of Battle: The Personal Journals of Colonel Charles S. Wainwright 1861–1865*. New York: Harcourt, Brace, and World, 1962.

Norton, Oliver Willcox. *Army Letters, 1861–1865*. Chicago: O. L. Deming, 1903.

O'Neill, Robert F. *Chasing Jeb Stuart and John Mosby: The Union Cavalry in Northern Virginia from Second Manassas to Gettysburg*. Jefferson, NC: McFarland, 2012.

Osceola, Lewis. *History of the One Hundred and Thirty Eighth Regiment, Pennsylvania Volunteer Infantry*. Norristown, PA: Wills, Iredell, and Jenkins, 1866.

Parker, Francis Jewett. *The Story of the Thirty-Second Regiment Massachusetts Infantry: Where It Went, What It Saw, and What It Did*. Boston: C. W. Calkins, 1880.

Parker, Sandra V. *Richmond's Civil War Prisons*. Lynchburg, VA: H. E. Howard, 1990.

Perry, Bliss. *The Life and Letters of Henry Lee Higginson*. Boston: Atlantic Monthly Press, 1921.

Perry, John Gardner. *Letters from a Surgeon of the Civil War*. Boston: Little, Brown, 1906.

Pfanz, Harry W. *Gettysburg: Culps Hill & Cemetery Hill*. Chapel Hill: Univ. of North Carolina Press, 1993.

Pierce, Solon W. *Battlefields and Camp Fires of the Thirty Eighth [Wisconsin Volunteers]*. Milwaukee: Daily Wisconsin Printing House, 1866.

Powell, William H. *The Fifth Army Corps (Army of the Potomac): A Record of Operations During the Civil War in the United States of America, 1861–1865*. New York: G. P. Putnam's Sons, 1896.

———, ed. *Officers of the Army and Navy (Volunteer) Who Served in the Civil War*. Philadelphia: L. R. Hamersly, 1893.

Power, J. Tracy. *Lee's Miserables: Life in the Army of Northern Virginia from the Wilderness to Appomattox.* Chapel Hill: Univ. of North Carolina Press, 1998.

Preston, Noble D. *History of the Tenth Regiment of Cavalry, New York State Volunteers, August 1861–August 1865.* New York: D. Appleton, 1892.

Pyne, Henry R. *The History of the First New Jersey Cavalry.* Trenton, NJ: J. A. Beecher, 1871.

Rauscher, Frank. *Music on the March, 1862–1865, with the Army of the Potomac.* Philadelphia: William F. Fell, 1892.

Rawle, Francis. *William Brooke Rawle: Reprinted from the Alumni Register of the University of Pennsylvania.* N.p., 1916.

Rawle, William Brooke. "Further Remarks on the Cavalry Fight on the Right Flank at Gettysburg." *Journal of the United States Cavalry Association* 4 (1891): 157–60.

———. *Gregg's Cavalry Fight at Gettysburg: Historical Address Delivered October 15th, 1884, upon the Occasion of the Dedication of the Monumental Shaft Erected upon the Site of the Cavalry Engagement on the Right Flank of the Army of the Potomac, July 3d, 1863, during the Battle of Gettysburg.* Philadelphia, 1884.

———. "Gregg's Cavalry Fight at Gettysburg, July 3, 1863." *Journal of the United States Cavalry Association* 4 (1891): 257–75.

———. *A Refutation by William Brooke Rawle of Certain False Statements Made by Corporal Andrew Jackson Speese Regarding the History of the Third Pennsylvania Volunteer Cavalry Regiment.* Philadelphia, 1907.

———. "The Right Flank at Gettysburg: An Account of the Operations of General David McM. Gregg's Cavalry Command and Their Important Bearing on the Results of the Battle." Philadelphia: Allen, Lane, and Scott's Print House, 1878.

———. "With Gregg in the Gettysburg Campaign." In *Annals of the War,* 467–84.

Rea, Lilian, ed. *War Record and Personal Experiences of Walter Raleigh Robbins, from April 22, 1861 to August 4, 1865.* Chicago: n.p., 1923.

Regimental Association. *Under the Maltese Cross: Antietam to Appomattox, the Loyal Uprising in Western Pennsylvania, 1861–1865.* Akron, OH: Werner, 1910.

Regimental History Committee. *History of the Third Pennsylvania Cavalry, Sixtieth Regiment Pennsylvania Volunteers, in the American Civil War, 1861–1865.* Philadelphia: Franklin Printing, 1905.

Reuther, Catherine, "Descendants of John Brooke." N.p., July 2014. Online at http://www.kennedyreuther.com/barlow/brooke_report.pdf.

Rhea, Gordon C. *The Battle of the Wilderness, May 5–6, 1864.* Baton Rouge: Louisiana State Univ. Press, 1994.

———. *The Battles for Spotsylvania Court House and the Road to Yellow Tavern, May 7–12, 1864.* Baton Rouge: Louisiana State Univ. Press, 1997.

———. *On to Petersburg: Grant and Lee, June 4–15, 1864.* Baton Rouge: Louisiana State Univ. Press, 2017.

———. *To the North Anna River: Grant and Lee, May 13–25, 1864.* Baton Rouge: Louisiana State Univ. Press, 2000.

Robertson, James I., Jr., ed. *The Civil War Letters of General Robert McAllister.* New Brunswick, NJ: Rutgers Univ. Press, 1965.

Rockwell, Alphonso D., M.D. *Rambling Recollections: An Autobiography.* New York: Paul B. Hoeber, 1920.

Roe, Alfred Seelye, "In a Rebel Prison: Or, Experiences in Danville, Va." In *Personal Narratives of the Soldiers and Sailors Historical Society of Rhode Island.* 4th ser., no. 16. Providence, RI: Snow and Farnham, 1891.

———. *The Thirty-Ninth Regiment Massachusetts Volunteers, 1862–1865.* Worcester, MA: Regimental Veteran Association, 1914.

Rosenblatt, Emil, and Ruth Rosenblatt, eds. *Anti-Rebel: The Civil War Letters of Wilbur Fisk.* New York: Emil Rosenblatt, 1983.

Sauers, Richard A. *Advance the Colors!: Pennsylvania Civil War Battle Flags.* 2 vols. Harrisburg, PA: Capitol Preservation Committee, 1987.

———. *Guide to Civil War Philadelphia.* Boston: Da Capo, 2003.

Schaff, Morris. *The Battle of the Wilderness.* Boston: Houghton Mifflin, 1910.

Scott, Robert Garth, ed. *Fallen Leaves: The Civil War Letters of Major Henry Livermore Abbott.* Kent, OH: Kent State Univ. Press, 1991.

———, ed. *Forgotten Valor: The Memoirs, Journals, & Civil War Letters of Orlando B. Willcox.* Kent, OH: Kent State Univ. Press, 1999.

———. *Into the Wilderness with the Army of the Potomac.* Bloomington: Indiana Univ. Press, 1985.

Sears, Stephen W. *Lincoln's Lieutenants: The High Command of the Army of the Potomac.* Boston: Houghton Mifflin Harcourt, 2017.

Sedgwick, Henry D., ed. *Correspondence of John Sedgwick, Major General.* New York: DeVinne, 1902.

Silliker, Ruth L., ed. *The Rebel Yell and the Yankee Hurrah: The Civil War Journal of a Maine Volunteer.* Camden, ME: Down East Books, 1985.

Sipes, William B. *The Seventh Pennsylvania Veteran Volunteer Cavalry, Its Record, Reminiscences, and Roster.* Pottsville, PA: Miners Journal Print, 1906.

Smith, John Day. *The History of the Nineteenth Regiment of Maine Volunteer Infantry, 1862–1865.* Minneapolis: Great Western Printing, 1909.

Sparks, David S., ed. *Inside Lincoln's Army: The Diary of General Marsena Rudolph Patrick, Provost Marshal General, Army of the Potomac.* New York: Thomas Yoseloff, 1964.

Spear, Abbott, et al., eds. *The Civil War Recollections of General Ellis Spear.* Orono, ME: Univ. of Maine Press, 1997.

Speese, Andrew J. *Story of Companies H, A, and C, Third Pennsylvania Cavalry, at Gettysburg, July 3, 1863.* Germantown, PA, 1906.

Starr, Stephen Z. *The Union Cavalry in the Civil War.* 3 vols. Baton Rouge: Louisiana State Univ. Press, 1979–84.

Stevens, C. A. *Berdan's United States Sharpshooters in the Army of the Potomac, 1861–1865.* St. Paul, MN: Price-McGill, 1892.

Stewart, Alexander M. *Camp, March, and Battlefield; or, Three Years and a Half with the Army of the Potomac.* Philadelphia: Jas. B. Rodgers, 1865.

Stine, John H. *History of the Army of the Potomac.* Philadelphia: J. B. Rodgers Printing, 1892.

Styple, William, ed. *Writing and Fighting the Civil War: Soldier Correspondence to the New York Sunday Mercury.* Kearny, NJ: Belle Grove, 2000.

Survivor's Association. *History of the Corn Exchange Regiment, 118th Pennsylvania Volunteers, from Their First Engagement at Antietam to Appomattox.* Philadelphia: John L. Smith, 1888.

Survivor's Association. *A History of the 121st Pennsylvania Volunteers. An Account from the Ranks.* Rev. ed. Philadelphia: Press of Catholic Standard and Times, 1906.

Sutherland, Daniel E. *A Savage Conflict: The Decisive Role of Guerilla Warfare in the American Civil War.* Chapel Hill: Univ. of North Carolina Press, 2009.

Taylor, Frank. *Philadelphia in the Civil War, 1861–1865.* Philadelphia: By the City, 1913.

Tenney, Luman H. *War Diary of Luman Harris Tenney, 1861–1865.* Cleveland: Evangelical Publishing House, 1914.

Thomas, Hampton Sidney. "Some Personal Reminiscences of Service in the Cavalry of the Army of the Potomac." Philadelphia: L. R. Hammersly, 1889.

Thomas, Milton Halsey. "Professor McCulloh of Princeton, Columbia, and Points South." *Princeton University Library Chronicle* 9, no. 1 (Nov. 1947): 17–29.

Tilney, Robert. *My Life in the Army: Three Years and a Half with the Fifth Army Corps, Army of the Potomac, 1862–1865.* Philadelphia: Ferris and Leach, 1912.

Tobie, Edward P. *History of the First Maine Cavalry, 1861–1865.* Boston: Emery and Hughes, 1887.

Trout, Robert J. *After Gettysburg: Cavalry Operations in the Eastern Theater, July 14, 1863, to December 31, 1863.* Hamilton, MT: Eagle Editions, 2011.

Trudeau, Noah Andre. *Bloody Roads South: The Wilderness to Cold Harbor, May–June 1864.* Boston: Little, Brown, 1989.

———. *The Last Citadel: Petersburg, Virginia, June 1864–April 1865.* Boston: Little, Brown, 1991.

———. *Out of the Storm: The End of the Civil War, April–June 1865.* Boston: Little, Brown, 1994.

US War Department. *The War of the Rebellion: A Compilation of the Official Records of the Union and Confederate Armies.* 70 vols. in 128 pts. plus *Atlas.* Washington, DC: Government Printing Office, 1890–1901.

Waitt, Robert W., Jr. *Confederate Military Hospitals in Richmond.* Richmond, VA: Richmond Civil War Centennial Committee, 1964. Reprint, Richmond, VA: Richmond Independence Bicentennial Commission, 1979.

Walker, Francis Amasa. *History of the Second Army Corps in the Army of the Potomac.* New York: Charles Scribner's Sons, 1886.

Ward, George W. *History of the Second Pennsylvania Veteran Heavy Artillery (112th Pennsylvania Volunteers), from 1861 to 1866, including the Provisional Second Penn'a Heavy Artillery.* Philadelphia: George W. Ward, 1904.

Weld, Stephen Minot. *War Diary and Letters of Stephen Minot Weld.* 2nd ed. Boston: Massachusetts Historical Society, 1979.

Wert, Jeffry D. *Custer: The Controversial Life of George Armstrong Custer.* New York: Simon and Schuster, 1996.

———. *Mosby's Rangers.* New York: Simon and Schuster, 1990.

———. *The Sword of Lincoln: The Army of the Potomac.* New York: Simon and Schuster, 2005.

White, Jonathan W., ed. *A Philadelphia Perspective: The Civil War Diary of Sidney George Fisher.* New York: Fordham Univ. Press, 2007.

Williamson, James J. *Mosby's Rangers: A Record of the Operations of the Forty-Third Battalion Virginia Cavalry, from Its Organization to the Surrender.* New York: Ralph B. Kenyon, 1896.

Wingate, George W. *History of the Twenty-Second Regiment of the National Guard of the State of New York.* New York: Edwin W. Dayton, 1896.

Wister, Sarah. *Walter S. Newhall: A Memoir.* Philadelphia: Press of C. Sherman Son, 1864.

Wittenberg, Eric J. *The Battle of Brandy Station: North America's Largest Cavalry Battle.* Charleston, SC: History Press, 2010.

———. *Protecting the Flank at Gettysburg: The Battles for Brinkerhoff's Ridge and East Cavalry Field, July 2–3, 1863.* El Dorado Hills, CA: Savas Beatie, 2013.

———. *Rush's Lancers: The Sixth Pennsylvania Cavalry in the Civil War.* Yardley, PA: Westholme, 2007.

———. *The Union Cavalry Comes of Age: Hartwood Church to Brandy Station, 1863.* Washington, DC: Brassey's, 2003.

———, ed. *We Have It Damn Hard Out Here: The Civil War Letters of Sergeant Thomas W. Smith, 6th Pennsylvania Cavalry.* Kent, OH: Kent State Univ. Press, 1999.

———, ed. *With Sheridan in the Final Campaign against Lee, by Lt. Col. Frederick C. Newhall, Sixth Pennsylvania Cavalry.* Baton Rouge: Louisiana State Univ. Press, 2002.

Wongsrichanalai, Kanisorn. *Northern Character: College-Educated New Englanders, Honor, Nationalism, and Leadership in the Civil War Era.* New York: Fordham Univ. Press, 2016.

Young, Carleton. *Voices from the Attic: The Williamstown Boys in the Civil War.* Syracuse, IN: William James Morris, 2015.

INDEX

Page numbers in italics refer to illustrations.